Harnessing the Potential of ICT for Education

A Multistakeholder Approach

*Proceedings from the Dublin Global Forum
of the United Nations ICT Task Force*

Edited by
Bonnie Bracey and Terry Culver

United Nations

United Nations
Information
and
**Communication
Technologies**
Task Force

gesci

Published by
The United Nations Information and Communication Technologies Task Force
One United Nations Plaza
New York, NY 10017
unicttaskforce@un.org

My best thanks go to Sergei Kambalov, Enrica Murmura, Robert de Jesus, Edoardo Zucchelli and Cheryl Stafford of the United Nations ICT Task Force Secretariat, for their input and encouragement as we collaborated to find the best stories and case studies from the Global Forum. Their assistance with this task was invaluable.

I also thank Terry Culver, of GeSCI, for helping to bring many of the participants to the conference, and for his assistance in identifying contributors and persuading them to lend their knowledge and insights.

This report would not have appeared without the support of my husband, Vic Sutton, who not only provided help and encouragement, but also tackled all the copy editing of the report with patience and professional skill, over a period of many weeks.

As a small child, I attended an Irish-supported mission school in the ghetto of Alexandria, Virginia. That gives me a special reason to thank the government of Ireland for its support for the Global Forum, and for its vision for the future – helping others.

Bonnie Bracey
13 October 2005

THE UNITED NATIONS ICT TASK FORCE

The United Nations ICT Task Force was established by Secretary-General Kofi Annan to help identify ways to harness the potential of ICT for economic and social development by promoting partnerships of public, private, non-profit and civil society stakeholders to advance the global effort to bridge the digital divide.

As a global forum for placing ICT at the service of development, the ICT Task Force has grown in stature and influence since its inauguration in 2001. With the potential of ICT to enable the attainment of internationally agreed development goals becoming widely embraced, the Task Force provides a platform to discuss international norms, policies and practices through the work of its networks, working groups and members.

The Task Force is not an operational, implementing or funding agency but provides a platform and focal point for discussing the ICT for development agenda, including issues related to strategic direction, policy coherence and coordination and advocacy in relation to the global ICT for development agenda. It has the mandate to help forge a strategic partnership between the United Nations system, private industry and other relevant stakeholders in putting ICT at the service of development.

Meetings, in particular a series of global forums focused on key issues held over the last two years, bring together Task Force members with international development and ICT experts, policy makers, leading private sector representatives and members of civil society and non governmental organizations and provide a platform for sharing experiences, exchanging views, catalyzing new partnerships and building consensus in complex and politically sensitive policy areas.

THE GLOBAL E-SCHOOLS AND COMMUNITIES INITIATIVE (GeSCI)

"The Global e-Schools and Communities Initiative matches the power of ICT with educational need, and has the potential not only to improve education, but also to empower people, strengthen governance, open up new markets and galvanize our efforts to achieve the Millennium Development Goals." - Kofi Annan

GeSCI was established in 2004 to harness the power of new technologies to strengthen education and communities around the world. GeSCI brings together actors to launch or coordinate national or regional efforts and to connect global partners to these efforts. In partnership with governments, the private sector, and civil society, GeSCI designs practical, long-term and sustainable solutions, and as an honest broker, cultivates the growth of ICT in education environments

The range of services GeSCI provides includes developing and implementing national or regional education strategies, building capacity of teachers, administrators, and policy makers, scaling up successful innovations, building and sharing knowledge, creating hands-on tools, mobilizing resources, and facilitating coordination among stakeholders.

GeSCI has significant activities underway in a number of countries and has established offices in Namibia to lead the Namibian National ICT in Education Initiative, and in India, where GeSCI is both working in a number of different states and advising the Federal Government on ICT in Education policy. GeSCI is also engaged in research and strategic planning activities in Ghana, Bolivia, Jordan, and Columbia, and will become involved in more countries in the near future.

To complement the national and regional work, GeSCI is also developing a Total Cost of Ownership Assessment Tool, to enable practitioners and policy makers to articulate educational needs and to determine ICT solutions with their different costs and benefits. GeSCI is also leading the Return on Investments in ICT in Education Study, which is a multi-year, multi-country research project to understand the long-term, quantifiable benefits a country can anticipate with investments in ICT in education.

The founding members of GeSCI are the United Nations and the governments of Switzerland, Canada, Sweden, and Ireland. GeSCI has also established a number of strategic partnerships in the private and public sector.

Why GeSCI?

Education is vital to economic growth by developing a skilled work force and increasing productivity. It is equally vital to social development, as it empowers people to improve their health, environment, and governance. But, education systems in the developing world are under strain. Many of the world's children receive no formal education or a sub-standard education. Those who are fortunate enough to attend schools lack books and materials, have poor infrastructure and little communication with the wider world, and their teachers are too few and inadequately trained. Strengthening education and communities is essential to cultivating sustained development.

GeSCI is committed to helping achieve several of the Millennium Development Goals (MDGs), a global compact to end human poverty among nations. GeSCI directly targets goals 2 and 3: achieving universal primary education and promoting gender equality, and goal 8: creating private-public partnerships to realise the potential of ICT for development. In addition, education underpins the realisation of all eight goals.

CONTENTS

MESSAGE[1]

Kofi Annan
Secretary-General, United Nations

I send my greetings to all participants in the Eighth Meeting of the United Nations Information and Communications Technologies Task Force.

Last month, in my report "In larger freedom", I proposed to the Member States of the United Nations an agenda for far-reaching policy commitments and institutional reforms in development, security and human rights. That agenda will be before world leaders in September, when they meet at a summit in New York to review progress in implementing the Millennium Declaration.

The cause of development occupies pride of place in my proposals – in particular, the need for urgent action in 2005 to ensure that our world starts to make real progress towards the Millennium Development Goals, and achieves them by 2015.

To achieve the goals, we must harness the potential of ICT. The September Summit, and the second phase of the World Summit on the Information Society to be held in November in Tunis, give us opportunities to make vital progress in doing so. In 2005, we must fully integrate the global ICT agenda into the broader United Nations development agenda. And we must ensure strategic coherence in implementing the decisions taken at these important meetings.

We also need to improve the use of ICT within the United Nations itself, so that the Organization's collective mindset and methods of work are brought fully into the digital age.

I thank the Task Force for its work, in which governments, civil society and the private sector have come together to forge a common approach. And I warmly welcome the attention that this meeting is giving to education. One of the Millennium Development Goals is achievement of universal primary education by 2015. We must ensure that ICT is used to help unlock the door to education, whether for young girls in Afghanistan, university students in Uganda, or workers in Brazil, so that they can fully seize economic opportunities, and live lives of dignity, free from want.

---

[1] Delivered by Mr. José Antonio Ocampo, Under-Secretary-General for Economic and Social Affairs, at the Eighth Meeting of the United Nations ICT Task Force (Dublin, 13-14 April 2005).

It is encouraging to know that Ireland and other Task Force members, in spearheading the Global e-Schools and Communities Initiative, have taken action to put ICT at the service of education in developing countries. We need to do much more work along these lines, and we need to be creative and ambitious. Let us therefore use 2005 to think and act urgently and boldly to ensure that ICT is used to advance education and development. In that spirit, I wish you every success for this important meeting.

PREFACE

Noel Dempsey T.D.
Minister for Communications, Marine and Natural Resources, Ireland

Education is a powerful tool. With it, whole communities can be empowered. People can be engaged to fully participate in their country's development and prosperity. Education can be the primary mechanism not only to raise standards of human capital but also to tackle such widespread issues such as the AIDS crisis, gender equality and fair trading rights.

Against this backdrop, more than 300 people traveled from across the world to meet in Dublin, Ireland to discuss the issue of Harnessing the Potential of ICTs for Education. The Global Forum was an incredible opportunity to share lessons and build partnerships on this crucial global issue. Over the few days of meetings, the wealth of knowledge that the participants shared forged stronger links between a myriad of sectors, backgrounds and experience, and generated a web of valuable relationships in the area of ICT and education.

This book continues what the Global Forum started, and I believe, advances an essential international dialogue on sustainable and lasting change. I have noticed that increasingly, it is this multistakeholder approach that creates an opportunity to further develop and exploit all our existing strengths. These relationships will provide the solutions to international development issues.

And there is no better time. The year 2005 is recognised as a key year for global initiatives overall and in particular; it is a watershed in relation to international development efforts. The second stage of the World Summit on the Information Society takes place in November. The annual G8 Summit has made development a clear international priority by placing the issue of "tackling poverty" on its agenda, and the deadline of the United Nations Millennium Development Goals by 2015 moves ever closer.

Personally, given Ireland's tradition of investing in education, I am pleased that we were able to support the United Nations in hosting the Forum and to contribute to its outcomes. As a country, Ireland have benefited considerably from a focused investment in fusing technology with the power of human capital. We recognize that investment in ICTs in education cannot merely be limited to these shores.

Through facilitation, understanding and consensus, it is the international organizations that will be able to see the "whole picture". Together, we will work towards finding solutions to these global challenges that we are beset with. And it will take the involvement of the private and the public and from the local to the global if we are to tackle the issues that strike at the heart of our international community.

It is through such events as the Forum that truly effective dialogue on these important matters can be achieved, and it is initiatives such as GeSCI and the leadership of the United Nations ICT Task Force that will create positive change on a global level.

INTRODUCTION: UNITING PEOPLE, TECHNOLOGY AND POWERFUL IDEAS FOR LEARNING

Bonnie Bracey

ICTs in Education

This book is a journey through some global uses of ICT and the ways in which various groups, individuals and partners have utilized technology in new ways to think about learning and teaching and reaching the Millennium Development Goals. We concentrate on the use of technologies in developing nations as a whole, but we are reflective of the new technologies that can serve us globally.

One of the purposes of the book is to give a vision, a perspective of the possibilities that will draw people to the cause and use of technology in ways that will take advantage of the opportunities the future will afford.

Another purpose is to provide case studies of ICT use that will create an understanding of the possibilities of use now and in local decisions that work for many of our participants today.

As Alvin Toffler observed: "The illiterate of the 21st century will not be those who cannot read and write, but those who cannot learn, unlearn, and relearn."

We know that the challenge to world leaders is to use technology in effective ways to create a bridge across the digital divide. As literacy is one of the problems, we address general educational goals, but also are devoted to the environment, science learning and literacy, and the use of national goals, with local content to create learning landscapes that reflect the goals of place.

The challenge to teachers is to be effective in using technology.

The problems in teaching and learning are not the technology, or just the wiring, it is this: after the wires (or wireless, or uses of ubiquitous devices) are provided, what happens then?

As Bertram Bruce puts it: "Learning in almost any subject today means not only learning the concepts within that area, but also, how to use technologies in that endeavour. Thus, the traditional lines between learning about technology and learning through technology

Eventually, simpler computers with fewer options and compact operating systems, costing a fraction of desktop computers, will be marketed to meet the needs of learners. We may start with "Text2Teach" as an example of leapfrogging technologies,[2] but go on, in fact, with many new ways of communication using simple devices.

Much is made about the fact that there are those who have grown up digitally (one contributor calls them "digital natives") and those of us who have converted to be able to be a part of the future of education.

To that end, we have included participants' contributions from the Youth Forum of the World Summit on the Information Society (WSIS), and some of their projects and practices. But make no mistake about it, educators and practitioners schooled in pedagogy will be a match for "digital natives" if they are afforded time to weave their knowledge into practical learning environments.

What Kinds of Technologies for the Future?

Community tools are technologies that foster new types of learning processes.

"Collaborative representations" are tools for supporting remote interactions mediated by diverse visualizations, notations, and models. The core idea is that the external, symbolic representations of information and knowledge provide grounding for discussions, reflections, and learning conversations. Therefore the interest in e-learning and the investment in Virtual Universities and professional development that make these tools user friendly.

There are new kinds of knowledge networking. Network improvement tools have the potential to enhance learning by linking individuals to new sources of knowledge, to like-minded peers, to subject matter experts, or to teachers. Scaffolding tools employ pedagogical principles to structure educational activities, and thus enable more advanced performances than learners would be capable of without such supports. Learning is more than reading, writing, and arithmetic; it requires posing productive questions, seeking diverse viewpoints, creating argumentation, and reflective analysis and revisions of one's beliefs or works based on critique. Research in networked interactive learning environment projects illustrates the importance of scaffolding to guide students toward appropriate forms of learning activities and outcomes.

In the future, as in the African Virtual University, new technologies will be used to create resources for those with the old technologies using the newest wave of innovation.

At the World Summit on the Information Society it was stated that the development of new ICTs "opens up unprecedented opportunities to ensure universal and equitable access to scientific data and information and to enhance the global knowledge pool.

---

[2] See the article in this volume, 'Teaching through Mobile Technology Debuts in Schools in the Philippines'.

Many of the building blocks of the information society are the result of scientific and technical advances made possible by the sharing of research results."[3]

[3] Excerpt from the World Summit on the Information Society Draft declaration of principles, http://cern.ch/rsis

INFORMATION AND COMMUNICATION TECHNOLOGIES FOR DEVELOPMENT

Jeffrey D. Sachs[1]

Looking beyond 2015[2] to the year 2025, we can see a path to the end of extreme poverty, the kind of poverty that still affects around one billion people on the planet. I believe that the Millennium Development Goals are fundamental steps but only the halfway house[3] to a poverty-free world. The extra decade could take us the rest of the way. The ICT sector and certainly science and technology in general will be instrumental in proceeding on that path.

The Millennium Project was initiated by the Secretary-General in 2001 out of concern that United Nations' goals are easily stated but not so easily achieved. The task for our Project was to recommend practical ways to achieve the MDGs. This was good judgment on the Secretary-General's part because, since the MDGs were announced, I think it is fair to say that having the goals has not yet changed very much of the on-the-ground realities.

The MDGs were adopted in September 2000. Unfortunately, we went to war for much of the intervening period. Some countries had been making progress as of September 2000 and, by and large, they continue to make progress. In some places, particularly in Asia, the progress is absolutely breathtaking and remarkable. Some parts of the world are not making progress, are in fact actually suffering regress, particularly Sub-Saharan Africa and more remote areas such as Central Asia and the Andean region. Those places have not been turned around by the mere announcement of the goals – not even close.

When the Millennium Project issued its report in January 2005, we concluded on the work of ten Task Forces; 13 monographs were submitted to the Secretary-General composed of 2,700 pages of studies, as well as a mercifully brief 74-page overview. In this report, the Millennium Project concluded that the MDGs can be met everywhere, but that they are not being met in dozens of countries, and that to meet the MDGs

---

[1] This is an edited statement, prepared by the United Nations ICT Task Force Secretariat, from a keynote address delivered by Jeffrey Sachs in Dublin on 14 April 2005, at the Global Forum on A Multistakeholder Approach to Harnessing the Potential of Information and Communication Technologies for Education.
[2] The target year set for the attainment of the Millennium Development Goals.
[3] Goal 1 is to halve poverty by 2015.

would require a decisive change of course. We believe that 2005 needs to be the year for that decisive change.

The report is titled "Investing in Development – A Practical Plan to Achieve the MDGs". The two words that are at the essence of what we are recommending are "investing" and "practical".

Investment

If we are going to meet the targets by 2015, we need to step up the rates of investment in the poorest countries. Those investments, by and large, have to be public investments because public investments are critical to meeting challenges of education, health, infrastructure and environmental management, and also because those public investments are a pre-requisite for a vigorous private sector. The report states that public investments are key to a breakthrough if we are going to enable healthy private sector development.

Do not look for micro-finance to carry Africa, especially rural Africa, out of extreme poverty if there is no water, electricity, roads, public health, basic education – it is getting the order wrong. Build the basic infrastructure, which will provide a base for all that goes on in the real economy. By and large, all that goes on in the poorest of the poor economies right now is subsistence agriculture, or people have just escaped it and are living in slums engaged in very informal activities. That is the reality for the billion people at the bottom of the world. If they do not have investments to empower them to be productive, it is a matter of wishful thinking to hope for their way out of poverty.

We identified three core areas of investments: 1) people; 2) the physical environment; and 3) infrastructure.

Investing in people, or human capital, means investing in four priority areas: education, health, nutrition and family planning.

Investing in the environment means investing in soils, water management, habitat preservation and preservation of ecosystem functions, whether it is corals or mangroves or tropical forests. All over the poorest world there is massive degradation of the environment and mining of natural capital. For instance, in Africa the most dramatic mining of natural capital is the depletion of soil nutrients because farmers do not use fertilizer. Fertilizer is sometimes viewed skeptically by environmentalists but actually soil is destroyed when fertilizers are not used as well as when they are overused. Farmers abandon farms and cut down the trees nearby, continuing a process of destroying the forest as well as facing an inability to grow enough food to become commercial farmers.

Investment in infrastructure is a big part of the ICT Task Force's work. This includes communications and, increasingly, data management networks. Infrastructure also includes basic all-weather roads, motor transport, electricity (which still eludes perhaps two billion people on the planet) and effective port services. It is all those network systems that are at the essence of breaking economic isolation, enabling trade and enabling exchange of ideas and information – all the elements that make for a real economy in terms of the underlying physical, non-natural capital base.

What the report shows is that these investments are not being made right now at anywhere near the scale that would be needed to actually help to achieve the MDGs. The report makes a basic point, on which there is a growing consensus (except in Washington, D.C.), that the poorest countries cannot afford to make these investments on their own. That is the essence of the international challenge. People can give lectures from here to 2015 without changing any realities for people who are too poor to undertake the investments that need to be made. Do not expect markets to rush in to make these investments. These are public goods and these governments are not credit-worthy because they are impoverished. That is why the IMF, the World Bank, the Africa Commission, the United Nations Millennium Project and the Secretary-General all have announced that aid must be doubled. The fact of the matter is that we are not mobilizing the resources that are needed to make the advances right now.

For a long time the discourse about poverty was that the poor had only themselves to blame, that they are living in corrupt countries and the corruption has blocked them from being a part of the world economy. This is false as a general diagnosis. The poor have extreme poverty to blame. And the reasons why poor people are trapped in extreme poverty is not incidental to where they live. If you live in a temperate zone near a port, something like Dublin, you are doing pretty well in the world, with very few exceptions. The one most notable exception is North Korea. There it really is politics. There, North Korea does have its leader to blame. But if you are living in the interior of Africa, in a Savannah climate, where the rains fail frequently, where the soils are depleted of nutrients, where malaria is endemic, where AIDS is ravaging the population, there you have a perfect storm of insufficient food production, massive disease burden – which is based on the local ecology to a crucial extent – and economic isolation.

I know many well-governed countries that cannot do anything in these circumstances except watch their children die. They do not have themselves to blame. They cannot get out of the poverty trap on their own. They need help. That is the essence of why we need official development assistance right now. We need it because people are trapped in poverty and because they are dying by the millions every year. I estimate 20,000 people a day die of extreme poverty – eight million a year. They are dying of chronic under-nutrition, malaria, AIDS, unsafe drinking water leading to diarrhea, and unsafe cooking fuels used at home leading to acute lower respiratory infection. They are dying in Darfur, not because of bloody-mindedness, but because there is not enough rain and not enough food production to support a population that has doubled in the last 20 years at the same time that the carrying capacity of the land has gone down significantly. There, it turns into violence because people are hungry, desperate and fighting for land to stay alive. We call that politics, but I call it ecology and poverty.

The Project produced estimates of what is actually needed to make these core investments. We found that what is needed is to go from the current level of aid, which is a rather inadequately targeted 0.25% of rich-world GNP, to a well-targeted 0.5% or 0.55% of GNP of the rich world. This 0.55% is aid for the poorest people in the world. That does not include the tsunamis that lie ahead, or other climate disasters, or where

All of us are productive because we have light bulbs above, we have computers at hand, because we have educations, because we go to our doctors regularly, and we have had a full run of immunizations.

Practical Solutions

Poor people are not our enemy, and they are not corrupt, they are just poor, they are hungry, and they are sick. We should figure out practical ways to help them get out of that situation.[6]

That Africa lives on rain-fed agriculture rather than irrigation agriculture is one of the most fundamental reasons why Africa is in extreme poverty right now. The major topographical difference between Asia and Africa is that Asia has the Himalayas, and the Himalayas mean great river systems with massive irrigation. In Africa you have 96% of staple food production in rain-fed places, and the rains are erratic.

Health issues are rampant in Africa. AIDS, malaria, malnutrition wrack the local populations who may have no clinic close by, and where there are clinics they may not have sufficient medicine. Many suffer because malaria medications have lost their efficacy and new drugs are 20 times as expensive – 1 dollar a treatment instead of 5 cents. Perhaps around three million children this year will die of malaria, which is an utterly treatable and largely preventable disease. The way we are approaching this disease is by trying to sell bed nets to poor people, to socially market them. This is a terrible idea. Give the nets away, you cannot sell things to people that have no money.

Kenya spends $7 per capita per year on health. But that is not Kenya's fault, that is the fault of poverty. It is about 2.5% of GNP. But if your GNP is $300 per capita, you do not get very far. Even if Kenya spent 4% – which would be a huge stretch because poor countries do not collect much revenue – that would be $12 per capita. That is still not enough per year to manage three pandemics – AIDS, TB and malaria – as well as to address women dying in childbirth, lack of emergency obstetrical care, acute lower respiratory infections, chronic under-nutrition, lack of immunization coverage, deaths from diarrheal diseases and so forth.

Many women in Africa spend six hours every day just getting water. What a life. You want to know why people are poor? Because instead of running a tap, they spend six hours a day fetching water. They do not have time to be productive. They are only fighting for daily survival. This is what extreme poverty is: fighting for daily survival.

We made indexes of ecological vulnerability or geographical vulnerability. Three factors proved to be influential: 1) do you live far from the coast? 2) do you live in an endemic malaria region? and 3) do you live in a sub-humid or arid, rain-fed agricultural system? Africa is all three; no other part of the world has this concatenation of problems. That is

---

[6] Here, Mr. Sachs presented a series of photographs of individuals and families with whom he met in his travels to illustrate the many problems facing the poor in Africa. This chapter retains only excerpts from his full presentation.

what makes Africa different from the other poorest places in the world. It is not that Africans are more corrupt. It is not that Africans do not care. It is not that Africans do not know what to do. They are facing water scarcity, lack of irrigation, endemic malaria, an AIDS pandemic. Most of the population lives great distances from the coast, because the concentration of African population is not coastal, it is interior. It is the highlands where food can be grown more easily – in places like Rwanda, Burundi and the highlands of Ethiopia – rather than on the coast of Somalia. But it takes people away from ports.

It is wonderful to talk to people in the villages. First, they know all of this. They have told us they need fertilizers, bed nets, doctors, and so on – very practical. The point of the Millennium Project is that there are practical things that can be done.

Take water management, for example. Treadle pumps cost $80, but the villages cannot afford them. Natural, green systems can replenish nitrogen-depleted soils. Investments like these can help farmers realize full crops. The difference between one ton of maize per hectare and three tons per hectare is the difference between life and death. It is the difference of the green revolution and Africa's predicament. Africa could have a green revolution. All it would take are simple things like rock beds, where you need just fencing over them to keep the soils from being depleted. Another example is the school meals programme, which is the single most proven intervention to get children into school.

But do you know how few school meal programmes there are in poor areas? They cost money and also they need more local production of food. The farmers need help growing more food and then part of that food should be used for school meal programmes. More examples: bed nets to fight malaria, anti-retroviral drugs to treat AIDS. These are drugs that cost 30 cents a day, $130 a year, and yet three million Africans will die this year of AIDS because they are not getting this right now, because we have not invested properly in helping Africa to scale up primary health at the local level. These are remarkably simple interventions. But they cost money, and that is what the Project priced in its report.

Communities want to work in partnership to solve their problems. We offered to provide a doctor to a community, and they said they would build a clinic, and they did it in five weeks. They asked us to provide the cement, the corrugated roof and the wiring, and they did everything else. That is the kind of partnership possible – people want to stay alive, they are thrilled to have a doctor, they are thrilled to build a building, and the whole community pitched in. Community health workers in western Kenya were asked what they need, and instead of asking for an ambulance or a four-wheel vehicle, the answer was better training to help them treat malaria and AIDS, to improve hygiene, and so forth. They wanted training, that was the basic answer.

The point is that the Project is stressing practical interventions that require modest financing and that are village-based. About 75% of Africa's poor live in rural areas, in villages.

The Promise of ICT

Now let me close with a couple of sentences about ICT. These villages – each one with about 5,000 people – should be on-line. The reason why that is important is that connectivity would first enable aid to work in a new way. We could get aid right down to the village level. We could monitor it, we could understand what is needed. There would not be a question of whether the money makes it to village level if it is given to the central government. We know it would not have to go through the six lines of government. Or we could deliver aid with agreement of the national government right down to the community, which is where it needs to be for probably about half of the total investment. Connectivity would be wonderful.

More development professionals need to be given the tools to know where connectivity is possible, where it is not, what are the right technologies, what can be done. There are schools that are not on-line, clinics that do not even have a phone – much less a computer or e-mail for a logistic system, for inventory management for referrals, for a hundred other things for which they would use connectivity. Villages can be connected. There are cell towers around, if people in the villages had access to phones. Most likely the phones are basically free, maybe $5 or $10 marginal cost, especially if someone would give last year's models. We could work country by country to find the best way to deliver the most basic services to the village level. I am not talking about using a microfinance model, which I also believe in, because these are often communities before that stage, and there is no market there because there is no income.

I know there is progress, some good progress. We need not just software, we need the hardware, we need the connectivity, right down to the ground level. We need ways for countries to implement the best way to have connectivity in their rural areas, clinics and schools. We need the engagement of private industry, which is already very active in many ways. Maybe Nokia will provide 100,000 phones for 100,000 villages. Or maybe Finland and Nokia do it together, or the United States and Motorola. But somebody needs to help on the basic questions.

As we come to September[7], I do not think we need a seminar about how important ICT is. I think we need agreed, practical, bold, scaled, country-scale works-in-progress that show that we are getting the villages, the schools and the clinics on-line, that we are connecting the poor of the world with the rest of the world. We should demonstrate how we help, how we connect, how markets can get connected, how people can be referred for medicines, how drug supplies can be managed, how children can be taught, how weather can be monitored, how prices can be monitored – share all the things we know and all the great stories we know. Let us come for the Millennium Summit +5 in September with true, national scale models, in enough places that we see we have made the break-through, that we have turned the corner, in which donor aid is coming now.

---

[7] In September 2005, a five-year review of progress toward the implementation of the Millennium Declaration will be held at a High-level meeting of the General Assembly in United Nations Headquarters in New York City.

I do not think we have the models fully in place. I know there is a great model on education under way,[8] but let us look at how can we get the countries we are working within the Millennium Project into the programme, so that every country that wants to do it can have this kind of scaled achievement of connectivity.

---

[8] Mr. Sachs was referring to the Global e-Schools and Communities Initiative (GeSCI), the co-organizer of the Global Forum. For more information, please see http://www.gesci.org.

PART ONE

THE CONTRIBUTION OF ICTs TO EDUCATION INITIATIVES

models in areas like e-commerce, health care and education. While many of these initiatives have yielded promising results, these have only begun to address the daunting challenges in these areas.

One of the most significant issues confronting developing countries, including India, is the task of empowering and providing productive skills and capabilities to its youth. While the increasingly globalized environment demands better educated and skilled labour, overall levels of literacy, education and skill-acquisition remain low. A sixth of children worldwide, amounting to a hundred million, do not attend school. India alone is estimated to have 40 million children out of school.

The obstacles to universal education are formidable and wide-ranging: the absence of school buildings and teachers, resource constraints, cultural barriers to formal education, poor community involvement, inadequacy of teaching tools, etc. However addressing these challenges has emerged as one of the top priorities of Government, and a recent amendment of the Indian Constitution obligates the Indian State to provide free and compulsory primary education for children between the ages of six and fourteen. The Indian Government has also stepped up the quantum of resources flowing into the school-education sector by instituting a special educational cess on taxpayers.

Given India's strengths in the ICT and software sectors, an array of innovations and experiments are underway for utilizing these tools and technologies to overcome educational challenges. India has recently launched its own educational satellite called Edusat for linking schools across the country on a remote learning platform, in order to mitigate the issue of absence of qualified teachers, as well as the lack of access to schools. The Indian Government has also launched key initiatives such as the ICT@ Schools programme and the Vidya Vahini project, to train children in frontline technologies, as well as to improve the efficacy and spread of teaching. Various State Governments in India have also launched path-breaking programmes for enabling remote access, improving pedagogic content, and for facilitating community involvement in teaching. India has also been partnering with countries in Africa in the area of ICT-enabled learning, and there is considerable potential for such international collaborative ventures between nations.

The private and civil society sector in India are also undertaking experimental projects in ICT for education. Noteworthy of mention would be the "Hole-in-the-Wall" project, where slum-children are provided free access to computers and the Internet in an interesting, and highly successful experiment in self-directed learning; and the Premji Foundation's work in using computers as an inducement to retain children, particularly girls, in schools.

The successful experiences of the past few years in deploying ICTs for education dramatically reveal the potential that that these new technologies have for advancing educational goals. As the world moves towards an integrated knowledge society, there will be an increasing need for a populace that is not just literate but also equipped to understand and effectively utilize ICTs.

Given the critical importance of this sector to advance development goals, and the key lessons that that have been learned in recent years, international efforts need to converge around the following key areas:

1. Higher allocation of resources, including multilateral and ODA assistance for mainstreaming ICTs in development;

2. Fostering collaborative partnerships between nations for sharing technology and best practices;

3. Facilitating and coordinating the energies of possible international partners in this effort, including private sector companies and civil society organizations; and

4. Supporting and leveraging the Global e-Schools and Communities Initiative [GeSCI], which has been specifically set up by the United Nations ICT Task Force to address ICT for education challenges in developing countries.

TWENTY-FIRST CENTURY LEARNERS: A NEED FOR TECH-SAVVY TEACHERS

Bonnie Bracey

"Teachers may be forgiven if they cling to old models of teaching that have served them well in the past. All of their formal instruction and role models were driven in the past by traditional teaching practices. Breaking away from traditional approaches to instruction means taking risks and venturing into the unknown. But this is precisely what is needed at the present time." – National Council For Accreditation of Teacher Education, U.S.A.[1]

The Good Old Days?

Dr. David Thornburg likes to tell the story of a teacher revived from a hundred years ago, who is brought to a modern classroom and who does remarkably well considering the time she has been out of the classroom.

He tells this story in conferences and we laugh out loud at how little education has changed. But it is really not a laughing matter, and we know it. At these digital campfires we realize the problem of creating teachers who love the use of technology. Many teachers are trapped in their educational practices by a lack of meaningful exposure to good information on the use of technology and of how to initiate new ways of sharing information that will help them to move forward. Some are hindered by the lack of understanding and inexperience of those in their immediate learning community. Others are restricted to the use of only vendor-supplied solutions in IT as selected by leaders in their educational community. Time is also a problem. Learning in many countries is a prisoner of time. Yet there are foundations and groups around the world attempting to make change and to show examples.

What Is Technology?

To cite the U.S. National Academy of Engineering, "In its broadest sense, technology is the process by which humans modify nature to meet their needs and wants. However, most people think of technology only in terms of its artifacts: computers and software, aircraft, pesticides, water-treatment plants, and microwave ovens, to name a few. But technology is more than its tangible products. An equally important aspect of technology

---

[1] http://pt3.org/technology/21century_learners.html

is the knowledge and processes necessary to create and operate those products, such as engineering know-how and design, manufacturing expertise, various technical skills, and so on. Technology also includes all the infrastructure necessary for the design, manufacture, operation, and repair of technological artifacts, from corporate headquarters and engineering schools to manufacturing plants and maintenance facilities."

NAP, Technically Speaking. http://www.nap.edu/books/0309082625/html/3.html

"Technology comprises the entire system of people and organizations, knowledge, processes, and devices that go into creating and operating technological artifacts, as well as the artifacts themselves."[2]

What Is Technological Literacy?

Technological literacy encompasses three interdependent dimensions – knowledge, ways of thinking and acting, and capabilities.

Like literacy in reading, mathematics, science, or history, the goal of technological literacy is to provide people with the tools to participate intelligently and thoughtfully in the world around them. The kinds of things a technologically literate person must know can vary from society to society and from era to era.

The goal for teachers worldwide is to establish technological literacy. There are groups that are in place to help teachers achieve these goals, as well as ministries of education with programmes toward this goal. Some examples will be found in Appendix 1.

Creating a Learning Landscape

We can use resources to change teaching and learning. We can help teachers by giving them a different perspective, by involving them in meaningful activities, and by allowing them entry into the knowledge networks that define teaching and learning. Giving them the hardware, and some technical training, is the first part of their learning journey. For some the journey is a hard slog. Mentoring helps. Friendly technical support and teaming also helps.

If we use the ideational scaffolding of Jennifer James, who has written about teachers moving toward the future with new eyes,[3] we can identify eight new skills that need to be taught to teachers:

- Seeing with New Eyes

- Recognizing the Future

- Harnessing the Power of Myths and Symbols

---

[2] See http://www.nap.edu/books/0309082625/html/3.html
[3] See her book 'Thinking in the Future Tense: Leadership Skills for a New Age', ISBN 0-684-81098-0

- Speeding Up Your Response Time

- Understanding the Past to Know the Future

- Doing More with More or Less

- Mastering New Forms of Intelligence

- Profiting from Diversity

Tomorrow's teachers will enter classrooms that will look and feel very different from the classrooms their education professors may have taught in 30 years ago. Globally, the ways we think about teaching and learning have been challenged and we need to establish new kinds of practice, and pre-service education. We also need to create an interface for those teachers already in the classroom, who will live out their teaching career with students so that they are up to the task and who should not be forgotten as the world of education changes.

Professional development using e-learning, and virtual opportunities, are among the ways in which some have attempted to change teaching and learning as a process.

Mastering new forms of intelligence requires an understanding of visualization and modeling, parallel computing, ubiquitous computing, and of the uses of technology.

What is Ubiquity?

As Bob Tinker, President of the Concord Consortium writes:[4] "In the rush to bring modern information technologies into schools, one group of technologies is being overlooked that can greatly improve learning. While people are starting to realize the huge impact that current desktop computer and network technologies could have on education, other extremely valuable information technologies are not being used or even being considered.

"Small, inexpensive, handheld computers and their associated communications channels and software tools could play an important role in education. The computational power and communications capacities of handhelds are increasingly impressive. Many pack the raw computer power of desktop computers only a few years old while having increasingly good communication channels, either through a wired cradle, infrared beams, or radio frequency radiation. These channels can be used with software tools for a broad range of sophisticated productivity and browser applications. These handheld technologies could greatly enhance learning in and out of schools.

"Yet this 'anytime, anywhere' computing goes beyond just handheld computers. Ubiquitous, mobile devices such as phones, wrist bands, wearable devices and intelligent structures are bound to impact the future of education."

---

[4] http://usight.concord.org/what/

What is Going On? Understanding the Past to Know the Future

Some good things are happening. A quiet revolution is taking hold in many schools of education all over the world. Criticized for offering programmes that are long on theory and short on practice, many schools have responded with new approaches to teacher education. Students in these programmes develop subject matter expertise, practice teaching in real classrooms, connect with mentor teachers and learn the skills to teach with technology as media.

Content has a new meaning, because of the information revolution. Depending on the skill of users, there is an abundance of information available. Students do not have to rely on the teacher for information in most subjects. Books are static, and while there are some learning places that have resource materials, many rural and distant groups of people do not have access to them. Moreover, there remain problems with training, access, resources, the hardware and software and the understanding of how technology should be deployed in most schools and learning communities.

Studies of the process of educational change show that access to new information, procedures or tools alone rarely leads to change. Teachers with limited reach cripple the future of the children they teach. Education policy often lacks a focus that encourages the integration of technology content into the learning landscapes of schools, in the standards, curricula, instructional material, and student assessments in non-technology subject areas. For technology to work well for students and schools, we must build human infrastructure at the same pace we are installing computers, systems, and hardware.

Personalization of technology by interactive use has taken place in digital story telling. How many teachers labour to have children write, using the textbook? Project-based work, and digital story telling, get more of their attention.

Project-based work succeeds, because they children talking to other students and a different audience. It also builds communities of learning that link them with national or worldwide audiences.

Harnessing the Power of Myths and Symbols

Storytelling, both digital and personal, has another appeal. Stories put us in touch with ourselves, with others, and with our surroundings.

There are many different definitions of digital storytelling, but in general, all of them revolve around the idea of combining the long-standing art of telling stories with any of a variety of available multimedia tools, including graphics, audio, video animation, and Web publishing.

Using innovations in multimedia technology, student and adult audiences can make personal connections to visual art and museum artifacts through new ways of storytelling.

Digital storytelling is a new medium for this age-old practice and one that is humanistic, culturally rich, and globally relevant. The value of digital storytelling – for teachers and for museums or other learning places – is that the interactivity gives ownership to the creators. For some the personalization of media use is the key to learning. Many of us learn new technologies in projects and in learning circles.

There is great concern that the increased use of computers in education will only drive another wedge between rich and poor, exacerbating the "digital divide". While schools struggle with this issue, the ongoing revolution in information technologies continues: computers will soon be very inexpensive and ubiquitous. Most people will own several, including toys, TVs, phones, pagers, handhelds, as well as general-purpose computers, and many will communicate through an ubiquitous network.

This means that the desktop computer and its close cousin, the full-featured portable, will represent just one end of a spectrum of intelligent personal assistants. Full-featured computers already have far more power than most educational applications need. Eventually, simpler computers with fewer options and compact operating systems costing a fraction of desktop computers will be marketed to meet the needs of learners.

Many countries have leap-frogged the technology and have transformed their communications technology using ubiquitous computing.[5]

It is important for knowledge networks to be developed that are inclusive of the people who are to use new ideas in teaching and learning, to bridge the educational communities. Education needs to be more inclusive as the depth of content available has been increased. This is best done by involving those who teach as a part of the team developing ideas.

The job is to turn information into knowledge that is meaningful. Informal education is using technological literacy to improve learning outside of the various ways in which we construct primary, junior and high schools or university settings. Formal learning needs to adapt the same ideas on technology. Technology is not magic and does not automatically make a powerful learning experience unless it is used with good teaching and curricula. There is no silver bullet.

Learning places such as museums, "newseums", science and agricultural centres, and television, radio, newspapers, magazines and other media comprise the informal education system which offers, to citizens of all ages and backgrounds, the opportunity to use, learn about, and be involved in a variety of learning experiences. We should build on those experiences by encouraging partnerships with parent and community groups, universities, and others who play a critical role in making schools true centres of learning in their communities, and in their nations.

As the Concord Consortium writes:[6] "It is important to understand the difference between today's reality, where students occasionally use a computer in school, often as

---

[5] See further http://www.concord.org/publications/newsletter/2005-spring/future.html
[6] http://usight.concord.org/new/

part of a group, and the future, where they will always have their personal handheld computer available. Few students and teachers today have sufficient exposure to computers to become fluid with them, to begin to use them to enhance personal expression and understanding. For most students, the term 'personal computer' is a misnomer; students use 'institutional computers'. Teachers have often even less time to incorporate the use of technology into practice.

"Low-cost handhelds should help bridge the 'digital divide' by putting affordable modern computational tools in the hands of all students. There is always the worry that some students will not take care of computers."

"Several studies have shown, however, that if the incentives are set up so the kids feel a sense of ownership, computers that travel home with students, even expensive portables, are handled responsibly in even the poorest communities."

How can Technology Help?

Technology is, and should be, a tool – the means to an end, not the end itself.

Technology can be used as for inquiry, communication, construction, and expression.

As Bertram Bruce and James Levin write,[7] regarding the interests of the learner: "We began to search for a way to organize the tools, techniques, and applications to accommodate better to a constructivist and integrated view of learning. We assumed that the ideal learning environment would, as Peter Marin once said, satisfy students or the learners' curiosity by presenting them with new things to be curious about. It would engage them in exploring, thinking, reading, writing, researching, inventing, problem-solving, and experiencing the world.

"Thus, the basis for learning would be what John Dewey (1943) identified nearly a century ago as the greatest educational resource--the natural impulses to inquire or to find out things; to use language and thereby to enter into the social world; to build or make things; and to express one's feelings and ideas. Dewey saw these impulses, rather than the traditional disciplines, as the foundation for the curriculum. The educational challenge is to nurture these impulses for lifelong learning."

Active Participation in Learning

One great feature of the Internet is the democratic participation in media: people can finally be more than just consumers of information. With tools such as community networks and blogs, podcasting, digital story telling, project based learning initiatives, video blogging and other new technologies, people can become *producers* of information, using the Internet for civic engagement, education, cultural prosperity and community development. The emerging new uses of technology such as Internet 2, parallel computing and new uses of serious games, computational science, as well as traditional uses, in e-learning, give interactive power to the participant.

---

[7] http://www.isrl.uiuc.edu/~chip/pubs/taxonomy/

Technical Skills

Teachers need to be able to master the hardware, and use the software and resources available to them on the Internet in tech-savvy ways.

As schools continue to move into different phases of educational reform, one factor that is consistent is the need for professional development. Every school-improvement effort hinges on the smallest unit; in education, that is the classroom (McLaughlin, 1991).

As Linda Darling Hammond points out,[8] "Educational reform requires teachers not only to update their skills and knowledge but also to totally transform their roles as educators. It establishes new expectations for students, teachers, and school communities that some educators may not be prepared to meet."

Seeing with New Eyes

Professional development is a key tool that keeps teachers abreast of current issues in education, helps them implement innovations, and refines their practice.

As we extend the information revolution, education and the use of technology in education must be more than just an afterthought – as it still is for many people. The explosion of new technologies has changed the way we live – from the way we do business to the way we communicate with each other. Technological advancements are also affecting the way we teach and learn. But there is one group of workers who may not be getting effective training, who touch the future in educating the children of the world.

Many teachers have little meaningful professional development. Students and teachers must learn new skills to live and work in this digital age. In many cases there is a tech person, but the teacher has had minimal use and training in technology use, at whatever level there is technology for their use.

In thinking about education, most people do not understand the impact that technology has on students in their daily lives. Technology in some schools is seen as an Internet connection or a "wired" solution. Actually ubiquitous computing and the third wave of technology may allow some world communities "leapfrog" stages of development, establishing new practices without employing the old.

Many of today's schools may have a wire that does not connect to anything. The ratio of computers to children is aggregated to make us think that students actually have hands-on technology in most schools. We know that the level of technology varies by country, and by the way the use of technology is taught. Many schools and students are missing out on the richness of this learning experience for various reasons.

---

[8] http://www.ncrel.org/sdrs/areas/issues/educatrs/profdevl/darlinga.mov

Interactive Multimedia Technology

Today, interactive, multimedia technology can provide us with new ways to draw upon children's natural impulses. These new media hold an abundance of materials including text, voice, music, graphics, photos, animation and video. But they provide more than abundance. Bringing all these media together means that we can vastly expand the range of learning experiences, opening up the social and natural worlds. Students can explore the relations among ideas and thus experience a more connected form of learning.

Perhaps most importantly, these new media are interactive, and conducive to active, engaged learning. Students can choose what to see and do, and they have media to record and extend what they learn. Learning is thus driven by the individual needs and interests of the learner.

A quiet revolution is taking hold in many schools of education all over the country. Criticized for offering programmes that are long on theory and short on practice, many schools have responded with new approaches to teacher education. Students in these programmes develop subject matter expertise, practice teaching in real classrooms, connect with mentor teachers and learn the skills to teach with technology as media.

However, there remain problems with training, access, resources, the hardware and software and the understanding of how technology should be deployed in schools and learning communities. Studies of the process of educational change show that access to new information, procedures or tools alone rarely leads to change.

The U.S. National Academy of Engineering, in its report "Technically Speaking: Why All Americans Need To Know More About Technology", addresses the question of fluency with technology as a national problem. However, the ideas represented are global in scope.[10]

All teachers do not have these skills. Children have grown up digitally and may be masters of the technology, but the teachers who touch their future have been handicapped with a lack of sufficient knowledge about the use of technology. Teachers who teach with limited reach cripple the future of the children they teach.

Missing in our education policy is a focus that encourages the integration of technology content into the learning landscapes of K-12, in the standards, curricula, instructional material, and student assessments in non-technology subject areas. For technology to work well for students and schools, we must build human infrastructure at the same pace we are installing computers, systems, and hardware.

---

[10] http://www.nap.edu/catalog/10250.html

Technological Literacy[10]

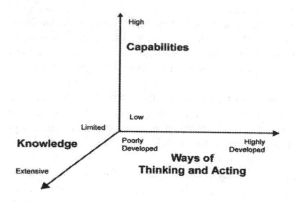

Information Literacy

Information literacy is a set of abilities requiring individuals to recognize when information is needed and have the ability to locate, evaluate, and use effectively the needed information.

Information literacy is also increasingly important in the contemporary environment of rapid technological change and proliferating information resources.

Because of the escalating complexity of this environment, individuals are faced with diverse and abundant information choices – in their academic studies, in the workplace, and in their personal lives.

Information is available through libraries, community resources, special interest organizations, media, and the Internet – and increasingly, information comes to individuals in unfiltered formats, raising questions about its authenticity, validity, and reliability."

So media literacy is needed, and a focus on the media as technology. As Dr. Bertram Bruce states[11] "At least three layers of meaning for technology are typically identified (see MacKenzie & Wajcman, 1999). First, there are physical devices, such as automobiles, telephones, or oil pipes. Second, there are the procedures, activities, or organizational systems that incorporate these devices. These may be represented in user manuals, but also in daily habits of users of the technologies.

---

[10] reproduced with the kind permission of the U.S. National Academy of Engineering, from http://www.nap.edu/books/0309082625/html/15html

[11] Bruce, B. C. (1999). Educational technology. In M. A. Peters & P. Ghiraldelli, Jr. (Eds.), Encyclopedia of philosophy of education (Enciclopédia de Filosofia da Educação). [Online: http://www.vusst.hr ENCYCLOPAEDIA/]

"Third, there is the technical knowledge that enables particular activities, for example, the accumulation of experiences by a midwife constitutes a technology for assisting in births. The line between these layers is not sharp. Devices can reify procedures, organizations are mutually constituted by their artifacts, and activities can be viewed as both knowledge and practices. This is in fact precisely the reason why people studying technology cannot restrict their view to physical components per se."

Returning to the question of what aspects of education, if any, are technological, the layered conception of technology suggests that technology is not a separable component of educational practice, but rather, a perspective, or set of perspectives, one may adopt on all educational activity. Some of the major perspectives are these.

First, educational technologies can be viewed as texts, as symbol systems to be interpreted by users. This perspective has led to a variety of analyses in the tradition of literary criticism. The prevalence and power of technologies as bearers of meaning leads for example to Heidegger's question concerning the essence of technology. His concept of Gestell (enframing) inscribes technology as a mode of thought prior to the scientific revolution, one which "reveals being" in a particular way. Thus, people are defined by the technological way of thought, and not simply users of technological devices.

However, not all interests are yet represented on the Internet. Communities need access to diverse and meaningful content in order for the Internet to have relevance.

Conclusion: the Need for A Knowledge Society

Nationally and internationally, it is crucial to work in ways that can narrow the "digital divide".

To quote from educators of the world, who issued this statement in July 2005 at a meeting held in Stellenbosch, South Africa:[12]

"Information and Communication Technologies are changing the World. We are now in the Information Society, a Society in which information is an essential and valuable commodity that one can buy, sell, store, or exchange. But this Society may also be the Society of the Digital Divide, enlarging the gap between the haves and the have-nots. As educators, we know that information and knowledge are not the same. We want not only an Information Society, but also a Knowledge Society in which Knowledge can be shared and distributed all around the world, enabling all children and all people to access Knowledge and to benefit from being educated. Education is a key issue in the Knowledge Society, and Educators have a major role and mission."

---

[12] http://www.unesco-iicba.org/index.php?option=com_content&task=view&id=76&Itemid=1

ENCOURAGING THE EFFECTIVE AND SUSTAINABLE USE OF INFORMATION AND COMMUNICATION TECHNOLOGIES FOR PROMOTING EDUCATION AND DEVELOPMENT

Titilayo Akinsanmi

Introduction: Promises Undelivered?

The use of information and communications technologies (ICT) in the educational sector, for poverty alleviation or in development in general, can potentially result – for those who have been empowered with the skills – in an increase in income, an increased quality of life, improved access to knowledge and change-makers, as well as providing the user with cultural and political advantages.

The unplanned introduction and adoption of ICT without a sustainable model that includes ownership by beneficiaries can intensify existing inequalities in society, and reinforce an internal chasm separating the "haves" and "have-nots" of society.

This "divide" is a complex problem that manifests itself in different ways across countries and communities. It presents both practical and policy challenges. Solutions that have been implemented successfully in developed countries cannot simply be transplanted to developing country environments or adapted haphazardly. While this could be seen as an obvious issue it is often neglected as a result of bad planning and time lines. The introduction of ICT must be based on an understanding of local needs, conditions and ownership.

ICTs have been punted as the "ultimate saviour" for reaching the Millennium Development Goal's and in particular the Education for All goals but they are more of an enabler – they have the potential to help reach both, but not without reliance on more traditional learning systems and technologies. This means an education-centred approach with ICTs adding pedagogical and learning value, enhancing the quality of, access to and the efficiency of the educational system in the classroom and beyond.

To date ICT initiatives have been failing to deliver on this potential because many initiatives lack credible knowledge of and experience with ICT. Many also fail to integrate and use effectively the knowledge that can be gained from past initiatives, both from a donor and from an implementing agency perspective.

ICTs for Development: the How, What and Why

In the first decade of ICTs taking up the role of an enabler in development and specifically in education most development initiatives were unable to provide sustainable, replicable models for community ICT use, and often erred with top-down approaches that were not grounded on the needs, interests, and active direction (or even participation) of local residents. Many government policies failed to provide a coherent long-term plan for prosperity, and actively obstructed efforts to address ICT disparities. The private sector, on the whole, initially failed to see the developing world as a valuable market and deliver targeted tailor-made products for the developing community. What was missing – and presumably still is, because of a myriad of reasons including donor focus – is an implementable and sustainable model for delivering ICT-enabled development at ground level based on local needs, local ownership and locally-led implementation.

A number of organizations and initiatives including SchoolNet Africa (education) and Bridges.Org (research oriented) have been examining the development of ICT, considering what works and what does not work, and why.

Bridges.Org building on its own experience and the thinking and work of a number of other organizations, has designed a holistic, integrated strategy it calls Real Access/Real Impact while SchoolNet Africa has what it terms the school networking value chain which is elaborated upon in its School Networking tool kit.

Real Access and Real Impact

The Real Access/Real Impact framework of Bridges.Org sets out the determining factors in whether there is *Real Access* to ICT: going beyond computers and connections such that a *Real Impact* on socio-economic development can be determined and not a focus on a specific technology application. It is "a roadmap to the digital divide that can be used to improve the way that ICT is integrated into initiatives in healthcare, education, small business development, government services and other programmes in the countries and communities that have the most to gain."[1]

The *Real Access* criteria are used as an analytical frame of all issues surrounding access to and use of ICT. They are designed to anticipate or detect the reasons that ICT development initiatives, government e-strategies, or grassroots projects fail to achieve their goals or highlight how and why these projects succeed.

ICT must be appropriate to local conditions, affordable and physically accessible. The people of the communities that the initiative is aimed at must also have at least a basic grasp of the benefits of the ICT via training and the deployment of relevant skills necessary to make use of it. This brings to the fore the issue of locally-relevant or locally-generated content and services which meet needs in the daily lives of the people without construing to be an added obstacle in the plethora of difficulties they are faced with.

---

[1] www.bridges.org

Socio-cultural factors must be addressed so they do not inhibit widespread ICT use – users must trust ICT in terms of security and privacy, amongst other issues.

Legal and regulatory frameworks must not limit the effective use of ICT, the local economic environment must be able to sustain its use, and national macro-economic policy must be conducive to widespread ICT use. Governments must have the political will to drive change, and the public must support government strategies to promote ICT use.

Sometimes initiatives address substantive issues effectively, but still fall short because of poor project administration. A set of guidelines for ICT development management advises projects to implement and disseminate best practice; ensure local ownership; do a needs-assessment; set concrete goals and take small achievable steps; critically evaluate efforts; address key external challenges; make it sustainable; and involve groups that are traditionally excluded.

Added Value in Education

Learning, it is said, occurs in four different streams in the 20th century.

1. Formal learning takes place in schools and higher education institutions providing systematic education.

2. Non-formal learning occurs outside the formal education system but is nevertheless an organized event with specific target groups or clients and learning objectives. This includes continuing education, adult education, professional training and literacy programmes.

3. Informal learning is the individual acquisition of skills, knowledge and attitudes from the everyday experience and environment. [2]

4. Virtual collaborative learning occurs both as an independent learning structure and or within networks made up of learners with similar learning needs in the case of initiatives like the African Virtual University and as an integrated strategy added on to "formal learning" experience within the classroom – an example of which is the Global Teenager Project (www.globalteenager.org).

The term distance education can be applied to the first two streams; the third is also becoming a major area in distance education while the fourth represents an area of learning merging the best of the first three options and needing more exploration as to what works in it. The term "lifelong learners" is increasingly used to describe the appropriation of learning tools combined with a depository of knowledge which the Internet has made readily accessible via a largely informal learning stream in the acquisition of skills and knowledge.

---

[2] www.col.org

The use of ICTs in education depends on a number of factors as depicted in the modified SchoolNet Africa value chain below. A few of these are elaborated upon below:

- *Geographical size and situation:* Large countries with dispersed people and communities, such as Nigeria, Argentina or Indonesia and island nations such as Madagascar, have an additional drive or motivation to use communications to deliver some educational services cost effectively

- *Policy on telecommunications, the Internet, IT and Education:* Privatization and liberalization of telecommunications and the Internet are improving quality, lowering costs and accelerating innovation around the world. A country's education and ICT policy is often key to raising awareness and providing leadership in educational use of ICTs.

- *Appropriate Technologies:* This includes the adoption of technologies that can be demonstrated to be most feasible in deployment for the specific situation in the community – school or centre – and not by the prevailing marketability or necessarily the newest technologies.

- *Funding Sustainability:* The means to address start-up investment challenges and the market affordability to attract commercial players are all-important ingredients to ease the way to change and growth.

- *Perceived educational or developmental needs (teacher and learner development):* These can relate to educational delivery challenges because of geographic or cultural isolation, or appreciation for the more systemic challenges – such as adapting to the demands of the information economy which can only be seriously addressed with ICTs.

SchoolNet Africa value chain

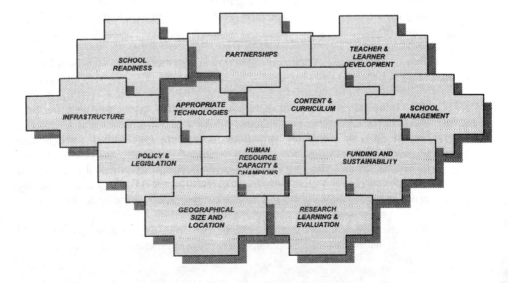

Many developing countries are facing fundamental problems with education delivery in which ICTs could assist. However, they face a severe challenge harnessing the necessary skills and resources to address the opportunity. Meanwhile high income countries can afford to address a wide range of felt needs. Not all their initiatives can be labeled as successes, but these countries can afford to experiment until they get it right.

Trends and Opportunities

Advances in telecommunications and related information technologies offer exciting new possibilities which have the power to transform the learning environment. Several terms are now seen as descriptive of current trends though they all too often contain a huge amount of rhetoric and "hype" as to how rapidly these new technologies can be adopted or provide impacts, for example:

- *Convergence:* the union of information, communications and media technologies, which brings about an almost seamless access to a full range of multi-media resources which educators and learners amongst others can use – an example is the use of hand-held devices including mobile phones in the healthcare sector and by nomads in northern Nigeria

- *Wireless and satellite:* the delivery of communications services by new technologies available at any time and anywhere at a lower cost – an example is satellite TV deployment in classrooms

- *Leapfrogging:* the opportunity for countries to jump to a new paradigm before problems associated with the delivery of high quality telecommunications or education services have been solved by traditional means

- *Privatization and liberalization:* seen as the twin vehicles for accelerating and facilitating technological advance and access to the wide range of options increasingly available to people living in high income and advanced countries – an example is the liberalization of Voice over Internet Protocol (VOIP) in South Africa.

It is clear that technological developments are coming together which offer the following benefits:

1. The Internet, worldwide Web, e-mail and other Internet-related feedback mechanisms offer new and enlarged sources of information and knowledge acquisition and exchange that offers to appropriately skilled teachers and learners opportunities for self-development as well as benefits from incorporation into classroom environments beyond their physical borders – as exemplified in the Virtual Learning Circles of the GTP. Greater opportunity exists to reduce the isolation and time delay associated with distance education.

2. With the extraordinary pace of software development, enriched teaching and learning with enhanced graphics, interaction, animation and visualization is accessible.

3. Through lowering telecommunications bandwidth costs and emergence of enhanced cable, wireless and satellite systems, greater opportunities for basic access, video-conferencing, on-line interactive learning, and live interaction within all streams of learning.

4. Through community access schemes, more often than not based within the "formal" school system, more potential exists to make the benefits of the four learning streams easily available to lower income people and rural communities. The tables beneath summarize some relevant trends in computers and local area networks (LANs) and the Internet and their current and potential impact on learning.[3]

COMPUTERS AND LANS		
CATEGORY	TREND	IMPACT
General	Higher operating speeds; lower cost of memory	Pictures, graphics and powerful software packages can be used economically. Education can thus harness ever-improving graphics capabilities to improve interest and acceptability to learners
PC development and marketing	Rapid pace of development will make more previous generation equipment available to education establishments which cannot afford their own.	More equipment availability at marginal cost (this may not be ideal in the rapid paced developed country environment, but could be significant at start-up level in some developing countries)
Software	Enhanced educational software: - integrates several elements seamlessly - offers learners, teachers and administrators control over the learning environment, results, records, etc.	More effectively moderated learning programmes are possible

THE INTERNET		
CATEGORY	TREND	IMPACT
General	Becoming ubiquitous as a service in urban and sub-urban areas at least, and becoming available in rural areas through various access strategies and technologies	On-line education techniques available to more and more students and lifelong learners
Web site technology	Web based learning becoming widespread	Making an incredible amount of information resources, learning management and student-system interaction available in very user-oriented fashion.
Desktop video	Teachers and students can create and exchange real-time or message based talking-head and multi-media materials from their office, school room or telecentre, without expensive production studio.	Easier and lower cost video-based lesson materials, and non real-time video clips will be sent by e-mail, enhancing contact between teacher and learner.
Special access hardware	Low priced Internet devices	These will make Internet-based computer use available to more and lower-income students, and facilitate more devices per classroom and more individualized usage.

---

[3] Commonwealth of Learning International: *Use of ICTs for Learning and Distance Education*

In summary, current trends are offering a combination of benefits that truly improve cost-effectiveness and make ICT-supported and enhanced learning an increasingly powerful alternative to the traditional classroom, even in developing countries. Importantly, this combination is also creating an "education market" in the technology and Internet service sectors which will, in turn, increase the level of core funding available from commercial companies who stand to benefit from the demand generated. This will supplement the funding from aid agencies.

The dilemma of developing countries is acute. Many are justifiably cautious that opening to new technology increases their dependency on outside resources. Nevertheless, they will have even fewer options and fall even further behind unless they open their markets sufficiently to improve their Internet access, and adopt policies that encourage the entry of private sector investors and service providers.

ICT Policy: What has Worked?

Education using information and communications technology, whether formal or informal, is to a large extent dependent on the reach and quality of a country's existing ICT infrastructure. For example, telephone density either limits or allows people to have access to the Internet, and the quality, and capacity of the network determines the potential for multi-media applications. Another key condition is the cost of access; high cost telecommunications severely limits the take-up of ICT enabled initiatives,

Privatization and liberalization as mentioned earlier are important steps in the ICT sector reform process, resulting in accelerated infrastructure development.

Privatization typically injects needed capital into the sector. In developing countries this often means foreign capital injection. The private investment allows a speedier network upgrade and roll-out than the state-owned or supported cash-strapped former monopoly operator could accomplish, either in the telecommunications or technology sector. National policies not only need to aim at privatizing operators but also to ensure that the investment climate is secure and attractive. With privatization comes a more entrepreneurial and efficient management of the telecom operation. However, this approach is highly contested in a wide variety of sectors.

The introduction of competition is the next step and an important condition for network development. Whereas privatization can bring needed investment to the sector and promote efficient management by the operators, competition is the factor that drives the prices down for telecommunications services and the technology sector. The strengthening of free and open source technologies has influenced the adoption and deployment of proprietary versions in most cases – though reactive in its response.

Although telecommunications sector reform is called deregulation, it is misleading to think regulation is no longer needed in a liberalized and competitive market, or that the market simply regulates itself. Governments faced with the need to liberalize often fear that national objectives and development goals will be neglected by the market, assuming that liberalization is synonymous with the absence of regulation. This is not the case if effective regulation is in place.

Deregulation means mainly that the government stops influencing the operation of telecommunications networks. Often the ministry responsible for telecommunications is the policy setting body, the regulator and the operator. This needs to end with privatization and liberalization. Effective liberalization requires an independent regulatory body outside the ministry responsible for telecommunications, since the ministry often still has an ownership interest in the former monopoly operator.

A recurrent key problem is that the former monopoly operator uses its market dominance to hinder new entrants. The regulator's role is to ensure a level playing field and fair competition.

The following policy principles and regulations are important:

- *Liberalization of Internet Service Providers (ISPs):* The majority of countries seem to be following this principle, including developing countries.

- *General "hands off" approach toward Internet regulation:* This approach recognizes the fact that the Internet has developed so rapidly, largely owing to the fact that it was free of hindering regulation. The Working Group on Internet Governance of the World Summit on the Information Society has recently submitted a report – in debate – on propositions for "governing" the Internet.[4]

- *Promoting broadband and advanced communications:* This can be achieved by allowing competition to flourish with the government and development agencies remaining "technology neutral".

- *Low import tax on computer hardware and software:* This applies also to telecommunications equipment.

- *Ensuring that transmission capacity pricing is low and cost-based:* Otherwise ISPs cannot offer affordable consumer prices to achieve a mass market. Again, competition is an important prerequisite for lower prices.

Similarly crucial is the pricing of local dial-up access to ISPs, which determines the speed of Internet take-up. There is an African policy initiative to guarantee local call prices for access to ISPs nationally, however only 13 countries had subscribed to the concept as of 2001.

Education Policy

The following policy initiatives are important conditions and facilitators of ICT based learning:

1. *Government awareness of the importance of ICTs for national education.* This calls for understanding that:

---

[4] www.wsis.org

    a.   ICTs are vitally important to the development of the economy and to participation in the global information society, with a corresponding need to develop appropriate skills, and

    b.   ICT based learning and distance education can play a crucial role in broadening access to education for the whole society and reaching the Education for All goal

2.   *A strategic plan or policy.* This must be based on an analysis of needs and priorities for the use of ICT to improve education – the SchoolNet Africa value chain being a possible basis to begin with. Some key elements and concrete steps of such a strategic plan include:

    a.   ICT skills integration in national curricula – in teacher training institutions and in-the classroom

    b.   Equipping schools with appropriate technologies such as computers

    c.   Teacher and administrator training on ICT

    d.   Initiatives and programmes which invite and attract private sector involvement.

2.   *The presence of local participation and initiative, and serious considerations regarding the self-sustainability of projects.* Financially; skills-wise (e.g. through train the trainers); equipping teachers to use these technologies in teaching; long-term maintenance of such technologies; support systems to ensure longevity to get optimal use from resources committed to such technologies. In order to develop sustainable ICT based education in developing countries, models of financing need to be devised which provide for transition from initial dependency on the international donor agencies to self-sustaining and continuing institutions.

A policy on ICT in education is just one facet of preparing the population and workforce in all parts of the country to be productive, competitive and at-ease in the information economy. Education is fundamental to achieving development – education not just in terms of skills acquisition, but in the application and implementation of skills to meet needs of the communities to bring about development.

ICT IN EDUCATION: A PRACTICAL APPROACH

Esther Wachira

Introduction

Information and communication technologies (ICTs) have become an indispensable tool in the fight against world poverty. ICTs provide the developing countries with an unprecedented opportunity to meet vital development goals such as poverty reduction, basic health care and education far more effectively than before. Those nations that succeed in harnessing the potential of ICTs can look forward to greatly expanded economic growth.

ICTs help us communicate more effectively. They provide capability to derive the economic and social benefits that electronic communications can bring. ICTs mean radio, television, satellite, fixed telephone, video, fax, and computers, wireless communication devices such as mobile phones, DVDs, CD-ROMs, voicemail and the Internet.

For the developing countries, access to a preferred type and quality of ICT is a dream. There are great numbers in the population owning radio and television assets. A computer is not common around houses. The goal is instead to gain access to where there is one – a costly attempt for an individual. Yet at the heart of ICT is computer-related technology. Without computer literacy one may be limited to earlier and almost archaic forms of ICTs. ICTs are to be fast, efficient, and intended to generate and allow quick processing and sharing of information. Digital alternatives play a significant role in this. Computer technology is the core of the digital alternative.

The Digital Divide

Though inequalities in the ICT access are more revealed across countries, inequalities exist within the countries where there is an information underclass. In developing countries where less than 1% of the population has access to ICTs, the digital divide is largely a rural-urban divide with those in the urban areas being on the vantage point.

Women in many developing countries constitute the majority of the urban and rural poor. Female-headed households have a higher level of poverty than male-headed ones. Women constitute the highest number of the unemployed and the illiterate. Because of the foregoing poverty related reasons, women in Kenya have a disproportionately low access to ICTs. The prevalence of illiteracy has denied them access to ICT and gainful employment. In situations where ICT facilities exist, the dominant use of English as the language of the Web has shut out many women from using ICTs. Beside the gender dimension, the rural populations have remained disadvantaged in accessing these vital technologies. The youth are critical in the uptake of information and communication technologies because the culture of utilizing ICTs needs to be cultivated early in life.

Technology to some brings the promise and benefit of inclusion, opportunity and wealth and still to others, greater isolation and increased poverty. It is necessary to greatly increase public access to ICT technology. Affordable access to information infrastructure and the effective use of the gained knowledge are key factors for economic sustainability and improved social conditions. The divide is based on insufficient infrastructure, high cost of access, inappropriate or weak policy regimes, inefficiencies in the provision of telecommunication networks and services and locally created content and the inability to derive economic and social benefits from information intensive activities.

To bridge the divide and harness potential benefits of ICTs, we need to build human capacity, develop appropriate content and increase competition especially in telecommunications and Internet-related business. The success of the ICT expanding initiative lies in the coordinated action and commitment of all stakeholders; the government, the citizenship, the donor organizations, private-public partnerships, NGOs and multilateral institutions.

The education sector is charged with the responsibility of producing an informed population for today and tomorrow. This sector should train and produce informed citizens who fit into the diverse sectors of the economy and properly function in society. Out of the education sector, other sectors draw information, manpower and ideas. It is the basic place to begin attempts at bridging the digital divide. Efforts must start from the primary, secondary, tertiary, diploma level and training institutes to the national and public universities and institutes

The challenge lies not in starting such programmes but in gaining support (technical and financial) for such programmes backed by strong institutional and policy framework. This should not be seen as a task for the public sector manager, but one among those rare "joint ventures" between the government, private sector, NGOs and other stakeholders in the education sector.

ICT in the Development Process

ICT should not be seen to offer panacea for social and economic development. There is a growing need to evaluate the social and economic impacts of ICTs and to create opportunities for capacity building that will ensure their beneficial use and absorption within national economies.

However ICT can be an enabler of the of the development goals because its unique characteristics improve communication and information exchange to strengthen and create new economic social networks. These characteristics include:

- ICT is pervasive and cross cutting;

- ICT is a key enabler in the creation of networks;

- ICT fosters dissemination of information and knowledge by separating content from the physical location;

- The "digital" and "virtual" nature of many ICTs products and services allows for zero or declining marginal costs;

- ICTs power to store, retrieve, sort and filter distribute and share information seamlessly can lead to substantial efficiency gains in production, distribution and markets;

- ICT makes it possible for users to acquire products and services directly from the original provider, reducing the need for intermediaries; and

- ICT is global and can transcend the cultural and linguistic barriers.

For ICT to facilitate crucial links in the process of development and spur economic growth, proper infrastructure and policies have to be in place. The potential of ICTs can be captured for sustainable development through applications in Health, Education, economic opportunities, empowerment and participation, sustainable environment management.

However to harness the potential of ICT in these areas:

- Initiatives should explicitly define their development goals and how they will directly impact the target group.

- Initiatives should be driven by user demand, identified and realized through direct participation and ownership

- ICTs solutions should be built to last

- Initiatives should be sensitive to local conditions and limitations, considering affordability, accessibility, maintenance and flexibility.

- The interest of key stakeholders must be broadly aligned with each other and with the goals of the intervention.

ICTs can be framed and applied as tools in alleviating poverty, extending health services, expanding educational opportunities and generally improving the quality of life for many of the disadvantaged. However such framing must realize the outcomes are only plausible when ICT deployment is accompanied by concurrent public policies supporting equitable access to social institutions such as health care, education, government and other benefits potentially available through the application of digital tools and communications.

Harnessing ICTs for Educational Programmes

There is an immense opportunity for the utilization of ICTs in the education sector, for learners, teachers and the administrators. Countries should analyze the opportunities that may be present to use ICTs in education, by weighing them against the constraints in their education systems. Education choices have to be made first in terms of objectives, methodologies, and roles of teachers and students before decisions on appropriate technologies can be made. No technology will fix bad educational philosophy and practice. Learning objective should be aligned with learning technologies.

There are four rationales for the use of computers in schools:

- Social rationale – this is the demystification of the importance of computers at school level;

- Vocational rationale – the need to prepare learners for employment through providing computer competencies, including educational programmes;

- Pedagogical rationale – the use of computers to improve on the delivery of education and as an aid in the teaching and learning process;

- Catalytic rationale – use of the computer in the overall performance of schools, integrating functions of teaching and learning management and administration.

Whereas the developed nations are placing emphasis on the development of e-commerce, the World Wide Web and Internet, the developing world is still grappling with attaining access to ICT equipment and gathering hands-on experience in operating ICT devices. Affordability should be addressed, as it is the largest single reason for the low use of ICTs in the developing world.

The capability of ICTs to achieve development goals will not be effectively leveraged without content that is responsive to user needs and local conditions. If ICTs are to be used for education purposes, the content should be relevant to the curricular requirements of the education system and the needs of the students, teachers and administrators.

Establishing the best policy framework is essential if the development potential of ICTs is to be fully realized. Effective introduction of ICTs requires policies and planning at various levels. At the national level, when leaders recognize the benefits of ICT it is easier to allocate funds for their support. Incentives can be provided to increase the involvement of the private sector. The government should show support and commitment and be involved in the democratization process of access to ICTs. The regulatory framework should be adaptable to allow faster expansion of ICT use and enterprise growth.

Capacity Building

There is need for low cost solutions, government support and increased involvement of the telecommunication providers in narrowing the gap between the capacities of urban and rural schools. Technology infrastructure needs upgrading, more so with poor telecommunications infrastructure in the developing world. Maintaining permanent qualified technical support is costly and trade-offs should be made. Teachers in the schools should be trained to cut across teaching as well as providing technical support. The success of ICTs will to a large extent be based on the cooperation between the technical and educational infrastructure. The quality of manpower and teachers in the ICT programmes has a great direct impact on the success of ICT learning. There is a need for dedicated human resources with several roles. A full time IT teacher who should have appropriate technical training for technical backstopping would be appropriate for each school.

Basic literacy is of crucial importance for the development of ICT. To deploy ICT for development, countries should develop a critical mass of trained personnel at various levels. Developing human capacity in ICT will be supported by the promotion of relevant educational curricula and the creation of new educational facilities with emphasis on ICT skills development. Teachers often do not know what they can do with technology and the tendency is to use ICT simply to automate traditional teaching methods. Teachers need to get critical guidelines and upgrading of their skills for effective use of ICT.

Partnerships

Partnerships between the various stakeholders in ICT programmes will be central to the full adoption of ICTs. Issues raised with partners revolve around the need for strong co-ordination and support from the government; active partnerships between the government, NGOs, the private sector, donors and telecommunication providers; private-public sector partnerships for long-term sustainability; and complementary donor funding for such programmes. Partnerships need to be flexible, strength-related, prioritized and have clearly defined goals. Of importance is the involvement of the implementers and members of the wider community. This group of people is often overlooked but forms the strongest basis for the sustainability and successful implementation of ICT projects.

MOVING BEYOND THE DIGITAL GAP: INVESTING IN THE YOUNG TO CREATE NEW LEARNING AND SOCIO-ECONOMIC OPPORTUNITIES[1]

Clotilde Fonseca

1.   From Digital Gap to Digital Opportunities

George Bernard Shaw, the English dramatist and social critic, said that at the age of five he was forced to abandon his education in order to attend school. Shaw's insightful statement undoubtedly throws light on the difference between learning and schooling, a distinction that has received significant attention in recent years. To most children in the developing world, school offers little beyond basic instruction. In the anxious race to respond to the necessary questions of basic literacy and job-related skills, teachers and institutions have frequently failed both in adequately teaching those skills and in responding to the children's interests and cognitive inclinations. Like Bernard Shaw, many would rather learn from more direct and vital sources.

Furthermore, in a world progressively subject to technological transformations, these children have had little, if any, contact with technology. As it was frequently pointed out, most children in developing countries have never made a phone call, let alone use a computer or browse the Internet.   Contact with technology marvels, but is generally elusive. The symbols of technology – which children normally perceive as symbols of future and progress – are, to children in the developing world and even in the less developed areas of more developed societies, distant symbols of a future that they are usually condemned to observe, slipping through the window – of a window that is, paradoxically, a technological one, that of the television screen.

Computers and access to networks, however, open up new cognitive and productive dimensions. They offer the means to turn elusive hopes into concrete opportunities. When adequately introduced in innovative formal or informal learning settings, they provide a context for the development of children's interests and talents. They support the development of new skills and competencies, as well as contribute to the formation of a positive vision about their own future, as well as to their self image and self efficacy.

---

[1] The present text is an updated and expanded version of the article "The Computer: A New Door to Educational and Social Opportunities", published originally in 1999 by LCSI, Canada in the book *Logo Philosophy and Implementation*. It has been reviewed for inclusion in this publication at the request of the editors.

To put it in the words of a Costa Rican teacher: "television is a window that lets you look into the future. Through it, we can get glimpses of what a future world for us might be like. But the computer offers us a door through which we can enter that future." Like this teacher, many of us are convinced that digital technologies have the potential to be a door to development, especially for the young in the more deprived sectors of society. This is particularly so when these technologies are seen not only as technological objects, as symbols of progress, but as part of an emerging culture that is generating powerful transformations in all areas of human activity, a culture that needs to be properly understood and appropriated.

Digital Technologies as Infrastructural Technologies

The importance and penetration of digital technologies – or ICT as they are frequently referred to[2] – has become so strong that today analysts refer to them as "infrastructural technologies," just like electricity and transportation. As we all know, digital technologies have become a fundamental platform for all productive, learning and communication processes in industry, business and society. As Carr has stated, as their ubiquity and power have grown, particularly in more developed sectors of society, they have become critical, not simply strategic. Their importance today depends much more on the innovative and creative capacity of the people who use them than on their availability. Robert McDowell, Vice President of Microsoft Corporation has expressed this new reality in quite descriptive terms, when he says that the real worth of these technologies is found "in what happens between the ears."[3]

The Digital Revolution and the Importance of Mind

Manuel Castells, one of the leading contemporary analysts and thinkers on issues of the information age and the knowledge economy, stated that "the human mind is for the first time a direct productive force and not just a decisive element of the production system" (Castells, 2002, p, 43). The real power associated to the IT revolution, he points out, is not in information and knowledge per se, but in the symbolic capacity required to handle and create symbolic material for the generation of products and services.

Paradoxically, within the context of the technology-intensive cultural and productive world in which we live, the most important tool is the human intellect, particularly human imagination and inventiveness, which are central to innovation and generation of

---

[2] The term "digital technologies" has been preferred to that of "information and communication technologies" or "ICT". The latter term is frequently clearly associated to a broadcasting paradigm. It tends to place too much weight on the "information" and "communication" dimension of these technologies and frequently leads to a reductionist view of the potential and possibilities of these technologies. This type of focus tends to leave out key aspects of digital technologies, such as computer programming, simulation, robotics, to name only a few. The real revolution of our times is the digital revolution, which is clearly much more than connectivity, downloading and uploading of information as a significant part of the education and development community tends to believe.

[3] Robert McDowell's statement was made during a videoconferencing segment of the debate "Nicholas Carr vs. Roberto Sasso: Is IT Strategic or Not?" held at the National Auditorium, San José, Costa Rica on August 24, 2005.

value. The development of mind and of human capacity is, therefore, central to socio-economic development. It is a key strategic element in poverty reduction efforts. Politicians and development experts alike need to take notice. This is obviously the greatest challenge, since it involves bridging the social and cognitive divide as well as the technology gap.

The cost effectiveness of the use of computers and networks in schools and communities must be seen, therefore, within the context of more complex and far reaching issues of human and national development. As Seymour Papert has warned us repeatedly, the educational community must transcend the common tendency to expect the computer, or access to the Internet, for that matter, to have an effect as a new teaching tool. The real task before us, Papert has noted, is to rethink and reformulate education in the presence of the computer and to exploit its power in the process of learning and creating.

2. Investing in the Young to Capture Digital Opportunities: The Case of Costa Rica

It is precisely for this reason that education and capacity building efforts have to transcend the still common focus on "computer literacy" or access to connectivity and content. Bridging the digital divide will never be achieved simply by providing access to computers and networks. The digital divide involves, as has been indicated, a social and cognitive divide as well as a technological one. The challenge is twofold. It must be addressed in unison.

Even though in general the social construct of the computer is still frequently that of a mathematical and word processing machine, a progressively higher number of individuals and professionals have committed their effort to its use as an option to bring about a process of transformation in the traditional school environment and to establish bridges among individuals and communities working for the higher goal of more humanized forms of development. One such instance has been an initiative put forth in Costa Rica in 1988, launched as an investment in the talent of Costa Rica's teachers and youth.

Origins of the Costa Rican Initiative

The way in which Costa Rica chose to introduce computer technology into its schools is an example of what a developing nation can accomplish with vision and sustained commitment. Seen in retrospect, what is today known as Costa Rica's National Educational Informatics Program involved commitment, risk taking and decisive investment. This initiative is today a fully developed program that has grown and consolidated over almost two decades of work.

The program was created and jointly implemented by the Costa Rican Ministry of Public Education and the Omar Dengo Foundation. For almost two decades, the program was sustained through different political, technological and economic contexts with the basic ongoing support of seven ministers of education throughout five different administrations. Even if levels of commitment and investment have varied, it is evident that program results and impacts on the lives of teachers and students has gained important national and political support.

Program design and implementation involved addressing issues of equity, access to technology, and the development of technology-enhanced learning environments for teachers and students. Special priority has always been given to students with special needs and to children and youth from rural, low income and marginalized communities that rapidly became part of the program and received the benefits not only of the technology, but of a series of important training and support services.

Pedagogical Focus and Program Approach

Costa Rica opted to provide these opportunities first to young children. For this reason, the program initiated in elementary school and provided services to K-6 grade students. With its children-oriented approach, Costa Rica broke away from what was at the time international standard for the introduction of computer technology in schools which was basically oriented to high school students for the development of job related skills. The main focus of attention became the development of cognitive, problem-solving and creative skills and capabilities. This approach, which the Costa Rican Ministry of Public Education and the Omar Dengo Foundation nurtured as early as 1987, during the planning period, is clearly responsible for the program's achievements throughout the years.

Since 1988, the program was conceived to bring about change in children and teachers, to rekindle interest in learning, and to develop technology skills within the school and the community where the computers are placed. Considering the program's objective of stimulating creativity, cognitive development and collaborative work, Logo was chosen as the main learning and exploration environment. In 1998, LogoWriter, the initial program used, was substituted by MicroWorlds, a multimedia program consistent with the Logo philosophy and environment which is used as a generic programming and educational tool. MicroWorlds[4] is the central tool used, though other Microsoft productivity and reference tools are also available and used when pertinent to the educational objectives.

The children's learning activities are project-based and curriculum-related. The development of computer literacy skills is seen as a valuable by-product of higher educational goals. The program has also generated other types learning situations and opportunities for students and teachers which provide additional enrichment opportunities, including access to themes, materials and experiences not normally present in the traditional school setting or in their normally more limited, if not deprived, community or home environment. Like the program that hosts them, these new educational situations attempt to relate learning and personal productivity and to help children develop an awareness of the potential contributions they can make to their own lives and communities.

---

[4] In 1997, the Costa Rican Ministry of Education purchased a national licences of MicroWorlds, thus making it possible for all students and teachers to have the software available in school, at home, and in other formal and informal learning and recreational environments.

Throughout the eighteen years of program implementation, Seymour Papert, Mitch Resnick, David Cavallo and other members of the Learning and Epistemology Group of MIT's Media Lab have provided support and ideas for program design and for the development of teacher training strategies. They have worked with Omar Dengo Foundation and Ministry of Education personnel both through ODF's Educational Innovation Center, and more recently through the Innov@ Institute on Learning and Technology. In order to provide sound understanding of theory and good implementation practice, ODF has generated initiatives for the academic and professional development of its teachers, trainers and advisors in the program. Training, support and follow up of professional development initiatives constitute a central part of program investment. In this process, ODF has always counted on the support of national universities as well as of other international research and development academic centers.

The Costa Rican Educational Informatics Program has been clearly centered on the development of teachers and children. Even though more than thirteen different project development options were considered during the planning phase back in 1987 the one finally selected was that which was more intensely teacher-dependent.[5] This was so because one of the main objectives of the program was to rekindle the teachers' interests in their own professional development and to help them value their role as apprentices. Instead of bypassing the teacher through the use of technology, as has frequently been the case, the Costa Rican program chose to focus on stimulating and developing teacher talent and knowledge about learning and technology. For this purpose, a strong and systemic teacher-training and follow up program was created (see Fonseca, 1993).

Teacher Development and Follow Up

Instead of by-passing the teacher through the use of technology, as has very frequently been attempted, the program chose to focus on teacher development precisely by using the stimulating potential of computers. For this purpose, a strong and systemic teacher-development and follow-up program was created (see Fonseca, 1993). The preparation of the tutors who work as lab attendants has been conceived as a continuing education effort which must transcend computer-related matters. Much time and effort have been devoted to aspects of educational philosophy and practice. Teacher development has throughout been seen as a process which requires different types of pedagogical, motivational, and technical inputs at different times. This fundamental component has been the responsibility of a group of advisors, a well-prepared and highly motivated permanent task force in charge of developing training materials and modules who also provide on-site and, more recently, virtual or on-line support.

As part of the teacher development activities, every two years, a national "Computers in Education Conference" is organized by the Omar Dengo Foundation. The conference promotes the exchange of experiences as well as the introduction to new ideas and initiatives undertaken by colleagues in other areas of the country. The conference, as well

---

[5] For a detailed analysis of how the Program was created and of the central criteria for its success, see Clotilde Fonseca, *Computadoras en la Escuela Pública Costarricense: La Puesta en Marcha de una Decisión*. San José, Ediciones de la Fundación Omar Dengo, 1991.

as the different training programs, is part of an effort to construct a truly professional program culture. This has been strongly stressed within the program, since in a new area such as that of educational computing, there is a need to generate a new set of attitudes and behaviors associated to this new educational context. The construction of this new culture is something that the program attempts to address not only through the work with teachers, tutors and advisors, but with school principals, supervisors, and other educational authorities as well.

Issues of Gender

An important aspect associated with teacher participation in the Costa Rican Computers in Education Program is the gender component. It is worthy of note that within this program, over 90 percent of the teachers working as tutors and 97 percent of advisors and program staff are women. Most of them had never had any prior experience with computer technology before joining the program. This fact is no doubt meaningful. While it is true that in Costa Rica most teachers are women, the fact that it has been mostly women who have chosen to become computer tutors says a lot about program perception and ability to respond to different teachers' learning styles and sources of motivation. To most of these women, participating in the program has been an act of self-assertion which has contributed to their self-esteem and their prestige within their own local and professional communities. This undoubtedly generates a new source of non-traditional role models for the thousands of girls in the program.

Program Beneficiaries: Students, Teachers, Principals and Community Members

Since the program has a strong and sound educational focus, the Foundation also provides intensive training and follow-up on how to use the computers and networking capabilities within a personally and educationally meaningful context. At present the Omar Dengo foundation provides annual training for thousands of lab tutors, program advisors, principals and educational authorities. On weekends, after school hours and during vacation periods, the Foundation also organizes courses directed to different members of the community. These courses help train individuals as well as company and community groups on productivity tools as well as special computer and Internet applications. Special efforts have also been made to integrate students from rural and less developed areas of the country. At present 57% of the children from cantons with special needs participate.

Over the years, the Costa Rican Educational Informatics Program has provided services to over 1.5 million children and teachers. The focus of the program has clearly been responsible for the achievements that the program has been able to document. The studies conducted by ODF's Research Department, show that children participating in the program have become professionals. They report the importance of what the early use of technology and the ways in which they were introduced to them, had a very important effect in the view they developed about their own future, and about their own capacities to tackle problems and challenges.[6] Changes in teachers, culture and practice have also been meaningful and salient.

New Learning and Exchange Opportunities and Environments

Throughout the years, the Costa Rican Program has created a series of extremely powerful and meaningful learning opportunities and environments that have allowed children and youth participating in the program to better understand their own creative and productive potential. Among these initiatives, the following have been particularly enriching and challenging and are cited as examples of the types of projects implemented both for elementary and high school teachers and students:

- The Children´s Conference: Created in 1989, the Children´s Computers in Education Conference gathers several hundred K-6 students in an environment that is both recreational and educational. The children work throughout the school year on different research and creative development projects. Each school selects two students to represent it at the Conference where the young students present their work and that of other classmates. They also participate in special activities ranging from new design, telecommunications, or robotics workshops to involvement in cultural and recreational experiences.

- The Teachers Conference: Launched initially in 1989, and organized every two years an Educational Informatics Teachers Conference that brings together hundreds of computer tutors and advisors from around the country. At this event, teachers present their experiences, exchange lessons learn and participate in different workshops of their interest.

- The Children´s Robotics Festival. Created in 2002, the festival is held every two years. Through this activity, young children who have developed an interest and experience in educational robotics within the program design themselves learning situations and workshops through which they share their own knowledge and skill with children from other public schools that do not yet have access to robotics initiatives. These experiences are part of the work of the Robotics and Learning through Design Area of the Center for Educational Innovation which provides support to the elementary schools and high schools that participate in the program.

- The Children´s Telematics Encounter: The program also hold a national Children´s Telematics Encounter through which students and teachers share their own web based productions and develop different types of activities to promote connectedness among participants, schools, and regions from around the country.

---

[6] Testimonials from children and youth who participated in the Program and are now professionals can be found in the Omar Dengo Foundation´s Research Department documents and publications. A video has also been produced with this material which is available on the web: www.fodweb.net or www,fod.ac.cr

- The New Millenium Electronic Magazine and the "Zone M" Journal: Emphasis on production and creation has been a key component of all educational experiences. Throughout the years, students have organized to produce different types of digital products, including journals and magazines that the students themselves design, produce and exchange, based on virtual meetings and agreements on line.

- "Ciudad Alegría": The program also has a series of web-based learning environments and productions that are free to use on-line. The "City of Joy" has been created as an innovative environment oriented to generate web-based learning experiences with high interactivity, thinking and creative dimensions. Among the different options students and children find in this enriched learning context are experiences and materials that range from productions oriented to "Reading the World" both through the understanding of texts as through the understanding of images and digital productions ("Lectores Interactivos"), as well as environments that stimulate students to create their own film ("Luces, Cámaras, Acción) and their own poems or even to travel through the world or Costa Rican art in order to understand better Costa Rican scenery and history ("Artistas y Viajeros").

- Active Citizenship through Deliberative Capacity (CADE): CADE is an initiative of ODF's Research Department that has been developed to stimulate active citizenship, dialogue, perspective taking and consensus building in elementary school children. The project focuses on the development of critical thinking and interpersonal skills. Through it the children address real problems that they select from their own communities and agree on solutions that they discuss and implement. CADE has developed its own "preferendum online," a powerful web-based tool that is used to discuss topics, vote, and reach agreements among children from different schools. This project has been developed in collaboration with the Harvard Task Force on Children and Democracy and with the Child Health and Social Ecology Group.

- Labor@: Practice firms and learning through simulated entrepreneurial environments. Labor@ is a high school enrichment program which allows young students ages 14-24 to operate a simulated technology-intensive practice firm. The project has developed a service center which provides a simulated environment through which students lean and experience different banking, tax payment, social security, marketing and financial transactions. This initiative counts with the ongoing pedagogical, organizational and technological support and follow up of Omar Dengo Foundation and Ministry of Public Education personnel. The initiative is currently being implemented in different high schools around the country.

Educational Innovation through the Meaningful Appropriation of Technology

Within this context the Omar Dengo Foundation developed a leadership role, particularly in areas of research and development both within the formal education program implemented jointly with the Ministry, as within the context of other programs and projects ODF implements directly in Costa Rica and in other countries in the region within its recently created Innov@ Institute on Learning, Technology and Development. The Institute brings together the different centers that ODF had created in order to be able to respond to the demands posed by the National Educational Informatics Program as well as by other sectors of the Costa Rican and Latin American public. Among these are the Center for On-Line Learning and Digital Production, the Center for Educational Innovation, the Center for Maintenance and Support, and the Center for Digital Citizenship and Productivity. [7] On-line and virtual learning experiences for both students and teachers are being developed. It must be noted that within the Costa Rican program networking has always been seen as an exploration and problem-solving tool to enable students and teachers to transcend their own geographical and cultural limitations, which include the lack of libraries and other enriching educational opportunities.

Research Findings

It is interesting to note that, as recent research has shown, participation in the Children's Conference generates an important impact on the children's self-esteem and perception of their own future. A contest held by the Foundation in 1997 made it possible to collect the experiences and stories of former program students, many of whom are now in high school or pursuing university careers. These stories revealed that the conference was of importance in the definition of the children's perception of themselves and of their possibility to organize a successful future. Many of the respondents narrated how their participation in the program and in the activity was the beginning of what they perceived as a change in their lives.

These findings are completely consistent with what research on the program has revealed throughout the years. It is interesting to note that one of the central impacts of the program has been identified is in the area of the development and strengthening of the children's and the teachers self-esteem and perception of the future, an impact that was not initially envisioned but that proves central to the development of the individual and of his or her learning capacity. The program has also had an important impact on the children's creativity as a 1993 study conducted by the Ministry of Education showed. It has also increased children's independence as well as the motivation to attend school.

3. Harnessing Digital Opportunities: Addressing Issues and Implementing Actions

In 1987, when the Omar Dengo Foundation was created, there was among the founders the clear conviction that investment in educational technology would have an impact on the country's socio-economic development. This was clearly reflected in the institution's constitutive documents. In 1992, many were still skeptical when some of us wrote that equitable access to the uses of technology to further educational goals could contribute to transforming a basically agricultural society to a service-oriented information age

---

[7] For a detailed description of the Omar Dengo Foundation educational and development programs as well as to know more about its educational innovation, research and training initiatives, see http://fodweb.net or http://www.fod.ac.cr

society, that is, towards new industries that are more productive and less taxing to the environment (Fonseca 1992).

Though changes of this systemic sort always arise as the result of complex and intricate processes, and it would be naive to establish a direct cause-effect relationship, it is worthy of notice that among the reasons mentioned for the selection of Costa Rica as a technology industry investment site by such corporations as Acer, Intel, Microsoft, Proctor and Gamble, and Hewlett Packard, among others, is the use of computers in education programs. Though access to broad band and high quality connectivity is still today a national challenge, Costa Rica is still among the countries in the hemisphere with more widespread use of computers. It is today one of the world's centers for outsourcing services[8]. This is no doubt due to the country's educational tradition and to the level of technology fluency in the Costa Rican population.

It is no doubt a symbolic coincidence that on the same day the first elementary school computer lab was inaugurated, exactly ten years later, on the 18th of March, 1998, Intel begun the operation of its microchip production plant, its first in all of Latin America. In the 2001 Technology Report of the United Nations Development Program, Costa Rica emerged as a potential leader within its Technology Advancement Index. The reason for this important placement was due to the technology diffusion efforts that the country has undertaken, and very particularly due to the achievements in widespread initiatives in human capacity building, particularly among the new generations.[9] As a matter of fact, many children who participated as students within the program in the late 80's and 90's have gone on to become professionals in different technology and software industries, as ODF Research Department has documented.

In Costa Rica harnessing digital opportunities to close the digital divide has also meant establishing strong multistakeholder partnerships.[10] The Costa Rican Educational Informatics Program is really an excellent example of how the public sector can join forces with a public interest non-profit organization such as the Omar Dengo Foundation and jointly channel the support of national and international academia, development agencies and international corporations. These partnerships have been grounded on ambitious projects with clear implementation goals that have at the base powerful education and social ideas and initiatives. Partnerships are undoubtedly one of the key components of technology in education and technology in community development efforts in Costa Rica and worldwide.

---

[8] Today Costa Rica holds the third position in the Global Outsourcing Report of 2005. It is preceded only by India and China. Source: Minevich, Mark and Richter, Frank- Jürgen Richter. Global Outsourcing Report 2005. Going Global Ventures, Inc. New York, March 2005.

[9] United Nations Development Program (2001) Human Development Report: "Placing Technological Progress at the Service of World Development" New York.

[10] The Omar Dengo Foundation has conducted a research project to document the development of multistakeholder partnerships within the National Educational Informatics Program. This project is part of an initiative sponsored by the Global Knowledge Partnership (GKP) which will be presented at the World Summit on the Information Society in November of 2005.

Optimistic Scenarios

Experienced and somewhat skeptical experts and professionals in the field may view Costa Rica as an optimistic case of the use of computers in schools and communities in the developing world. And, as Peter Schwartz has warned us, people refer to optimistic views of the future as unrealistic, and, what is more, according to a notion we have tended to import from business: that it is particularly negative to be unrealistic (*The Art of Long View*, 1991).

However, if countries really want to start generating change in education, they must abandon the dictatorship of a linear view of development which does not allow for leaps that can bring about qualitative changes. If attempting to do so is unrealistic, then we must be so. It is in the dialectic tension between the real and the possible, between down-to-earth everyday reality and the dream, that social systems undergo transformations. The only sin we cannot forgive politicians and policy makers, somebody once said, is their inability to dream, to envision new options.

Investing in the young

And why must we emphasize the politician's need to dream? Well, precisely because education has become a political matter. There is hardly any doubt that the need to invest in the preparation of new generations is one of the central problems faced by governments, private sector and international organizations alike. Education has stopped being a concern of educators and parents. It has further become a central issue to economists, manufacturers, entrepreneurs as well as of those involved in international development. In a world progressively concerned about globalization of the economy, issues of efficiency and productivity have taken center stage, both in developed and developing countries.

But the economic reference implicit in the term investment should not mislead us. A look at the etymology of the word can be very enlightening. Investment means empowering, granting control or authority, arraying in the symbols of office or honor. To understand investments in technology for schools solely under the perspective of economic or quantitative returns is to miss completely the higher social function of education. We must invest in the young, and we must invest in them with the energizing power of the technological and cultural developments of their time.

Redefining Priorities

To do this, however, we must redefine our priorities. It is true that the key explanation most frequently provided to justify the lack of investment in educational projects, particularly when associated with technology, is cost. However, problems of funding are not exclusively economic problems. Deep down, they are political problems because they involve the definition of priorities. The art or science of governing an organization, a community or a nation, is that of making choices.

This can clearly be understood through some examples: In 1999, a very poor Latin American country purchased 18 MIG-29 planes at a price of US$39 million each. With the sum payed for each one of those planes, at least 1.026 new computer labs, similar to the ones existing in the Costa Rican program, could have been provided to schools and communities in that nation. With the sum allocated for those eighteen planes, over 18.468.000 students could have benefited. Furthermore, the yearly maintenance of each of those planes—that is, US$1.9 million—could have been used for the training and follow up of teacher development efforts as well as for technical maintenance of the equipment. This would no doubt have been a substantially more productive social and economic investment.

Just as this article is being reviewed, another South American country is in the process of acquiring ten F-16 combat planes, at a cost of US$65 million each. The US$650 million allocated to this investment could easily have purchased brand new computers and networks for approximately 16,250,000 students. The resources paid to cover maintenance and basic repair could pay for ongoing support, maintenance and permanent teacher training. Between 2002 and 2004, a South American country purchase 8 A532 U2/AS-332L2 helicopters from France. It spent US$160 million,[11] an amount that could have made it possible to purchase approximately 4.000 computer labs to service over 4.000.000 students.

These are issues of critical importance worldwide. According to the Bonn International Center for Conversion, official development aid rose by about $10 billion worldwide between 1999 and 2003, while military spending increased by almost three ties that much ($28 billion). Even within the context of clear consciousness of the need to reduce poverty and close the digital gap, military expenditures now stand at 2.6% of national income worldwide. This means that there has been a 0.2% increase from 2000.[12] Just in Latin America, in 2003 governments spent $26 billion on their military ($22.2 billion in South America, $3.8 billion in Central America).[13] Just in the United States, the proposed increase in defense spending for 2006 amounts to US$19.2 billion. These resources could have been used to hire more than 330,000 elementary school teachers or provide around 3.7 million university scholarships.

This analysis clearly shows that, even in less developed countries, lack of resources for technology investments for education and development cannot really be used as an excuse. The real issue is certainly that of redefining priorities. It is therefore an issue of leadership and vision, much more than one of lack of resources and investment capacity.

The Subversive Power of Computers

Allowing children and teachers to develop their own talent and potential has been at the core of this Costa Rican initiative. This, of course, can be a highly political matter. As a Latin American journalist who visited the program once noted: "if children learn to think as these kids are doing, if they become autonomous and critical, they may question the system, and that is dangerously subversive."

---

[11] SIPRI *Yearbook 2005: Armaments, Disarmament and International Security,* p. 461.
[12] Bonn Internacional Center for Conversion. *Conversion Survey,* 2005.
[13] *Ibid.,* p. 151.

Few people have understood more deeply the potential involved in innovative uses of computers in education, particularly in the developing world. However, the subversion involved is not the violent political activism to which many Latin American youngsters have been drawn for decades, but the subversion of the mental patterns which lie at the base of underdevelopment, the subversion of the patterns that keep human talent trapped generation after generation.

This fact was very well understood by the principal of a poor rural school in Costa Rica, when he made the decision to invest funds collected for a soccer field in the preparation of the facilities for a computer lab. As he put it: "What these children really need--he noted--are soccer fields for the mind" (Fonseca, 1991, p. 54). The dynamic nature of this metaphor seems to be right on target. It is highly consistent with the emphasis on the mind which characterizes the most of the social and economic developments of this century, particularly when one analyzes the trends in work and power relations being generated by the emerging information culture (Zuboff, 1988) and the skills and preparation being demanded by present changes in industry, which progressively call for symbolic analysts more than the routine producers which characterized the industrial age (Reich, 1992).

It is evident that computers cannot change certain human conditions; they have no way of overcoming certain limits. However, when placed within the context of enriching educational ideas and seen with a humanistic focus, they can help generate change in schools, communities, and even in the lives of the children and teachers involved in their use. Perhaps one of the most valuable contributions that the Costa Rican Computers in Elementary Education Program has made to the international community resides in the fact that it has shown that it is possible to introduce new technological and educational opportunities to children and teachers from deprived communities and to obtain significant results.

Two decades of experience in the implementation of the Costa Rican Program has shown that computers in schools and communities can have a multifaceted potential to bring about change, including frequently some which were not originally expected. For this to happen, however, the traditional linear view of change in education must be abandoned. To bring about systemic change in education, qualitatively new options and new approaches must be sought. The energizing effect generated by the presence of computers in schools (World Bank Report on Computers in Costa Rica and Chile, 1998)) must be used to the benefit of educational and socio-economic change.

4. Final Remarks: About the Construction of the Future

A brief look at the political and economic situation around the world will make us realize that significant masses of the planet's population will remain unaffected by the outbreak of the new millennium, no matter how symbolic the change may be to some of us. No doubt that under these conditions the twenty-first century will reach very few people, if by twenty-first century we mean space-age development, quality of life, and access to the technological and social benefits of the time.

Furthermore, the impact that technology will have on our lives depends on social, political and economic decisions, not on the potential of the technology itself. It depends more on issues and decisions that are more political and ethical than technological, because, as is historically evident, technological developments have not necessarily benefited all. Progress, as Paul Kennedy has observed, "benefits those groups or nations that are able to take advantage of the newer methods of science, just as it damages others that are less prepared, technologically, culturally and politically to respond to change" (1993, p. 15).

We must analyze the changes that have been introduced in education and learning throughout the last two or three decades and study carefully the real impact that digital technologies have had. We need to view in depth what has change, but above all, what has not changed. It is necessary to transcend the naïve enthusiasm that frequently surrounds technological revolutions. As David Rothkopf would say, "only through the recognition [of what has not changed] will we begin to focus on the truly critical issues" (in Friedman, p. 451).

Clearly the world challenge is today in the process of widespread cultural appropriation of technology and of its use to stimulate learning and the development of human imagination, talent and mind We cannot refrain from facing these realities, particularly because the digital gap forces us to tackle also the literacy and cognitive gap. Issues of equity and solidarity must regain their due place so that the times to come may be marked by developments more coherent with our democratic values and global consciousness. Investing in the human aspects of development is no longer an altruistic matter. It is a matter of survival--economic, national, and international survival. As Thomas Friedman has suggested, we need to encourage people to focus on productive outcomes that may create environments conducive to the advancement of modern societies and civilization. Imagination is the one thing that cannot be commoditized. But we need, as he points out, "peaceful imaginations" that can help us minimize alienation and exclusion and celebrate interdependence and solidarity (Friedman, p. 443).

The Need for Vision and Direction

Allowing children and teachers to emerge from behind their mental parapets, from behind their deprived cognitive and cultural windows, is one of the megachanges that education must bring about. Creating learning environments that allow children to appropriate the world of knowledge--of technology, science, art,--is more than a problem of pedagogical dimension, it is a problem of social policy, of risk taking, of capacity to tap on to situations that can nurture meaningful change. As Papert noted in *Mindstorms* almost two decades ago, "what is happening now is an empirical question. What can happen is a technical question, but what will happen is a political question, depending on social choices" (1980, p. 29). And this is the key issue. Will technology continue to slip through the television window or will it become a door opening up to new opportunities and change?

Fortunately for the children, youth, teachers and communities from deprived socio-economic contexts there is real hope in the making. Knowledge, leadership and will have come together in extraordinary ways to surmount the cost and availability barriers withholding them from being apart of the digital world. The initiative just launched by the MIT Media Lab to produce by late 2006 or early 2007 a $100 laptop computer to provide new learning opportunities for children from around the world offers real possibilities. It is no doubt an extraordinary initiative that brings together high level science and technology with productive capacity and educational vision. The project is led by Nicholas Negroponte, Joe Jacobson, and Seymour Papert.

The new computer, a Linux-based, full-color, full screen laptop has been designed to use innovative power supply (which can even include, winding up facilities) and will have WIFI and will be cell phone enabled. Its specifications include 500 MHz, 1GB, 1 Megapixel. It has been designed to provide young students with mobility so that they can use it in school, home and community. The project, which has been conceived as an MIT Media Lab research initiative, will be operated through a non-profit association, the One Laptop per Child or OLPC.[14] Not surprisingly, Nicholas Negroponte has indicated that this is basically an education project, not necessarily a laptop project. His deep conviction is, as he indicated during a presentation on the Technology Review's Emerging Technologies Conference at MIT is that "if we can make education better—particularly primary and secondary education—it will be a better world."[15]

It is precisely for this reason, and in view of the potential that technology will soon make available, we need to focus on the ways in which we will move beyond concerns of digital divide in order to create new learning and socio-economic opportunities. Once more, knowledge, leadership and will are required to rethink the learning processes within which these new tools will be made available and exploited. This is a wonderful new challenge for education leaders and teachers on the ground. It cannot however be bypassed or overlooked. As Negroponte and Papert have insisted, the central thrust needs to be educational. To make this transformation as powerful and meaningful as it needs to be, the main focus needs to be on the creation of opportunities for the young.

Slightly over a century ago, Costa Rica had a visionary and strongly determined President. His name was Jose Figueres-Ferrer. He abolished the army and committed himself to the construction of what could have easily been interpreted, within the context of the region and the times, as an "unrealistic scenario." He was a forward looking leader who had the foresight and the will to adhere to Emerson's principle that, in decision making we should "hitch the wagon to a star." Because of its applicability to the problems that concern us in rethinking the role of technology in education and development, I would like to close these remarks by quoting what he wrote in 1949, one year before he took that radical and path-breaking step:

> First there should be a philosophy to light the way. Then come all the technical plans ... guided by a central idea and by the most noble spirit that we can snatch from our hearts. All of us know that stars cannot be reached by the hand. But we must agree that men and associations and nations need to know exactly the star to which they will hitch their wagon in order to be able to distinguish, at crossroads along the way which paths lead forward, which are simply deviations, which will rather lead us back . . . (Figueres, *Escritos y Discursos*, 1986)

---

[14] http://laptop.media.mit.edu/
[15] Mike Ricciuti, "The $100 laptop moves closer to reality" in http://news.com.com/ September 28, 2005.

No doubt the time has come to define precisely the star to which the leaders in the field of education and development will hitch the technology wagon.

REFERENCES

Carr, Nicholas (2003). "IT Doesn't Matter." Cambridge: *Harvard Business Review*.

Castells, Manuel (2002). *La era de la Información, Sociedad y Cultura. La sociedad de la Red.* Tomo 1, Volumen 1. México: Editorial Siglo XXI.

Figueres-Ferrer, José (1986). *Escritos y Discursos: 1942-1962*. San José: Editorial Costa Rica.

Florida, Richard (2005). *The Flight of the Creative Class: The New Global Competition for Talent.* New York, Harper Business.

Fonseca, Clotilde (1991). *Computadoras en la Escuela Pública Costarricense: La Puesta en Marcha de una Decisión*. San José: Ediciones de la Fundación Omar Dengo.

Fonseca, Clotilde (1999). "The Computer: A New Door to Educational and Social Opportunities". *Logo Philosophy and Implementation*. Canada: LCSI.

Fonseca, Clotilde (1993). "A Systemic Approach to Teacher Development: Lessons Learned from a National Logo-Based Computers in Education Program." Cambridge: *Journal of Information Technology for Teacher Education*, Vol. 2. No. 2.

Friedman, Thomas L (2005). *The World is Flat: A brief History of the Twenty First Century.* New York: Farrar, Straus and Giroux.

Kennedy, Paul (1993). *Preparing for the Twenty-First Century*. New York: Random House.

Ministerio de Educación Pública (1993). *Evaluación del Programa de Informática de I y II Ciclos*. San José, Costa Rica.

McDowell, Robert and William L. Simons (2004). *In Search of Business Value: Insuring a Return on Your Technology Investment*. New York: Selected Books, Inc.

Papert, Seymour (1980). *Mindstorms*. New York: Basic Books.

Reggini, Horacio (2005) . El Futuro no es más lo que era: La tecnología y la gente en tiempos de Internet. Buenos Aires, Argentina: Editorial de la Universidad Católica Argentina (EDUCA).

Reich, Robert (1991). *The Work of Nations: Preparing Ourselves for 21st Century Capitalism.* New York: Vintage Books.

Schwartz, Peter (1991). *The Art of Long View*. New York: Doubleday Currency.

United Nations Development Program (2001). *Human Development Report*: "Placing Technological Progress at the Service of World Development. New York.

Vogel, Jr., Thomas. "Alta Tecnología en Costa Rica." The Wall Street Journal Americas, in *La Nación*, April 7, 1998.

World Bank. "Computers in Schools: A Qualitative Study of Chile and   Costa Rica. A Summary Report of a Collaborative Research Project." April, 1998.

Zuboff, Shoshana (1988). *In the Age of the Smart Machine: The Future of Work and Power*. New York: Basic Books.

PART TWO

HARNESSING THE POTENTIAL OF ICTs FOR EDUCATION

Section One

MAXIMIZING THE COMPLEMENTARY STRENGTHS OF
PARTNERSHIPS

GeSCI: ICTs FOR GLOBAL EDUCATION AND COMMUNITY DEVELOPMENT

Astrid Dufborg

Introduction

In 2003, a milestone year in the evolution of the global Information Society, the United Nations ICT Task Force, promoted by Sweden, Switzerland, Ireland and Canada, established the concept of the Global e-Schools & Communities Initiative (GeSCI). Taking up the challenge of the Millennium Development Goals, GeSCI's purpose is the comprehensive deployment of ICTs as a tool to raise global standards in education through multistakeholder partnerships. The Initiative works at regional, national, and local levels to support developing countries as they create and implement strategies for ICTs in education and community development. Its imperative is to be demand driven and to respond to the needs of real people – and real gaps in educational strategies and community development.

With the concept launched by Mrs. Nane Annan at the first United Nations World Summit on the Information Society (WSIS), GeSCI was welcomed as an exemplifier of how a people-centred, inclusive development ideal could be implemented in education. GeSCI looks to bring all stakeholders to the table in a collaborative way, and to complement and coordinate existing efforts already underway. It does not come to knock on any government's door with a pre-conceived road map in hand, but comes open handed, with a clear willingness to walk the road and create the map together. When GeSCI sits down with stakeholders it looks to understand the context and then clearly articulate where it can add value. Typically its value is inherent in its ability to bring stakeholders to the table, build and implement a plan and to mobilize resources to do so.

Four countries – Bolivia, Ghana, India and Namibia – were chosen as starting places. They were chosen on the basis of criteria which balanced need against readiness plus willingness to take on an ICT in education programme (including the importance of ICTs in government policies), and the potential for impact.

Global Forum

Having held wide-scale consultations and surveyed the spectrum in the four partner countries, GeSCI co-hosted a Global Forum in Dublin in April 2004 with the United Nations ICT Task Force to share findings and plan the next steps. This exceptional set of round tables brought together experts, education ministers from India and Namibia, representatives of industry, implementing NGOs, ICT and education specialists from all around the world, from many different walks of life. In the words of Joseph O. Opaku, it is this "galvanisation of a collective genius" which is needed to be able to realize the promise of ICTs in education and their knock-on effects in community development.

The forum was an important milestone for GeSCI. It sharpened its mandate and honed its focus on the most important challenges in education and ICTs. The plenaries and break-out sessions got to the core of the ambitions and challenges faced. Comprehensive strategies in programme countries would have to take the following priority issues into realistic account:

- It is teachers who shape the future through their work. They are multipliers, authority figures and agents of socio-economic change that must be empowered. Therefore, they should have all available tools at their disposal, including the full range of information and communication technologies – not just the Internet, but also stand-alone computers, radio, TV and telephones. However, in order to provide them with the skills they need to become "facilitators of learning", to improve their own effectiveness and to insure that the ICTs that are finding their ways into schools in the developing world are put to good use, teachers urgently require training in ICT. However, it was recognized that educators who had been trained in ICT often abandon their teaching careers for jobs that pay better salaries – a form of teacher brain-drain.

- Many excellent ICT for education projects cannot be implemented on a large scale or in a sustainable manner due to a fundamental lack of support. Ways to overcome such challenges were suggested. One of them was to urge the private sector not only to be innovative in addressing hardware, software and connectivity issues, but also to invest in schools and to support teacher training programmes. Universities in the South were also encouraged to act as incubators and supporters of community centres to bring educational opportunities to adult learners.

- ICT needs to be integrated into all national education systems in order to realize a higher quantity and quality of education. But in order to succeed in this effort, it is imperative to have a strong institutional commitment and well-defined political will. The integration of ICT into education systems is of particular value to developing countries because it gives them an opportunity to leapfrog inherent limitations and to acquire new resources and formulate innovative strategies.

- New models of capacity development of teachers and administrators are key to the success and sustainability of education strategies and to a systematic approach in the use of ICT for education.

- Creating more knowledge of and experience with multistakeholder partnerships in ICT for education efforts. Multistakeholder partnerships have become a popular vehicle for addressing development challenges, and their use in the ICT for education efforts is relatively new.

- ICT for education efforts should be targeted at all age levels, and in particular there was a call to develop a research framework to engage young people further.

- There was also a call to further engage universities in both identifying models for sustainability for ICT for development projects, and to encourage universities in developing countries to participate in ICT for development activities.

- The results of the GeSCI experiment have a bearing on other initiatives aimed at addressing the Millennium Development Goals.

Invigorated by the success and support of the Global Forum, and with a new international team in place, GeSCI set about its work in programme countries with increased energies. It knew there was much to do and much yet to learn. The powerful testimony of a ten-year-old Irish boy, Patrick Dempsey, whose life had been transformed through access to ICTs in his own disadvantaged classroom, reminded the Dublin Forum that ICTs in education are not a simple gift that a perfect North can bequeath a struggling South. No one stakeholder and no one region has everything to teach and nothing to learn. To succeed, the approach must be truly collaborative and genuinely reciprocal.

Next Steps

Two months after the Global Forum, in June 2005 GeSCI signed a MoU with Namibia. An implementation schedule has just been completed. Mapping exercises to determine ICT availability and use in all educational institutions are to be carried out. GeSCI in partnership with the Namibian Ministry of Education will deploy ICTs into the four National Colleges of Education. Secondary schools and teacher training centres will be fitted with resource labs and supporting software and hardware over the next three years. On the content and curriculum front, GeSCI is consulting with all relevant stakeholders towards the development of a Namibia-wide ICT competency certificate, a methodology to integrate ICTs in cross curricula and a plan to localise e-content to support the integration of ICTs into the whole curriculum. Added to this, GeSCI is working to create an e-learning centre to house all e-content and provide training for content development, instructional design, e-learning management and virtual learning communities in Namibia.

Infodev of the World Bank, the Minister for Education and SchoolNet Namibia are among the critical members of impactful partnerships in Namibia. The success of the partnerships here, GeSCI hopes, will catalyze other programmes. On a parallel track to this, GeSCI is forging networks between initiatives in different places to share information, and disseminate knowledge about promising practices in key aspects of ICTs in schools.

GeSCI's work in India is also developing at a promising pace. The link-up between existing ICT for education efforts and the planning of overall ICTs for education strategies are being explored. Plans and proposals come directly from the States involved. GeSCI's country programme facilitator is in discussions with States aimed at coming to a collective understanding of priorities and possibilities for GeSCI to add value. The discussions are wide and broad and aimed at encompassing a wide range of issues before agreements on cooperation are made. The Ministry for Education in India, local authorities, implementing NGOs and community stakeholders are all involved. Memoranda of understanding will soon be signed. The action of the implementation plan will follow.

In Bolivia, GeSCI has had listening, exploratory talks with a range of actors and interests. Key government departments and agencies, NGOs and universities, bilateral donors, and multilateral agencies, and other stakeholders in ICTs in schools have shared their visions and expectations. The work of translating that into a memorandum of understanding, and from there a programme of implementation starts now.

Meanwhile GeSCI's work in Ghana is gathering a striking momentum. Information about major actors, aspirations and activities in ICTs in schools has been compiled. Based on this overview and the existing national educational strategy a MoU is in draft stages. This – the collaborative action plan, co-written by all major stakeholders – teachers, Ministry, NGOs, and private sector representatives – will be presented to the government. Appropriate educational and community objectives and strategies for an overall deployment of ICTs to schools, consistent with national policies, expressed in documents such as national development plans, and consistent with the Millennium Development Goals, should be the final result.

On another front, GeSCI's knowledge work, to provide educators and decision-makers with comprehensive and accessible tools for understanding both the country-specific value and the feasibility of different technology options, is in the latter stages of completion. GeSCI believes that this one-of-a-kind calculator will go a long way to demystifying, and ultimately increasing access to ICTs in education – for both developed and developing countries.

Concluding Outlook

Going forward, GeSCI glimpses exponential growth on the horizon, as its models start to have a large-scale impact on the ground. In Tunis, GeSCI will report back to the WSIS II, on its progress from conceptual origin to organization in action. It looks ahead to working with its partners – in Namibia, in India, with the World Bank, UNESCO, and others – as it pushes forward in its mission to harness ICTs for education and community development, in ever new and extensive ways.

BUILDING A MULTISTAKEHOLDER ALLIANCE FOR ICT IN EDUCATION IN LATIN AMERICA

Irene Hardy de Gómez

Introduction

In December 2003, the United Nations organized the first meeting of the World Summit on the Information Society in Geneva. The main goal of the conference was to define an action plan for promoting the use of the information and communication technologies (ICTs) in meeting the Millennium Developmental Goals.

Among the items established in the Action Plan for bridging the digital divide are two that are relevant to this article:

- The integration of ICTs in education, and

- Training in the use of ICT.

In its report entitled "Closing the gap in education and technology", the World Bank points out that economic growth is crucial if Latin America and the Caribbean are to reduce their poverty levels, but in order to achieve an improvement in their economic perspectives, it is indispensable that they increase their productivity. Governments of the region have to adopt urgent measures that counter the deficit in the areas of knowledge and skills in technology.

The reality is that Latin America is at a significant disadvantage in the adoption, adaptation and creation of technologies designed to increase productivity, but is hindered by its weaknesses in the realm of achievements and educational enrolment. It is therefore recommended that countries build their own skills and technology levels from the bottom to the top, in a fast, coordinated and sequential manner.

The World Bank also points out that the majority of countries show high enrolment numbers in primary school but present a massive deficit in enrolment at the high school level, in part because of the high rates of repeated years and late registrations at the primary level.

One of the reasons for this failure in primary education is the poor preparation of teachers, for the following reasons:

- The education they receive before beginning training programmes, either in elementary or secondary school, is generally poor in quality. They have up to two years less studies than teachers from Japan, the United States and Europe;

- Pre-service training courses are generally short, highly theoretical and sacrifice real practice in class; there is little emphasis on appropriate techniques for disadvantaged students;

- Many programmes are poor in quality and have no relevance or impact in improving the skills of teachers;

- Standards have not been established for teachers and their performance is not evaluated;

- Teachers do not receive adequate support for class preparation nor for working in groups;

- Beginning teachers are not trained by more experienced ones;

- Coherent groups of teachers are not formed in the schools and the good teachers generally receive little recognition from the school administrators or parents;

- Teachers do not feel the reforms introduced into schools as their own and therefore have little incentive to change their methods in class;

- Even though they are in direct contact with their students, they are seldom taken into account in the design of reforms but are expected to implement them. The teachers' participation is reduced to designing teaching projects but they are not involved in the handling and planning of these reforms.

Recommendations for strengthening the training of teachers include:

- Improving the knowledge and pedagogical tools of less-qualified teachers;

- Providing specialized skills in areas where weaknesses are diagnosed; and

- Training teachers in the use of ICT as support for their research and teaching activities.

Functioning of the AME Programme

Actualización de Maestros en Educación (AME) can be translated as "Updating the skills of school teachers". AME is an interactive programme designed for the basic education of teachers in Latin America, using television and e-learning.

AME contributes to improving the quality of training for teachers in the information and communication technologies, in specific areas of knowledge and values. It also facilitates the contact of teachers with new forms of knowledge and information and allows their participation in virtual communities capable of promoting innovation in educational processes. The programme is currently running in Argentina, Colombia, Costa Rica, the Dominican Republic, Guatemala, Panama, Peru and Venezuela.

Figure 1 shows the functioning of the programme. Five universities from Latin America and Spain generate the didactic contents in two forms: as a television mini-series with a duration of 6 to 12 hours, and as written material that is posted on the virtual classroom of the Web page: www.ame.cisneros.org. The teachers form groups of two to three persons and watch the classes in the educational centres, and at the same time carry out the activities posted on the virtual classroom, always under the tutoring of the university professors that created the contents.

Figure 1. Functioning of AME

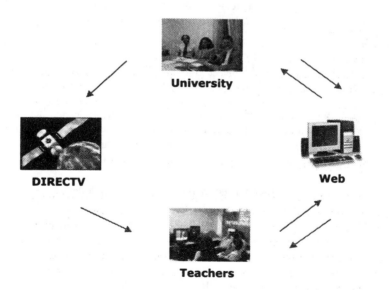

The courses include topics that are strictly academic as well as topics that help the teacher do their job in a holistic fashion, in the context where they are working and compatible with their culture, their sensibility and their local language. The courses go for approximately eight weeks and are dictated for all Latin America in two periods per year so that each period consists of two courses. It is estimated that the groups have to work for 100 to 140 hours to complete the courses.

Figure 2. Courses of the AME programme

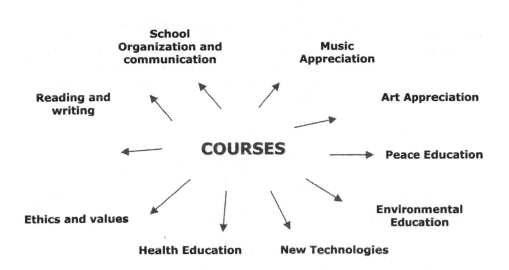

Internally, AME functions as the administration of a school would work. Externally, the programme is implemented in educational centres, which can be individual schools or training centres for teachers. The training centres could be university extension programmes. Each centre has a person that supervises the implementation of the programme. Various training centres can form a network and this happens when, for example, a university implements the programme in different parts of a country and for these a coordinator supervises the centres that form the network. The programme is currently implemented in 163 training centres for 1,341 teachers.

Constructing a Multistakeholder Alliance for AME

The basic principles included in the digital solidarity agenda established in Geneva during the World Summit on the Information Society point out the need to establish the conditions for mobilizing human, economic and technological resources to include all men and women in the information society. Moreover, they suggest that it is necessary for governments, international organizations and the private sector to work together in creating the proper conditions that would trigger the effective mobilization of these resources to finance development.

This point was taken up during the conference on "Financing and Management of Education in Latin America and the Caribbean" which took place in Puerto Rico in 2004 and was sponsored by the United Nations, UNESCO and ECLAC. The conference concluded that the mobilization of private and public resources is necessary to meet the educational targets of the Millennium Development Goals.

Within this context, the Cisneros Group of Companies though the Fundación Cisneros has established multistakeholder alliances at the national, regional and international level. The strategies for the creation of these alliances have changed throughout time through a complex, progressive and voluntary process and have taken into account aspects like politics and infrastructure. The models for these alliances are established in the organizational manual of the programme.

The alliances have been built on complementary strengths, mutual respect and shared responsibilities. The negotiations are in a face-to-face fashion that later evolve into direct channels of communication that allow for the improvement of the programme and that help in solving the problems that arise. The partners include governments, private enterprise, academia, and civil society.

Thus:

- The Fundación Cisneros has provided the necessary monetary resources to finance the programme and provides the strategic planning as well as the administrative support that assures its transparency and functioning;

- Five universities generate the contents, evaluate and certify the teachers;

- DIRECTV Latin America provides the satellite space for the transmission of the audiovisual contents, the decodifiers and the satellite connection to the teacher training centres;

- A private television channel, Cl@se, and a university channel, Simon TV from the Universidad Simón Bolívar in Venezuela, transmit the audiovisual contents free of charge;

- Cable operators like Magic Cable in Peru transmit the Cl@se programming;

- Local schools, public, private, rural, urban, training centres for teachers (Fe y Alegría Network), academic sectors (Universidad Central de Venezuela, Universidad Central de Panama, Fundación La Salle in Venezuela), private foundations (Fundación Backus in Peru), Governments (State Secretary of Education from the Dominican Republic and Argentina), and indigenous communities (Pemón in Venezuela), provide the necessary infrastructure (television, VHS, computers), connectivity to the Internet and the facilitators in new technologies *in situ* so that the teachers will be supported at every stage of the programme. All the previous institutions select the teachers that will participate in the programme following pre-established policies and some of them even copy and distribute the audiovisual material necessary if no other access to them is available; and

- Two Ministries of Education (Costa Rica and Dominican Republic) certify the accreditations granted by the universities and the Fundación Cisneros.

Bibliography

De Ferranti D., Perry G.F.; Gill I., Guasch J.L., Maloney W.F. Sanchez Páramo C., Schady N. (2003) Closing the gap in education and technology. The World Bank Washington, D. C

Draft Plan of Action (2003) Secretary General of de World Summit on the information society. Document WSIS-03 /GENEVA/ DOC 5 – E

Lagging Behind: A Report Card on Education in Latin America (2002) PREAL Task Force on Education, Equity, and Economic Competitiveness in the Americas. http://www.iadialog.org/programs/policy/social/education/

Machado A.L. (2004) Financiamiento y gestión de la educación en América latina y el Caribe. En Seminario de la Gestión de la Educación en América Latina y el Caribe: ¿Vamos por buen camino? CEPAL / UNESCO. Puerto Rico

Objetivos de Desarrollo de la ONU para el Milenio http://www.un.org/spanish/millenniumgoals/

Tomorrow is Too Late PREAL (2000) Task Force on Education Reform in Central America. http://www.iadialog.org/programs/policy/social/education/

STMICROELECTRONICS FOUNDATION AND THE DIGITAL UNIFY

Elena Pistorio

The 8th Meeting of the United Nations ICT Task Force and the Global Forum on Harnessing ICT for Education held in Dublin, Ireland on 13-14 April 2005 highlighted the importance and need for multistakeholder partnership and multisectoral participation in scaling innovation and investment in ICT for Education. Extensive debate, consultations and discussions on what improvements have been made and what still needs to be done to eradicate poverty and achieve the millennium development goals and mainstreaming ICTs in education took place in the Global Forum, in roundtable meetings, break-out sessions and working group meetings. Debate focused on the multiple opportunities and challenges faced by multistakeholder partnerships in ICT4D, of the need of scaling innovative strategies for access to ICTs in Education, of "maximizing" complementary strengths, of the role each sector and stakeholder can play, and of the need of building capacity for government leaders, management, teachers and administrators.

Education includes not only formal, primary and secondary and higher education, but also non-formal, continuing education as learning must be a life-long process. The same nature of rapid, constant innovation of media forms and computer technology requires developing a culture that is sensitive to the need for continuous learning and updating.

Numerous significant projects have demonstrated how effective ICTs can be in primary and secondary schools in increasing both attendance rates as well as student performance. Educational software programs and didactical material can be selected and used by teachers to complement curriculum of given courses (sciences, mathematics, etc). The PC and office tools and specially designed software programs can assist teachers in organizing the school year planning, individual class lessons, student reporting, monitoring of students' performance, and their work in general. Teaching, in many countries under paid profession, becomes more gratifying when student attendance and performance increases. Teachers often change career for a better paid jobs, and a more gratifying working environment can represent a motivation to stick to their jobs.

There is no single formula as to how to introduce ICTs in formal education. ICTs includes the new digital technologies as well as the traditional media of communication of radio, television, mobile telephony. Successful projects range from the introduction of multimedia centers consisting of audio-visual equipment and mobile telephony in the classroom to the set up of one or more PCs in the classroom or to the set up of a separate computer and multimedia lab in the school.

A multimedia center or PC in the classroom is useful to complement and enrich the lesson of any subject with audio visual material. The impact of seeing on video a volcano erupting or a heart beating is stronger than describing it in words or in a textbook. Audio visual tools solicit another type of learning experience that can enhance student participation and performance.

In a computer lab, students can acquire advanced computer skills as well complementing curriculum material outside the classroom through selected educational software material. Software programs also allow students to compose music, create art work, edit videos, and express themselves artistically. Office tools such as word processors, excel sheets, enable student to do their homework more quickly and efficiently.

Teachers, schools staff, administration and even the local community can benefit from a computer lab in a school. The internet accessed in such a lab also represents an important door to the external world, with possibilities of interacting with teachers and school staff from other schools nationwide or abroad, of comparing educational programs and curricula, of sourcing new material and information.

In any program that seeks to implement ICTs in formal primary and secondary education, a multistakeholder approach that involves the participation of national or regional boards of education is a necessary prerequisite. Private sector initiatives must work in unison with public institutions of education. Collaboration is needed to maximize complementary strengths. Often, the public sector cannot go about such a massive task as mainstreaming ICTs in education alone due to the lack of financial resources or of technological and entrepreneurial know-how. Likewise, the private sector alone cannot work with schools without the blessing and cooperation of the public sector. Academia can also provide informed consultancy on best practices and best educational programs, and insight into the evolution of education. They are a bridge between the world of education and the working world. Professors and students represent together a generational bridge and know at one time what the new generation wants and how the older generation can fulfill emerging needs. Also, professors and students alike are an invaluable untapped resource of volunteer work and source of knowledge on the local reality. The potential of the academia and universities in partnerships for ICT in Education is far from fully exploited.

NGOs have cumulated years of experience on the field, have learned from best practices, are familiar with the local needs and reality and also must be consulted and represented from the start in a multistakeholder partnership for development.

Similarly, civil society must not be excluded from the loop. ICTs in schools, especially in underdeveloped regions, can work best if the local community is also involved and informed on the benefits of ICT4D. Community members could benefit from ICTs in schools by receiving after school classes in the school's computer lab. This would serve to raise awareness of the importance of education in families and help improve attendance.

Multistakeholder partnerships must have a clear objective and strategy. Single party interests, in particular from the private sector which may be motivated by publicity or immediate financial return, must be made clear from the start and resolved to avoid deception along the way. It is important that private sector companies learn to have a longer term vision when dealing with issues of poverty reduction and equal rights in education, health, gender parity, etc. Citizens, companies, government, must all share responsibility and work together and contribute to the achievement of the millennium goals as objectives in themselves. Companies should appreciate that working for such a cause in itself brings its rewards in the long run: a better distribution of wealth in the world means a safer world and a better working place for all, healthier economies, larger markets and more business opportunities in the future. Looking for immediate financial return is a short-sighted and obsolete view that the world cannot afford right now. With over 2 billion people living at less than two dollars a day, 1 billion in extreme poverty, and only one child in four attending school, the world can no longer wait to alleviate poverty while companies find the best formula for getting financial return out of their socially responsible actions. Human beings do voluntary work such as donating blood not because they are paid for it or because they think he or she will be more popular in his or her neighborhood. Thinking of a company only in terms of pure business is not only outdated, old-fashioned, surpassed, but it is also paradoxically detrimental to the company business, to the working environment within the company and to its image amongst its stakeholders and shareholders.

There is evidence showing that more and more investors prefer to invest in socially conscientious companies. Companies that perform poorly in corporate citizenships are being a priori discarded by those investors. Regulations and benchmarks for social reports are becoming ever more demanding. As citizens are becoming more concerned about their environment they are demanding that companies also abide to regulations that respect human rights and the environment. Consumers will boycott products known to have been produced by companies that do not respect human rights or environmental standards. Shareholders are interested in companies that have a strong social agenda where investors will be happy and proud to pour their money in.

A company operates in communities, not markets. Companies are made by people and relationships within and without the company. People that work for a socially committed company are more proud of their company and work better because they are happier and more satisfied at their workplace. It has been proven that the best performing companies are those in which the people working within the company are happiest. Clients receive better service when the supplier providing the service is happier and content with his/her job. But their satisfaction also depends on the satisfaction of the people that person is interacting with within the company. Doing "good" for the surrounding communities and environment increases the employees' level of satisfaction and belonging and therefore improves company performance. At the same time, the acceptance of that company within the community and amongst all stakeholders is increased.

A lot of important urgent projects in developing countries die because of insufficient funding. In 2005, STMicroelectronics Foundation spent only 62 000 Euros to create wells and provide safe drinking water to 4 villages in north east India. 9000 people benefited from this project, forever changing their lives. Little investment can indeed go a long way.

In multistakeholder partnerships for achieving development goals, whether it be education, health, poverty alleviation, etc, companies should put to service and offer what they are competent in, whether it is technology, know-how, business consulting, as well contributing financial resources. The private sector can be useful in developing and supporting financing models to accomplish projects or scaling them.

Only with the collaboration of the public and private sector can funds be stretched and adequate. Governments should also respect their commitment made to development aid. The type of government aid that was pledged by donor countries years ago, namely 0,7 of their GDP, has yet to materialize averaging less than 0,3 of GDP for most countries. Richer countries must appreciate the fact that their lack of compliance detracts the largest portions from total development aid. Governments of developing countries should also harness partnerships with other sectors and promote an enabling environment to facilitate and attract investment and implementation of ICT4D. By including and mainstreaming ICTs in Poverty Reduction Strategies governments could trigger more investment by donors in ICT4D.

In every partnership, each partner should be transparent and clear from the start on what his expectations are and what is expected from every other partner at every stage of development of a given project. A multistakeholder partnership in ICT4D must also evaluate the "sustainability" of any project, what will happen to the partnership once the mission is accomplished and how will the project continue and be sustained in the long run.

A project must be designed with in mind the group of people, such as teachers or students, who will ultimately benefit from it. Such group should be represented in the partnership from the beginning. The project must fully take into account what the needs of the end-users are. Projects should be "pulled in" rather than imposed.

In multistakeholder partnerships, partners come from different working worlds, accustomed to different needs, paces, and requirements. Partners must have the will to cooperate and patiently adapt to the modus operandi of the other. Successful cooperation can come via consensus over a clearly defined goal and strategy.

Partnerships should be aware of existing programs and avoid duplication. When possible, donors and partners should concentrate and build on valid existing multistakeholder partnerships, such as the GeSCI initiative.

In embarking on new initiatives, partners should consult the existing information compiled by agencies on best practices in ICT4D and study and learn from successful projects as well as from failures to avoid repeating errors. Partnerships must also work at bringing to scale successful projects.

STMicroelectronics has decided to take up the challenge of contributing to bridge the digital divide and has proposed in 2001 that every company, with over 250 employees, contribute up to 0,1 % of revenues and up to 0,1% of hours worked to provide both the necessary technology and training to those who do not have the means and resources to access a PC and the internet. The aim is to connect villages, provide hardware and basic training to people so that they can use a PC and the internet and be included as citizens of the digital era and reap the benefits of the digital revolution.

Access to information means access to knowledge, which in turn means empowerment and therefore human progress. Just as access to education, water, food, shelter, electricity, are basic human rights, in the same way access to information should be considered a right and not a luxury. Equal opportunities in education mean also equal opportunities in access to digital technology and information which is an integral part of education in the western world. During a forum of a Task Force meeting in New York, one civil society representative from sub-Saharan Africa stood up and mentioned energetically that her desire was simply to connect to the internet and send emails to her friends but that the first internet point was way too far for her to do this on a daily basis. The feeling of belonging to the digital era is an achievement in itself and a right of all people.

It has been shown that there is a direct correlation in a study conducted on a number of sub-Saharan African countries between the increase in the ownership of cellular phones per 100 people and the growth of a country's GDP. Mobile phones make it easier for people to find jobs, to compare market prices for their businesses in different locations in a short time, to make payments, etc. Clearly the internet would be an even more powerful tool of communication and source of information and the impact on the economy would be even more significant. Bringing computer and internet training and access to a greater portion of the world population can have obvious positive impact on their lives and on the economies of their countries.

STMicroelectronics has translated its proposal into action by developing the Digital Unify program with the mission of providing free computer literacy training and computer and internet access to 1 million people up to the year 2014. STMicroelectronics has confided the sponsorship and coordination of the program to STMicroelectronics Foundation to separate the program completely from the business activities of the company. The scope of the Digital Unify program is not to improve STMicroelectronics' sales or image but to contribute to the well-being and progress of underprivileged communities.

In 2002 the Foundation asked the IT division of STMicroelectronics and ST University to develop a comprehensive introductory course on the computer and the internet. The 5 module, 20 hour course, entitled "Informatics and Computer Basics" currently exist in English, Italian, French and Hindi. A "Train the trainer" course was also devised to train trainers that would deliver the ICB.

An initial debugging phase consisted in delivering ICB courses directly at STMicroelectronics sites. Courses were delivered to ST employees and their family members. All trainers were volunteer ST staff trained via a "Train the trainer" program. ICB courses were delivered throughout 2003 at ST sites in Italy, Malta, Morocco, and India.

The next phase entailed training the local community at training centers at ST sites and creating external training centers in collaboration with local partners. In 2004, the Foundation, with the help of local volunteer ST staff, forged partnerships in each country with local schools, universities, administrations, and NGOs. Many times, local partners were identified with the help of Regional Education or Social Welfare Departments or Local Administrations.

STMicroelectronics has maintained historically a very strong social agenda in every country in which it operates, guided at the very top management levels by a strong commitment to values of social responsibility and environmental protection. It has earned itself a reputation as a socially responsible company amongst the communities it operates, often cited by local government representatives as an example to follow, and recipient of numerous recognitions world wide for its commitment to the environment and corporate citizenship, such as the European Quality Award, the Malcolm Baldridge Award, the Environmental Protection Agency Award, etc, and among the first to be listed in indexes such as the Dow Jones Sustainability Index.

STMicroelectronics has also harnessed close collaborations with Universities worldwide where it is present. In countries such as Morocco, Tunisia, India, Italy, France, US, Singapore, STMicroelectronics has a history recruiting local engineers, providing training and internships to university students, interacting with professors, sponsoring research at universities, etc. These ties have proven beneficial both to the company and universities, while positively impacting the local community and economy at large. STMicroelectronics has also earned itself a reputation for its ecological concerns and commitment. As early as 1994 STMicroelectronics established a corporate Environmental Decalogue for recycling, reusing and reducing consumption of energy, water, paper and raw materials. Convinced that existing laws are not stringent enough to safeguard the environment, STMicroelectronics imposed on itself more rigid standards. STMicroelectronics chose to apply the strictest existing regulations in one country to the entire company worldwide. The program has had outstanding results. Today, in Morocco, for example, no waste goes to landfill. Paper consumption has been reduced worldwide by over 80 % in STMicroelectronics in the past 10 years. The ultimate aim of the company is to have 0 impact on the environment, and it is a goal it hopes to reach by 2015. Every year since 1994, the company spends approximately 30 million US dollars on programs related to the environment. Using the 1994 baseline consumption per unit of production, applied to the volumes of 2004, total savings resulting from the environmental programs amounted to 170 million US dollars (of which over 100 million in energy savings sparing the environment the impact of a plant of 150 MW). Overall the environmental programs added 140 million dollars to the bottom line. STMicroelectronics has been a pioneer in demonstrating that going green is not only good for the environment but it is also good for the bottom line and therefore makes also business sense.

People are caring more about the consequences of global warming and pollution, they are demanding that companies pollute less and use alternative energies. Consumers prefer products that use recycled paper, that are biodegradable, and that consume less energy. Companies that consume less raw materials and energy will have a competitive advantage with respect to those that will be forced to comply in the future to stricter environmental regulations. Also companies that are able to manufacture products that are "greener" will have a competitive advantage as consumers prefer to buy products that have a lesser impact on the environment.

ST sites worldwide have also been historically involved every year in large social programs in every country it operates, leading blood donation campaigns, for example, earning itself the respect of governments and local administrations and communities.

Therefore, local ST staff is an important resource for the Digital Unify as they are well positioned to identify ideal local partners. The Foundation then sponsors and oversees the establishment of a fully equipped computer lab with internet access at the premises of the local partner. Volunteer ST trainers train volunteers or staff from the local partner to become trainers through the "Train the trainer" program. The local partner commits to organizing classes and cascading for free the ICB course to the local community. The Foundation also requires that a certain amount of time is allotted daily for participants and those who have completed the ICB course to access the training and use the PCs and the internet. The Foundation provides training manuals to trainers and participants distributes certificates upon successful completion of course and ensures maintenance of the computer lab for the first 3 years.

In Morocco, the Foundation has already set up over 15 training centers in 5 different regions (Casablanca, Rabat, Ifrane, Meknes, Rachidia). In many instances, our training center complements an NGO's or local administration's program for women or youth. The Foundation has set up computer training centers at universities where university students volunteer to train the local community. Computer training centers have been set up at schools where teachers become trainers who in turn train other teachers, school staff, and students. We have set up training centers at local administrations where trainers train their own staff and the local community. Usually, once Digital Unify deployment takes off in one country, NGOs, institutions, local administrations themselves approach the Foundation to partner with their existing education programs or ICT4D strategies.

In developed countries where the program is deployed in a reduced scale, the Foundation targets schools in poor neighborhoods, prisons, immigrants living in difficult socio-economic conditions, elderly, disabled, and in general marginalized and underprivileged groups.

The Digital Unify is currently being deployed in Italy, Malta, Morocco, Tunisia, India, Malaysia, where STMicroelectronics is present, but also in countries where STMicroelectronics does not operate, such as Congo and Nepal, and it is planning to start in Ethiopia. In such countries the Foundation partners with local or international NGOs with field experience in ICT4D.

So far, our program counts over 300 volunteer trainers worldwide and we will have trained over 15 000 people by the end of 2005. We intend to set up dozens of new training centers every year in selected countries of deployment, and therefore the number of people trained is set to increase exponentially via the "train the trainer" scheme and the ongoing delivery of ICB classes throughout the year for the next 10 years at each training center.

Our course is revised and updated on a yearly basis, in consultation with volunteer trainers worldwide, by volunteer ST University and IT staff at STMicroelectronics.

Following the request of most participants, the Foundation is currently evaluating ways in which to offer participants free on-line training for advanced computer skills. The Foundation is also looking at educational and didactical software programs including language courses that can be accessed at our training centers. For the learning centers that are set up in schools, the Foundation is currently evaluating teacher training programs that the Foundation could direct schools to. The Foundation is also creating for each training center a list of websites with relevant local content that can be useful for participants at each center.

The Digital Unify's main focus is computer literacy and computer and internet access, and the aim is to reach one million people by cascading the ICB course at training centers in collaboration with local partnerships but also by involving other companies to adopt the course and extend the program to their company. The Foundation is willing to share the course and provide the course for free to any company who wishes to follow our example. The effort of contributing to bridge the digital divide should not be limited to high-tech companies, who seem to be the only ones so far actively implementing programs for mainstreaming ICTs in education.

The Digital Unify program is easily replicable and scalable by any company.

Why should a company get involved in such a program or any other type of social project? To respond to an ethical mandate; to generate a sense of belonging and motivation amongst employees; to increase acceptance within the local community where companies operate; and in the long term, to open new markets through the generation of wealth and therefore to establish the condition for future business opportunities

ST volunteer trainers and DU team organizers spend many hours out of their own free time to help out with the Digital Unify. These may be people who were already involved in volunteer work and are inclined towards social work. Trainers claim they are gratified by discovering the art and challenges of teaching. They are proud to help out their fellow nationals and teach the basics of computers to people who were even afraid of touching a PC. Educated professionals from a private company can represent positive role models for youth coming from difficult socio-economic backgrounds.

There is also an important element of self-esteem and confidence that education gives to people. During a ceremony for the delivery of certificates to participants in Morocco, one elder woman claimed it was the "first certificate she received in her life!" The director of a shelter for women under-18 mentioned that the learning center set up by the Foundation at their institution had changed the lives of the girls. Illiterate girls managed to learn how to use programs on the PC. The PCs have become a medium of expression for many girls who use them to make drawings, write poetry, and communicate with the external world.

In the same center, the directors had been struggling for years to find extra financing to construct an extension to the overcrowded building where the girls where housed. Lack of sufficient space created other problems of disputes and violence among the girls, reduced hygiene standards, and made life in the community much more difficult. Only a few months after the opening of our learning center was announced in the media, public and private donors increased their support so that the institute was able to construct two new wings to the building. Good actions can be contagious and often trigger other channels of aid and assistance.

YOUNG VOICES ON ICT FOR EDUCATION – FOUR REGIONAL INSIGHTS

Introduction by Julia Christina Fauth

It was surely an innovation in the United Nations ICT Task Force when at its eighth meeting young people were asked to share their views about the potential of ICT for education and the meaning of ICT for the empowerment of young people. Thanks have to go to the Irish government which supported this involvement of youth and to the GeSCI team. The participation of young people on the panels in the Global Forum of the eighth United Nations ICT Task Force meeting can truly be seen as a breakthrough towards a higher perception of them as a key stakeholder in the proceedings of the United Nations ICT Task Force.

Education is central to the lives of young people, but not only through the fact that they are the beneficiaries of educational methods and models. Young people should be included in evaluation and the development of learning methods, in particular for the reason that they are the ones most closely tied to it. Their involvement should be considered as a premise for further proceedings in the area of ICT in education and their policies.

Young people should not be seen only as a target group for the policies of ICT for education but also as viable knowledge consultants for shaping these policies in terms of appropriate content, language and connectivity.

Young people these days grow up as citizens of a "global village" that still leaves people all over the world amazed by the way in which new information and communication technologies are able to cross distances within milliseconds and open unprecedented opportunities for global dialogue and exchange. People can cross borders by driving along the Internet highway and young people are the ones who are most open to these intercultural or cross-border encounters. A huge traffic of chats and other forms of instant messaging from South Korea to Saudi Arabia, Australia, Europe or Africa is nothing spectacular but an aspect of daily life among the networked youth community around the globe.

Against this background young people have a remarkable potential to enhance peaceful development and integration in the global village. But they are paradoxically also the group which illustrates exclusion and disconnection from the global village to a large extent. We cannot overlook the disconnected parts of the world, mainly in the developing countries where young people have to face big disadvantages regarding their education.

The Global Forum on ICT for education in Dublin drew particular attention to these inequalities and involved the voices of a group of young people from different regions in the panel discussion of the Global Forum. These different youth insights into ICT for education initiatives and projects in different regions left a strong impression there and have also since emerged in successful youth involvement in the civil society forum of the World Summit on the Information Society. The involvement of young people is truly a gain for ICT for development discussion and policy making.

The following four articles written by young authors from Nigeria, Ireland, Brazil and Germany provide us with diverse regional pictures on ICT for education projects through young people's eyes. The individual articles show us on the one hand what kind of ICT education may be needed in the national contexts. On the other hand, the compilation provides evidence of ways in which global approaches to ICT for education can be harnessed for establishing networks and the sharing of best practices.

An overall thread of the compilation is also worth mentioning here. The youth insights are based on the premise that technologies do not have a natural bias to be harnessed for only one particular way of learning. On the contrary, they allow us to be creative young thinkers and to develop our own content and context. ICT can enable us to act creatively as individuals and that evidence might be one of the most important aspects of the new knowledge of the Information Society.

This compilation of articles lets us look at ICT for education through five individual youth perspectives. We encounter young authors who are a target group of ICT for education policies, but who are not just to be seen as "end-users", as used to be the case. The different regional insights increase our awareness of the need for joint efforts and approaches in ICT for education policies but they also remind us to focus on the young individuals who are at the receiving end of each policy.

1. E-EDUCATION IN NIGERIA: CHALLENGES AND PROSPECTS

Dabesaki Mac-Ikemenjima

Introduction

Information and communication technologies (ICTs) have become key tools in service delivery across various sectors of society. This phenomenon has given birth to the contemporary e-commerce, e-government, e-medicine and e-education, which is the primary focus of this chapter. ICT is revolutionizing educational methodology globally. The concepts of computer aided teaching and computer aided learning have given birth to computer aided instruction, which represents a combination of both teaching and learning.[1] However, this revolution is not widespread and needs to be strengthened to reach a large percentage of the population. What is required now is for government and all stakeholders to insist on the best standards and approaches to ensure effective ICT for education service delivery in institutions of learning.

E-education is an electronic mode of knowledge sharing and transmission which may not necessarily involve physical contact between teacher and student.[2] Access to instruction is flexible, ensures broad viability and availability of educational opportunities. It is a cost effective system of instruction and learning materials can be accessed irrespective of time and space. This is a great area of investment which will be of great value to the young people of this generation now and in the future and will definitely mitigate the impact of the current population explosion and poverty which has led to massive unemployment in many developing countries.

Nigeria: Education Overview

The Nigerian educational system has evolved through various phases of development over the last three decades. In 1973, the educational system was reviewed to the 6-3-3-4 system and in 1979 the first National Policy on Education was developed and adopted. Since then, the educational system has witnessed many changes and modifications at various levels. The current phase of evolution is a transition from traditional pedagogical

---

[1] Osah-Ogulu, D and Mac-Ikemenjima, D. (2004). Shaping attitudes: care and appreciation of the virtual Library. In Journal of Psychology and Pedagogy. Port Harcourt.
[2] Mac-Ikemenjima, D. (2003) The Integration of ICT into the school system: Our roles. *Paper presented at the student leaders IT Conference.*

methodology to more sophisticated, but user friendly, technology-based instructional methodology.

Nigeria currently runs the 6-3-3-4 system of education (6 years primary, 3 years junior secondary, 3 years of senior secondary and 4 years of tertiary education). The educational sector is guided by the National Policy on Education and several co-ordination mechanisms have been put in place to ensure that the highest standards are maintained in curriculum, infrastructure and manpower requirements. The primary and secondary schools are directly under the Ministry of Education either at the state or federal level, the universities are under the National Universities Commission (NUC), the polytechnics fall under the National Board for Vocational Colleges and Technical Education (NABTECH), while the National Commission for Colleges of Education (NCCE) oversees the activities of the Colleges of Education.

The institutions under each of these coordinating mechanisms are enormous and diverse in many respects. The numbers involved are as follows:

University Institutions - 58[3]

- 26 federal

- 19 state

- 8 private

- 5 federal inter-university centres

Polytechnic Institutions - 48[4]

- 17 federal

- 29 state[5]

- 2 private

Colleges of Education - 67[6]

- 21 federal

- 41 state

---

[3] Aminu, I. (2003) The Higher Education Environment and Users of the Nigerian Virtual Library. Working Paper at UNESCO Virtual Library Feasibility Study Workshop
[4] Yakubu, N.A. (2003) The Virtual Library and the Polytechnic system. Paper presented At Feasibility Study on the development of a virtual Library for Nigeria
[5] Ibid.
[6] Isyaku, K. (2003) Virtual Library and Colleges of Education in Nigeria.

- 5 private

Other institutions include 44,000 primary schools, 9,000 secondary schools, 3 specialist postgraduate institutions, 26 federal vocational colleges and schools, 15 university teaching hospitals and 61 research institutions.

E-education in Nigeria

E-education is not new to Nigeria. One may say that it had started even before the present digital revolution began taking place. In 1972, the Ahmadu Bello University had a "university of the air" programme. In 1983, the Nigerian Television Authority ran a distance learning programme. The methodology for communication was through the TV and the course content was basic arithmetic, English and science. Each of these courses was taught on a weekly basis and assignments were given. During the following week, the assignments were reviewed and the participants allowed self-assessment if they had provided the correct answers to the questions. During 1983, the first National Open University was launched but was however short-lived as a result of military intervention in 1985.

e-Education in Nigeria: Present Initiatives

There are several ICT for education initiatives in Nigeria. These initiatives are either being undertaken by government, civil society or the private sector.

Government e-Education Initiatives

There are presently at least nine ICT for education initiatives at various stages of development being carried out by the education coordinating agencies of government and the Ministry of Education. They include:

1. The Nigerian Universities Network (NUNet) Project

2. The Polytechnics Network (PolyNet) Project

3. The SchoolNet Project

4. The Nigerian Education, Academic and Research Network (NEARNet)

5. The Teachers Network (TeachNet) Project

6. National Open University

7. National Virtual (Digital) Library (Ministry of Education/ NUC)

8. National Virtual Library (Ministry of Science and Technology/NITDA)

9. National Information, communication and education programme of the Presidency.[7]

Four of these are described in more detail below: NUNet, NOU and the virtual libraries.

National Universities Network (NUNet)[8]

The origins of NUNet dates back to 1994 when it was realized that it was increasingly becoming necessary for universities to be connected electronically, at least through e-mail. However, it was later realized that interconnectivity issues for institutions of higher learning were far greater than e-mail alone. Following this, partnerships were built with several institutions and NUC staff were trained in various IT related skills.

In 1996, the NUC signed a MoU with the International Centre for Theoretical Physics in Italy and secured 3 IDD and 9 telephone lines for NUNet, procured equipment, registered a domain name and introduced dial-up e-mail services.

The objectives of NUNET are:

- To end the isolation of Nigerian academic staff and students from each other and from the global academic community;

- To ameliorate staff shortages arising from the brain-drain, by providing the ICT facility required by Nigerian academic staff-in-Diaspora to make their contributions regardless of where they live or work;

- To encourage the sharing of resources, foster academic and research collaborations among Nigerian universities, and with their counterparts throughout the world;

- To provide universities with access to electronic databases, journals and books many of which are increasingly available only in digital formats;

- To serve as a vehicle to expand access to education at minimal cost of capital building expenditure; and

- To place Nigerian universities at the forefront of the information revolution, that they might serve their proper roles as foci for national development.

There are currently 52 university centres and colleges of education who have their domain names registered, while 15 are active e-mail users.

---

[7] Same as 3 above
[8] Russel & Dlamini, H (2002) Mission Report (4-18 November, 2002) with the purpose of launching the feasibility study for the development of a Virtual Library for Universities and Institutions of Higher Learning in Nigeria.

The National Open University of Nigeria

The National Open University of Nigeria (NOUN) first began in 1983 but was suspended in 1985 by the then military government. The resuscitation of NOUN is part of the commitment of the present government towards universal basic education. The justifications for the establishment of the Open University are clear; there are approximately 1.5 million applications per year for a place to attend university. However, the university system can only accommodate 20% of this number.[26]

The course delivery will be through a combination of Web-based modules, textual materials, audio and video tapes as well as CD ROMs. The university currently has 18 study centres and plans to have at least one study centre in each of the 774 local government areas of Nigeria. It runs programmes in education, arts and humanities, business and human resource management and science and technology.

Virtual Library Initiatives

There are several virtual library initiatives in Nigeria. The National Virtual (Digital) Library project of the Ministry of Education is supervised by the National Universities Commission, the National Virtual Library Project of the Ministry of Science and Technology is supervised by the National IT Development Agency and there is currently an ongoing effort by UNESCO to develop a virtual library for all higher education institutions in Nigeria.

In summary, the objectives of the national virtual library include: improving the quality of teaching and research institutions through the provision of current books, journal and other library resources, enhancing access of academic libraries to global library and information resources, enhancing scholarship and lifelong learning through the establishment of permanent access to shared digital archival collections, provision of guidance to academic libraries on ways of applying appropriate technologies for production of digital library resources, and to advance the use and usability of globally distributed networks library resources.

The virtual library project at the NUC is currently undergoing a review and hopefully this will lead to the upgrading and improvement of the virtual library. The portal for the Nigerian Virtual Library is www.nigerianvirtuallibrary.com.

Civil Society e-Education Initiatives

These include:

1. Community Teaching and Learning Centres

2. Lagos Digital Village by Junior Achievement Nigeria

---

[26] Ibid.

3. Owerri Digital Village by Youth for Technology Foundation

4. Computer Literacy for Older Persons Programme by Mercy Mission

Further details follow of two of these initiatives, Community Teaching and Learning Centres and the Owerri Digital Village.

Community Teaching and Learning Centres (CTLCs) are locally run and managed places strategically placed in or close to schools and businesses in order to serve as local, practical education centres[27]. CTLCs are an initiative of Teachers Without Borders, an international NGO that seeks to connect teachers globally, to each other and to resources.

The centres currently exist in various parts of Nigeria and comprise on-line and off-line rooms. At each centre, the community provides space and manpower for the CTLC, while Teachers Without Borders provides equipment, technology and training. CTLCs serve to provide education where none existed before and improves learning by using technology to access and share latest knowledge.

Programmes run at the CTLCs include early childhood education, HIV/AIDS training, literacy and teacher education- leading to the award of a Certificate of Teaching Mastery.

Owerri Digital Village (ODV) was launched in September 2001 by the Youth for Technology Foundation (YTF), an international non-profit organization based in the United States and Nigeria. The mission of ODV is to promote rural community development by providing technical, educational and entrepreneurship skills training to disadvantaged individuals in the effort to create social and economic opportunities that can change people's lives and transform communities.

The Owerri Digital Village currently runs four programmes; Tech Kids, Tech Teens, Tech Communities and Tech Enhancement.

Challenges for e-Education in Nigeria

Although ICT holds great potential to support ongoing educational as well as national development efforts, several challenges have affected its large-scale deployment and utilization for educational purposes, and these have very much reduced its capacity to do the nation good. Some of the factors which have affected the effective deployment and utilization of ICT for educational purposes in Nigeria include:

- Inadequate ICT infrastructure including computer hardware and software, and bandwidth/access;

- A lack of skilled manpower, to manage available systems and inadequate training facilities for ICT education at the tertiary level;

---

[27] www.teacherswithoutborders.org/html/ctlc.html

- Resistance to change from traditional pedagogical methods to more innovative, technology-based teaching and learning methods, by both students and academics;

- The overall educational system is under funded, therefore, available funds are used to meet survival needs by the institutions;

- The over-dependence of educational institutions on government for everything has limited institutions' ability to partner with the private sector or seek alternative funding sources for ICT educational initiatives.

- Lack of effective co-ordination of all the various ICT for education initiatives.

This list is not exhaustive but represents the major problems faced in the development of ICT for education in Nigeria. If these are adequately addressed, e-education will thrive in Nigeria.

Forward-looking Strategies and Prospects for e-Education in Nigeria

The core of the recommendations contained in this chapter point above all to ways in which policy makers and government can work with civil society and the private sector to mainstream ICT in the overall educational development process. Although this chapter is focused on e-education in Nigeria, its implications will mostly also apply to other developing countries as the challenges faced in the deployment of ICT for educational purposes are largely similar and can be addressed using cross-cutting recommendations and strategies.

The following key points maybe considered as key points and recommendations for the development of e-education in Nigeria:

- e-education has great potential to assist in achieving Nigeria's goal to achieve education for all by the year 2015 and therefore should be maximally harnessed by every possible avenue;

- IT education should be included in the educational curriculum including the provision of necessary infrastructural support and massive training and deployment of skilled manpower into both secondary and tertiary institutions;

- Young software developers should be trained and supported with the necessary equipment to develop nationally usable e-education software;

- The various government education coordinating agencies should work together to develop an integrated broad-based model/ strategy for e-education with a definitive timeline for its completion;

- Government should increase funding for the entire educational sector with particular emphasis on ICT;

- Government should work with the private sector and civil society to ensure affordable and sustainable access to ICT infrastructure;

- A policy environment which encourages investment in ICT should be put in place including tariffs on import of ICT infrastructure, in order to promote affordability and wide range usage at all levels of the educational system;

- The importance of youth participation in ICT decision making processes cannot be over emphasized; therefore, their participation in ICT policy-making processes at the national and other levels should be encouraged and supported by all stakeholders.

"If ever there was an area where young people were the leaders, not only of the future, but also of today, it is in the emerging information society."[28]

Youth Participation in ICT for Education

Young people have begun mobilizing and carrying out initiatives that support the efforts to move ICT-aided education forward in Nigeria.

For example, student leaders recently came together from various institutions in Port Harcourt, Nigeria, for an IT Conference. Apparently worried that the potentials of ICT in the effective delivery of educational services are not being maximally harnessed, the young leaders made several commitments and called on all stakeholders to ensure that they play their roles in the process to integrate IT into the educational system.

As follow-up to the conference, the student leaders have made plans to develop a Web portal where information, resources, research findings and profiles of their institutions can be posted and regularly updated. They recommended: that ICT related courses be included in the school curriculum at all levels, the development of infrastructure at institutional level, the participation of young leaders in IT policy making, utilization of virtual teaching and learning opportunities/environments, and prioritization of access to ICT infrastructure at the institutional level.

Their conference declaration stated: "...as young Nigerians and heads of our various campus organizations, we have committed ourselves to ensuring that we work with our mentors at the higher levels to ensure the actualization of the e-education integration initiatives and goals, for the good of our today and tomorrow."

---

[28] Moraitis, N. (2002) World Summit on Information Society Youth Caucus Strategic Plan Draft v.1

2. THE IMPORTANCE OF LEARNING HOW TO LEARN

Mike Griffin

The harsh and saddening reality is that kids globally are looking everywhere else bar school in order to be stimulated. Traditional schooling has changed very little since the 1800s bar the odd crack of the cane. It is not beyond the scope of imagination to realise that a teacher from Victorian times could well walk into any classroom today and do a reasonably good job in educating our school children. Teachers are still relying on undeveloped, archaic teaching methods. "Chalk and talk" is for the most part the scope of their methodology. The teacher is still regarded as the sage on the stage.

ICTs have an enormous role in developing the effectiveness and efficiency of education but only, in my opinion, once we acknowledge and come to the full realisation that the greatest and most important technology in the world lies between our ears. I see little point in creating more expensive blackboards per se to facilitate education unless we are fully determined to release the genius potential in each of our children, bar none. Our heritage means that there is no dismissing the fact that our brain can operate at genius level. Learning to learn is the vital step into this genius realm at which we are all capable of operating.

There are two types of education. One teaches you how to earn a living; the other teaches you how to live. Education for the 21st century needs to move more into the latter category. The real secret is for ICTs to move in harmonious line with brain-based research and development. Education could be making us more aware of our inherent, amazing human capabilities. Learning should always be an adventure, creative and fun.

Schooling today for the most part, unfortunately, is based on competition and not cooperation. This is absurd. In my opinion, we need to look seriously at the nature and the volume of examinations children are subjected to in school. Examinations, by their very nature, are set up in such a way that the student immediately feels under threat and puts teachers under pressure too. It limits their own creative and imaginative potential because they must get the course covered for the exam. It is extremely difficult for the students to "claim ownership" of the material they are studying if they feel they are being judged. This should never be the case. We are human beings, we cannot limit ourselves to silly, outdated modes of trying to verify competency.

It is important to realise that when learning anything new the brain goes through four stages of development as identified by the eminent psychologist Abraham Maslow. The brain loves to succeed at anything it undertakes, whether it is solving complex mathematical problems or simply making a cup of tea. The stages one goes through are first Unconscious Incompetence, Conscious Incompetence, Conscious Competence and finally Unconscious Competence.

To illustrate this let us use an example. Let us say you get up one morning and decide you would love to learn how to fly an airplane. The first stage, unconscious incompetence, simply means you do not know what you do not know. Yesterday you were completely unaware of how to fly an airplane. Today your outlook has shifted and you have moved into the second stage, conscious incompetence. You will experience a mixture of frustration and confusion. You know what you would like to accomplish but have no idea as yet about how to fly, you are consciously incompetent. After a number of weeks of study and practicing under the tuition of your trainer you begin to feel that you have begun to integrate the necessary skills but are not fully confident of flying without the supervision of an expert, you are consciously competent. The final stage you can call mastery is when you can fly comfortably and confidently on your own. You are no longer under supervision and have taken to the sky on numerous occasions, performing at an unconscious competent level.

For the most part, when we begin to learn something new we are unaware of this learning developmental model. A failure to recognise this means when we say that we have for example, thirty years experience, in reality what we have is perhaps six months to a year and a further twenty-nine of this repeated behaviour. It means that people avoid undertaking a new learning challenge even though they would really like to. They begin to oscillate from their current position to where they would like to be. We can all get stuck within our own cushy prisons, refusing to step out of our own self imposed hang-ups to learning. But once this cycle is recognised and understood then the learner can realise that it is all part of the learning process.

Mistakes are simply a necessary ingredient and should be viewed upon as a sign that the learner is showing a willingness to stretch themselves out of their comfort zone. So called "mistakes" should be embraced wholeheartedly. School should provide a safe haven for students to undergo learning and experimentation. It should acknowledge that it is all learning, regardless of momentary setbacks. These setbacks are merely stepping stones to greater and richer learning experiences. Such a positive feedback loop would encourage students to explore. The study is always us personally. Teachers are not teaching subjects. They are teaching people. This must never be forgotten.

Emotions can play a vital role, when left up to their own devices in any learning experience. But emotions are simply emotions. They are energy in motion, passing through us. There is simply no need to identify and judge them. Emotion literally means "disturbance". The word comes from the Latin *emovere*, meaning "to disturb". All too often students are turned off from learning in school because of so-called negative emotions. An understanding of how best to deal with these debilitating monsters in the closet is vital to helping students overcome self-imposed hang-ups to learning. We all have gremlins when it comes to learning. Some of these are clever and remain hidden in the backs of our minds. These shadows, when immediately recognised for what they are, limitations to learning, can be removed when we know how.

One of the greatest techniques for freeing ourselves from self-limiting and self-defeating emotions is simply to release from them. Recognise that they are not us. We are beyond and we are something deeper than our thoughts and emotions. There is an old Indian saying that they are like guests in a hotel; our thoughts and emotions simply check in and then check out again. Just simply releasing from our emotions may seem incredibly simplistic at first. But like an old Chinese saying goes "the truth is simple. If it were complicated then everybody would understand".

To fully understand the power or releasing from our emotions it obviously needs to be experienced, like jam needs to be tasted rather than read about. ICT is of little use if we have all the greatest technology in the world inside a classroom but nobody is able to handle it due to self-imposed limitations to learning that go unrecognised within students. There are a number of barriers that school must first recognise so that they can be removed to enable students to learn in the optimum environment and state of mind.

"You cannot teach people anything. You can only help them discover it within themselves," said Galileo. School should instill in students the conviction that their potential is limitless and set about uplifting students' negative attitudes, beliefs and false assumptions to learning. The first step to this is to educate our educators. One of the problems that exists in today's schooling is that the people who traditionally do well in school return to teach. But they return with the belief, understanding and continued practice of an old paradigm of learning and teaching. Unwittingly they are not relieving the problems but for the most part feeding into them.

This old paradigm, where students were taught that academic success was only achieved through hard, disciplined work, is in line with the Puritan work ethic that was characterised during the time of the Industrial Revolution. Industry became highly mechanised and everything had to be somewhat logical and concrete. Education to its detriment began to be recognised in the same light. You were no longer encouraged to use right brain activities such as imagination and intuition, such esoteric mind tools were frowned upon.

So unfortunately we have educators coming back believing that learning is somewhat of an arduous task, with a "no pain, no gain" mentality. This is in direct opposition to the accelerated learning to learn movement that is in operation and needs to be implemented inside every classroom globally if we are to supply students with the necessary tools to help them empower themselves. Because it is natural, it is easier; because it is easier, it is faster. That's why we call it Accelerated Learning.

Mind mapping is a fabulous whole brain enhancing thinking technique developed by Tony Buzan. Mind mapping originated as an initial study aiding memory technique into an all round "Swiss army knife" tool kit for the brain. It can be used for all types of thinking: logical, analytical, creative, note taking and making and because it uses your full cortical abilities is highly memorable. Mind mapping taps into your brain's latent capabilities by utilising both the left and right hemispheres.

The left is often referred to as "the analyst" specialising in what are commonly labeled "academic" aspects of learning – language and mathematical processes, logical thoughts, sequences and analysis. The right brain "aesthe" is principally concerned with "creative" activities utilising rhyme, rhythm, music, visual impressions, colour and pictures. Researches also ascribe to the right brain the ability to deal with certain kinds of conceptual thought – intangible "ideas" such as love, beauty and loyalty. With a mind map the student can immediately see the entire structure and outlay of whatever they happen to be studying at once. The old adage "a picture tells a thousand words" is never truer when dealing with mind mapping, or cerebral calligraphy as many of its users like to call it.

The advantage of mind mapping over traditional note making and taking is enormous. Up to ninety per cent of time is saved when returning to review notes as only the key words, ideas, issues and concepts are noted. Notes taken in a singular mono colour unwittingly send the brain to sleep; the root of the word monotonous is mono and what does a brain that is bored do? It goes to sleep! The brain becomes frustrated by traditional linear notes as it tries to decipher the relevant information from pages and pages of notes. It is extremely difficult to grasp the thread of what is being studied when one has to plough through reams of monotonous notes to figure out key concepts and the associative relationship between ideas.

Mind mapping is highly individualised, working with the individual's own unique brain. There are not so much "rules" to follow, merely guidelines on how best to utilise this thinking tool. A student should always start with a central image in the middle of a horizontally placed page. It is laid out in this format to encourage expansive thinking and idea formulating. Inadvertently ideas placed in a linear bullet point form guillotine the brain's ability to generate new ideas; it simply looks at the list thinking "that's it"; whereas the mind map is unrestrained and encourages the brain to think more deeply about a subject. So, unintentionally the majority of people are still using a system that hinders rather than develops learning, cognition, creativity and memory. The great news about this is that once it is noticed and made aware of, we can set about correcting it. We can save the next generation of students by standing on the shoulders of Mr. Buzan's ingenious mind mapping system.

Mind mapping should be a standard affair for the 21st century student. Teachers no longer need to laboriously read through pages of notes trying to decipher whether or not the student has a firm grasp of what they are studying. A quick glance at the mind map reveals at what stage the student is at and where gaps exist in their current knowledge base. This intelligent gap management system provides an efficient, effective and positive feedback loop of encouragement for the student.

Mind mapping technological software can greatly enhance the interdependent learning capabilities of students globally. Study buddies from all over the world can be working on the same mind map generating an infinite number of ideas and creative solutions to whatever area of knowledge captures their imagination. This is the proper role for education in the 21st century, ICTs and brain based knowledge mixed to form a cocktail of interdependent action among students globally.

The PhotoReading Whole Mind System is a state of the art learning to learn technique developed by Paul Scheele of Learning Strategies Corporation in Minneapolis, USA.

PhotoReading enables the reader to process information at rates of 25,000 words a minute, minimum. What might you say? This is impossible! The mind cannot possibly achieve such a feat!

The secret of PhotoReading lies in its use of the non conscious mind. The conscious mind can only hold roughly seven items of information at any one given time; whereas the non conscious part of our brain receives millions of items of information per second. If it were to send all of this information to the conscious fanatic-in-the-attic it would completely overwhelm it. To highlight this difference place your two feet together on the floor and observe the space underneath. This is the narrow information bandwidth of the conscious mind. Now look at all the surrounding floor space around you, not only in this room but up to eleven miles in all directions around you. This is the information playing field of our other than conscious mind. We can draw on information, creativity insights and solve problems using an eleven mile radius if we only allow ourselves to do so. All we have to do is get out of our own way and let it happen.

While PhotoReading, the reader takes mental snapshots of the written page. This bypasses the critical editing function of the conscious mind. The information goes directly to the non conscious where the brain begins to do its magic by sorting and coding the information for us. It is like a magical genie within, doing all the work for us. All we have to do is learn to relax, use our intuition let the PhotoReading Whole Mind System work for us. The greatest obstacle for many learners is that they do not know how to unlearn their self imposed delusions and hang-ups to learning and allow the process to work.

Years of false identification that learning is arduous can be hard to undo for some. PhotoReading offers the reader choices and enables them to get their reading done in the time and comprehension they need. First time PhotoReaders can expect to get through books at least one third of the time it would normally take them. After playing with the system and going through Maslow's four developmental stages of learning i.e. unconscious incompetence, conscious incompetence, conscious competence and unconscious competence, the PhotoReader is open to a limitless potential for improvement.

Pete Bissonette, the Chairman of Learning Strategies has been recorded on hundreds of radio and TV shows; on one such exhibition of how PhotoReading works, he read very technical law reports at a rate of over 600,000 words a minute and later answered questions with over seventy percent comprehension. Not bad! Especially considering when you read at a normal average speed, word for word for word, the reader can expect no more than a twenty percent comprehension rate. Who in their right mind would not want to become a PhotoReader!

PhotoReading is exactly how it should be for the 21st Century student.

We must adopt a playful, receptive attitude to learning. Leave our hang-ups outside. Let your mind set be relaxed, willing to have fun and allow whatever you require to come naturally and effortlessly to you. This is in direct accordance with the universal law of least effort seen ubiquitously in nature. The grass doesn't strain and make an effort trying to grow, it just grows.

The basic steps of the PhotoReading Whole Mind System are:

Prepare: You enter your ideal state of mind for learning by centering yourself. While in this state of relaxed alertness you quietly affirm your purpose for reading.

Preview: You perform a simple mental reconnaissance for your genius mind. You preview whatever you are about to read whether it's a book, journal, report or whatever; scanning the contents, quickly looking at chapter headings and anything else that may catch your eye.

PhotoRead: This is where you mentally photograph the text by entering into the photo focus state and bypass the critical editing function of your conscious mind.

Activation: Through a number of different activation techniques such as super reading and dipping, mind mapping, skittering, mind probing, you get what you require from the book, completely guilt free and ignoring parts of the text that are not in accordance with your purpose. No longer do you need to read a book for ten hours only to realise that it wasn't what you have been looking for!

Rapid Read: This is an optional step that can be employed; it keeps the fanatic-in-the-attic quiet, should he need it!

One of the greatest ways to bring to light, overcome and get in touch with the reality that we are all magnificent learners is through what is known as "The Work", by Byron Katie. The work consists of four questions and a turnaround of the original belief that you subjected to inquiry. It can radically transform not only students but people of all ages by awakening them out of their self-defeating, self-limiting daily trances that they may have unconsciously slipped into. Byron Katie's "The Work" is a way out of such self-delusion. It can reawaken the joy and love of learning that is our inherent birth right.

Let's take a closer examination of how "The Work" can free a student from self imposed hang ups to learning. In this example a student Aoife, 16, is experiencing difficulty with the concept that she is terrible at all things mathematical. The belief she subscribes to is: "I have always been terrible at maths". The first question the teacher asks Aoife in the process is: "Is this true?" Aoife: "Yes it is true. I have always been terrible at maths." Second question the teacher asks: "Can you absolutely know that it is true?" Aoife: "Well…I guess that I cannot absolutely know that it is true. I mean… I can remember a time when I sort of enjoyed maths. But it was a long time ago, back when I was about six or seven I reckon. So no I cannot absolutely know that it is true that I have been terrible at maths."

The third question in this process the teacher asks is: "How do you react when you think that thought?" Aoife: "It makes me feel sick in my stomach. My head begins to fill with negative thoughts about not only maths but learning in general. I get tense and quickly try and shift this feeling by either ignoring it or trying to blast it away by claiming that maths is silly anyway and I will never need it. I treat myself badly when I believe this thought. It does nothing to promote action in trying to overcome my obstacle to maths. When I hold this belief all I get out of it is unnecessary stress."

The fourth question the teacher asks in this inquiry process is: "Who would you be without the thought?"

Aoife: "Without this thought I would be much happier. I would be more relaxed and better able to accept myself. I would begin to enjoy maths, I think, once I dropped this thought. I would feel free, more adventurous and would be willing to play and experiment with maths. I definitely see no valid stress free reason to hold onto this thought."

The final process in "The Work" is when you turn around the original belief statement which in Aoife's case was "I have always been terrible at maths". Here Aoife turns it around to "I choose to allow myself to become terrific at maths". Her mindset has completely been changed. She no longer views maths as a disguised demon, out to fill her with dread and induce anxiety in her. Such brain-based knowledge work is a terrific example of how we must first acknowledge the self imposed hang-ups to each individual learner first, before we can successfully implement technology into the classroom. The two together can obviously set alight the latent learning capabilities within each student.

Such a simple and profound process can create the optimum learning environment within each student as well as the outside classroom environment. It is a great example too, of the changing role of the teacher, which I believe needs to take place within education. The educator's role should be one of coach and facilitator of learning, guiding the student along so that the answer can be found within, where it always really lies. This Socratic method is the true basis for education; the word "education" is derived from the Latin educare, which literally means "drawing out".

The teacher should no longer be the omnipotent presence at the top of the classroom asking the student for the "correct" answer. Such a situation puts the mind set of a student into the wrong gear for learning. It is not about "correct" answers. It should always be about the questions you ask and your willingness to explore new avenues of knowledge, to bring classroom information to life and to the outside world.

Howard Gardner's original theory of multiple intelligences when integrated with ICTs of today and the future will greatly benefit students. He said the question should no longer be "How smart are we?" but "How are we smart?" When learning anything a student needs to exercise as many of their senses – sight, taste, sound, touch, and smell – as possible. Gardner identified that people have a multiple number of intelligences.

Mathematical/logical intelligence, simply put, is a skill with numbers and reasoning. Linguistic intelligence is the ability to articulate ideas in our own language; it is a skill with words and semantics. Visual/spatial intelligence is the ability to think visually and in three dimensions. Physical intelligence is the ability to use our musculature and physical awareness to get the results we want. Intrapersonal intelligence is the ability to "go inside" and make connections. Interpersonal intelligence, simply put, is a skill with people. Musical intelligence is the ability to articulate ideas and emotions through music. A student's understanding, retention, recall, ability to use and communicate information is greatly enhanced when they can activate at least three of their intelligences.

Gardner's theory is completely congruent with the holistic approach that education in the 21st century should be taking. We can no longer afford to stifle and tread upon young minds by backing them into a meaningless scenario whereby they are forced to rote memorise school work and then regurgitate this disjointed information come exam time. This pandemic of rote learning is creating a myriad of problems and unnecessary stress among students and only promotes a surface, superficial type of learning. It does nothing to promote our inherent love of learning, so obvious in young school children before school tarnishes them.

Everybody has experienced this sort of scenario before; you cram your study just before an exam with a desperate, panicky sense of urgency; almost holding your head going inside the exam hall in case some of your newly squeezed knowledge were to fall out! You then proceed to pour out the information during the exam only to completely forget the entire relevant meaning and understanding the very next day. This is the reality and it is completely unnecessary. We can make this scenario a thing of the past for future generations. There is no mystery to how we can achieve this. The information and know how is already here. Let us integrate brain-based knowledge with ICTs to create stimulating, nurturing and creative learning environments for students.

People do not need to be taught how to see, they merely need to be saved from schools that blind them. I strongly believe that learning how to learn is the only way forward for students of the 21st century. We can no longer keep stifling and straining young minds by telling them what to learn. By coaching them in accelerated learning techniques designed to bring out their inherent genius, we empower them with a passion for life-long learning and give them the necessary tools to invent the future.

It is a reality that the greatest technology in the universe lies between our ears. By gaining a more intelligent understanding of how we can better use our brains we can then leap into the fabulous ICT facilities becoming more accessible to students globally. By creating the optimum learning environments both internally and externally for students we can truly create an interdependent global network of scholars. The technology is there waiting to be used and further developed, but we must further understand the basic learning styles, hang-ups and needs of each individual learner.

By doing so we fully release the resistance to learning that school unwittingly creates by constantly examining students thereby always setting learning up as a threat; with students going about their study with a grim determination to succeed and get through the system. Learning should not be separate from life, it should be life.

Imagine the scenario in the near future when every student is confident with their ability to learn anything. They have an arsenal of accelerated learning tools at their disposal. Each student is fully confident in centering themselves into the required state of relaxed alertness, the communication channel whereby learning is greatly facilitated. They have a firm understanding of how to motivate and direct themselves; can mind map with students across the globe; are proficient PhotoReaders; can gain creative insights and solve problems by self directing out the knowledge held from within; have a firm understanding of how to train and manage their memories; realise that emotions are simply an energy in motion and can fully release from their debilitating, suffocating nature; can rise above their self limiting and self defeating delusions that the ego mind likes to implant in order to prove that it is right by having the awareness to do so; and can therefore tap into a deeper more intuitive intelligence that lies within. Learning will no longer be a dull, conscious, limiting, threat induced state, but will be an adventurous, exciting and imaginative journey into the wondrous universes of knowledge that lie all around us. School with ICTs will become the best party in town!

3. PROMOTING PARTICIPATION AND ENCOURAGING EMPOWERMENT – EXAMPLES OF GERMAN ICT FOR EDUCATION INITIATIVES

Geraldine de Bastion

Information and communication technologies (ICTs) are more than useful – they have become an indispensable means to increase the availability of educational services and the efficient administration of educational institutions. School computer labs with maths self-help tutorials, online library catalogues and book order services, electronic scientific article databases, and of course the Internet, are just a few examples of how ICTs influence the education of students in Germany on a daily basis.

ICTs have changed the way people educate themselves and the way educational institutions operate in many countries. Making the benefits of ICT in education available to all is one of the goals of German development cooperation. The German Ministry for Economic Cooperation and Development (BMZ) considers education to be "a prerequisite to health, economic prosperity and socio-political participation." Seeing that "ICTs facilitate cost-effective access (…) furthering education, equality of opportunity and, thereby, empowerment"[1] they have been integrated into a number of development programmes and are continually gaining in importance.

The German Gesellschaft für Technische Zusammenarbeit (GTZ)[2] implements development programmes on behalf of the BMZ and partner countries in the formal education sector and helps to create non-formal educational opportunities. ICT solutions are included in the education programmes and projects whenever suitable, be it in form of large training schemes, administrative reforms or smaller projects that aim to increase the availability of information and educational services to specific target groups. Of course, there is no one-fits-all patent and ICT solutions have to be tailored to suit the demands of the people, the available infrastructure as well as the local learning culture. A few examples, to demonstrate the scope of the projects supported by GTZ during the last years, are the following.

---

[1] Federal Ministry for Economic Cooperation and Development: "Information and Communication Technology – Harnessing Partnership and Unleashing Potential for Development," Division of Development Education and Information, June 2005.

[2] The Deutsche Gesellschaft für Technische Zusammenarbeit (GTZ - German Organisation for Technical Cooperation) is one of the world's largest organizations for development cooperation. On behalf of the Federal Ministry for Economic Cooperation and Development (BMZ), as well as other funding organizations, GTZ implements bilateral and multilateral technical cooperation activities in more than 130 countries. http://www.gtz.de/en

ICT for Education: Building Competencies

The 'Africa Drive Project' (ADP) is a response to the shortage of qualified primary and secondary school educators in the South African education system. According to President Thabo Mbeki, "Special attention needs to be given to the compelling evidence that the country has a critical shortage of mathematics, science and language teachers, and to the demands of the new information and communication technologies".[3] Designed to alleviate this shortage, the ADP introduced ICT into teacher training. Innovative learning strategies such as blended learning are improving the competencies of educators so that they in turn can provide students with relevant, quality education.

Initiated by the South African Department of Education in a public-private partnership with the University of the North-West, GTZ, SAP Research, Siemens Business Services, eDegree, and a number of other local partners, the implementation of the ADP started in July 2003. Since then the ADP learning portal has been set up and a number of learning centres have opened. Formal learning, preceded by basic computer training, commenced in July 2004. Now, the first graduates are already "applying the lessons learned in their own classrooms. ICTs have been accepted as a supplement to existing methodologies" as Christian Merz SAP employee and member of the project team confirms. In addition to improving the competencies of secondary school educators in subject areas such as science, mathematics, technology, business studies, English and computer literacy, the curriculum of the ADP addresses the role of the educator with regard to social issues such as HIV/AIDS, TB and conservation. Beyond these immediate goals, the project aims to encourage the rollout of blended learning in a developing society and create new business opportunities related to the education training sector.

ICT for Education: Creating Opportunities

ICTs also play an important role in the creation of informal educational opportunities. Sometimes this is a part of larger sector projects, for example the Web site www.chezasalama.com, a user-friendly information portal on reproductive health which was developed within the health sector reform programme in Tanzania. It can also be a supplement to existing educational services, as in the case of the project started by Chilecalifica and GTZ in 2004 entitled 'Occupational Guidance for Youth', aimed at improving counselling services and occupational guidance for Chilean youth.

The project is employing the software JOBLAB as an e-learning medium. Originally developed in order to guarantee equal opportunities for girls in Germany's labour market, JOBLAB has been tailored to provide career counselling meeting the needs of the youth in Chile. The software is being made available on CD-Rom along with other information on non-university training paths and typical career options on the labour market. Moreover, together with the accompanying educational material, the programme will be made available to teachers and counsellors at secondary schools, multipliers at youth information centres and local employment agencies.

---

[3] Cited from the Africa Drive Project Website: http://www.adp.org.za

ICT for Education: Promoting Participation

Participatory project planning is an important means to ensure the sustainability of development projects. Thus, it is not only important to consider the youth as a target group, but also to include them in the planning and implementation of projects. This was the case in the project 'Espacio Libre Joven' in which young people from Chile, Guatemala, Honduras and Paraguay were engaged in creating cross-regional cultural exchange between young people and initiating their own media-projects. After an initial conference in 2001 different 'open spaces' for young people were established in the countries involved.

In Paraguay for example, ten open spaces have been created since 2003 – in youth centres, town halls, and universities and even in the GTZ office in Paraguay. These open spaces take on many different forms, depending on the concepts developed by the young people involved: not all of them offer Internet access because of the limited access in rural regions, but all of them provide computer access and cross-media libraries where young people can research as well as offering workshops to enable young people to gain IT skills. Some have implemented youth employment programmes to ensure sustainable long-term financing. The open spaces offer young people the room to learn, exchange and create – with the aim of empowering young people, helping them to gain a voice and asserting themselves in today's information society.[4]

ICT for Education: Encouraging Empowerment

Education is a fundamental human right and the engine of sustainable development. Therefore, ways to increase the availability and impact of educational opportunities and services need to be promoted – ICT is one. Even though many advances have been made during the past years, many challenges still lie ahead in making the benefits of ICT available to all. Access to ICTs remains one of the obstacles to overcome, especially in rural areas of developing countries.

In order to harness ICT for education, development cooperation activities need to promote sustainable, affordable ICT infrastructure and applications, encouraging local ownership. Furthermore, ICTs should be used to enable young people to voice their needs and demands, allowing them to take an active role in the planning and implementation of development schemes.

---

[4] http://www2.gtz.de/interspacio/

4. TECHNOLOGY AND EDUCATION IN BRAZIL

Diogo André de Assumpção

"Learning is ever in the freshness of its youth, even for the old." – Aeschilus

Brazil is a diverse country, like many others in Latin America. The size of its land imposes great differences in the population's characteristics, habits, traditions and way of living. Even with a huge diversity of ethnicities, we still speak one language. The same Portuguese is spoken all the way from the cities near the border of Uruguay, to the lands above the Equator. This is one heritage that we received from the centuries under Portuguese dominion.

What we also got from years of being a colony of Portugal was a lack of interest and investment in education. Back in the 1800s, even rich businessmen were illiterate. Literacy was not a requirement to vote, as long as you had land titles and property. The deficiencies in the education system in Brazil have their roots in that time, when Brazil was still an untamed territory with just its coast inhabited and formal knowledge not being the main concern of the government, or large parts of the population.

Back to our time, we now have 180 million people distributed in 8.5 million square kilometres, divided into 26 states, all speaking the same language. Education is stated as one of the most important social rights by the Constitution, along with health, security and work; but providing education to all has always been one of the major challenges for Brazil.

In the matter of literacy, we have always been behind our neighbors. Argentina, Chile and Colombia have much better literacy rates than Brazil. Twenty years ago, illiteracy rates were around 25%.[1] In the early 1990s they were still around 20%, with large regional disparities, with the northeast region by far the most illiterate, and the south and southeast the most literate region. This scenario resembles the economic disparities in Brazil, where the economy is much stronger in the south and southeast, and the northeast is the poorest of all regions.

Things started to change a few years ago. With a bold approach to basic education, the government managed to change the scenario and put 96%[2] of children between 7 and 14 years of age, into school. This was something never seen before, a true achievement with the potential to change the face of the Brazilian education system and foster development throughout all the different regions of Brazil.

Brazil is now realizing that putting kids into schools is only the first step to improve education, It is also necessary to improve schools, and in particular what is taught and how it is taught. This is the real challenge.

Focusing on how things are taught in Brazil, it is safe to say that it has not changed substantially in the last 10 or 15 years. This is certainly a small timeframe to promote deep changes in the education system, and it would not be a major issue if we were talking about the decade of the 1950s or 1960s. However, we are talking about the 1990s and it is completely clear that the world is today very different from what it was 15 years ago.

If we put aside the geopolitical changes that occurred in that period, there is really just one other big change: computers, ICTs, or the digital revolution to use a wider term.

Bringing it to a more local perspective, we can reduce the timeframe for the last ten years, when the Internet really made an impact in Brazil, when computers were beginning to be more popular and affordable, and the first mobile phones were being sold. It was in 1994-95 when ICTs really started to change the way we lived here in Brazil.

That is when I was in high school, 14 years old, and lucky enough to have a personal computer. Also lucky to be in private school, where education is supposedly better.

At the time, computers were mostly stand-alone machines. If they were connected, it was with low-speed dial-up, basically for chatting, maybe e-email and some browsing, that is from a teenager's perspective.

Education and technology were then disconnected. Even if some schools had computers, they were not sure how students could benefit from them. The teaching methods were classroom-based, dependent on books and infinitely boring. Classrooms were the place where everything was supposed to happen, all gains in knowledge should happen there, transferred from the teacher's brain to the empty minds of youth. Very little effort was made to make students interact, learn by doing, learn by experimenting, exchanging experiences or connecting.

Nowadays, computers are common, at least to those who can afford it, Connections are via broadband, and there are thousands of possibilities. The technology is there to make our lives easier, searching for information is easier, publishing information is simple, finding people to chat is instantaneous, sending a message to Japan takes only a minute. The way we live has completely changed because of ICTs, either you have access or not. Education now is dynamic; students are all connected and can exchange ideas and experiences,

Right? Well, unfortunately not. Being a student today is basically the same as being a student ten years ago.

Education did not follow the pace of technological developments, It was left behind. Schools failed to integrate technology in education; a few tried but soon realized that computer classes are not real integration. Technology should not be treated as just another subject, the best approach would be not just to teach how to use a computer, but allow students to experiment with the technology. The integration will come when the use of technology is part of the normal activities in school and not a separate thing that is used in just one or two special classes.

For the incorporation of technology into the education system, not only students have to experiment with computers, but also teachers. The ICTs bring the opportunity of borderless collaboration; teachers can connect to discuss ideas and new methodologies, to develop new material, to organize events, to exchange experiences and knowledge. The possibilities created by technology are huge. They range from simply making study more fun, to improving the education system, and modifying the way we learn.

With all the promises the digital revolution brings, there is a need to start putting the right things in the right place. Incorporating technology into education is not just providing a laptop computer to each student, and is not just creating multimedia presentations in the classroom. We need to start thinking how communications can be improved using the ICTs; how content can be produced in collaboration with the teachers; how students can connect to each other and learn about the different aspects of their lives.

In Brazil, the reality of a child in Rio de Janeiro is totally different from the reality of a child living in the northern region, in the middle of the Amazon forest, or a child living in the northeast, the poorest region of the country. Today, the education those kids receive is the same, they usually have exactly the same book, featuring exactly the same pictures and examples. Those books are produced, mostly, in the states of Sao Paulo and Rio de Janeiro, the richest, most developed and most politically important states, and very often reflect the reality of those states.

The content produced by the most developed regions is used everywhere else, with no adaptation to the local reality. This lack of "localization" is often a problem when teaching younger children. In basic school for example, where kids learn to read and write, the examples used usually talk about avenues, apples, shopping malls, and other things not coherent to the local reality of poor regions. The kids may learn to read and write the letters and words, but may never understand the meaning of those words. The opposite also occurs, children in big cities have never heard of animals or fruits that children in other regions find common.

The information and communication technologies can bring dynamic content to the classroom, wherever it is. Wireless communication technologies, like digital radio, can bring not only sound but text and images to remote areas. A classroom in the Amazon forest can connect to a classroom in a big city, bringing exciting experiences to both sides. New content can be produced with the input of local teachers to make learning a more diverse experience, mixing important cultural aspects of the different regions of Brazil.

The solution is here and can be used anytime. What is needed now is the political will to make ICTs accessible to the education system, build infrastructure, and transfer knowledge to teachers and others involved in creating content for education. Brazil is making some good moves, investing in free software, reducing taxes and developing lower cost computers. This is certainly good progress on the part of the government, achieved in partnership with other sectors of the society. Civil society has the responsibility to monitor and evaluate governmental actions. The private sector must invest in social responsibility, building partnerships with other sectors of society, creating new ways of interaction between education and technology and making solutions available for wider use.

Brazil has all the conditions to make a positive change in the education system. The environment is encouraging; public and private investments are available; civil society is willing to collaborate; the economy is stable and relatively prosperous. The next ten years are crucial to the future of education in Brazil, the system has to change and adapt, it cannot be left behind again. The government is the main body responsible for changing, but collaboration and partnership are crucial to a relevant and positive shift.

GIVING EVERY MACEDONIAN STUDENT A GATEWAY TO THE WORLD

Leigh Shamblin

A Dream Becomes a Reality

Just a little over three years ago the President of Macedonia left for an official visit to China and returned with a promise and a dream: to increase the number of computers available to school children. Macedonia, a land-locked country about the size of the US state of Vermont, has over 400 primary and secondary schools scattered across its mountains, deep basins and valleys. In 2002, it is estimated that less than half of them had working computers.

As of September 2005, labs filled with computers running new Microsoft software are operating in all primary and secondary schools. An army of teachers, 6,000 strong, newly trained in basic IT, are ready to help students get started.

Schools which two years ago did not even have a telephone, now have a link to the entire world. Every lab has broadband Internet access via the country's first nationwide wireless broadband network – a direct result of the complex consortium of many partners that emerged from a seemingly straightforward donation of 2,000 basic computers.

Like many consortia, this one was not born naturally – it evolved.

And like most ambitious dreams, this one did not "just happen" – it depended on visionaries and creative thinkers to make it a reality.

The public-private consortium which managed the initiative includes the Government of Macedonia (GoM), its Ministry of Education and Science (MoES), the US Agency for International Development (USAID), the People's Republic of China (PRC), and Microsoft.

What have we Learned?

Partnerships can work. Donations cost money. Timing is important. Having the right regulatory environment is critical for Internet growth. Basics – such as security, insurance and maintenance – matter. If possible, think globally. And finally, the real work is just beginning. Each of these lessons learned will be discussed in detail later in this article.

Hardware: the First Donation

During the official visit of the late President of Macedonia Boris Trajkovski to the PRC in May 2002, the Government of the PRC offered a grant to the GoM. Trajkovski, a champion of youth and a strong believer in the need for children to learn twenty-first century IT skills, advocated that a large portion of the grant be used to purchase computers for schools. Later that year, Trajkovski made a pitch for USAID to introduce Internet in all schools.

Both the PRC and USAID responded positively. The first donation from the PRC of 2,000 computers, plus some peripherals and spare parts, was received in the summer of 2003. MoES distributed the computers to the schools. USAID's E-School project installed wired computer labs in all 100 secondary schools and provided training to secondary schools teachers in integrating ICT into education.

Hardware: the Second Wave

One month before his tragic death in February 2003, Trajkovski asked the GoM to use remaining grant funds from the PRC to purchase more computers for primary schools. The GoM and the PRC agreed; in the spring of 2005, a shipment of 3,300 computers and 300 printers arrived in Macedonia.

The MoES distributed these computers to 360 primary schools throughout the country during summer 2005. USAID again supported the donation through its E-School project, this time linking computers in primary schools via wireless LANs to allow more flexibility for teachers.

Software Packages

The first 2,000 computer donation included an operating system but not educational software. Open source software had to be installed for basic word processing etc. Meanwhile, the GoM negotiated with Microsoft, resulting in a donation of over 6,000 licenses for a package of software which includes the XP Operating System, Microsoft Office, Frontpage, and Encarta. Microsoft also donated Microsoft Server.

Software licenses arrived in early summer 2005; software was installed in primary schools by USAID as labs were created.

The Cost of Accessing the World

The regulatory environment in Macedonia proved to be one of the project's biggest challenges. At the start of the initiative few Internet service providers were operating, all buying access from Macedonia Telecom (MakTel). The monthly cost for a dial-up 56k line using a private ISP and MakTel averaged over €150.[1] The prospects for increasing Internet access were bleak.

The high cost of access, combined with the poor quality of communications services, and limited, costly access to broadband impeded economic growth and hindered development efforts. Macedonia's household Internet penetration rate (quoted at 4% in 2003) lagged behind that of its neighbors in southeast Europe.

The consequences for Macedonia's schools were evident; only a small percentage could afford to provide Internet access to students and teachers. Although MakTel had provided a discounted school package for its ADSL service in larger areas, schools in smaller, rural areas only had access via costly dial-up options.

The End of a Monopoly – the Beginning of a New Era

On December 31, 2004, legislation came into effect that ended MakTel's monopoly. Earlier in 2004, USAID/Macedonia launched the Macedonia Connects project, not only to help schools, but to make broadband Internet access readily available and affordable throughout the country and facilitate its use by all sectors of society.

Macedonia Connects issued a request for bids in December 2004 to select the ISP that would provide broadband nationally. MakTel was excluded as a prime bidder due to its government ownership but was allowed to be a subcontractor to an ISP for the purposes of bidding.

The ISP On.Net was selected in April 2005 because its proposal represented best value. To reach the schools, and insure that rural markets would have broadband access, On.Net completed installation of a nationwide wireless backbone in August 2005. The backbone provides 155MB x 2 access via a connection to Serbia and will substantially increase availability and bandwidth in Macedonia.

Who Gets What?

After a review of the budget,[2] USAID's Macedonia Connects project decided to provide free broadband access to 460 primary and secondary schools and 71 other sites from September 2005 through September 2007.

Of the 71 additional sites, 50 are directly related to education, including dormitories for secondary school students, faculties at universities not currently supported by other programmes and the offices of the Bureau for Development of Education, which sets the curriculum for all subjects in primary and secondary education. Twenty sites were chosen through a competitive grant process; most are NGOs which support education, economic growth, or democracy and governance. The final site, a residential institution

---

[1] 12 hours a day.
[2] And consultations with MoES and other stakeholders such as the Macedonian Academic and Research Network (MARNET) which provides high-speed Internet to Macedonia's universities and academic community.

for the physically and mentally handicapped, hopes to use computers and the Internet to help deinstitutionalize its residents.

Table 1: Sites supported by USAID's Macedonia Connects project

Secondary schools (with labs)	100	
Primary schools (with labs)	360	
Subtotal		**460**
Secondary school dormitories	24	
University faculties	11	
Bureau for Development of Education offices	15	
Free Connectivity Grant Winners (NGOs)	20	
Residential institution for physically/mentally handicapped	1	
Subtotal		**71**
TOTAL		**531**

Lessons Learned: Partnerships can Work

This is a good example of how something that started out rather serendipitously worked in the end. Partnerships can slow down the process, but the benefits outweigh the inconveniences.

Lessons Learned: Donations Cost Money

In order for the schools to utilize the generous donations of computers and software from the PRC and Microsoft effectively, much work had to be done to distribute the computers, install them, and train IT and other teachers how to use them. USAID's project costs alone are estimated at US $1.3 million for installing the 5,300 computers and 300 printers in labs and US $400,000 for training 6,000 teachers in basic IT skills. These estimates do not include administrative time, or contributions by other partners.

If procurement regulations allow and goods are available on the local market, organizations might consider providing grants for equipment and letting the Ministry of Education or the schools themselves procure computers, equipment and installation locally. This helps the local economy and will likely mean that the money will go further, resulting in more computers.

Lessons Learned: Timing is Important

Each of the organizations involved in bringing computers and Internet access to Macedonia's schools has different business issues, different stakeholders to which they must answer, and different processes for procurement. As a result, it was not easy to put the pieces of this partnership together in such a way that the timing always worked.

The first tranche of computers from the PRC arrived and were distributed to schools by MoES in 2003. They were not installed into labs in secondary schools by USAID until summer 2004, due to the time it took to start the E-School project and subcontract locally for the installation. This understandably caused frustration for all involved. To ensure more success and less frustration with installation of the second tranche of computers, and later with the Internet, representatives from MoES, USAID, and USAID's E-School projects established a bi-weekly co-ordination meeting. The team was later joined by representatives of the Bureau for Development of Education (BDE) to help coordinate training, Macedonia Connects for Internet, and, as needed, representatives of the Education Modernization Project (EMP)[3] which helped schools with needed electrical repairs. Through these meetings, transparency and communication helped resolve problems quickly.

Microsoft's donation arrived in spring 2005, in time for the installation of labs in the primary schools. However, because the first 2,000 computers for the secondary schools were received and installed prior to receipt of the donated software, as mentioned earlier, open source software had to be installed to make these operational for the schools for the 2004 school year. Now IT teachers in the schools must go back and install the donated software on all computers.

The first tranche of computers were installed in secondary schools in wired labs. When the second tranche of 3,300 computers were ordered, it was anticipated that they would be installed in wired labs as well. However, while the computers were in transit, the team agreed that having wireless LANs in the primary school would give the schools more flexibility. Making this happen required the purchase and installation of 3,300 wireless cards.

Summer means vacation time in Macedonia's schools. As a result, both the E-School and Macedonia Connects projects had difficulty finding school directors or their designees to open schools during July and August 2005. Coordinating with the Ministry on a daily basis was critical to keep the schools open and keep the installation on schedule.

The Macedonia Connects project started in September 2004 but an ISP was not chosen until April 2005 because of the competitive bid process. This delay was actually positive for the project in that the telecom monopoly was dissolved allowing for more growth in the market and new technologies emerged to make building an effective network cheaper and easier.

There is a clear need to start off with co-ordination meetings and include everyone that might need to be involved from the start. Information sharing is valuable and individuals can always withdraw later if their participation is not needed.

Lessons Learned: the Regulatory Environment is Critical

Another USAID project, the WTO Compliance Activity, worked with the GoM to develop a new telecom law to help open the market prior to the end of the MakTel monopoly on December 31, 2004. Without the end of the monopoly and strong regulations in place, it would not have been possible to set up a nationwide wireless broadband network or to increase competition in the Internet market and introduce services such as VOIP effectively.

---

[3] EMP is funded through the World Bank and the Dutch Government.

Lessons Learned: Basics Matter

Security, insurance, and maintenance of the computers were not widely considered in the initial planning stages and caused problems during secondary school installation. Problems with electricity became an issue for the primary school installation.

During the first installation of computers in secondary schools, computers were stolen from three of the 100 computer labs. These schools did not have insurance to cover the loss. Even when schools were insured, many secondary school labs remained locked due to a lack of awareness by the school directors that the insurance policy they already had covered the new computers.

Some labs remained locked while not in use because of a lack of funds to maintain the equipment and general security concerns.

USAID worked with the school directors' association to raise the issues of security, maintenance and insurance on a post-installation basis for the secondary schools and held pre-installation meetings with the primary schools to try to head off some of the problems. Despite the precautions and the fact that there were bars on the windows, three primary schools lost their computers, one just two hours after installation.

Over 100 of the 360 primary schools needed basic electrical repairs before installing a safe computer lab in the building was possible. Several of the schools were able to complete the repairs themselves. MoES, through EMP, arranged for schools that were not able to do the repairs themselves to get advances on individual grants that were to be given to each school as part of the education decentralization process in Macedonia.

It makes sense to require evidence of security and insurance before transferring equipment or installing computers. Schools can often purchase inexpensive insurance through a private insurance company. The ideal will be to sign an agreement with each school that they will be responsible for maintenance of the computers, and encourage schools to develop regional maintenance pools, including using local technical schools to do the work. Training for LAN administration may also be needed.

Lessons Learned: if Possible, Think Globally

Because Macedonia is relatively small in land size, it is possible, and even more cost effective, to do programmes on a national, rather than a pilot scale. Macedonia Connects is a good example of scalability. By using the schools as a platform across the country, On.Net was able to build a network to a scale large enough so that the resulting market would increase the chances of Internet sustainability, especially in rural areas. With this scale, On.Net is able to lower the prices of connectivity dramatically and offer a special teacher/student package at €9 - €15 per month.

Lessons Learned: the Real Work is Just Beginning

Installing hardware and software and seeing new labs in new schools certainly feels like an accomplishment. Add Internet access for every school and it feels better. However, the real work starts once the computers and connectivity are in place.

How are teachers and students to be motivated to use the increased ICT capacity? Students currently study IT (or infomatics) in Macedonia starting in 5th grade. How will the curriculum be revised to integrate ICT in early primary school? Who will help teachers create digital content in Macedonian, Albanian, and other languages in use in the country? And how will it be possible to get even more computers and Internet access in classrooms in Macedonia so that the nation's 330,000 primary and secondary school students are able to learn twenty-first century IT skills and be more competitive in the labour market?

These are the next issues for the consortium to tackle.

GLORIAD: AN ADVANCED NETWORK FOR SCIENCE AND EDUCATION

Gregory Cole and Natasha Bulashova

The Global Ring Network for Advanced Applications Development (GLORIAD) rings the northern hemisphere of the earth in an ambitious effort to link the research and education communities of the three organizing nations – the US, Russia and China – in close cooperation with core partners in Korea, Netherlands and Canada.

In late December, 2004 GLORIAD received a five-year US funding commitment from the National Science Foundation, as part of an international package of funding with its partners in Russia, China and Korea and with additional contributions from CANARIE (Canada) and SURFnet (Netherlands)) to develop a hybrid (circuit-/packet-switched) network, aiming for multiple 10 Gbps wavelengths around the earth by 2008. The project is naturally interesting for the geo-political story of the three organizing countries undertaking the joint construction and shared management of such a network crossing their territories and the oceans and continents between and linking their scientists, educators and students. It is also interesting for the changes in network service and telecommunications provisioning it requires.

GLORIAD's supporters include the US National Science Foundation, a consortium of science organizations and Ministries in Russia, the Chinese Academy of Sciences, the Ministry of Science and Technology of Korea, the Canadian CANARIE network, the Netherlands SURFnet team and with some telecommunications services donated by Tyco Telecommunications.

New Technologies

GLORIAD provides scientists around the globe with tools that improve communications and data exchange, enabling active, daily collaboration on common problems. With GLORIAD, the scientific community can move unprecedented volumes of valuable data effortlessly, stream video and communicate through quality audio- and video-conferencing.

The benefits of this advanced network are shared with science and engineering communities throughout Europe, Asia and the Americas. The advanced network leapfrogs old technologies using parallel computing to link to other sites. There are other advanced networking tools in use. The advanced networking tools allow groups to download and to share advanced technologies using traditional networking.

The broad range of scientific pursuits supported include the most advanced areas of collaborative research involving the partnering countries in high energy, nuclear and fusion energy physics, atmospheric science, astronomical observation, geological sciences, environmental monitoring, bioinformatics, nuclear materials protection and a host of others.

International Cooperation

GLORIAD provides more than a network; it provides a stable, persistent, non-threatening means of facilitating dialogue and increased cooperation between nations that have often been at odds through the past century. This new era of cooperation will provide benefits not only to the science and education communities but to every citizen in the partner countries through:

- Improved weather forecasting and atmospheric modeling through live sharing of monitoring data;

- New discoveries into the basic nature and structure of the universe through advanced network connections between high energy physicists and astronomers - and the expensive facilities GLORIAD makes it possible to share;

- Support of the global community building the International Thermonuclear Experimental Reactor (ITER), creating a technology which will someday provide a practically limitless supply of energy;

- Advancing joint geological sciences related to seismic monitoring and earthquake prediction;

- Enabling new joint telemedical applications and practices;

- Strengthening current programmes in nuclear weapons disposal, nuclear materials protection, accounting and control and active discussions on combating terrorist threats.

- Increasing classroom-to-classroom cooperation to accessible scientists and students in other countries through the 24/7 EduCultural Channel, the Virtual Science Museum of China, the Russian-developed "Simple Words" global essay contest, and a special partnership with International Junior Achievement.

At its core, GLORIAD connects communities, be they scientists, educators or students, by operating an advanced, stable and robust network infrastructure to better support collaborations. The programme is just as focused on expanding quantity and quality of collaborative opportunities – believing that broader exposure to Science and Education

(S&E) programmes in Russia and China promises direct benefit for the US S&E community, and vice versa.

GLORIAD EduCultural Channel

The EduCultural Channel is a 24/7 streaming video service. Its goal is to broker content and in some cases, stage and develop content, making high-end science applications utilizing the GLORIAD network understandable and accessible to the general public and to young people.

Junior Achievement

Junior Achievement's interest in GLORIAD centers on its ability to provide an advanced network service to enable young people in the US, Russia and China (and beyond) to engage in its various business development programmes, shared lectures, and joint educational programmes related to international business development. More details can be found at:

http://www.gloriad.org/gloriad/eot/ja/index.html(opt,mozilla,unix,english,,default)

Simple Words

Simple Words is a global essay contest for young people pioneered in Russia by GLORIAD leader Dr. E. P. Velikhov. Simple Words introduces young people in the GLORIAD countries by enabling them to share their thoughts via on-line submitted essays about certain core human concepts – such as faith, hope, love, death, friends, war – and then providing a structured, teacher-supervised setting to discuss their thoughts and opinions.

The GLORIAD team has enthusiastically agreed to develop a global "Simple Words" essay contest based on the contest piloted in Russia. The US GLORIAD investigators have already developed a complex software system for managing essay submissions (including software for teachers and sponsors). The Chicago Public Schools will be piloting this activity during the coming months.

Virtual Science Museum of China

The Virtual Science Museum of China (VSMC) is an enormous undertaking of GLORIAD's China partner, Computer Network Information Center, to provide high quality content about scientific subjects in a manner appealing to students of all ages. It now comprises 60 separate on-line museums available for on-line browsing.

In 1999, Internet users were looking for science and technical information, but there was a serious shortage of Chinese on-line content in those areas. The Computer Network Information Center of the Chinese Academy of Sciences (CAS) applied the technical advantages accumulated in the process of researching and applying the next-generation Internet technologies toward the creation of the Virtual Science Museum network of China.

CAS harnessed a great deal of scientific information and resources when building the VSMC. It united thousands of experts in the subject areas and the young IT technical staffs, took CSTNet as the platform, applied Web multimedia technology and constructed the virtual museums – http://www.kepu.net.cn. In this way the CAS became a forerunner in China in applying the advanced network media technology to carry out scientific propagation.

After five years of development and construction, now VSMC has grown from 4 virtual museums to 60. Additionally, VSMC now includes a simplified Chinese version, traditional Chinese version and an English version. These virtual museums have been constructed by experts applying the first-grade network multimedia technologies facing the future Internet freeway and have become a popular and unique resource on the Internet for providing excellent popular science content. The 320,000+ of daily page hits at the virtual museums, both domestic and international, indicate the broad appeal the virtual museum concept has with the public.

Conclusion

The current GLORIAD ring network will expand from today's (primarily) 155- and 622-Mbps circuit to 10 Gbps by year three of the project, and will enable scientists around the globe to manage their own network service requirements quickly and efficiently.

Already, the GLORIAD project has fostered stronger ties and working relationships between three large countries that did not embrace the benefits of cooperation with one another in the past century. Beyond the direct science benefits, these relationships help to dispel myths and misinformation and build trust and understanding from the highest levels of government and science down to the next generation of leaders still in the classroom. Additionally, the GLORIAD ring activity championed by the partnering countries has already encouraged other regions near the ring, particularly in central and east Asia, to address network infrastructure requirements to attach to this ring, someday establishing additional benefits for scientists, educators and students in their respective countries, as well as for citizens more broadly across the globe.

INTEGRATED WATER CONCEPTS IN THE NATIONAL CURRICULUM IN JORDAN

Mayyada Abu Jaber and Mona Grieser

Introduction

The need to tackle water issues in the Jordanian school curricula emerged from a national need to protect diminishing water resources in a semi-arid region of the world. With the present level of consumption of resources, Jordan's fragile environment has reached the limits of its carrying capacity.

Jordan is a water-poor country with the lowest rate of water consumption per capita in the world. Demand for water far exceeds supply and the country has continuously sought to increase its water supply to meet the rising demand. Yet a bigger responsibility lies with the Jordanian citizen to conserve water. It is by educating the young population that the message will reach one third of the Jordanian population.

This was the background to the project known as Water Efficiency and Public Information for Action (WEPIA), an initiative of the Jordanian Ministry of Water and Irrigation and the Academy for Educational Development launched with funding support from USAID.

Environmental Education

Environmental education in schools started in the late eighties by setting up nature conservation clubs, through the ambitious initiatives of the Royal Society for the Conservation of Nature (RSCN). The first nature conservation club was set up in the city of Salt. At present, there are as many as 1,000 nature clubs in schools throughout Jordan. For a comprehensive education programme, the non-formal curriculum needs to build on the material introduced into the textbooks.

Environmental education was implemented in the national Jordanian curriculum in 1996. The Ministry of Education (MOE), in collaboration with UNDP, developed an environment conceptual framework. In the framework, environmental concepts that needed to be introduced in the textbooks were identified. A comprehensive environmental education reform programme was introduced.

A multidisciplinary approach was used to introduce environmental education into the curriculum. The material was introduced as either separate units or as lessons in all subjects throughout the schooling year. For grades 11 and 12, separate environmental education and chemistry textbooks were introduced.

Much of the environmental education material introduced back then is now outdated and the need to build on new approaches in learning became vital. Current curricula in subject areas such as science and social studies frequently attempt to cover as much environmental content as possible, regard all content as equal, and divide content into artificial categories that bear little relationship to how individuals use content in the world beyond school. Furthermore, students' attitudes about subject matter, and the skills and strategies that they need to learn, are rarely addressed. Traditional curricula emphasize isolated, low-level skills, to the neglect of meaningful content and higher-order thinking skills.

Furthermore, the Ministry of Educations began implementing its new vision to develop a culture of information literacy in schools throughout the kingdom. This was accomplished through the creation of e-learning material for schools supported by Internet laboratories placed in these schools. Access to the information is managed by a central administrator at the Ministry of Education (MOE). The e-learning initiative was driven by technology companies and little emphasis was given to the pedagogy and content evaluation by educationists in the field.

To facilitate the coordination between the different stakeholders involved in the project (Ministry of Education, Ministry of Water and Irrigation, Royal Society for the Conservation of Nature and WEPIA), a higher committee was formed by the MOE headed by the Secretary General of the Ministry of Education and the membership of the Secretary General of the Ministry of Water and Irrigation, and other decision-makers. The committee met three times during the course of the project.

A technical committee headed by the author and several consultants was formed. The participants were specialists in both education and water from universities and schools. Representatives from the Ministry of Education and Ministry of Water and Irrigation were also present. The committee had monthly meetings throughout the course of the project until it was wound up upon the finalization of the first stage of the curriculum reform (research stage).

A writers committee was also formed during the second stage of the project (writing of material stage). The committee included writing and water specialists as well as a writer for each targeted subject.

A training committee was formed during the third stage of the project. The main task of the committee is to prepare training of teachers, finalize material for the teachers' guide and train trainers on the material contained in the textbook.

In this chapter, the process of the review and reform of water education in the national curriculum will be highlighted and the new approaches and methodologies to shape the learning process will be introduced. Through the research, a distinction is made between creating the content and the process of learning. The content approach includes concepts, principles, generalizations, problems, facts, definitions, etc. While the approach used relies more on the process of learning strategies and skills, creative and critical thinking, thinking about thinking (meta-cognition), social skills, and so on.

A needs analysis survey will also be explained, followed by the curriculum development process. A description of the methodologies used to write the curriculum will follow and the teacher training and assessment programmes.

Knowledge, Attitude and Practice (KAP) survey

A knowledge, attitude and practice survey was carried out on 520 sample persons involved in education. 413 students were randomly approached in the different regions of the country. A sample questionnaire was given to them and results were analyzed. Similarly 107 teachers were also identified and sampled.

Results show that those questioned felt that Jordan was not ranked worldwide as a country suffering from water shortages and that it was amongst the least suffering from water shortages, or not suffering shortages at all. This is despite the fact that Jordan is classified as one of the water-poor countries in the world, as the per capita consumption of water is the lowest in the world.

Very few of those sampled also recognized that the water reaching their home is subsidized by the government and almost 20% were not sure how the billing system worked. 60% of those questioned felt that the price reflects their water usage at home and could be higher, and thus there was a general census that water prices are high.

At present a further need has risen to embed water management issues into the existing curriculum.

Educational Goals and Objectives

The goal identified at this stage was based on the knowledge, attitude and practice survey conducted in the earlier stage. The reason to recognize the goal in the early stage is to make the reform process output-oriented rather than being led by pure knowledge and content.

The goal of environmental education is to make students environmentally-aware, knowledgeable, skilled, dedicated citizens that are committed to act individually and collectively to defend and sustain water resources for the present and future generation.[1]

The objectives identified for the curriculum are:

1. Perceptual awareness: to make the student capable of perceiving and distinguishing among different stimuli; to process, refine, and extend these

---

[1] Engleson, D., & Yockers, D. (1994). *A guide to curriculum planning in environmental education.* Madison, WI: Wisconsin Department of Public Instruction.

perceptions to appreciate and acquire sensitivity to the natural and human made environment.

2. Knowledge: to help students comprehend and understand how the water system functions, the dependence of humans on the water system and the equilibrium reached between them.

3. Environmental ethics: to make students develop universal ethics that they can act upon and defend, improve and sustain the water system.

4. Citizen action skills: to make students develop proficiency to identify, investigate, communicate and be prepared to take action towards the prevention and resolving of water issues.

5. Citizen action experience: to make students apply the acquired perceptual awareness, knowledge, and environmental skills and ethics to take action towards the prevention and resolution of water issues at different levels of the society.[2]

The objective of curriculum reform is for the students to develop positive environmental behaviour through changing the way they behave with regards to an environmental issue. The lowest variable level is the energy in which the student is involved with water issues, this is followed by an ownership variable in which the student makes issues very important at a personal level to the individual and finally empowerment variables are those crucial to training students as good citizens, able to act affectively.

These objectives were distributed on the different grades as follows.[3]

The objective of the new curriculum begins at its lowest level with perceptual awareness, which develops when a stimulus from outside the body combines with thoughts and feelings inside the body to produce meaning. Perceptual awareness is a prerequisite for the construction of meaningful knowledge about the environment. It is different to knowledge as the learner does not recall a fact but rather becomes conscious of something. Knowledge is the second level of development for the learner, once an awareness of issues is completed; the learner shows curiosity to learn facts about issues. These facts will be used later on to develop his environmental citizen skills and citizen action.

The citizen action skill needs to be acquired in the learner to work toward the resolution of issues. In order for these citizens to be active participants, they must have both training and experience in citizen action. The highest level for environmental education includes utilizing various methods of citizen action; analyzing situations to determine if action is wise and warranted; and evaluating the effectiveness of actions taken. This level should be accomplished in the higher grades when all other objectives are met.

---

[2] Ibid.
[3] Ibid.

As for the values and attitudes objectives, it is assumed when all other four objectives are met, this objective automatically is met and the child become sensitive to issue around him and thus changes his behavior and attitudes to resolve environmental issues.

1. The Research Stage: Preparing the Conceptual Framework

The conceptual framework is primarily based on knowledge, which is one of the five goals identified for water education. For water education is the scientific base that the curriculum reform programme is measured against. The conceptual framework was prepared to cover seven themes: the unusual properties of water, water eco-system, water resources in Jordan, water pollution, supply management, demand management and water and civilization. Each of the seven themes is divided into sub themes.

Water Curriculum Mapping

Mapping the textbooks at this early stage of curriculum reform is crucial to determine learning outcomes and link it to the new objectives set for the water curriculum. It determines the sequence in which the identified learning outcomes will be taught and determines a congruence between the "written" curriculum, the "tested" curriculum and the "taught" curriculum.

One hundred and sixty textbooks and twenty teachers' guides were mapped. The textbooks covered five subjects: social studies (including geography, history and civics), science (including physics, chemistry and geology and earth science), mathematics, ICT and vocational studies. The textbooks mapped covered grades one to eleven. The teachers' guides mapped were for the targeted subjects covering grades seven through nine.

The curriculum mapping process was accomplished using a three dimensional matrix. The matrix identified where in the curriculum water concepts were covered and the environmental education objectives that it fulfilled.

A sample mapping matrix for a social studies lesson in grade four shows a lesson that tackles water and energy conservation through sets of pictures referring to wrong action by cleaning the car using a hose and the right action, cleaning the car using a bucket. This concept was covered similarly in the vocational studies grade 4 textbook. There is no skill taught through the lesson and thus, the learner is not motivated to make a change or instigate it.

As many as 482 water concepts were covered in the curriculum. However, 289 concepts were covered in the first two scientific water themes; the unusual properties of water and the water ecosystem. Application of these concepts to Jordan which is covered in water theme three covered the lowest concept, thus, most of what the student is learning is not applied to his local environment. The link between pure scientific knowledge and application is missing. Water pollution themes that are one of the crucial problems in Jordan also carried very little weight in the curriculum and so did the demand management concepts, which are only covered by 37 concepts.

Concepts were distributed equally in all targeted subjects, although higher emphasis was given in the social studies and science subjects. Greater emphasis for water education was given in the higher grades with as many as 154 concepts in grades 9 onwards. When analyzing the extent to which the existing concepts are met by the new reformed curriculum, it was clear that the water concepts only fulfilled one of the five objectives. The concepts were content-driven with many facts and figures to support the water content. Very little emphasis was given to building environmental skills and encouragement for students to participate in their local community to alleviate water-related problems. Thus, the curriculum was not shaping the values and attitudes of the student, but was rather an exam-driven content

Following this survey, it was clear that the water concepts in the curriculum needed a review and that very few new concepts needed to be added to the current curriculum as it was overloaded with vast water content.

Scope and Sequence Charts

Following the mapping survey of the textbooks, a scope and sequence matrix was prepared. The matrix shows where each water concept is covered in the targeted curriculum and in the grade levels surveyed. It allows the educationist to assess the spiral development of the water concept with the cognitive development of the child.

Unlike conventional scope and sequence charts, this one had the water concepts covered in the textbooks and the curriculum development objectives that it fulfils.

The scope and sequence chart mapped water pricing and billing and the economic benefits of conservation. Water pricing and billing is not covered in any of the targeted subjects in any of the grade levels. However, the economic benefits of conservation are covered extensively from grades 1 through 9 mainly in science, social studies, maths and vocational studies. However, much of the material covered is in the form of knowledge, thus, inapplicable and difficult to relate to real life.

Overall, very few knowledge gaps were found and most water material was covered from upper elementary to high school. However, when analyzing skills and participation gaps, it was apparent that most water concepts covered in the textbooks needed comprehensive review.

Identify Gaps and Repetitions: Concepts Reviewed in the Curriculum

Based on the scope and sequence charts, gaps and repetitions were identified. There were minor content gaps and mainly the skills participation gaps were highlighted. In the above example, it is clear that there is a gap in the first concept – water billing and pricing – while there is a repetition in the second concept, the benefits of conserving water.

Suggestions to review the content, skills and participation gaps/repetitions were then made and raised to the National Education Higher Council. The Council, headed by the Minister of Education and with the membership of eleven ministers in the current cabinet, reviewed these suggestions and approved the review process of the water curriculum.

Demand management and crisis management concepts are now tackled in the higher grades. Water auditing and reading the water meter, measuring individual use of water, as well as individual practices in conservation, are tackled throughout the schooling years.

By introducing these concepts in a multidisciplinary approach, the student builds positive attitudes and behaviour towards environmental issues and thus becomes environmentally active – willing to accept and make change.

2. Writing the curriculum: Textbook Writing Methodology

Writing textbooks in Jordan is the sole responsibility of the Ministry of Education/Curriculum Development Division. When preparing new textbooks, the curriculum division members sub-contract consultants from the universities to write different chapters of the textbook. The curriculum division members then compile all chapters into one textbook. Thus, the textbook is driven by the content prepared by specialists in the field rather it being pedagogy-driven to help students become active learners.

In Lebanon, educational goals and strategies for the country are set as a basis for preparing and producing the textbooks by the public sector. Different publishing companies have produced series of textbooks covering all grade levels and subjects. These books were then reviewed and approved by the Lebanese Ministry of Education.

Khoury library is one of the Lebanese textbook printing editing and publishing houses of local textbooks. The writing of units and activities was adopted by the Lebanese writer Sami Khoury, who conducted several training session with twenty Jordanian writers. The methodology of writing was implemented in four stages.

(a) The Motivation Stage

The first stage begins with a brainstorming session in which the student is motivated with a set of questions raising his curiosity and recalling much of the information he has acquired in earlier years.

The student then begins to anticipate the topics that will be covered in the lesson.

(b) The Exploration Stage

The units are explained by illustrations of pictures, graphs, sketches, cartoon presentations and newspaper cuttings, etc. Any new information given to the child is supported by these illustrations. Real life data and problems that stimulate group discussions are portrayed and illustrated.

During the exploration stage the child is involved in analyzing the information through sets of questions. Each of these questions clarifies the many aspects of the technical water concepts being taught.

(c) The Investigation Stage

During the investigation stage several interactive applications are introduced. These help the student to understand the technical concepts while acquiring new educational skills. The skills vary from analyzing to synthesizing and application of environmental concepts. During this stage the student is fully aware of the material in the unit and is using it to enhance his understanding.

(d) The Application Stage

Here the student utilizes his understanding of the concepts into real life applications. This is the highest level of environmental education that the child should reach in his process of learning. The student thus takes a personal initiative in making a change in his local community starting from his school (his environmental laboratory) to his home, and further, in order to influence his local community.

One hundred concepts were introduced into the year 2003 curriculum. The concepts mainly covered demand management and water pollution themes.

The following year, another 100 concepts were suggested to be introduced into the textbook for the year 2004. These covered the remaining themes.

Teachers' Guide

To support the water curriculum a teachers' guide was designed to clarify instructional methodologies, resources available, and assessment of the water lesson. The teachers' guide produced by the Ministry of Education did not match the textbook, since reviews in the textbook content were not reflected in the teachers' guide. As a result, the guide was outdated and difficult to use.

Consequently, a separate water education teachers' guide was produced which includes five sections as follows.

(a) The Preparation Section

In this stage the "big idea" is presented to the child. This covers the major concepts that will be covered in the lesson and the main sub-concepts. This section also covers the amount of time required for this lesson.

(b) The Motivation Stage

This is also the warm-up stage where sets of questions are given to the child to capture his attention and begin the discussion (brain storming session). The section also includes a resource management sub-section in preparation for the lesson. Management of resources also includes tying this lesson to previous knowledge.

(c) The Teach – Explore Stage

This section includes the following:

- CD- ROM link

- Teaching strategy

- Learning strategy

- Water words

- Caption answers

- Transparencies.

(d) The Assessment Stage

Within the water curriculum, continuous assessment should be an integral part of teaching. The use of assessment in a formative sense, to judge regularly the effectiveness of both teaching and learning processes, is essential to allow teachers and students to identify strengths and weaknesses. The purpose and means of assessment should be clearly explained to students.

The assessment criteria published in this section of the guide correspond to the objectives of the water curriculum programme. The levels of achievement described have been written with assessment of all grades in mind. Schools should adapt the relative importance, focus and expected levels of achievement for each criterion according to the progression of learning organized by each school. Some other criteria may also be added by school and reported on internally to parents and students.

The assessment criteria are reflected into rubrics or a specific task for each of the water lessons introduced in the textbook. These rubrics are added into the teacher guide and the teacher has the option of using it.

(e) The Closing Stage

A wrap-up activity to end the lesson.

E-learning

The main page for the e-learning material is linked to a page showing the water concepts covered in the textbooks. Grades and subjects index these concepts.

This page has four windows – each serves to fulfill an educational outcome. Each lesson has these four windows, and the windows are set so that the learner can spend 40 minutes to an hour, which is the duration of a lesson in school.

The windows are:

- What do you think?

- My experiments

- Games

- Learn more.

What Do You Think Window

This window will vary for the different grades, as follows.

For grades 1-7 the window will present a character called Abu-Tawfeer as he tackles water issues during his daily routine. His story is shown in an animated format, several critical questions are asked and the child is able to stop the story to answer these questions.

For the higher grades 8-11, the character disappears and the animation is related to environmental skills, such as newspaper article analysis, simulations and real life case studies.

My Experiments Window

Under this window hands-on experiments will be simulated for the learner. Learners are able to make decisions, taking different factors into considerations. Learners also document their findings on a note pad to be printed, thus showing results. The learner at this point is fully aware of the content covered in the textbook and is able to manipulate results and come up with conclusions.

However, if the students find difficulty working with this window, they can enter into the "learn more" window.

Learn More Window

This is a non-interactive window that shows a 3D video explanation of the lesson. This window is designed for students to learn the basic content and is a substitute for the content in the textbook.

Games Window

This window is for assessing and evaluating the core concept presented in the lesson. Several questions are given to the children that are timed. These questions are presented in the form of a maze or puzzle, and as the students play they enhance their learning and evaluate their work.

3. Teacher Training

New teaching approaches have changed the characteristics of all phases of the traditional learning process. The traditional features of technical education (i.e. presentation of theory and concepts, their explanation, verification of learning and design practice) have, of course, to be maintained, but redefined to take into account the specificity of the new delivery media. In the traditional lecture, the learner is a quasi-passive observer and listener of knowledge transmitted by an external centre (the teacher). With the use of new pedagogy supported by the multimedia, the student is the new centre of the learning process, exploring the environment and building knowledge and skills using simulation-based instruction tools. This implies that the student plays an active role that is an essential ingredient for a successful environmental education curriculum.

On the basis of these assumptions, in the teacher training programme proposed will develop new pedagogical approaches supported by IT to introduce the environmental education programme in which appropriate interaction with a rich environment is emphasized, and the application of the "learning-by-doing" approach. The pedagogical methodologies adopted are demonstrative, interactive, measurable and practical. A detailed description of each one is the object of the following sections.

The training programme included the training of 60 Ministry of Education supervisors from different regions in the kingdom. These will later train teachers in the region assigned to them. Ten exceptional supervisors will be identified and an assignment will be introduced to be accomplished by the end of the school year.

Part of this assignment will be to apply what the supervisors have learnt through the interactive teacher training session in selected schools in the kingdom.

Interactive Learning Course

The course will be divided into five stages namely:

(a) Preparing Trainers Committee

A committee has been formed to brainstorm and discuss the work plan and training activities associated. The committee includes members from the Ministry of Education.

(b) Producing a Training of Teachers Manual

The main task for the committee is to produce a training of teachers manual to be used during the training sessions.

(c) Training of Selected Teacher Groups:

In this first training of teachers session a total of 60 supervisors from all 32 departments of the Ministry of Education distributed throughout the kingdom will be selected and trained in the use of interactive methodologies in the delivery of the water curriculum.

Out of the 60 supervisors, only 10 will be selected to work on the assignment in selected schools. Each then will then train five other teachers from their selected schools and carry out the assignment.

The teachers will be trained on the goals and objectives of environmental education, and the expectation of the water curriculum.

The training will focus on the use of different pedagogical methods in the delivery of the curriculum, such as the use of:

- Drama in the delivery of the geography lesson;

- The use of art in the delivery of the geology and chemistry lesson;

- The use of debate in the delivery of the social studies lesson;

- The integrative approach in teaching water auditing, by joining maths and IT and social studies classes;

- Demonstration for the building of a drip irrigation system;

- e-Learning training on the interactive water CD;

- The use of movement in the delivery of the water curriculum.

The teachers will be trained to use standards for evaluating tasks carried out by their students. They will also be trained on creating their on rubrics benchmarked by the set environmental education standards.

(d) Assignment preparation stage

The 10 supervisors were assigned the task of preparing a training portfolio. The assignment will include:

- a plan for an interactive training programme using preferably an integrative approach of one of the demand management lessons;

- two other classroom assignments, prepared using interactive teaching methodologies for the delivery of any chosen environmental lesson; and

- a case study of the learning styles of students in one grade level – using a pre-prepared questionnaire – and analyzing the results. The case study was presented as part of the assignment.

The teachers evaluated the understanding of the concepts using a rubric that was earlier prepared for each of the three lessons prepared for the assignment.

Conclusion

The water education curriculum reform programme tackled the review of 200 water concepts. The material was introduced in textbooks in an interactive manner. The first e-learning material in Jordan was produced to support the water curriculum along with a teachers' guide and a curriculum guide. Phase 1 research was completed in electronic format to be used for future review of the water curriculum.

The Ministry of Education is now embarking upon a complete curriculum reform programme for all subjects throughout the grade levels. The vision for the new reform is to build a knowledge economy. The new water curriculum will be re-evaluated to be introduced in the reform process.

By the end of this programme, a pool of trained supervisors at the Ministry of Education had been trained in water education and the use of interactive instructional methodologies. Sixty teachers were also trained on phase 1 of the project, the curriculum research stage. These teachers are mainly from private schools. The programme implementation was purely participatory, using national and regional expertise.

ICT: A POWERFUL NEW TOOL TO TEACH LITERACY

Bonnie Bracey

There are few people in the world who seem to have a mission for literacy. One of the pioneering stakeholders for the promotion of literacy is Wendy Pye of New Zealand.

Wendy Pye has been a leader and a catalyst for change, infusing the idea of literacy into many different parts of the world. Stakeholders are individuals, associations, or organizations with an interest in a particular issue. Because of their varied backgrounds, affiliations, and interests they often hold different, and even divergent, perspectives on how to best manage the issue and even what the final objectives should be. However, despite dissimilar value systems and the potential for conflict, stakeholders can develop innovative, creative, and positive strategic alliances that often result in formal partnerships. Drawing from each other's strengths, such alliances and partnerships can pool and leverage collective knowledge, expertise, and resources – be they human, technical, or financial – to achieve mutually desired outcomes.

For the past 30 years, Wendy Pye has been engaged in the development of literacy programmes in partnership with countries worldwide, both as a supplier of specialized content through printed and multimedia materials, and in the development of skilled professional training for teachers.

Dedicated community-based leaders and change agents are often needed to help create, form and shape ICT applications at the local level. They are often the best situated to identify, establish, and cultivate the key opportunities for building collaborations that lead to successful projects. Stakeholders in the private sector can provide financial, technological, and leadership support to create these collaborations or knowledge networks. Wendy Pye has created ways to create a knowledge network that is inclusive of local, regional and national ideas with the infusion of new technology and involving local and national content.

The partnerships created by her company, the Wendy Pye Group, provide an example of literacy programmes that are shared are between New Zealand (where the company is based) and South Africa, Malaysia, Singapore, China, Taiwan, Korea, and Chile. The partnerships have greatly improved the literacy skills of children aged 5 to 9 years in each respective country. If we think of the Millennium Development Goals and the effort to achieve universal primary education, we know that literacy is a crucial enabling factor, and reading skills can help to ensure that all boys and girls are able to participate in a full course of primary schooling.

The Challenge of Using ICT in the Classroom

With the recent development of ICT initiatives around the world creating global opportunities for communication, the company began to develop new strategies for teaching literacy using ICT with printed text. The challenge was to create twenty-first century resources for the children of today, to make their learning relevant to "now" rather than the past. There was also a challenge to upgrade the ICT skills of the teachers so that the programmes would be effective as teachers moved into new ways of working using technology with support, mentoring and feedback. One of the problems in the use of technology programmes has been the education of teachers for fluency with the programmes, and the use of new technologies.

The introduction of print and technology linked together with professional training for teachers proved very successful and is now used in many countries as the basic method for teaching literacy. In particular, the use of has proved very successful with learners for whom English is a second or foreign language.

In the world of global communications, it is critical to ensure that we bridge the digital divide between developing and developed countries through the introduction of ICT into elementary school systems where early learning begins. The challenge for all is to make use of new technologies in meaningful ways to maximize their value to learners, teachers and others involved in the dissemination of the uses of technology.

Case studies

- ## South Africa

In South Africa a reading programme was developed called Sunshine in South Africa, designed to create a positive impact on the English reading and language skills of primary school children in disadvantaged schools.

Staff from the Wendy Pye Group trained trainers from READ, a South African NGO closely involved in literary programmes, to use the Sunshine Programme. This train the trainers model was successful as a model of excellence.

Trainers received the programme enthusiastically and trained new staff as demonstrated by the results of research. This training was not a one time initiative but was supported by continuing support, monitoring, which involved a number of strategies to help teachers, including visits, group seminars , and sessions where classroom ideas, strategies, and ways of using the technology and problems were solved together. From these efforts an extensive guidance handbook was written. Since the teachers were involved in the process of developing it, the guidance handbook proved to be most effective to explain the use of new technologies and the training model was very effective.

Reading Progress in the South African Study

The following conclusions can be drawn from the evaluation of pupils' language growth.

In Grade 2 Reading, pupils in the "Sunshine" schools achieved at a level which was over 13% higher than pupils who followed the normal textbook programmes. Sunshine pupils had a larger reading vocabulary and understood better what they read. Grade 2 children in the project improved at twice the normal rate.

In Grade 3 Reading, children in the "Sunshine" schools showed a healthy growth of 17% from pre-test to post-test, which was nearly 7% more than control groups. Some classes doubled their expected rate of progress, but a few were not able to implement the programme properly because of staff changes and other problems.

Listening and writing

"Sunshine" pupils also showed greater gains in listening and writing. They were better at comprehending stories read to them and at matching pictures with sentences read aloud. They also wrote better, more interesting sentences and were better able to describe pictures in their own words.

An analysis by province showed very similar trends in each case. "Sunshine" children achieved well in every one of the six South African provinces involved in the study. The programme also proved effective for slow learners. There was not enough evidence to show how well it would impact on the progress of pupils in predominantly Coloured schools, but it was certainly very popular in these schools.

- **Chile**

Research recently undertaken in Chile highlighted how important ICT can be when teaching English as a foreign language. A programme entitled Galaxy Kids English links books with CD-ROMs, a teacher training programme, and follow-up training and monitoring with university personnel. The programme was used in a pilot research project with the involvement of the Universidad De Los Andes In Santiago. There were six experimental schools and half of these were in areas of the digital divide, the poorest areas of Santiago.

Three trainers were initially trained in New Zealand and then became mentors to the teachers they served in the Chilean programme.

The study shows that the areas in which there was greatest improvement after the implementation of the Galaxy Kids Programme, were oral expression and reading comprehension.

In general, the improvement of pilot groups was on average at a rate of 20 percentage points above those of the control groups. This is very clear in the results of individual tests, which also constituted an accurate measure of student achievement, performance, since each student was personally assisted by his/her English teacher.

Positive aspects of the programme were that there was greater improvement after the implementation of the Galaxy Kids Programme in oral expression and reading comprehension. Another positive aspect of the programme was pronunciation and fluency.

Motivation and student interest in English language learning also appear as key elements in the application of this programme.

- **China**

The use of ICT is also being initiated in China, with a major project using Galaxy Kids English in the city of Tianjin. The model is the same, books and CD-ROMs with an extensive professional development component of the programme.

As a result of the success of the pilot programmes, there is a global application, a complete reading and maths programme which is available on the Internet. This is available in Korean, Chinese, and English. This is a world first attempt to change the literacy boundaries and to develop a global kind of strategy.

Where ICT has been used with print as a main form in instruction, as in Australia and New Zealand, children have not only gained an understanding of computer skills, but have achieved outstanding results in learning to read, write and to communicate.

Section Two

ACCESS TO ICTs IN EDUCATION

ACCESS TO ICTs FOR EDUCATION

Rahul Tongia

Introduction – the Knowledge Economy

Education has always played a central role in human development. While today the world accepts universal primary education as an achievable goal, formal schooling for everyone is a relatively recent phenomenon. Even when it was less formalized or standardized, scientific and technical curiosity helped move mankind from the agricultural to the industrial and now into the knowledge economy. At a personal level, education helps individuals move beyond subsistence agriculture, and helps them compete against their peers. However, in today's globalized world, the competition is not just with people of the same village or region, but across continents.

A century ago, improving transportation was a driving force behind globalization. Now, information and communications technology (ICT) is a major factor. ICT's role in spurring development is positive, but it has also been seen as asymmetric. While it has the potential to be the great equalizer and democratizer, those who have been left outside its purview, or who fail to harness its potential, are increasingly at risk of falling further behind.

The Digital Divide

The digital divide, however defined, is a stark divide and a challenge for development and technology professionals. It is actually a manifestation of other underlying divides, spanning economic, social, geographic, gender, and other divides.[1] Attempting to address the digital divide as a cause instead of a symptom of other divides has led to many failures of ICT driven development projects.

If we consider the digital divide, it can be at four levels: Awareness, Availability, Accessibility, and Affordability.

    a.   ***Awareness:*** relates to knowing what can be done with ICT; people must also be open to using ICT (attitudes)

---

[1] *Sustainable ICT for Emerging Economies: Mythology and Reality of the Digital Divide Problem – A Discussion Note* (2004). Raj Reddy, V. S. Arunachalam, Rahul Tongia, Eswaran Subrahmanian, and N. Balakrishnan

b. *Availability:* ICT must be offered within reasonable proximity, with appropriate hardware/software

c. *Accessibility:* relates to the ability to use the ICT (spanning literacy, e-literacy, language, interfaces, etc.)

d. *Affordability:* All ICT usage together should, ideally, be only a few percent of one's income (under 10% maximum); this covers life-cycle costs (termed total costs of ownership—TCO), spanning hardware, software, connectivity, education, etc.

Reducing the divide requires improvements across all the dimensions of ICT (dubbed the 4C Framework: Computing, Connectivity, Content, and human Capacity.

a. *Computing:* Personal computers (PCs) are prohibitively expensive for most people, and shared access (e.g. schools, community centres or cybercafés) becomes inevitable. PCs today are very difficult to use, and even "experts" spend a lot of time maintaining their machines, worrying about upgrades, security, compatibility of hardware, etc. As a complementary (but not substitutive) technology, non-PC devices are an important option, e.g. mobile phones.

b. *Connectivity:* While mobile telephony is improving worldwide (witness in Africa it is now twice the number of landlines) it remains expensive, limited in rural areas, and poor at providing data connectivity. Many areas are now grappling with limited connected options, such as dial-up. Instead, broadband connectivity can be affordable, even in rural areas, with the right network and business models (detailed subsequently).

c. *Content:* Meaningful content is lacking in many languages, and most content is not locally relevant. Today's systems tend to make people passive consumers of information, instead of enabling the generation of local information. In addition, rich content demands multimedia (useful to overcome literacy issues), which, in turn, requires broadband connectivity.

d. Human *Capacity:* Users need to be aware, literate, and innovative to harness the power of ICT. They also should be empowered to use ICT, societally and governmentally.

Of course, ICT usage does not occur in a vacuum, rather within social and cultural norms that also shape the divide. In addition, ICT usage is based on policy and business models, especially regulation. In the long run, ICT must provide value and be sustainable from both a user and a provider perspective. As the Markle Foundation's Report on *National Strategies of "ICT for Development"* (2003) states, "Digital divides are not just the result of economic differences in access to technologies (*Have's* vs. *Have-Not's*), but also in cultural capacity and political will to apply these technologies for development impact

(*Do's* vs. *Do- Not's*)."[2] However, affordability is certainly a limiting factor, since we have seen that many people *could* access of some form of ICT but do not (e.g. mobile telephony's footprint extends to over 80% of developing country populations, but the actual usage rates are much lower).

Access is a Fundamental Requirement

If we consider the desired end-goals of empowerment and opportunities, access leads to information, which can lead to knowledge, leading to empowerment and opportunities. Of course, it is not linear, and one requires complementary capabilities, especially to interpret information into usable knowledge. In fact, knowledge is an interpreted extension of information that captures relevance and context, and it is tightly coupled with opportunities.

We revisit the important issue of *access* to ICT, especially for education, later in this article.

ICT and Education

ICT can help education and literacy, as it has the technological prowess of extensive reach, and provides options to tailor the output to meet individual needs at anytime of his or her choosing. More than such conveniences, ICT can overcome some of the major handicaps inherent in conventional education. For instance, it can provide quality education with appropriate graphics and experimental presentations that are today available only in a few select urban schools; it does not inherently discriminate on the basis of gender or income, and can be made available in any language. These characteristics of ICT-enabled education are available at any level including for courses in practical training, adult education or continuing education.

However, ICT as used for education cannot be a replacement for, but rather must be incorporated into existing systems. In particular, it must help teachers instead of becoming an additional task for them. They themselves are the first destination on the road to overcoming the digital divide in education.

Ultimately, ICT for education must be sustainable and provide value. ICT is a moving target, requiring continuous effort and integration. Areas where connectivity is available through dial-up may soon seek broadband, e.g. rural USA. While the fact that ICT keeps evolving represents a challenge for policy- and decision-makers, there are some benefits to this.

The first, of course, is that solutions are continuously becoming more powerful and cheaper (and over time, these should allow them to become more robust and easy to

---

[2] http://www.markle.org/downloadable_assets/gdoi_1223.pdf

use). Some day, hand-held devices will be able to perform voice recognition and translation between any pair of languages. Thus, any information in English, German or Chinese will be accessible to those who speak, say, Arabic, French, or Wolof. Of course, a harder challenge is contextual translation of information, presenting it in a meaningful format, i.e. that conforms to the user's literacy level and background. In fact, one of the goals for ICT must be to enable the Information Age "Bill of Rights": [3] providing the right information to the right people in the right language in the right timeframe in the right level of detail.

The second possibility is that ICT, with its new and evolving capabilities, can enable new formats, styles and levels of education. While everyone needs some comparable basic (primary) education (including literacy), there are many new possibilities ICT can enable for advanced education (including technical and vocational education). Here, ICT can allow for more customization and specialization, opening a floodgate of possibilities that traditional education was unable to deliver. In fact, advanced education is sometimes a better candidate for ICT based education because it demands higher-skilled instructors and specialized content.

Education using ICT is especially difficult as it involves specialized knowledge of both ICT and education. Many electronic/distance educational models failed because existing providers thought it was enough to digitize and put their current material on the Web. In fact, a number of reputed schools and universities failed or saw enormous setbacks in such efforts. To succeed in the long run, new content, and, ideally, new methods of instruction are key. Students learn and retain far more by doing than by "taking in". This also relates to the failure of many syllabi or curricula in being relevant for either rural areas or the modern (global) economy.

ICT is not yet at a stage where it can substitute for humans. It is best used to enhance and extend humans' capabilities. Globally, there is a lot of information available, but how correct, helpful, or relevant it is to someone trying to learn about a particular topic is unknown. One model talks of raw information soon becoming free, with payments or fees (sometimes borne by taxpayers) for the professionals who provide feedback, evaluation, and certification. Such a model is relevant to developing countries given the wide disparity in preparedness and infrastructure within countries (e.g. rural vs. urban). One major challenge is balancing meeting minimum skill sets for all students while allowing those who are able to progress rapidly. The catch is that some can progress rapidly not only due to skills but also due to advantages of family support, infrastructure, etc.

Access and Connectivity

Data connectivity is especially lacking across much of the world. While mobile communications have helped bring connectivity to many parts of the world, the impact in education has been limited, especially compared to uses in commerce or even agriculture. In contrast, broadcast technologies such as radio and television have played and continue to play a large role in education, especially where there is less of a need for

---

[3] Jaime Carbonell, CMU (1997)

real-time interaction. A number of countries have used such solutions effectively, ranging from Australia to China (where 44% of higher education students in the 1980s were using radio- or TV-based distance education (in combination with post).[4]

Why is there limited connectivity in the developing world? An obvious answer is affordability, but prices are linked to system design and policies. Given limited resources domestically, and a failure of "market"-like mechanisms, interventions and guided effort become inevitable. Government programmes are often required to bring ICT to under-funded schools. Chile's educational reforms of the 1990s included integrating ICT, and the *Enlaces* programme of providing computers, connectivity, and software now reaches over 90% of students in government-assisted schools.[5]

Even the developed world has universal service, subsidies, cross-subsidies and other mechanisms for spreading connectivity across the population, e.g. the e-Rate programme for schools in the US (which subsidizes the overwhelming fraction of connectivity costs for schools, libraries, etc.). However, this programme was sometimes inefficient, leading to gold-plating and high costs, and it was restrictive in how the infrastructure could be used. Underserved schools in the developing world are inevitably in areas underserved overall. Thus, it makes sense to synergize ICT with both existing/alternative (non-computer) technologies and also to use computers/connectivity for non-school uses during after-school hours. While there is no easy (or universal) solution to such issues, there are many good ideas and innovations worth attempting, and decision-makers should encourage such experiments and policies.

Our experience is that meaningful ICT based on models of interconnection should utilize broadband connectivity. If this is not feasible, then one need not design systems for synchronous interconnection.[6] We are especially skeptical of proposals that utilize outdated, interim or hand-me-down solutions that ultimately end up costing as much or more for far lower performance. In fact, it is patronizing to assume developing countries should make do with "enough" bandwidth.[7]

There is connectivity to almost any point on the earth using satellite communications. Africa alone has over 45 satellites with a footprint over some part of the continent. While satellite communications are a good niche technology, they do not scale for continental, widespread, usage. Not only is satellite connectivity expensive, typically

---

[4] ICT and MDGs: World Bank Group Perspective, December 2003
[5] ICT and MDGs: World Bank Group Perspective, December 2003
[6] An interesting "broadband" option is delivery via CD or DVD. These can be shipped via mail or other delivery means, and can hold hundreds of megabytes or even gigabytes of data, enough for many interactive lectures, exercises, and other teaching material.
[7] The simple act of regular anti-virus and software updates and patches can lead to weekly downloads on the order of 5 megabytes in size. If we consider the typical dial-up speed in many parts of the world, 28.8 kbps, and then factor in poor line conditions, dropped connections, and oversubscription of the uplinking, this translates into roughly an hour of being on-line, perhaps significantly more. This implies weekly connectivity costs just for this update on the order of the average weekly income in some countries in Sub-Saharan Africa! In contrast, those with a broadband (flat-rate) connection pay nothing extra for such an update, and even for those who dial-up to connect, the incremental costs for such an update can be well below 0.1% of incomes in developed nations.

costing several dollars per kbps (kilobits per second) per month in Africa, the total bandwidth is limited, especially in the uploading direction.

Mobile communications are less expensive, but their reach into rural areas is still limited, and the bandwidth is quite limited. Such systems are largely designed for voice networking, and data, even though now available, is modest in speed and has relatively high delay ("latency"). Even the much-touted third generation of mobile (3G) is at most a few hundred kbps, and is simply unaffordable for most users.[8]

If the above two technologies are not enough to bring connectivity to rural areas, especially schools, what technologies and solutions are there? Parts of the developing world – especially China and India – have shown consumer broadband can be offered for only around $10-15 per month. While their population density and development levels may not translate to other developing countries, there are new designs, both in *technology* and in *business models*, that can bring affordable connectivity to developing regions. Recent developments in optical fibres and wireless technologies indicate that these are optimal solutions for broadband for much of the world.

FiberAfrica Model

Affordable broadband for rural developing areas is possible if we think of the right scale and design. Today, connectivity is geared for a fraction of a percent of such populations. On the other hand, designed for tens of percent of the population, the costs could be brought down dramatically. In fact, a new model using optical fibres and broadband fixed wireless, dubbed FiberAfrica,[9] has such enormous capacity that educational users could avail of free connectivity, with the system sustaining itself from other users and/or modest charges paid by the government. For just about $1/person one-time capital costs, the majority of Africans could avail of (virtually) free data connectivity within walking or cycling distance.[10] However, this leapfrog network requires a rethink of how networks are built, owned, operated, and utilized.

Using a Geographic Information Systems (GIS) model, we found that approximately 70,000 km of optical fibres could be routed through all the major population centres, not just capital cities (routed along existing roads). This could be used for a multi-gigabit optical network, which would have enough capacity for almost all potential users. A core (backbone) network, like a single international gateway, is of little use without *access* to the network. Here, we envision a two-tier system of broadband fixed wireless – core hubs spreading connectivity from the entire core to several tens of kilometres nearby, and secondary distribution from such sites to nearby users using standard, off-the-shelf, inexpensive wireless.

---

[8] A recent check on-line for pricing indicated South African 3G services cost roughly 2 rand per megabyte (MB) outside a bundled package (just over US $0.30/MB); bundled packages are lower per MB, but can cost many tens if not hundreds of US$ per month. Given a school might go through hundreds of megabytes in a single day, this becomes very expensive, very quickly. Even 'all you can use' high-speed data plans, where available, are geared towards business users (e.g. in the US, which has relatively inexpensive plans, these are at least $80/month.)

[9] http://www.contrib.andrew.cmu.edu/~tongia/FiberAfrica--ending_a_digital_divide.pdf

[10] This excludes end-user equipment such as computers or wireless modems, which would be a distributed cost that scales with usage.

At the edge, there would be tens of thousands of community access centres or kiosks, potentially operated by entrepreneurs.[11] There would also be about 35,000 km of spur fibres to extend this system and interconnect additional wireless hubs. Such a system would provide broadband connectivity to the majority of the population of Africa. While any such network would be built in several stages, beginning with certain regions, the aim is within 2-3 years of operation to span the entire continent. The benefits would be available immediately, without waiting for full deployment.

The proposed business model is one of a public-private partnership, where private service providers and kiosk operators can compete for services over an *open-access* (low-cost) uplink – with the requirement that public users gain essentially free access. Such a separation of the underlying physical infrastructure from the services that run on top of it is not a new idea (an open access framework), but it is only now gaining acceptance in parts of the world. If we treat the physical infrastructure for connectivity as a public infrastructure, it can be built for much less than what people's mental models indicate.

Roads are a good example of an analogous system that allows open access on top of public infrastructure – we don't want ten highways in parallel under the aim of competition. But, there remains significant competition and private participation, ranging from hardware (e.g. cars) to maintenance (e.g. outsourcing or tendering for toll-booth operations or even building the roads) to services riding on the infrastructure (e.g. courier and delivery companies). Of course, highways and roads cost some 100 times more per kilometer. [12]

How would this network sustain itself? The one-time capital investment, for the optical fibres, installation, optical electronic equipment, core wireless hubs, towers, back-up power, gateways, etc. all come to about $900 million.[13] Of this amount, a large fraction would be for physical infrastructure that lasts for decades. This is an additional reason for separating the physical infrastructure and basic services from the retail services (where edge equipment might need to be upgraded every 5-7 years).

The operational costs, including maintenance, international connectivity, R&D, insurance, electricity, etc., would all come to roughly $100 million per year.[14] While this may sound like a large amount, this is a fraction of the annual expenditure on other telecom services, which only reach a modest fraction of the population. While basic public access would be free, additional (value-added) services would entail fees, and there would be additional revenues from private users of the network.

Why does such a model make the most sense? The rationale for the FiberAfrica as proposed is based on several realizations:

---

[11] The kiosks could operate on solar or other renewable power, where electricity is unavailable. These would be candidates for development aid and external grants, as they must also provide computers. But, the cost of a personal computer (PC) is only a few hundred dollars one-time cost, which is less than the cost for connectivity (or even standalone power systems).

[12] Terrestrial optical fibre deployments can be done for only a few thousand dollars per kilometre, as experience from India and China shows (utilizing inexpensive local labor).

[13] These are using today's technology, and we expect significant improvements in wireless and other technologies within a few years.

[14] Again, this excludes distributed costs at the community centres or with end-users.

a. ***Small "Internet Size" of most countries requires unique scaling and design.*** Most countries in Sub-Saharan Africa are very small in terms of "Internet size", and even the obvious exceptions are themselves modest in the scheme of the Internet overall. The number of users, hosts, content, and present interconnections is proportionately much lower than even their GDP when compared to most other nations. Today, most countries are attempting to "reinvent the wheel" with their individual international fibre-connected gateways, data centres, security centres, etc. Instead, they could save significant costs by sharing many of these features (with appropriate security mechanisms and sovereign control, of course). A single large-scale core router could handle all the traffic going in or out of Africa today with ease. But, we have countries with a few million people, and less bandwidth than a small city in the US, building out their own networks without optimizing them for the size or scale possible under a transnational network.

b. ***Domestic content and connectivity are required.*** Without meaningful penetration within the country, building out international connectivity does not achieve much. Meaningful penetration will only be driven by content that meets domestic (local) needs, and such content is unlikely to be made available from abroad, especially not in local languages. To that end, while international connectivity via optical fibre can be justified, it should be the cart that follows the horse (local needs), and not the other way around. Using international connectivity as the backbone for interconnections is poor and expensive design[15] – domestic fibers will be much less expensive and easier to scale. We already have significant global fibre capacity (potentially, hundreds of Gbps) landing at multiple points in Africa (in multiple countries). However, has this done much for bringing down connectivity/uplinking costs in those countries?

c. ***Big bang approaches can sometimes be more acceptable than small interventions that keep the underlying system (and divides) in place.*** Envisioning any two neighboring countries cooperating might be more difficult in some cases than creating a common playing field at the continental level. In addition, the vision of FiberAfrica ensures that a new divide between African countries is not created – market-driven solutions would otherwise only connect a subset of countries in a meaningful manner. This also makes it more likely for donors to consider investing in such infrastructure. There are certainly interim solutions and technologies that may be less expensive, with the trade-off that they are less scalable. FiberAfrica will not be built out at once, rather beginning in certain regions first. However, the vision and end-goal should be continental. Interim solutions will take enormous effort and cost to upgrade the solution down the road.

d. ***There is no lower barrier to entry than free.*** In addition to innovations in technology, FiberAfrica has a unique business model, whereby public users (schools, hospitals, libraries, etc.) can get free or nearly free broadband access,

---

[15] Even India had segments until the late 1990s where e-mail from one city to the other would go through the US!

and end-users can also get free basic connectivity in community access points, distributed throughout Africa. Such access points would themselves receive either free or virtually free connectivity, and would charge for value-added services or assistance with transactions and fulfillment. Affordability is a key aspect of the digital divide.

e. ***The best model is one of public and private partnerships, on an "open access" model.*** Optical fibres are a preferred technology for connectivity, but can we expect three or more independent fibre networks being deployed across Africa in the near term? If we treat optical fibres like a utility, built everywhere (or deeply enough) just once, then different players could compete to provide *services* on top of this infrastructure.[16] For rural or underserved areas, free or nearly free connectivity could be given for community access points. In urban areas, this could provide much cheaper uplinking bandwidth for service providers.

The suggested use of donors is only one option, and private funds could also be used (leveraged through multilateral agencies, perhaps, who help reduce risks). It is worth emphasizing that donors would only pay for the lowest level of open infrastructure; the actual retail services would be provided by other public or private providers, whose total investment would be much larger in the long run.

One striking aspect of the proposed FiberAfrica model is that while African countries become stakeholders in the network, they do not need to invest any money to have it built – the amount is modest enough for grant-based construction. Instead, they need to enable and allow the network through *appropriate policies*. These include allowing convergence technologies such as multimedia and voice over IP (Internet Protocol), waiving rights-of-way charges for the optical fibre, making appropriate spectrum available, etc. Without such policies, the same physical network can be built, but at much higher cost. Governments may feel they are losing tax or equivalent revenues through such policies, but they would not necessarily. Higher economic activity would ensue, leading to overall improvements in taxes and government earnings. In addition, instead of up-front fees, governments could ask for a modest revenue share. Such a policy would reduce barriers to entry and allow more competition, innovation and entrepreneurship, which now would occur at the services and application level, which is where we should focus development.

FiberAfrica challenges many trickle-down, mobile-centric or other traditional telecom models. Governments should be willing to embrace such disruptive technologies and business models. It is only reasonable to ask for special policies (such as the waivers listed above) for a public network – one would not want the same concessions given to a private enterprise. But, public uses, such as for education, are too important to wait for incremental solutions that will take years if not decades to reach the rural underserved. And without bold innovations, we do not foresee affordable broadband reaching the population at large in the coming years.

---

[16] This has parallels to the Utopia network model in the state of Utah, USA, and projects in Sweden.

ICT Needs to be in Context

As professionals recognize, ICT is not a silver bullet for education, or other development. It is simply a means, and not an end. However, it holds enormous promise for improving all aspects of life, especially because its capabilities are yet growing and its uses in the long run are limited only by our imagination. It is especially an empowering technology, providing access to information and opportunities.

Optimal levels of investments in ICT are hard to judge *a priori*. Like all development, complementary efforts and investments may lead to dramatic improvements in education, especially in enrollment. Positive externalities are hard to predict, especially the "free-rider" effects these can have. In some parts of India, free mid-day meal schemes were offered for education. The aim was to draw more girls into school. The hope was that these girls would be educated, perhaps get jobs, and perhaps marry later in life. Delayed childbirth would then lead to declines in population within a generation. To their pleasant surprise, demographers found sharp decreases in population growth rate within just a few years. It turns out the girls who were now going to school used to be babysitters at home (with the mother working in the fields). Now, the mothers started having fewer children.

The potential for similar free-rider effects and spin-off benefits from ICT are enormous. Not only could the efficacy of education improve and enrolments increase, ICT done right may also draw more people into the teaching profession. Students could also learn about the capabilities of ICT, and begin to use ICT for their own development (personally and professionally). This does not just mean ICT-related jobs but integrating ICT into all spheres of life. The Internet is exceptional in that true innovations occur at the edges, by end-users, who utilize the technologies for new and varied uses.

There are many components of ICT for education that require investment. These include hardware (computers), software, training/education, supporting infrastructure such as electricity, and connectivity. The design we propose for connectivity is promising since it not only provides affordable connectivity for education, all public uses of connectivity (such as healthcare, government offices, libraries, etc.) would also benefit.

INNOVATION TO IMPROVE ACCESS TO ICT IN EDUCATION

Martin Curley

We are living in an agenda of dramatic change. However, conventional thinking and technology will lead to conventional solutions to improve access to ICT in education. In fact if we continue to follow the conventional approaches that exist for ICT in education, the digital divide will in fact get worse, not better. Even in the developed countries, governments worldwide are experiencing difficulty in keeping pace with technology change and the acceleration of the information society. Despite this, it is clear that societies which invest in ICT are those that will reap the digital dividend whilst laggards will be left behind on the other side of the digital divide. To drive a more concerted adoption of ICT in education worldwide, different and more lateral thinking is required.

Whilst governments in developed countries face economic and political pressure to demonstrate that their investment in ICT increases the effectiveness and efficiency of services, governments in developing countries face the real challenges of leveraging ICT to improve basic national services such as education and health care. It is increasingly clear that while IT is an unconventional resource, there are few models or role models to help governments manage their IT portfolio in a holistic fashion.

Integrated Digital Strategy and Common Infrastructure and Services

Governments should not address ICT in education in a vacuum, nor can they afford to. Rather, they need to address it as part of an integrated digital strategy for their country and for the different services that need to be provided. There is increasing logic to suggest that governments should manage their IT infrastructure and the applications in the same way that enterprises run their IT infrastructure and applications. A key tenet of this approach is the concept of shared infrastructure and services where common infrastructure and services provide a foundation for better service at lower cost. The idea of having a common approach to supporting solutions covering the range of solutions which governments need to operate on a standardized architecture and converged platform may sound like nirvana, but this makes sense from an economic, integration and functionality perspective. Where multiple government departments and solutions share the same backend infrastructure, support approaches and common network, these costs can be shared across all the different departments, giving an overall lower cost of ownership for each type of solution.

Appointment of a national chief information officer (CIO) to work on developing a national infrastructure and a common services and support approach to best meet the evolving needs of the country, whilst working within constrained budgets would seem to make much sense. From one perspective developing countries may be in a better position that the more developed countries as they typically will have fewer legacy systems in place and can adopt a common services based approach. Indeed the emergence of Services Oriented Architecture is a key enabler to allow this common services and infrastructure type of approach.

One example of the common infrastructure approach at work is in Westminster City Council (WCC) in the UK where they are deploying a wireless infrastructure to support a closed circuit television network for use for multiple usage models including surveillance, noise monitoring and viewing street lights for operation. Additionally WCC plans to deploy other services such as eLearning and eHealth solutions over the same network, increasing the utilization of the deployed assets and significantly reducing the unit cost per solution and user.

Lowering ICT Unit Costs through Improved IT Management Practices

Governments can significantly increase access to ICTs in education if they can lower ICT unit costs, thereby allowing much more to be done with the same money. Thus a key strategy for governments should be to attempt to lower ICT unit costs on an ongoing basis. This can be done through a combination of things including taking advantage of Moore's Law [1] and improving the management practices used for managing IT in the country.

We also require new approaches to cost effective deployment models, learning from the lessons that many global corporations have learned in deploying technology. Central procurement, standardized platforms and builds, buying PC's with headroom to maximize useful life, central support centres and down the wire management are all practices which are used effectively today by many corporations and these practices must be implemented by governments and regions to drive down Total Cost of Ownership (TCO).

Standardizing on a standard infrastructure for both front end and back end computing saves money from both a capital and operating expenditure standpoint. Governments that can aggregate demand and negotiate volume discounts from vendors for a standard platform will typically receive significant cost reductions. Often the benefits of standardization in terms of ICT unit cost reduction are even more strongly felt in operating expenditure savings as this means that typically less staff and overall spare parts may be required to support systems thereby lowing overall cost. (Typically organizations may spend three to five times the original capital investment in a system to maintain it over its lifetime).

---

[1] Moore's law was forecast by Gordon Moore in 1965 and today means that raw computing performance effectively doubles every eighteen months or so at less or equal cost than the previous capability.

In terms of choosing front end computers for education, governments may very well be tempted to buy the lowest specification of PC available to maximize the access to PCs. This might not be the wisest strategy. At Intel we made the decision in the late nineteen nineties to purchase value PCs instead of Performance PCs for Intel employees – this turned out to be a poor decision as we had to write off the twenty thousand PC's purchased after only one and a half years when we needed to do an operating system upgrade and install some new applications which needed more computing horsepower. Specifying the right PC is a key decision in better enabling access to ICT's in education.

One method of calculating what specification to buy and what the appropriate refresh cycle should be is to calculate the "equivalent annual cost" (EAC) of different specifications and different refresh cycles. (EAC is a fairly common financial method to compare capital investments with different lifetimes and is an annuity that has the same present value and life as the underlying cost flow). In determining Total Cost of Ownership for PCs governments should to take into account all the cost components of a PC's lifecycle including PC deployment, PC usage, PC support and PC retirement costs. Calculating the lowest equivalent annual cost of different configurations helps in choosing the right system and refresh cycle for PCs in education.

Consolidating backend systems to reduce the number of servers required can be a significant tactic in reducing unit cost of ICT. Again this is a practice that many corporations have used to reduce ICT unit costs with typically e-mail servers being a frequent target for quick cost reduction. The ever-improving price/performance ratio of communications, particularly the role of wireless as a disruptive technology, is also an enabler to consolidate multiple data centres into fewer larger data centres. Also as blade technology becomes more mainstream, computer density in computer rooms can be significantly increased, again lowering cost.[2]

Disruptive Technology and Win-Win Business Cases

Countries also require a new kind of "ICT in education" *business case*, one which takes advantage of Moore's Law and delivers both new business value in education and also improves ICT efficiency. Collectively we need to understand how ICT can be used to catalyze and transform education, not merely enhance education. As ICT becomes more pervasive we need to find solutions which actually lower aggregate and unit IT operating costs whilst at the same time increasing penetration and coverage.

We require disruptive and breakthrough thinking and technology. Emerging technologies such as WiMAX and peer to peer computing hold great promise. WiFi networks already enable fast and low cost establishment of local area networks – this is already changing the speed at which schools can be networked and significantly improving the economics as provisioning a wireless LAN network is significantly cheaper than having to cable a school. WiMAX will likely have a more dramatic impact as it will enable broadband

---

[2] Blade servers are the next step in the evolution of dense rack mounted computers and typically comprise of a complete computer system. The dimensions of blade servers can allow more than 300 blades to be housed on a single rack.

connections at high speed at distances of over 20 km from a single base station, which will enable cost effective broadband enablement of rural areas.

And WiMAX is not just hype, it is real. As the people of Banda Aceh, Indonesia have been rebuilding their lives after December 2004's catastrophic Indian Ocean tsunami, Intel has quietly been helping reconnect that part of south Asia with the rest of the world. This is in the form of a very large wireless broadband "umbrella" that lets humanitarian and disaster relief groups in hard-hit Banda Aceh communicate with each other and the outside world.

In June 2005, engineers flipped on a pre-WiMAX network that today covers some 600 square miles (1,500 square kilometres) of Aceh province, where the tsunami wreaked the greatest destruction. The network consists of three pre-WiMAX base stations providing high-speed Internet data connection at speeds up to 6 megabits per second within the coverage area, and 28 megabit per second backhaul connections between base stations and connections to multiple small satellite terminals, called VSATs. This relief project demonstrates that the technology both works and can operate in the harshest of environments. The economics are compelling and WiMax will enable new connectivity in the coming years that was inconceivable due to both cost and distribution factors.

Meanwhile peer-to-peer computing can enable pseudo-broadband performance over narrowband pipes and drive network efficiencies by moving a significant proportion of large files transfer off expensive wide are network connections onto local area networks. The benefits of this are two fold – first large eLearning files can be downloaded much faster and cost savings can be achieved through minimising wide area network transfer of files.

In parallel, new virtualization technologies will allow multiple users to run different eLearning applications simultaneously on the same PC with multiple screen interfaces.

New hardware such as the HP 441 allows four simultaneous users to interact with a PC, driving down both capital requirements and overall TCO – (estimated 50% reduction in capital acquisition costs and 65% in systems management costs). Also open source can be a key tool in particular circumstances to lower overall TCO. All in all, disruptive technologies continue to emerge which will continue to dramatically improve access to ICTs in education.

In some cases Governments can over invest in ICT with respect to other resources to drive lower overall total cost of operating of the complete education system – for example the Higher Colleges of Technology in Abu Dhabi invested in a wireless notebook approach for students which avoided the building of fifty computer labs, lowering the overall total cost of operation for the college. Moving from a lab based computer approach to an integrated wireless notebook approach can deliver a significant improvement in education performance as well as lowering overall total cost of operation of the education systems.

In developing countries, government policy changes will likely need to change to drive better adoption of ICT. For example only 41% of developing countries allow use of WiFi in unlicensed spectrum whilst more than 95% of developed countries allow this.

Conclusion

Many people acknowledge that curriculum-based rich content is the biggest gap or issue in increased adoption of ICT in education. Armed with the appropriate tools and the appropriate standards, teachers can and should be encouraged to develop curriculum-focused content which can be re-used by other teachers. The Intel ® Teach to the Future programme has trained more than two million teachers worldwide and these kind of programmes rapidly improve teacher competency in using laptops in the classroom. A disruptive innovation that could transform the development and proliferation of content is the establishment of a Napster-like solution based on Peer-to-Peer networks which could enable easy sharing of teacher prepared content between schools and across borders.

Another tactic to improve access to ICTs in education is the increasingly popular concept of public private partnership. This occurs when both public and private sector organizations come together to fund, develop and operate solutions or services. As we move into an era of third generation corporate social responsibility, corporations and governments can increase their collaboration to drive large-scale changes which produce win-win outcomes. While developing overarching strategies which address this, we also need to continue to drive pilots and leverage learning from rapid solution prototyping.

Finally, governments should try to create virtuous circles of innovation through coordinated strategies on broadband deployment, PC purchase programmes, digital literacy programmes and on-line e-services provisioning. While each of these components have value in isolation, a network effect in education can only be achieved through the co-management and co-evolution of strategies which co-evolve the 4C's of ICT – Computing, Connectivity, Content and (Human) Capacity.

Section Three

LEARNING STRATEGIES

"AGAINST ALL ODDS": REFLECTIONS ON THE CHALLENGES OF SCHOOLNET AFRICA

Shafika Isaacs

"When you can share knowledge then you can make the world a better place. Computers and e-mail allow new ways to share knowledge. This is why we need the computers and the e-mail because through it we can improve our chances to deal with problems of crime and HIV/Aids." (Grade 10 learner, Alexandra High School, South Africa)

In August 2005, SchoolNet Africa (SNA) prepared to carry out a student training programme on virtual collaborative learning at Alexandra High School in South Africa, attended by fifteen Grade 10 students (eight girls, seven boys, aged between 15 and 18). SNA's questions revealed that:

- The school had two PC labs: one established three years ago and another more recently.

- The lab to which SNA was assigned was set up in a spacious room with 15 Pentium III PCs (of which only five were in working order), each cased inside a customized lockable desk. The lab was very well secured with burglar bars on all windows and a security gate attached to the door.

- The lab did not have access to the Internet and e-mail.

- The second computer room's server was down but had e-mail and Internet access "most of the time".

- Seven of the 15 learners had used a computer in their lives before, at cyber cafés, in previous schools and in Saturday schools but not at their school. Of the seven, one student had used the Internet before and one student had a computer at home.

- Three of the seven students used the computer to type essays beforehand.

- All the students had cell phones.

- It appeared that the PCs were mainly used by teachers in the lab assigned to SNA and that mainly grade 11 and 12 learners have access to the other PC lab.

- All the students articulated expectations to understand how the computer works, understand the background of computers and the Internet, know what was meant by Google, how software programming works, how viruses work and two boys expressed surprise that SNA facilitators for the workshop were women instead of men.

The SNA facilitators were to train the learners on how to engage in a global virtual collaborative learning, in the absence of e-mail and Internet access and a workable computer local area network. The facilitators resorted to impromptu participative learning methods to demonstrate in practice, without the use of the PCs, how e-learning works. They divided the students into three groups, each representing a school based in a different country and allowed them to write notes on paper, hand them to the facilitator who represented the e-mail and who then delivered the message to the designated schools accordingly.

Whilst SNA could not fulfill their immediate expectations, despite the obstacles, the objective of the exercise was achieved to a large extent; all learners shared knowledge and views through animated discussion and debate reflecting an enthusiasm and passion for learning and a loyalty to their school and its teachers. When asked what they valued most about the exercise, all of the students who spoke said that they liked the idea of learning from schools and learners from other cultures and countries. And then came the hard question: *"Now that we know all of this, how do we participate in your global learning programme because we would love to be in touch with learners our age in other countries but we don't have the Internet and e-mail"*.

An estimated 5,000 schools in South Africa have PCs and of these, an estimated 2,000 have Internet access, out of a total number of approximately 28,000 schools. Alexandra High is an urban public school in a former "black township" of South Africa with 1,820 learners and 57 teachers. The school has a legacy of relentless struggle against apartheid education. With an estimated 20 workable PCs in the school if both labs are considered, the PC: student ratio is 1:91. The second PC lab was set up by Gauteng Online, a flagship programme of the government of South Africa's Gauteng Province which had a start-up budget of ZAR 500 million (approximately US $77 million). The server in the second PC lab set up by Gauteng Online broke down only recently according to one teacher, but because the school no longer has a computer teacher responsible for the lab, the situation was not reported to Gauteng Online.

If access to PCs (albeit limited) and the support of a dedicated government budget are considered indicators of resource privilege, then Alexandra High represents a relatively privileged school in the South African context and an absolutely privileged school in the broader African context. The SNA experience at Alexandra High provides a snapshot of one reality of "school networking" activity in Africa. It demonstrates how the international discourse on access to e-learning opportunities in an African context is often considered in a vacuum. It illustrates the importance yet again of getting the support system working properly for optimal use of the limited technological access that some schools have. And it highlights the substantive effort and strategies required to move towards universal access to e-learning opportunities in schools at a national level.

The role and function of SchoolNet organizations that have evolved and grown in a number of countries across Africa, that form part of the SchoolNet Africa network, is to challenge the harsh realities that obstruct the promotion of e-learning access to African youth and teachers by continuously developing qualitative workable models of technology access to support e-learning programmes. In their attempts to achieve these objectives, African SchoolNet practitioners and policymakers are often swimming against a tide of skepticism, declining donor aid for ICTs in African education, limited private sector support, limited government buy-in, limited international exposure and a doubtful attitude towards African civil society leadership. Attempts at gaining additional support are often confronted with conditions to first demonstrate sustainability, affordability, replicability, scaleability and of course, "impact", to warrant significant support.

Networks and Networks of Networks

The SNA network needs to be viewed against the backdrop of a growing movement towards the provision of e-learning opportunities for African youth that has had an estimated 10 to 15 year evolution. SNA was formally constituted in 2001 on the back of the growth of individual projects and national SchoolNet organizations already in operation in more than 20 African countries at the time. The SNA network can be defined as both a pan-African and global network of learning communities of practice comprising networks of SchoolNet organizations, networks of technology practitioners, networks of teachers in the form of the African Teachers Network, networks of learners in the form of the Global Teenager Project and Mtandao Afrika (formerly known as ThinkQuest Africa), networks of policymakers who are often based in national ministries of education and networks of partner organizations who are usually representatives of donor and development agencies and private sector groups..

Inclusion in the SNA network is defined by virtue of sustained Internet and e-mail access, a common interest in a spectrum of issues pertaining to technology-mediated education in African schools and access to the team of individuals who lead the network.

Quantifying the SNA network in Africa, based on programme reports, on-line interactions, attendance at workshops and conferences reveals the involvement of:

- An estimated 200 African general SchoolNet practitioners spread across 35 countries;

- An estimated 50 champions who more often show leadership both within the regional and national networks;

- An estimated 1,000 schools involved in the SNA-specific programmes;

- An estimated 3,000 teachers engaged in various SNA-specific teacher training and learner-centred programmes; and

- An estimated 4,000 learners involved in various SNA learner-centred virtual collaborative programmes.

Thus the regional network comprises a limited number of individuals and communities who interact regularly as a pan-African network. In turn however the regional network is linked to national SchoolNet networks which have stronger and wider interactions with schools, teachers and learners within their respective countries. For instance, SchoolNet Nigeria currently works with an estimated 50 schools and is planning ICT rollout to 1,000 schools, SchoolNet Uganda works with an estimated 30 schools, SchoolNet Mali works with an estimated 10 schools. Here the numbers of schools, teachers, learners and practitioners vary from country to country.

In addition there are independent initiatives that are often government-led (such as the e-Schools programme of the New Partnership for Africa's Development, NEPAD) or private sector-led (such as the Intel Teach to the Future programme) or research-led such as the African "hole in the wall" equivalent in the Eastern Cape of South Africa. A study by SchoolNet South Africa in 2002 revealed that there were an estimated 34 individual projects on ICTs for education in South Africa at the time. Today this number probably stands at about 40. There is limited interconnection and interaction between the "independent" projects and the SchoolNet organizations at both national and regional levels.

The cumulative effect of all of these processes and formations however, suggests a growing movement with both bottom-up (largely civil society-led) and top-down (largely government-led) initiatives. If these were to be quantified then the most optimistic guesstimates would suggest:

Table 1: Network Reach[1] in Africa

	Pan African Estimated Total	Network Reach*
Schools**	600,000	27,000***
Teachers	5 million	10,000
Young Learners in School	44 million[2]	30,000
Young Learners Not in School (Sub Saharan Africa only)	43 million[3]	Unknown

* reach denotes those who have been drawn into the most basic ICT programme
**denotes public, private, primary, secondary, independent and middle schools
*** this includes approximately 20,000 schools in Egypt and 5,000 schools in South Africa which means that outside South African and Egypt, only an estimated 2,000 schools have been reached.

Whilst the figures in table one provide an idea of how far the African Information Society has reached learners and teachers, there remains limited indication of the quality

[1] The figures in table one are based entirely on guesstimates. The dearth of accurate statistical information in general and ICT for education in particular makes it difficult to provide exact information.
[2] Unesco Institute of Statistics (2005): '*Table 1: How have enrolment grown in primary, secondary education* in *Global Education Digest 2005. Comparing Education Statistics across the World*, Montreal, Canada
[3] UNDP Human Report Office (2005): *Sub-Saharan Africa - the Human Costs of the 2015 'business-as-usual' scenario*:
http://hdr.undp.org/docs/publications/background_papers/2005/HDR2005_Note_Africa_Child_Mortality.pdf

of reach. Furthermore, whilst the SNA network cannot at all lay claim to being a monopolistic network on the continent, it has assumed an influential role as one of the very few internationally-vocal, experienced, consolidated networks which has consciously and actively promoted e-learning opportunities for African learners and teachers with a distinctly African voice.

Conceptual Challenges

School principal: Oh, so you want to teach our kids about computers. That's very good. The computer is very important in today's world.

SchoolNet practitioner: Yes, but more importantly, we want to show how computers can enable learners to learn better by connecting with learners across the world and enable teachers to teach better and collaborate with teachers all over the world.

School principal: You mean the computer can do all that as well?

Many African policymakers and school managers believed that SchoolNet Africa and its network of national SchoolNets were simply promoting access to PCs in schools or that SNA was encouraging teaching about PCs and how they work, or promoting computer science as a subject. SNA was confronted with the need to clarify its conceptual framework in a way that accommodates further learning over time because it was aware that SNA still had much to learn as well. SNA also had to demonstrate the educational value of the use of ICTs in schools in an attempt to shift from the technology-push approach which was predominant at the time. SNA had to demonstrate repeatedly that school networking was about a system of interconnected activities that were geared towards improving learning and teaching practice in schools and providing greater opportunities for learning to African youth. SNA developed a "SchoolNet value chain"[4] to make the point that using the school as the agency for delivery required the consideration of a chain of activities ranging from school readiness to partnership development to resource mobilization and monitoring and evaluation. Within each of the chains of activity were a plethora of contentious issues which were animatedly debated in the networks in the quest for workable models.

The Flagship Programme Approach

Any significant ICT-enabling education initiative has to be integrated within the national education systems and needs to be developed on a national scale, for it to work sustainably. National SchoolNet organizations however, were predominantly civil society organizations who were in their first phase of evolution and whose activities reached

---

[4] The SchoolNet value chain is explained in the African SchoolNet Toolkit available at http://www.SchoolNetafrica.net/1500.0.html and http://www.i4donline.net/april05/april05.pdf as well as in Isaacs S (2002): IT is Hot for Girls: ICTs as an instrument in advancing girls' and women's capabilities in school education in Africa. Paper presented to the United Nations Division for the Advancement of Women Expert Group Meeting on "Informationand Communication Technologies and their impact on and use as an instrument for the advancement and empowerment of women" Seoul, Republic of Korea, 11-14 November 2002.

only a few, largely urban secondary schools on a range of inter-related projects as part of a grand experiment in demonstrating the worthiness for larger scale investment in ICTs for education. SNA's mission was to develop value-adding regional programmes to support and enhance the work of the national SchoolNets. Here SNA focused on programmes which sought to demonstrate African-appropriate, replicable models on affordable and sustainable access to ICTs (such as the "Campaign for 1 Million PCs"), on ICT-enabling teacher professional development (such as the African Teachers Network and the Connecting Africa's Teacher Training Institutions project), and on learner-centred education content development (such as ThinkQuest Africa/Mtandao Afrika and the Global Teenager Project).

SNA was always acutely aware that flagship programmes and projects had serious limitations in diffusing through the education system and that their impact would be on an insignificantly small scale. The thinking was that the success of small scale national projects, supported and promoted by a unified continental network of practitioners, would catalyse increasing government and multistakeholder support in order to develop national integrated policies and strategies that would eventually permeate to all schools and communities.

Model-building, growing knowledge networks of African practitioners and policymakers in which SNA could foster continuous learning, characterized the way in which SNA conducted its work. In practice, this approach evolved unevenly across Africa with a few countries having national programmes to reach all schools at least at a policy level with some degree of implementation process in practice. Here Ghana, Namibia, Egypt, Botswana, Zambia, South Africa and more recently Tanzania and Rwanda offer some prominent examples. The emergence of the NEPAD e-Schools Programme in 2002 provided an important value adding opportunity in catalyzing the growth of ICT for education as government-led integrated national programmes.

Debates on Access to ICTs

"Please can you link us up with schools in Africa so that we can work on collaborative learning projects with African students and teachers?"

As the Alexandra High case demonstrates, many international e-learning and ICT for development programmes offered virtual collaboration projects and training support to African schools but very few, if any, were involved with the promotion of access to the technologies that would enable African learners, communities and schools to participate in these programmes. SNA was at times told by its partners that its focus should really be on the educational use of ICTs and not so much on the technologies. Alas, if no-one rallies for access to ICTs in schools in the first place, then there can be no involvement in e-learning programmes, content development initiatives and teacher training in the use of ICTs. Indeed, access to technologies for schools remains the core business of the national SchoolNet organizations.

Along with its work on learning strategies in using new technologies, SNA and its local SchoolNet partners launched the "Campaign for 1 Million PCs for African Schools" in an attempt to highlight the importance of universal access to ICTs as a crucial starting point for African community involvement in the Information Society.

SNA promoted a model of access that encompasses a broad definition of ICTs and one which does not just confine itself to the use of PCs only, thus including the use of traditional technologies such as radio, television, video, print media as well as high-end PCs, e-mail and the Internet.

SNA considered the prospects for the adoption of policies on universal access in various African countries which could consider *inter alia*:

- The promotion of an education rate or e-rate which refers to subsidized access to telecommunication services including subsidized Internet access to schools.

- The promotion of free and open source software.

- Preferential pricing mechanisms for large-scale purchases of new technologies and services from the private sector.

- Consideration for the use of second hand and refurbished PCs within an established support system.

- The relaxation of tariffs on imported technologies designated for education institutions and schools.

- The establishment of a Universal Service Fund to support affordable access to ICTs in schools at national level.

With reference to implementation of the above, national SchoolNet organizations promoted this strategy at local level with research, lobbying and advocacy support from SNA. With particular reference to the campaign for an e-rate, there have been successes in Egypt, Senegal and South Africa by way of national policy. In South Africa, the e-Schools Network (formerly known as the Western Cape Schools Network) has been in the forefront of a campaign to implement the policy of a 50% discount on Internet access for schools. SNA conducted workshops and produced a research report on "Affordable Bandwidth for African Schools". Whilst policy formation happens at government level, SNA has learned that the local SchoolNets who are mainly civil society institutions had to lobby to ensure policy implementation. The e-Schools Network[5] example is one case in point.

The Refurb and Software Debate

The Campaign for 1 Million PCs was confronted with substantial criticism. SNA was told that the campaign was "irresponsible" and that the volume was unachievable; and that it was making Africa one grand landfill by encouraging technology dumping from

---

[5] www.esn.org.za/news.php

Europe and the USA. The criticism came mainly from non-SchoolNet practitioners. The regional network of SchoolNet organizations and practitioners throughout Africa unanimously agreed to the ideas of the campaign which was discussed extensively at an ICTs for African Schools Workshop held in Botswana in April 2003.[6]

SNA prepared a detailed document[7] which explained that something had to be done to shift the prevailing paradigm from accepting small-scale PC donations towards a mass model that would make the impact that SNA was pressured to demonstrate. The terms included setting minimum standards of second-hand technologies that will be distributed to the schools, establishing local refurbishment and solution provision centres (called Technical Service Centres[8]) , developing technical skills for boys and girls, men and women to assist with the system of deploying educational technology solutions to schools.

The campaign was not so much about old PCs as about a lobbying opportunity to promote a resource strategy for the education system that shifts from the acceptance of "dribs and drabs", small scale and piecemeal donations for which SNA was meant to be grateful. De facto, the campaign highlights an access model that goes beyond just PC access and covers the range of issues relating to universal access to ICTs in an African context. Here the continuing commitment and support of African-based organizations like the Open Society Initiative for Southern Africa (OSISA) has been instrumental in the success of the campaign to date. The details of the "refurb debate" can be found on the SNA Web site along with a policy statement supported by the network.[9]

Infused within the refurb debate was the debate on software choice. SNA adopted a position of platform independence and software choice[10] which was also supported by the entire network of SchoolNet organizations, the vast majority of which have a similar policy. Here too SNA was criticized for supporting the use of proprietary software whilst at the same time promoting free and open source software.

These debates were often highly emotive and sometimes devoid of facts and empirical evidence. In an attempt to take sober-minded decisions on these matters, SNA partnered with and supported various research agencies to conduct research in these areas. These included a software comparison study conducted in partnership with bridges.org, OSI and IDRC,[11] a study on the use of second hand PCs in African schools,[12] a study on total cost of ownership (TCO) produced by OpenReseach on behalf of the Department for International Development (DFID)'s CATIA programme.[13]

These studies were the first of their kind in providing much needed empirical data that would encourage an atmosphere of learning instead of blaming. The TCO study proved

---

[6] http://www.SchoolNetafrica.net/fileadmin/resources/Workshop_Report.zip
[7] Isaacs, S (2003): One Million Computers for African Schools: A Call for Partners -
http://www.SchoolNetafrica.net/fileadmin/resources/Call_for_Partners.pdf
[8] www.SchoolNetafrica.net/fileadmin/1MillionPCsTraining/Index.htm
[9] http://www.SchoolNetafrica.net/1491.0.html
[10] http://www.SchoolNetafrica.net/fileadmin/resources/policy_on_technology_choice.pdf
[11] http://www.SchoolNetafrica.net/1502.0.html
[12] http://www.SchoolNetafrica.net/fileadmin/resources/Refurbished_computers_ResearchReport.pdf
[13] www.catia.org

extremely valuable in that it shifted the focus of the debate on the costs borne by the entire pipeline of activities that moves beyond software issues alone. SchoolNet Namibia,[14] one of the champion SchoolNet organizations, went further in developing a model on total cost of ownership for the consumption of other African SchoolNets,[15] a model which is currently being developed further by the recently established Global e-Schools and Communities Initiative (GeSCI).[16]

Partnership with the Private Sector

NGOs internationally are challenged with being financially sustainable. The discourse on sustainability in the ICT for development community strongly points to the merits of multistakeholder partnership in general and with the private sector in particular, as part of a sustainability strategy.

In its experience with partnership development SNA has had many experiences with promises of support after the submission of detailed time-consuming proposals, only to have its hopes dashed. This taught SNA to work out ways not to have its expectations raised and to ascertain upfront how serious the donor's interest was. In the end, SNA has learned to act only once an agreement for funding support had been signed. On the other hand SNA also learned that it too should not raise expectations about its delivery capability on the ground.

SNA also learned that multistakeholder partnerships in general sometimes required complex balancing acts in managing competing and contradictory interests. SNA is still learning how best competing interests can be managed within the ICT for development sector.

On the basis of SNA's limited experience, a partnership development framework has emerged that is premised on a relationship-building model. This means that partnerships are not just forged for the purposes of resource acquisition but also for mutual value addition to the aims, objectives, vision and mission of the parties concerned. Here SNA drew a distinction between resource partners who tend to provide financial support (and who are often donor partners), implementation partners who arguably are the most important in support of realizing SNA's vision (and who are often the national SchoolNet partners) and network partners who tend to add value by virtue of global and local networks (such as the Global Knowledge Partnership[17] of which SNA is a member).

The strongest partners of SNA were partners with whom it had established quality relationships in which mutual trust, respect, transparency, and integrity featured highly. One of the many relationships that stand out in this regard, is its partnership with the International Institute for Communication and Development (IICD) who at the worst of times and the best of times demonstrated in action the extent to which they respected its autonomy, its vision, mission and policies.

---

[14] www.SchoolNet.na
[15] www.SchoolNetafrica.net/fileadmin/1MillionPCsTraining/Index.htm
[16] www.gesci.org
[17] www.gkp.org

As with UNESCO and UNDP, a matter which caused much consternation however was SNA's partnership with Microsoft. The assumptions by those who criticized SNA were that Microsoft was going to use SNA in their desire for market access in Africa, they were going to encourage SNA to buy and sell their products thus putting the open source lobby out of business[18] and that SNA was legitimizing Microsoft's interventions across Africa. Like with the software and refurb debate, the issue became emotive and personalized.

At the time of writing, it had been 16 months since SNA signed its partnership agreement with Microsoft.[19] What has been the experience? Microsoft, like many multinational companies such as Intel, HP, IBM, Oracle, have a strategy of market expansion in Africa which involves relationship building with governments and civil society organizations in a manner that is independent of any one particular NGO. In fact, multinationals do not need civil society to facilitate market access as they often have willing partners within government. Thus, like others, Microsoft had a strategy of engaging in specific partnerships particularly with governments across Africa, quite independent of SNA and for which SNA could not be held responsible.

Secondly, the MoU with Microsoft is emphatically non-exclusive. This means that SNA reserved the right to partner with a range of competing firms and reserved the right to promote alternative software solutions. In practice, this is exactly how it panned out. SNA continued to partner with companies who considered themselves competitors of Microsoft, SNA continued to promote free and open source software (FOSS) and continued to engage with FOSS partners.

Thirdly, the partnership in concrete terms meant that Microsoft's "Partners in Learning" and "Unlimited Potential" programmes supported the participation of 1,034 learners and teachers in SNA's ThinkQuest Africa programme where they formed multinational teams to develop educational Web sites, some of which were in local African languages. Microsoft also supported the training of 1,385 teachers in basic ICT skills and their participation in virtual collaborative learning programmes such as ThinkQuest Africa and the Global Teenager Project.

In addition, Partners in Learning supported research into the African experience with ICT-enabled teacher training with a view to promoting the professional development of African teachers at pre-service level. Here SNA developed a strategy to connect all of Africa's teacher training colleges, which was to include a host of partner organizations. In the context of the bigger African picture, these numbers represent a drop in the ocean. However, in comparison with numbers of teachers and learners reached across Africa beyond individual country SchoolNets with bigger programmes, they represent a huge progress. For example, they compare with 145 teachers trained in the period 2002-2004. More about teacher training below.

---

[18] Much of this debate was captured on the mailing list of the Free and Open Source Software For Africa (FOSSFA) www.fossfa.org

[19] http://www.SchoolNetafrica.net/282.0.html?&L=0

SNA spoke at length with Microsoft about partnership on its Campaign for 1 Million PCs but since the signing of the MOU, in practice nothing concrete has as yet emerged from these discussions.

The creation of market access as a result of the partnership with SNA never arose, nor was SNA imposed upon to sell or promote Microsoft products.

Those who criticized the partnership with Microsoft often did so without any factual basis for their criticisms. More importantly though, from the perspective of fostering a learning culture within the networks, no-one was putting forward a coherent alternative. It was unclear whether SNA was being asked to partner exclusively with firms, big or small, who promoted only FOSS. SNA attempted to develop a policy for guidance on this matter, and its policy statement on partnership with the private sector[20] was widely distributed. As with the policy on refurbished PCs and technology choice, SNA received no comments, nor any constructive suggestions on how to improve the policy. SNA also found that no-one came forward to demonstrate clearly what alternative SNA could subscribe to by way of a policy framework on partnership with the private sector.

Moreover, outside of South Africa where the Shuttleworth Foundation has invested millions of rand in the promotion of open source in education, SNA has yet to find serious commitment by way of resources to promote FOSS in education across Africa.

Above all, the debates often perhaps lost sight of the fact that all SNA's actions and policies were consistent in promoting its mission and vision. Many have lost sight of the glaring reality that the education system in Africa is in dire crisis and that every effort that enhances access to learning should be encouraged. In the absence of a clear alternative, had SNA not forged ahead with its partnership with Microsoft, it would not have had the opportunity to reach the learners and teachers that it subsequently.

With reference to the controversy between Microsoft and SchoolNet Namibia, SNA remained implacably and consistently in support of SchoolNet Namibia as its longstanding partner in Namibia, a stance articulated to Microsoft at the start of the negotiations which they respected. In the same way SNA consciously continued to promote FOSS solutions and the development of technical support where the resources allowed this opportunity. This position was clearly articulated to Microsoft at the outset and was consistently respected.

Finally, one of the underlying assumptions about the partnership with Microsoft in particular was the implied view that an African NGO like SNA had no agency in the face of its dealings with a multi-billion dollar multinational like Microsoft. If anything, SNA demonstrated amidst all the sound and fury that a modest NGO could exercise influence, could act autonomously and above all, could promote the best interests in advancing education in Africa. This represents perhaps the most important learning from the entire saga.

---

[20] http://www.SchoolNetafrica.net/fileadmin/resources/Policy_on_private_sector_relationships.pdf

Teacher Professional Development

Whilst many of the national SchoolNet programmes have demonstrated tremendous innovation and enthusiasm among learners in schools sometimes independent of their teachers' influence, the reality is that often learner participation in SchoolNet programmes was a function of the influence of a teacher champion. Teacher professional development both in terms of overcoming technophobia and in using the technologies to promote learning, proved an important entry point into any systematic attempt at diffusing the use of ICTs in learning and teaching.

A research report produced by SNA and a range of partners, found an estimated 61 different ICT-enabled teacher training programmes in Africa.[21] These range from courses targeting several thousand teachers and spread across several countries (e.g. World Links) to those targeting fewer than 100 teachers and confined to a specific region within a country (e.g. LearnLinks projects in Zambia, Namibia and Morocco). In addition, there are also courses that are delivered entirely through distance learning on-line (e.g. Educator Development Network of SchoolNet South Africa), and there are those that are delivered entirely through face-to-face instruction (e.g., University based programmes).

The research also found that:

- The biggest problem with encouraging African teachers to use ICT in their teaching is the lack of suitable access to ICT.

- There is both the space and the demand for all types of course delivery in the African teaching context. The critical thing is to recognize the relative strengths and weaknesses of each course and ensure that the delivery of a chosen course is appropriate for the specific environment.

- There are enormous contextual, cultural and sociological differences within the African continent and enormous differences in teaching requirements within the category of "teachers" and differences in levels of formal training, both in teaching and ICT skills.

- Teacher motivation to participate in professional development courses in the use of technology remains limited. While some teachers will request and seek out professional development opportunities in the use of technology, many teachers will not.

The demographics within the teacher community are such that in most countries, the vast majority of teachers are women and this correlates positively with the small numbers of teachers involved in ICT programmes in schools. The average teacher participant in

---

[21] http://www.SchoolNetafrica.net/1489.0.html

SNA teacher training activities was male, based in an urban area, aged between 26 and 34 and taught in a secondary school. The gender disparity in terms of access to ICTs among teachers as well as access to training in the use of ICTs remains substantial, as a recent internal report on the experience with teacher training in the Global Teenager Project revealed.

In general it appears that most ICT-enabled teacher development programmes were of an ad-hoc nature and offered once-off training for a period ranging from two to six days with no follow up programmes.

One of the major shortcomings SNA faced in its teacher professional development strategies was the profound disconnect with their social realities in the schools. These include *inter alia*, the low wages earned by African teachers, the serious shortage of teachers worldwide and in Africa, influenced by the consistent recruitment of African teachers to teach in Europe and the USA, as well as the effects of the HIV/Aids pandemic. Recent figures from a World Bank report indicate: "HIV/AIDS kills teachers faster than they can be trained, makes orphans of students, and threatens to derail efforts by highly-infected countries to get all boys and girls into primary school by 2015." [22]

This report quotes figures that illustrate a disturbing trend, e.g. in the Central African Republic, 85% of teachers who died between 1996–1998 were HIV-positive. In Zambia, 1,300 teachers died in the first 10 months of 1998 compared with 680 teachers in 1996.

HIV/AIDS will rewrite the teacher supply and demand equations on current projections. The implications are as yet poorly understood but evidently very extensive. New systems of training and deployment are likely to be needed to meet this challenge. Whilst SNA has proposed various options for consideration including national strategies to target teachers at pre-service level with technology-mediated learning SNA has yet to make the link effectively with the effects of the HIV/AIDS pandemic and similar social realities such as in food security and learner safety in schools, particularly in countries where there have been significant incidences of violence in schools.

In view of the above, the key lesson is that addressing the crisis in teacher availability requires the search for systemic solutions on a national and regional scale. The role of any ICT for education programme for teachers needs to add value to such a strategy. In the absence of such strategies however, SNA is left with the task of continuing with limited, independent, once-off, externally-driven project-based interventions with the hope that over time their numbers add value and reach critical mass to influence the system positively. Such a perspective however, is naïve given the smallness of the numbers involved.

---

[22]

http://lnweb18.worldbank.org/news/pressrelease.nsf/673fa6c5a2d50a67852565e200692a79/d85862c24b5d549d85256bb2006e517e?OpenDocument

Content Development

If content is king, then learning strategies to use and produce content must be the ace.

Over the past few decades, there has been a sea change towards curriculum that is inter-disciplinary, tailored to flexible, collaborative, learner-centred learning methodologies and more suited to the needs of a global knowledge-based economy. In Africa however, the curriculum frameworks remain confined to the discipline of subjects, are based on instructive, rote-learning and drill and practice methodologies and are premised on the needs largely of subsistence, agricultural and industrial economies. This explains partly the generalized lack of access to African local digitized education content and concomitant learning and teaching methodologies in using and producing the content.

There are a few initiatives in the SNA network that attempt to address these challenges. The CurriculumNet project of the National Curriculum Development Centre (NCDC) in Uganda initiated the development of mathematics and geography materials in both digitised and print formats in an comprehensive, action-research based project which also involved the provision of technology access, teacher and learner training and monitoring and evaluation. The report on this pilot, supported by the IDRC, revealed that the effects on learners were such that they became more interested in geography and mathematics, displayed eagerness to learn and could engage in self-directed learning.

Within the SNA network however, much of work on content development and learning strategies has been programme-based. The Global Teenager Project incorporates two projects entitled the Learning Circles project and the Understanding Diversity project. Both of these involve learners from different schools in different countries exchanging information on selected topics that are curriculum-related, thereby producing content that is available in English, Spanish and French. An estimated 7,200 learners participated in the March 2005 Learning Circles from 33 countries globally.

Similarly, through the ThinkQuest African programme, learners predominantly from African countries form teams, led by a coach who is usually a teacher. Together they develop educational Web sites which are awarded in accordance with a range of categories and criteria. Here too, a number of educational sites were produced in local African languages as well as in English and SNA has records of some of the sites being used for learning and teaching in schools. These programmes demonstrate the potential that virtual collaborative learning has in promoting intercultural understanding and in building a range of skills from Web design, research and social skills among learners and teachers.

The most effective way for content development and learning strategies to be pursued in a sustainable way is if it assumes the form of a national, government-led strategy. This is evidenced by the success of the South African Ministry of Education's education portal called Thutong[23] and its support for the establishment and promotion of the Mindset Network.[24] Together they provide among the most advanced scaleable work on content

---

[23] www.thutong.org
[24] www.mindset.co.za

development and learning strategies in Africa. Mindset addresses inter-related challenges of schooling, health and livelihoods in South Africa. It develops educational resources and delivers them freely via satellite networks in the form of computer-based video, multimedia and print educational content.

Through its learning programme, learners and teachers have access to vast qualitative global and local educational resources which can be obtained via the Internet, and also via print media through inserts in the weekly Sunday newspapers and a dedicated television channel which broadcasts lessons on a wide variety of subjects. In this way, learners and teachers can be reached in large numbers and in remote areas. Both Mindset and Thutong are the outcome of many years of accumulated experience by dedicated champions as well as dedicated budgetary support both from the national Ministry of Education and various private sector partners.

Gender Equality Perspectives

Perhaps one of the most visible and sustained contributions made by SNA has been its consistent integration in practice, of a gender equality and women's empowerment perspective within its universal access, teacher and learner-based programmes. In addition to attempts to engender the ICT for Education agenda through the adoption of a gender mainstreaming approach, SNA also promoted preferential treatment of women and girls and the development of a cadre of women leaders as part of a strategy for awareness raising and challenging unequal gender power relations. A dedicated project entitled "SchoolNets in Africa: the Fe-mail Face" documents stories of leading women digital pioneers in African education, in an attempt to demonstrate how ICTs have contributed to the empowerment of women and shifts in perceptions on the capability of women. This work was reinforced by SNA's active participation in the WSIS Gender Caucus[25] during its first phase as well as in the United Nations Division for the Advancement of Women's interventions to determine the extent to which ICTs empower and advance women and girls.[26]

Whilst as a network, SNA has made some inroads in demonstrating how ICTs are not gender neutral and why conscious interventions that challenge existing gender power relations are necessary, the struggle for gender equality remains an uphill battle within the education sector in general and in ICTs for education in particular. Here consistent awareness raising, gender sensitization, capacity building and gender responsive policy will be contribute towards a transformative perspectives. However as the SNA case demonstrates, for this, leadership and conscious and consistent struggle, is key.

Further Conceptual Disconnects

Despite the pertinence of the issues that have emerged over the past decade, there were and remain significant disconnects between current conceptual frameworks and learning

---

[25] www.genderwsis.org
[26] United Nations Division for the Advancement of Women Expert Group Meeting on Information and Communication Technologies and their impact on and use as an instrument for the advancement and empowerment of women' Seoul, Republic of Korea, 11-14 November 2002.

and the glaring social realities of the education and schooling systems in many African countries. Reference has already been made to the conditions of African teachers and the effects of the HIV/AIDS pandemic and the serious limitations with which practitioners and policymakers have integrated the struggle against the pandemic with ICT for education strategically and consistently.

Similarly, whilst SNA has made overtures towards encompassing the achievement of the Education For All (EFA) objectives by demonstrating the potential of ICTs, there remain extremely limited interventions targeted specifically at youth not in school, thereby demonstrating a profound shortcoming with its interventions to date. Whilst the attainment of EFA moves beyond universal primary education and also addresses issues of quality education at all levels, conceptually however SNA has not moved significantly towards reaching the "extreme poor" referred to by Jeffrey Sachs (2004) and those not in the formal education system. In Africa, this is an estimated 43 million youth.

There is also a "pipeline disconnect" between initiatives and processes related to ICTs for education in the school system and developments at both ends of the education pipeline including early childhood development, basic education, tertiary and further education and perhaps more importantly their linkages to an evolving knowledge-based labor market.

Quo Vadis?

The mission of SNA when it was established in 2001, was to catalyze support for national SchoolNets and e-learning opportunities at national level. Many African countries today have some process under way which promote ICTs for education. A number of African countries have adopted or are in the process of adopting national policies and strategies on ICTs for education which serve to provide the supportive environment for the further growth of e-learning opportunities particularly in schools.

It can be argued that school networking in Africa has now reached a turning point in the fulfillment of SNA's mission. The advent of the e-Schools Programme of the New Partnership for Africa's Development (NEPAD) and its influence on and support from national ministries of education from 20 African countries, represents a value added step in the direction towards the proposed systemic model referred to earlier. Similarly, the approach adopted by the recently established Global e-Schools and Communities Initiative (GeSCI) towards supporting national government-led programmes to promote ICTs for education with a bias towards Africa, represents an added advantage. This allows for an opportunity for national SchoolNet organizations as civil society formations to engage directly with the NEPAD e-Schools and GeSCI processes in their respective countries as SNA endeavours towards more pervasive levels of ICT access to schools and greater possibilities for learners and teachers to share knowledge, as articulated by the Grade 10 learner from Alexandra High School.

Conclusion

Working in a geographically dispersed, culturally diverse, virtual environment in an African context forces one to face demanding situations which require courage and boldness even at the risk of becoming unpopular. Contrary to the findings of studies based on experiences in the US where learners are demotivated by the prevalence of computer access, in Africa, under conditions of scarcity and where the odds are stacked against the use of ICTs at community level, there appears to be greater enthusiasm to learn in a way that transcends the difficulties. This optimism of the will is a boon for the continent and should be the basis for encouraging greater support for the promotion of e-learning in Africa.

Bibliography

Broekman I, Isaacs S and Mogale T (2004): "Contextualising Education in Africa" in James T (ed): *The Role of ICTs. In Networking Institutions of Learning – SchoolNet*, Information and Communication Technologies for Development in Africa, Volume 3. IDRC and CODESRIA, Senegal

Butcher, N (2001). New information and learning technologies in South Africa: Pitfalls and possibilities. In C. Stilwell, A. Leach, & S. Burton (eds). *Knowledge, information and development: an African Perspective*. School of Human and Social Studies, University of Natal, Pietermaritzburg

Compaigne, B (2002) The Vanishing Digital Divide – unpublished paper

Lesoba Consult (2001): Affordable Bandwidth for African Schools, SchoolNet Africa, www.SchoolNetafrica.net

Haddad, W. D., & Draxler, A. (2002). *Technologies for Education*. Paris: UNESCO and the Academy for Educational Development.

Heppell, S. (2000). The online learning revolution in schools and beyond. In B. Lucas & T. Greany (Eds.), *Schools in the Learning Age* (pp. 51-56). London: Campaign of Learning.

Isaacs (2002): ICTs in African Schools: A Multi-Media Approach for Enhancing Learning and Teaching. *TechKnowLogia,, Jan-March*, 32-34.

Isaacs S (2002): IT is Hot for Girls: ICTs as an instrument in advancing girls' and women's capabilities in school education in Africa. Paper presented to the United Nations Division for the Advancement of Women Expert Group Meeting on "Information and Communication Technologies and their impact on and use as an instrument for the advancement and empowerment of women" Seoul, Republic of Korea, 11-14 November 2002

Isaacs S and Naidoo V (2003): A Schoolnet Value Chain for Africa – An integrated model enhancing education through the use of ICTs (unpublished)

Isaacs S (2005: "Reaching MDG2. SchoolNet Africa" in I4D Online. Centre for Development and Media Studies, India

Naidoo V and Ramzy H (2005): Emerging Trends in School Networking. Commonwealth of Learning. Vancouver, Canda

Sachs, J (2004): The End of Poverty

SchoolNet South Africa. (2002). *Audit of Major Educational ICT Projects in South Africa*. World Economic Forum Global Digital Divide Initiative.

UNDP Human Report Office (2005):

Sub-Saharan Africa-the Human Costs of the 2015 "business-as-usual" scenario: http://hdr.undp.org/docs/publications/background_papers/2005/HDR2005_Note_Af rica_Child_Mortality.pdf

UNESCO Institute of Statistics (2005): Global Education Digest 2005. Comparing Education Statistics across the World. Montreal, Canada

UNESCO (2002) The Eighth Conference of Ministers of Education of African Member States (MINEDAF VIII), Statement of Commitment, Dar-es-Salaam, Tanzania, 2-6 December 2002; www.unesco.org

UNESCO (2002): EFA Global Monitoring Report 2002: Is the World on Track, UNESCO Paris

LEARNING AND GROWING BY GIVING: CHILDREN AS AGENTS OF ICT

Edna Aphek

Children and the New Technologies

"The kids really do know how to use the Internet and they want it to be exploited in the ways they know it can be exploited. Outside the classroom and outside of any formal instruction, the Internet is a key part of their educational instruction." (Pew Internet and American Life Project August 2002).

It is a well-known fact that children nowadays master computer skills at a very early age and often better than adults. Youngsters also master many qualities usually attributed to grown-ups.

In a book called "Growing Up Digital", Don Tapscott describes the youngsters, whom he calls the n-Generation (net generation), as: Tolerant, Curious, Assertive and more Self assured Emotionally and intellectually open. "The Net Generation", summarizes Tapscott, "is a generation that combines the values of humanism with social and technical aspects".

Educational systems have been investing much time, money and energy in teaching teachers computer and Internet skills, often without spectacular results.

This process of teaching grown-ups a skill in order that later on they should teach it to youngsters, coincides with traditional and old assumptions – that the older teacher is the ultimate source of knowledge.

There has been a shift in the role and status of children caused by children's mastery of computers. Children speak the language of high-tech as their mother tongue whereas older people are "immigrants" in the land of technology, not familiar with its language.

In a world where many children speak the language of the computer and the Internet as their "mother tongue", where many of them possess the qualities that make good teachers, it would be most appropriate and only logical to put children's mastery of computer and Internet skills to use for the benefit of society at large in various ways and by means of different projects.

The digital divide has been looked upon in many countries and rightly so as a major problem. In Israel, people try to look upon it as a "probotunity". I learned of this term from the Brainstorming site – http://www.brainstorming.co.uk/.

This term "probotunity" means looking at a problem as an opportunity.

The opportunity is there, in combining the deep thorough knowledge of computer and Internet skills in the hands of our youth with the giving of this vast knowledge to others.

The following are a number of on-going projects in Israel. In all of them, young children, computer- and Internet-savvy, give of their knowledge to others, be it their peers, other children, their teachers or senior citizens. By so doing, they themselves are empowered: they take upon themselves new responsibilities and acquire new meaning in their lives, by extending beyond themselves.[1]

These "computer kids" serve as "computer trustees" in their schools and in the community. The term "computer trustees" refers to a multi-age group of volunteering students, computer oriented, with high emotional intelligence, responsible, and willing to give others of their time and knowledge. These students are not necessarily the traditionally "good" students.

Supporting Teachers and Students

In this project initiated by Dorit Bachar, students tutor and coach their teachers in computer and Internet skills on a one to one basis. They serve as their teacher's private tutor and help the teacher and work with him/her according to the teacher's pace and needs.

These youngsters also serve as trouble-shooters in school, at the computer lab and during class as they solve computer problems encountered in the classroom. A survey conducted in 2002 by the National School Boards Foundation in 90 schools in the US reports that "Fifty-four percent of the schools surveyed said that students provide technical support and 43 percent said students troubleshoot hardware and software problems."

Computer Trustees Serving as Telephone Helpdesk for the Community

The youngsters' knowledge and mastery of the ICT is very impressive. They also seem to enjoy immensely their new role as tutors, teachers and coaches. They do it at home with their family and they help their friends over the phone. Now they are also serving as a helpdesk for the community: giving telephone support in the afternoons, providing the public with hardware, software and Web support.

---

[1] The description of some of the projects listed in this chapter (tutoring teachers, expert groups, help desk, working with children in special education and the computer youth movement) is based on information supplied by Dorit Bachar of the Ministry of Education, Israel.

Constructing School Web Sites

In many schools worldwide, students build their school's Web site and often maintain it. They help in creating databases and assist teachers in uploading educational materials to Internet sites.

Tutoring Special Education Children

The computer, in addition to being the playground of the children of the Information Age, also serves as a meeting ground for children coming from different backgrounds and educational frameworks, who might not have met but for the new meeting place, the computer. In this project computer trustees tutor other computer trustees, who have learning disabilities or who study in special education classes: Together they clean computers, install software, create work sheets, surf the Web, etc.

Forming Expert Groups

This programme is geared to connecting industry and business with the school. In this project, a few students from each school and a teacher are trained by computer experts in the industry. They learn how to programme and develop new software. The trainees, in turn, teach what they have learnt to all other computer trustees in their school.

The Inter-Generation Connection Programme

This programme, initiated by the author, aims at minimizing the inter-generation gap and the digital divide by having school children tutor seniors in computer and Internet skills, and at the same time write together with the seniors a digital "mini e-book" based on a chapter from the senior's personal history.

The cooperative work of children and seniors enables youngsters to enhance their inter-personal intelligence through a process of teaching-learning and at the same time enables seniors to overcome the digital gap and become connected, involved and active. The programme also helps in debunking unfounded myth and prejudice, and creates heart-warming inter-generational connections.

And last but not least this programme, which combines the old and the new, helps us in preserving knowledge at risk of disappearance.

Children Tutor Other Children

In many schools computer literate children tutor other children, less knowledgeable at computer and Internet skills, in these skills and in other skills, such as reading, as well.

The process of reading acquisition lies right now at the centre of the Israeli educational scene. In a few schools older children (classes 4+) tutor the first graders in reading and in some of the cases the children use the computer as a mediating tool to accelerate the acquisition of reading.

In one school (the Alon school in Mate Yehuda) a group of fourth graders in 2005 tutored the first graders in reading, while using the computer, in the following specific areas:

- letter recognition;

- discerning final letters from letters in the beginning and the middle of the word (in Hebrew there are two sets of letters, according to the place of the letter in the word); and

- understanding the role of punctuation – the function of the period and the spaces.

In addition to the above the "young tutors" also taught the younger children how to write a very short paper using Word, and how to download pictures and to combine them with their writing.

Children Tutor Children in Other Schools

In 2000, the author initiated a project in the Alon School in Mate Yehuda where she served as an academic adviser. In this project, pupils from Alon School teach the use of the computer and the Internet to pupils from other schools in the Mate region, who have not yet learned the skills. The pupils are taught the basic skills needed for the preparation of a digital text, Powerpoint ® presentations, and the use of the Internet. These skills include an introduction to the computer and its workings, how to manage files and folders, how to use hyper-links between different information sources, the use of various graphic elements, use of the Internet and information retrieval and its use as a means toward a goal, basic knowledge of word-processing, spreadsheets and slideshow presentations, and an introduction to the Internet as a means for gathering information to be used in conjunction with other information sources.

Reviving the Youth Movement: Computer Youth Movement

In Israel, many of the youth movements have lost their appeal for the youngsters. Combining the ideas of the youth movements with ICTs might prove very beneficial.

In light of the aforementioned projects, the Israeli Ministry of Education is building a Computer Youth Movement. The goals of the movement are to involve as many youngsters as possible in the information revolution and the meaningful use of ICT by contributing to others in their community. In addition, the movement aims at training the youngsters as leaders in the ethical, social and legal problems of the IT world and initiating innovative programmes in the various fields of the ICT and implementing them in the community.

What these Programmes have in Common

All these programmes in which children impart of their knowledge of the ICTs also teach the values of caring, sharing, cooperation and volunteering. These programmes improve the social climate in schools and open up new avenues of expression and excellence for young computer savvies. The programmes also help to create a cadre of young ICT professionals and assist in minimizing the digital divide, caused by the introduction of the ICT into our lives.

The idea of sharing knowledge is an integral part of my philosophy. I strongly believe that pupils who are skilled in the use of the computer should be sharing their skills with others who are at the beginning stages or who have not been introduced at all to these technological skills.

What these projects also share is the principle of connecting between seemingly "foreign" elements. A close look at the projects mentioned in this paper will reveal that almost all of them are based on the creative idea of combining populations that usually don't "go together". The Israeli society is a torn society. Each group, whether secular or religious, is enclosed within itself. Projects of this kind foster meetings from a very young age of groups that otherwise would not meet. The goals of these programmes go beyond the teaching of the ICTs, they include the development of the values of responsibility and giving of oneself, the development of the values of patience and tolerance and teaching others in a technological environment and overcoming the differences of culture.

An End Note

There is no doubt in my mind that the new technologies are offering new ways for learning and bridging gaps in society.

I strongly believe that our children could and should share the knowledge they have acquired, whether through us, or through others, with other children (and adults) less knowledgeable.

The new technologies prompt us to redefine many aspects in our life in general and of school life in particular. There is a shift in the role and place of children. Children's mastery of the computer and the language of high-tech give a new status, unknown in the past. In many schools children become young computer technicians, as they maintain school computers and in many others they serve as young computer teachers and tutor other children in various subjects. These "computer children" who tutor other children, adults and seniors and who build amazing Internet sites, do what they are doing not because they are looking for a reward or for monetary compensation. Their compensation lies in the experience of giving to others.

Not only do the new technologies redefine the role of students but they also usher in what might be a new pedagogy which places much emphasis on the inter-personal element and on human values. Children who tutor others, be it children or adults, learn the values of tolerance, patience, giving and understanding the other.

Impact on Society

The postmodern era is often characterized by individualism and alienation. In a world where each is to his/her own, and people are takers, there is fear of the other and much loneliness. In one of his stories, the late Leo Buscaglia (http://www.buscaglia.com/felice.htm) tells about a person he gave some money to so that the latter could complete his studies. In a few years that person came and wanted to repay his debt. Buscaglia told him to give the money to someone else who needed it and thus to start an ever-widening chain of giving. I believe that our youngsters have started such a chain. It is now our turn as adults to join this chain of giving.

THE RISING TIDE OF ICT FLUENCY IN EDUCATION: "POWER USERS OF ICT"[1]

Joyce Malyn-Smith

Introduction

"Power users of ICT" are a critical factor in strategic planning for information and communication technologies (ICTs) in education. The name refers to youth with access to technology at home, in school, in telecentres and cybernet cafés. They play video games, talk to friends using instant messaging, listen to music and do homework all at the same time, – multitasking, shifting focus from one task to another seamlessly, without effort. They seek information, learn what they want to know and when to satisfy their needs and interests, on a just-in-time basis. We call upon them at home to programme our video recorders, troubleshoot our software and hardware problems, and advise us on specifications for technology purchases. They are our technology advisors.

"International Power Users of ICT" Research Initiative

Recent research[2] tells us that experience shapes learning. If this is so, then long-term, intensive experiences using technology tools and systems are shaping the ways young people think, learn and solve problems. What are the implications for our education systems when more and more youth are entering our classrooms as experts rather than novices? New ways of technologically-influenced thinking, combined with sophisticated technology skills, create learners that challenge teachers in classrooms around the world where youth have been provided with access to technology.

After a decade of work that focused on building capacity of youth and adults to use technology as a tool for living, learning and working, the Education, Employment and Community programmes of the Education Development Center, Inc. (EDC) began an initiative to learn from and with children who are "power users" of ICT and to organize a global network of policy-makers and practitioners who will work together to seek out,

---

[1] Adapted from an article published in the UN Chronicle
[2] Bransford, 1999

create and share new knowledge on these youth to inform policy and practice related to ICTs in education and development.[3]

The "Power users of ICT" initiative asks these central questions: What happens to youth when their technology capacity is highly developed? How does this capacity shape thinking and reasoning, educational and career decisions, family and social interactions? How do youth translate their technology skills and interests into "currency" in a global information society?

"Power Users of Information and Communications Technology are individuals who break out of the confines of traditional learning, demographic, or technological barriers by constantly using, sharing, creating, producing, or changing information in creative, innovative, and/or unintended ways so that they become force multipliers in their own environments" (Power Users Global Advisory Panel, 2002).

Several short-term goals set a foundation for the long-term research needed to support ICTs for education and development. They include:

- Raising awareness among leaders in learning, workforce and human development that "Power users of ICT" is an emerging global phenomenon with important implications for policy and practice;

- Establishing an international research base that connects researchers in many disciplines from countries around the world into a global research network; and

- Engaging an international community of practice to learn from and with "Power users of ICT" about living, learning and working with technology.

The First International Power Users of ICT Symposium was held in San José, Costa Rica in August 2005. This Symposium engaged youth who are power users of technology from countries around the world in teams with adult experts from education, psychology, sociology, cultural anthropology, learning and cognition. Together they solved problems using technology tools. From this experience valuable new knowledge is emerging about the technology capacities, habits of mind, and ways that "power users" work together to solve problems. Based on a long-term research framework validated through symposium activities, the "power users" initiative aims to conduct research that informs policy and practice on ICTs in Education and development on a regular basis over the long term through publications, Web activities and active utilization of an international network of partners.

"Our goal is not simply to nurture these unusual and masterful young Power Users to create a new elite… but to understand better what is at the heart of their thinking and to be far more intentional in bringing this knowledge together to give *all* children the opportunity to take advantage of what technology can offer… and most importantly, to create welcoming environments that encourage young people to be creators and

---

[3] EDC is a non-profit research and development firm with more than 320 projects in 40 countries around the globe

inventors of new technologies that connect us and improve our world" (Vivian Guilfoy, Senior Vice President, EDC, 2004).

Aligned with the United Nations Millennium Development Goals and in keeping with Kofi Annan's challenge to Silicon Valley, the "power users" initiative focuses on achieving its long-term research goals through an international network of public/private partnerships that invites participation of organizations from all countries in the world. Why is this initiative important to the United Nations community?

"You have to have ICT. If you don't, you will be left behind," says Dr. Mahathir Mohamad, Malaysia's former Prime Minister.[4]

More and more, information and communications technology is recognized as an important tool for development in our emerging global information society. ICT for development was a focal point at the World Summit on the Information Society (WSIS) in Geneva in December, 2003. By the end of the third day approximately 40,000 people had visited the expo and engaged in thoughtful discussion with international representatives, technology companies and non-governmental organizations (NGOs). The role that ICT for development will play in our changing world will continue to be important as WSIS plans the 2005 programme agenda.

A global sense of urgency in ensuring access to technology for all nations and peoples is emerging, along with an increasing set of questions around the impact that access will have on individuals, families and communities shaping our global information society.

According to Amir Dossal, Executive Director of the United Nations Fund for International Partnerships (UNFIP), "Power Users of ICT are seen to be emerging in countries around the world that have provided youth with access to technology. This is an important initiative that must include participation of youth in countries around the world, north, south, east and west." It is of special significance to developing nations that are leapfrogging into a knowledge economy.

The power of computers and the Internet is growing exponentially. "Between 1975 and 2000, the computing power per dollar has increased 66,000 times. By 2010, this figure will reach 10 million. There were 200 million Internet users in 2000, 600 million in 2002, and one billion by 2005. Developing countries' share of Internet users was 2% in 1991, 23% in 2001."[5]

"A highly skilled workforce is seen as the key to economic growth and prosperity and the quest for economic growth and prosperity remains at the core of public policy. It is now more and more accepted that knowledge and skills are at the heart of the development and diffusion of new technologies and crucial to technical innovation."[6]

---

[4] UNDP "Choices" magazine, December 2003
[5] UNDP "Choices" magazine, December 2003
[6] Overarching Framework, Statistics Canada, 2002

Countries are working to connect education and employment activities in ICTs. These efforts can help emerging "power users" make a smooth transition from school to work. Examples from Estonia, Malaysia, and Afghanistan have been highlighted in UNDP's "Choices" magazine. In Macedonia, EDC is working with both the public and private sectors to connect technology learning in schools with technology skills needed for success in a developing economy. USAID's project Dot.Edu is helping to develop a national e-schools initiative in Macedonia by supporting a community of practice among teachers in these schools who will integrate ICTs into curriculum. Exchanges between YouthLearn and villages in the Congo guide educators in developing technology-rich learning experiences and project-based learning.

A critical question related to ICTs in education is what happens to people once they have access to technology. What do they do to produce outcomes that matter to individuals, groups and societies? Costa Rica is a good example of the growing phenomenon of youth who are becoming "power users" of ICTs. It has made a commitment to building national technology capacity in the education and economic sectors, and is the first country to offer its citizens a free national e-mail account: *costarricense.cr*.

Public schools in Costa Rica integrate ICTs into the curriculum beginning at the primary level. The Omar Dengo Foundation is helping to achieve this goal by guiding and supporting students and teachers in public schools to use technology as a tool for living, learning and working. It has taken only ten years for Costa Rica to develop a technology economy that, according to economic indicators, has surpassed its coffee economy. The economic benefits of this bilateral investment are already seen in Costa Rica through increases in direct foreign investment (from 1US $62 million in 1990 to US $448 million in 2001), and the percentage of software companies in the region that are based in Costa Rica, 78%.[7]

Dr. Olman Segura-Bonilla, Rector of the Universidad Nacional' de Costa Rica describes the "power users" of ICT emerging in Costa Rica: "We are seeing youth that have a potential, a capability of working very fast and learning very quickly from computers. They are self-directed learners, constructing new learning in virtual environments and learning more from each other and from their own use of technology than from many of their teachers. We are talking about young individuals who get very bored in their class because they are able to learn faster and quicker and therefore we need to change curriculum somehow to capture their interest." In this sense, it seems that "power users" may help to close the digital divide, especially if we pay much more attention to the phenomena and develop national policies in that direction.

Similar issues are being discussed in the European Union. The COQS Index of Digital Literacy, a measure that combines four types of skills in using the Internet into an overall "digital literacy" score, indicates that youth in European countries consistently have significantly higher levels of "digital literacy" compared to the general population.

These trends throughout the European Union raise questions of national significance. They were interpreted, along with current research, at the ICT4D Power Users of ICT

---

[7] "Estrategia & Negocios" magazine, June 2001

roundtable at the WSIS by Dr. Lone Dirckinck-Holmfeld, Director E-learning Lab, Department of Communication, Aalborg University (AAU) in Denmark and Director of the Doctoral School on Human-Centered Informatics. "We are in a unique situation in our history," she said, "where we can observe and learn from a new culture that is evolving, one in which children as early adopters of technology are knowing more than their teachers within specific areas.

She states that "power users of ICT are brokering new ways of learning, challenging our institutions and our society." She asks: "What is the impact of power users on our institutions and how will the institutions be able to adapt? What is the social impact? Will some developing countries be able to skip the industrialized paradigm? Is it possible that some developing countries will be more advantaged and competitive because they move directly into a knowledge and learning society? Are our industrialised societies too slow to change holding back progress towards the learning society? How will this impact the global balance of power?"

To help answer these questions, EDC is establishing networks of supporters and collaborators. Frans Rameckers, Director of EDC Europe, is developing partnerships within the European Union, building awareness of this emerging phenomenon among institutions such as the European SchoolNet and Bertelsmann Foundation, and coordinating student interns to review relevant research and pose new questions for consideration.

"The Power Users initiative deals with what people in schools can learn about children in their classes who have developed sophisticated technology skills. It is just one example of changing patterns of learning challenging schools. It raises important questions on behalf of educators. The challenge of the Power Users initiative will be how to translate the long term research into a continuous flow of information to inform education ministries for purposes of developing education policy."[8]

Six "power users" international research centres are being established to create a global presence for this work and ensure participation of all regions in the world. The Power Users of ICT Global Research Network will develop a shared research agenda. With EDC, the centres will develop partnerships, projects, and research activities that contribute to the power users' mission and goals.

To date, two centres have come forward: the Universidad Nacional de Costa Rica will serve as the coordinating institution in Latin America, and Aalborg University's E-Learning Lab will serve in Europe. The Power Users Directorate at EDC is seeking additional partner institutions to join this initiative to represent the interests of North America, Asia, Africa, and Australia. The "power users" initiative is advised and supported by a wide range of partners including EDC Europe, Intel, Macromedia, Adobe Systems Inc., Verizon Foundation, Microsoft, the George Lucas Educational Foundation, DigiPen Institute of Technology, University of Aalborg, Denmark, the California State University at Sacramento, the Kempster Group, Learning Times, PTC and the United Nations Fund for International Partnerships.

---

[8] Dr. Ulf Lundin, Executive Director of European Schoolnet at WSIS, Geneva, 2003

There are several ways in which individuals and organizations can participate in and support the sharing of new knowledge on "power users" of ICTs and their impact on education in communities around the world:

- *Raise awareness of the "power users" initiative within your own schools and networks.* Link the "power users" initiative research sites to your Web site, create new venues to share information; invite the Initiative to present at conferences and author publications or articles of interest to your stakeholders.

- *Join the "Power Users of ICT Global Research Network".* Become active in the international "power users" community. Join the on-line discussion groups. Respond to the call for papers to synthesize existing research on "power users" of ICT and/or test new hypotheses.

- *Provide internship opportunities for students* to participate in "power user" of ICT research, projects, and activities.

- *Join the International Council of Partners,* which provides guidance and support for the "power users" initiative.

- *Participate in and support regional "power users" research and activities* and partner by engaging in your own research and programme efforts to learn more about the impact of "power users" of ICT in your community.

Understanding how "power users" of ICT learn and their impact on schools, culture, families and communities will help all nations develop more effective programmes that support ICTs in education for all youth. Policy makers and practitioners are invited to join the global research effort in this exploratory learning community – working together to understand and nurture the tremendous potential of young people around the world and to help the next generation take on the mantle of leadership that will make this world a better one.

ENGENDERING ICTs FOR EDUCATION

Claudia Morrell and Sophia Huyer

In the past few years, much has been written relating to the gendered dimensions of the opportunities and challenges brought about by the new information and communication technologies (ICTs). In 2002 the United Nations Division for the Advancement of Women (DAW), the International Telecommunication Union (ITU) and the United Nations ICT Task Force Secretariat developed and disseminated a Report of the Expert Group Meeting on "Information and Communication Technologies and their Impact on and Use as an Instrument for the Advancement and Empowerment of Women".[1]

In that report, the group clearly spelled out the recommendations for action at the World Summit on the Information Society (WSIS) including a call to the United Nations ICT Taskforce to "highlight the gender dimension in the WSIS process and enhance gender perspectives in its own work."[2] The WSIS Gender Caucus was formed in support of this call during the African regional preparatory conference in the same year and works collaboratively to gather and disseminate information and ideas on strategies for achieving gender equality goals both at WSIS and afterwards in follow-up programmes. The Gender Caucus recognizes that "integrating gender equality issues are a critical means as well as a goal in creating a World Information Society that supports and promotes human development and improvement in quality of life."[3]

In 2003, the Commission on the Status of Women developed Agreed Conclusions during its 47th session that were consistent with and in support of the DAW report. Specifically, the Commission noted that "media and ICT... offer tools for enhancing women's full access to the benefits of information and new technologies and can become central tools for women's empowerment and the promotion of gender equality. Efforts are therefore necessary to increase women's access to and participation in the media and ICT, including their decision-making processes and new opportunities created through

---

[1] United Nations Division for the Advancement of Women Department of Economic and Social Affairs. 2002. "Information and Communication Technologies and their Impact on and Use as an Instrument for the Advancement and Empowerment of Women." Report of the Expert Group Meeting, Seoul, Republic of Korea, 11 – 14 November. www.un.org/womenwatch/daw
[2] Ibid. p. 47.
[3] http://www.genderwsis.org/aboutus.0.html

ICT." [4] In addition, they welcomed the convening of the two World Summits on the Information Society and urged all participants "to integrate gender perspectives in every facet of the Summit."[5]

The WSIS as a body agreed and stated in the Declaration of Principles that "we affirm that development of ICTs provides enormous opportunities for women, who should be an integral part of, and key actors, in the Information Society. We are committed to ensuring that the Information Society enables women's empowerment and their full participation on the basis of equality in all spheres of society and in all decision-making processes. To this end, we should mainstream a gender equality perspective and use ICTs as a tool to that end."[6] In the same year, the Association for Progressive Communications (APC) published a handbook to initiate newcomers to the global issues and impact of ICT and included a chapter dedicated to gender.[7]

In all cases, ICT has been seen as both an opportunity for supporting women's social, political, and economic empowerment, and as a threat: the potential for increased gender inequality when access is denied and for the spread of harmful and exploitative practices such as trafficking and violence against women, is great. We must ensure that women are equal and active participants in and creators of the information society. Suggested areas for action to accomplish this can be grouped into four areas:

1. Girls' and women's increased access to ICT globally;

2. Girls' and women's improved ICT literacy and usability skills;

3. Women's full participation in the development and design of ICT hardware, software and content to ensure women's equitable participation in the information society; and

4. Women's increasing presence and leadership in all aspects of ICT, including policy and decision making, regulation, programme development, and the workforce.

The ability of the international community to adequately address these areas is confounded by the continuing challenge of girls' and women's unequal access to education. Limited national level sex-disaggregated data on participation in ICT education currently exists, but the available data and research indicate that women and girls are poorly placed to benefit from the information society. They tend to have less access to scientific and technical education specifically, and to education in general. They

---

[4] Forty-seventh Session of the Commission on the Status of Women. 2003. "Participation and Access of Women to the Media, and Information and Communications Technologies and Their Impact on and Use as an Instrument for the Advancement and Empowerment of Women," Agreed Conclusions. 14 March. p.1.
[5] Ibid.
[6] World Summit on the Information Society Declaration of Principles: Building the Information Society: A Global Challenge in the New Millennium. 2003. Document WSIS-03/GENEVA/DOC/4-E. 12 August. http://www.itu.int/wsis/docs/geneva/official/dop.html
[7] Nicol, Chris. Ed. 2003. ICT Policy, A Beginner's Handbook. Association for Progressive Communication. pp. 76 – 84.

have less access to skills training and development, which will enable them to gain employment in the information technology (IT) sector, and when they do, they generally get work at the lower levels, for less pay.[8] The Education for All initiative has recognized that girls and women lag significantly behind boys and men in both access to education at all levels of literacy: two out of three of the 110 million children in the world who do not attend school are girls, and there are 42 million fewer girls than boys in primary school (UNESCO, 2003).[9]

And while there is not a systematic measure of technological or scientific literacy internationally, "there is a strong indication that there is an under-representation of women in computing worldwide, at least in terms of undergraduate participation"[10] making access to careers in ICT development and design for women low. For all these reasons it can be said that the single most important factor in ensuring that girls and women benefit from and participate in the information society is education.

International organizations have long been concerned with the gender imbalance in education, dating from the UNESCO International Convention Against Discrimination in Education in 1960, and leading up to the current UNESCO-led Education for All initiative.[11] Goal 3 of the Millennium Development Goals includes as its target the elimination of gender disparity in primary and secondary education preferably by 2005 and at all levels of education by 2015.

Paradoxically, ICT provides opportunities to develop solutions to these challenges, which the global community has not been able to resolve over the past 45 years. ICT can support both the formal and non-formal education of women and girls through distance education and e-learning; literacy training; teacher training; and access to learning materials in remote communities. It provides the flexibility of scheduling and location which suit women's obligations and daily activities. Given the policy efforts and guidelines established to date, what remains is the action needed to carry the agenda forward.

Numerous efforts have been developed to increase girls' and women's participation and leadership in science and technology as well as ICTs. Organizations such as Women in Global Science and Technology (WIGSAT),[12] the Global Alliance for Diversifying the Science and Engineering Workforce,[13] the International Network of Women in Engineering and Science (INWES),[14] the Association for Progressive Communications

---

[8] See, Huyer, S. and Westholm, G. "Toolkit on Gender Indicators in Engineering, Science and Technology." UNESCO and the Gender Advisory Board, UNCSTD. Paris: UNESCO, 2005; and Huyer, S., N, Hafkin, H. Ert. and H. Dryburgh, "Women in the Information Society" in *From the Digital Divide to Digital Opportunities: Measuring Infostates for Development.* Ed. G. Sciadis. Montreal: Orbicom, 2005.

[9] UNESCO. (2003). Gender and Education for All: The Leap to Equality. Summary Report. Paris: UNESCO.

[10] Galpin, Vashti. (2002) "Women in Computing Around the World: an Initial Comparison of International Statistics." School of Computer Science, University of Witwatersrand, South Africa. SIGSCE Bulletin. Vol. 34, No. 2, June, p.99

[11] UNESCO International Convention Against Discrimination in Education. 1960.

[12] http://www.wigsat.org/

[13] http://www.globalalliancesmet.org/

[14] http://www.inwes.org/

Women's Networking Support Programme (APC – WNSP),[15] the Asian Women's Resource Exchange (AWORC),[16] MentorNet,[17] the Center for Women and Information Technology,[18] Gender and Science and Technology (GASAT), Gender Perspectives Increasing Diversity for Information Society Technology (GIST),[19] QUIN,[20] Women in Science, Engineering and Technology (WiTEC)[21] and FEMTEK,[22] among others, are generating models for research and action, influencing policy, and developing networking opportunities through the dissemination of information and resources and through conferences and local meetings and programmes.

Businesses are also taking action, either by providing resources to support these organizations or through their own efforts. Microsoft, Cisco Systems, L'Oreal, Intel, Dell, AT&T, Xerox and IBM are examples of companies that provide funding, software, curriculum, training and technology assistance to develop women's and girls' access to technology in an effort both to increase markets and to generate a skilled and diverse workforce. National efforts have also sprung up in many regions. The UK Resource Centre for Women is an excellent example of a recent collaboration between multiple stakeholders, including the government, business, and non-government organizations to develop and disseminate resources for women to improve their participation and progression in science, engineering and technology.[23]

The European Union has also demonstrated leadership in implementation of such initiatives through meetings and the development of several important documents that served as roadmaps for the European approach to mobilizing the contributions of women in science and technology. The ETAN Expert Working Group on Women and Science report, released by the European Commission Research Directorate-General in 2000 and focusing on the interests of women in Western Europe, was welcomed by women in the academic, corporate and government communities.[24]

The "Helsinki Group on Women and Science" released its first report in 2001 to promote the participation and equality of women in the sciences on a European-wide basis. They continue to meet twice a year and provide an important forum for dialogue about national policies.[25] The ENWISE Expert Group, which was created in 2002 to address the situation of women scientists in the Eastern and Central European countries and the Baltic States, released a report in 2004 and continues to work toward implementation and action.[26]

---

[15] http://www.apcwomen.org/
[16] http://www.aworc.org/org/front.html
[17] http://www.mentornet.net/
[18] http://www.umbc.edu/cwit/
[19] http://kitkat.informatik.uni-bremen.de/new/egist/html/
[20] http://www.quinest.ee/
[21] http://www.witec-eu.net/
[22] http://www.femtec-network.de/
[23] www.setwomenresource.org.uk
[24] "ETAN Expert Working Group on Women and Science Report." 2000. European Commission Research-Directorate General.
Learning.
[25] http://europa.eu.int/comm/research/science-society/women-science/helsinki_en.html
[26] http://europa.eu.int/comm/research/science-society/women/enwise/index_en.html

A wide range of research and programming is taking place at the grassroots level in all regions. Asha Kanwar and Margaret Taplin have documented the value of combining ICTs and education in the form of distance education. Together they documented 23 cases of women in challenging circumstances who were able to use distance learning to advance their economic and social well-being.[27] The Final Report of the Strategies of Inclusion: Gender and the Information Society (SIGIS) project found that ICTs can offer women, particularly those with low self-esteem, a safe and supportive women-only or women-friendly space for education and training.[28]

The India Technician Education Project assists industrially and economically underdeveloped and geographically remote regions in India by providing increased access to technical education and training for disadvantaged students, including women.[29] In Senegal, a Multimedia Caravan project exposed rural women to the benefits of ICT for development and provided important opportunities for women to contribute their perspectives on how ICT can be used to serve their needs. The National Alliance of Caregiving provides opportunities for education in rural areas where teachers and texts are difficult to provide.[30] INWES, WIGSAT, CWIT and the Global Alliance are only four of the many associations for women mentioned above that provide opportunities for networking among women ICT professionals, that conduct gender-related ICT and education research, and support programme development for women and girls through a variety of resources.

The results of these and the many other efforts at grassroots, national, regional and international levels are evidence of a growing momentum. But despite these glimmers of hope, we still face many challenges. A primary barrier is simply recognition of the issue. The International Journal of Education and Development using Information and Communication Technology (IJEDICT) is a new e-journal focusing on the developing world that provides free and open access to all of its content.[31] While the publication is only in its infancy (second issue released August 2005) to date there has been no reference to gender equality as a primary component in closing the digital and educational divides.

Individual efforts by stakeholders cannot address the vast array of challenges that exist in promoting the access, use and design of ICTs for increasing the representation of women and girls in formal and non-formal education and their active and equal participation in the information society. Recognizing both the current international policy context and the size of the task ahead, in June 2005 representatives of international, regional, and national organizations, including government bodies, NGOs,

---

[27] Kanwar, Asha and Margaret Taplin, eds. 2001. "Brave New World of Asia: How Distance Education Changed Their Lives." The Commonwealth of Learning.

[28] Faulkner, Wendy. 2004. "strategies of Inclusion: Gender and the Information Society. Final Report. European Commission IST Programme. p.19

[29] Huyer, Sophia. 2003. Gender, ICT, and Education. June. p. 109.

[30] United Nations Division for the Advancement of Women Department of Economic and Social Affairs. 2002. "Information and Communication Technologies and their Impact on and Use as an Instrument for the Advancement and Empowerment of Women." Report of the Expert Group Meeting, Seoul, Republic of Korea, 11 14 November. p.14. www.un.org/womenwatch/daw.

[31] International Journal of Education and Development using Information and Communication Technology. http://ijedict.dec.uwi.edu//index.php

research institutions, professional associations and the private sector, gathered in Baltimore, Maryland for an international symposium on women and ICT hosted by CWIT, WIGSAT, the World Bank, the World Trade Center Institute, and the Association of Computing Machinery (ACM). 230 women and men representing 29 countries, 49 international organizations, and 17 global corporations met to create a coordinated plan of action for both WSIS and beyond. Through two planning meetings and the final symposium, the group identified five areas that will need to be targeted in order to create change. These are as follows:

1. **Policy and Action:** Legislative, regulatory and administrative policies must be adopted at the international, national, and local levels as well as in the workplace to ensure access to ICT for women and girls. Action will be needed to make sure legislation goes beyond rhetoric and translates into action on the ground.

2. **Research and Collaboration**: Research needs to be directed at the issue of the identification of effective practices and programmes for the use of ICT to benefit women and girls. It also needs to include women, which means academic scholarships, internships, and promotion of women faculty in ICT fields, as well as inclusion of women and other stakeholders in research design, implementation and analysis. We also need to understand better the systems for effective learning and training for women and girls

3. **Dissemination and Communication:** Effective practices must be communicated broadly to allow for modified duplication and scaling up of success. For education, this may mean learning about effective educational efforts in rural India that can be implemented effectively in other countries. This will require the collaboration of governments, international bodies, associations and organizations to develop methods of data collection and to monitor progress towards goals.

4. **Resource Development**: Creating the infrastructure necessary to increase access for women and girls to education through ICT and other economic, social, and political uses will require the collaboration of organizations and governments. The goal is to better identify and allocate limited resources to those areas most likely to effectively use them to benefit all learners, including girls and women.

5. **Context and Culture**: Female representation and participation in the education system as well as the information society are shaped by cultural influences from the media, parents, peers, teachers, co-workers, and others. In many ways this is the most pervasive and most difficult barrier to overcome. Situational factors may also play a role in influencing access to education. Understanding these factors and working collaboratively towards equity in education may be facilitated through ICT. Once achieved, gender equity in education can also contribute to the achievement of equitable access of girls and women to ICT. But access insufficient for full and equal participation in the information society. Access without literacy, either because of lack of computer skills or lack

of content in the language of the end user, limits the level of benefit. And even if a girl has the basic usability skills, that does not necessarily augur for a career in ICT, as is seen in the United States.[32] Finally, equal education between men and women does not mean equal advancement in the workplace. Too often women get trapped in low level jobs and fail to advance.

The group agreed to take several specific actions with the goal of achieving increased participation of girls and women in scientific and technological education and training and the information society by 2010. Those actions include the following:

1. Develop strategies for collaboration cross-culturally to promote the increased representation and participation of women in scientific and technological education and in the design and development of the information society.

2. Create a Web hub for key stakeholders to communicate and coordinate existing global data bases, knowledge resources, and links.

3. Find out who is doing what. Create a mapping of activities being done by people or organizations to further the cause of women in ICT.

4. Build links with, between, and among professional organizations.

5. Develop a Declaration of Agreement and Plan of Actions. Individuals and organizations are encouraged to sign this document which calls for a commitment to move beyond an agreement in principle to individual and organizational responsibility for action.

This informal consortium of groups agreed that WSIS will provide an opportunity for the range of organizations representing education, gender, and ICTs to collaborate and advocate around these issues in support of the efforts currently underway by the WSIS Gender Caucus. WSIS represents the second of two world summits and will finalize many of the tasks outlined in 2002. While the primary focus of the 2005 WSIS meeting in Tunis will be on ICT policy issues such as universal access, regulatory frameworks, licensing, tariffs, spectrum allocation and infrastructure, the summit will also be the place where discussion will occur around continued leadership, representation, and future organization. To that end, the groups represented at the international symposium agreed to promote the following strategies to influence the WSIS process and follow-up:

- Engineer access to decision-making levels in order to pass on the aforementioned messages. This could be done by setting up a dialogue with the main public and private actors in the ICT domain, possibly at a pre-conference level.

---

[32] Janowski, Pat. 2004. "Guiding Women in Engineering Careers." November 5. http://www.theinstitute.ieee.org/portal/sitc/tionline/menuitem.be4d708ccca114d8fb22758 Accessed November 23, 2004.

- Lobby official delegations in order to raise awareness at national level. It is necessary to set up a long-term dialogue where wishes/demands are discussed. The aim is to engage national administrations to support envisaged action plans to further women's participation in ICT.

- Engage women and men at executive levels to act as ambassadors for the efforts and communicate gender-related information both during and after the Summit.

- Lobby the industry by helping its leaders recognize that any action relating to gender and ICT in the developing countries would assure them an early entry into emerging markets.

- Emphasize common threads and work on schemes by understanding the different cultures involved, encouraging world-wide mentoring systems, finding ways to measure success, involving all stake holders, sharing any progress made with interested parties, and defining projects based on differing needs.

The main action for the Summit in coordination with other like-minded groups is to generate leadership and collaboration (public and private i.e. governments and industry) to commit to implementing decisions, financing projects, adopting proven practices and ensuring that women are at the decision table on all policy efforts to advance the participation and leadership of women in the use of ICTs for promoting education and their active participation in the information society.

HARNESSING THE POTENTIAL OF ICT IN EDUCATION IN LATIN AMERICA AND THE CARIBBEAN

Danilo Piaggesi and Juan Carlos Navarro[1]

Introduction

In the year 2000, the international community adopted a set of objectives and targets, the Millennium Development Goals (MDGs), to set targets for major international development objectives. The MDGs provided a common policy framework and a number of sectoral directions in which the international community can now work with a higher degree of efficacy and value. Information and communication technologies (ICTs) were identified as a tool for development, and connectivity has been described as an indicator for development.

The integration of ICTs and science and technology in education strategies, technologies and their use in developing countries are seen as tools facilitating the acquisition and absorption of knowledge, offering unprecedented opportunities to enhance educational systems, improve policy formulation and execution, and expand the range of opportunities for social change in even the poorest communities.

The third of the MDGs sets a target of 2015 by when "all children everywhere should be able to complete a full course of primary schooling." But for ICT to make a difference to education and development in the Latin American and Caribbean region, there must be a formulation of policies, plans and strategies for implementation, the identification of local champions and committed staff, the prioritization of ICT for funding, as well as continued support of scientific research with increased linkages with technology.

"The approach determines what can be harnessed!"

How a phenomenon or process is perceived determines the options that emerge and the resources that are mobilized for addressing it. The predominant attitude towards

---

[1] Francisco Vieira, (SDS/ICT), Robert Vitro (SDS/ICT), Freddy Bentancurt (SDS/ICT) and Enrica Murmura (SDS/ICT) contributed to the preparation of this chapter.

information and knowledge defines, to a large measure, what a society is, how it will evolve and what it will become. If that attitude reflects a belief that information and knowledge are fixed and absolute, one type of society will evolve most likely closed, doctrinaire and authoritarian. If the predominant attitude is open-ended and expanding, another type of society might evolve most likely curious, deliberative and better able to deal with complexity. An expanding knowledge economy is a product of change, provokes change and is a vehicle for managing change throughout the society, it contributes to and emerges from a democratic process of efficient, equitable and sustainable development. It is important to view human development from the demand perspective of learning, learning environments and learning agents in building human capital rather than supply orientation reflected in the term "education".

Soedjatmoko, former Rector of the United Nations University, asked us to consider development as a learning process. It is essential to constantly evolve the mechanisms and instruments needed to match the diverse volume of demand for learning. A pluralistic learning marketplace already exists; the challenge is to recognize and integrate this new reality into development planning and to push ourselves to deepen our understanding about how a flexible and dynamic learning society/human capital industry might actually operate.

The Inter-American Development Bank (IDB) considers knowledge economy expansion as a conceptual and programmatic "bridge" between sustainable economic growth and the reduction of poverty while promoting equity. Dialogue within the Bank and with our partnering countries in Latin America and the Caribbean increasingly focuses on the practical implications of this approach in development strategy and project design. It is a fundamental premise of our perception that the profound changes in the organization, contents, financing, evaluation and timing of learning resulting from knowledge economy expansion have not yet been felt. Furthermore, we believe that unless an enabling environment for promoting fundamental innovation and building a capacity to manage change in these areas is encouraged, the human resource base needed to carry out a democratic process of efficient, equitable and sustainable development will not emerge.

IDB Strategies and Policies in Education and ICT

Can ICTs make a difference to development and education? Are ICTs fully integrated into the system or simply added extras? How are they being used in teaching and learning? Given the high costs and shrinking resources in education, are ICTs a wise investment? What investment is being made in teachers and other roles necessary to support ICTs applications? Are ICTs being used to bridge gaps or are they creating new ones?

Policy makers have been asking a different set of questions:

- What can be done to improve the education system so that we can increase access, improve quality and build a more skilled and informed citizenry?

- What can be done to encourage the marginalized sections of our society, whether they are girls and women, displaced people or rural people, to enter into the education system?

We know that ICT is not the only answer to all of these challenges, but it has been demonstrated that it can contribute to implementing innovative solutions contributing new learning, teaching and management processes.

However, in our view the central question is how to find a systemic approach to integrate ICT into the national education system. This can only be achieved through clear policy and transparent implementation processes and plans.

The Inter-American Development Bank is committed to assist Latin American and Caribbean countries in their efforts to promote macroeconomic equilibrium, to mobilize private sector capital, to improve the delivery of public services and to reduce poverty while advancing social reform. The Bank understands that education is central to these challenges and has been a very active player in the financing of the sector. Support to education initiatives is not new to the Inter-American Development Bank: from 1965 to 1999 a total of US $5 billion has been lent to members countries, with education representing roughly 4.6% of the Bank's portfolio.

The experience gathered during this period has identified some instances that are imperative in order to fine-tune and orient the Bank's activities in the present and its future course:

- greater and better quality access to the education system in order to better compete in world markets;

- programmes designed to reinforce equity, particularly focused on the poorest segments of the population;

- specific interventions both on the demand and the supply side;

- clear understanding of the goals and objectives of education strategies in the region; and

- effectively leverage the existing infrastructure and sustainability of strategies

It is under such a set of basic assumptions that information and communication technologies are more and more participating in education projects financed by the Bank. This paper addresses briefly the topic, presenting some of recent experiences with projects in countries of Latin America and the Caribbean.

Two sets of strategies guide the IDB operations with regards to the application of ICT in education: the Education Strategy and the ICT for Development Strategy.

The Education Strategy reflects the concern for equity and quality briefly mentioned above. It deals with primary and secondary education, technical and vocational training and with higher education. It focuses on teacher training, careers, and incentives as mechanisms available to improve education and to spur innovations within the sector. According to a recent evaluation of the current portfolio, almost one in five of all teachers in the region have been or will be trained within the context of an IDB loan. As acknowledged in the Bank's strategy, borrowing member countries have been going through a long path of educational development and reform. Several challenges are being faced and five major cross-cutting issues have been identified: institutions, information, teachers, technology and finance.

The Vocational and Technical Training Strategy, for example, explicitly calls for the creation of "training programmes using distance education, radio, television and satellites which may allow reaching further lowering the costs or improving the impact of training. Computers, the Internet and other more sophisticated technologies promise much as future alternatives". Distance education has also been the focus of discussion in the Regional Policy Dialogue initiative of the Education Unit. It has been analyzed under the lenses of how to reduce high school dropouts and improve learning in secondary education. In a paper produced by the Regional Policy Dialogue, recommendation number 6 asserts: "introduce computer technology intensively and system-wide, as means of changing the character of teaching and learning."

The Information Technology for Development Division (SDS/ICT), which develops and performs under the Bank's ICT strategy, has among its objectives to enhance human resource development through increased access to education, training and knowledge acquisition opportunities. This mandate was given from consultative meetings attended by representatives of all countries of the Latin American and Caribbean region in 1998 and in 2002.

The Division has provided technical assistance to several education projects funded by the Bank, and has assisted governments in the development of their national ICT strategy. Its basic assumption is that ICT can help in the efficiency and effectiveness of public sector activities, the participation of civil society in the development process, and the just distribution of the benefits of development.

The Division focuses on marginalized and less favoured geographic areas and populations, and aims to contribute to the reduction of the digital gap. It advocates that ICT can and should be used as an instrument to improve social policy, support change in governments and in the way they interact with their citizens. In the implementation of its projects the Division favors economies of scale, the exchange of already existing resources and the accomplishment of individual organization's full potential of contribution to projects or initiatives. Pilot projects, in instances where experience is minimal, are always recommended by the Division.

ICT in Education – IDB Basic Tenets Consolidated from Experience

In the support of initiatives to apply technology to the teaching and learning experience two groups in the Bank have been active: the Education Unit and the SDS/ICT

Division. Both groups of professionals have teamed up with education specialists in the design and implementation of projects and technical cooperation assistance in the region.

Some basic tenets and guidelines in the development and implementation of our work have been:

a.   Integrating ICT to national education systems

ICT in teaching and learning is not the panacea and the solution to all education's problems. Awareness seminars have proved to be a beneficial initiative to instill in our clients the understanding that technology is one ingredient in the education process and not a replacement to all other traditional resources. In many cases it is important to make clear that technologies are not the education reform *per se*, but one significant component of such a reform. It is equally important to emphasize that education problems come first, and then ICT can be introduced to the extent that is part of the solution, and not for its own sake.

b.   Preparing all sectors of national education systems to understand the value and significance of ICT

Central education authorities must be prepared and equipped for the use of ICT in national education systems. This includes a number of aspects: firstly the understanding and acceptance that information retained by them will be decentralized, even though they will maintain their decision-making power. This will lead to improving/adapting the institutional arrangements in order to cope with managing, maintaining and making proper use of the technologies. Secondly, more adequate planning for the integration of ICT will have to be provided: new staff must be trained and old staff need to have skills updated or polished; physical space must be refurbished to create an environment adequate to housing new equipment; processes must be formalized, in the form of written records and manuals, to guarantee basic operational conditions and continuity in the work. Lastly, government support and external assistance have to provide clear backing in order to give programmes and plans a reasonable chance of implementation.

c.   Developing and strengthening human capacity

Human resources development in ICT and education policy and plans are of paramount importance. The Bank does not finance the purchase of equipment for schools unless it is certain that local communities are able to capably make use of this investment. Even if the number of computers already available is mediocre, it is always possible to train a number of people per school that suffice the initial activities after the computer laboratories are in place. The IDB, through its programmes intends to establish a critical mass of competent staff, the promotion of local champions and innovators as well as the creation of relevant content infrastructure.

d.   Providing ongoing technical support

Maintenance policy and procedures are vital. The use of ICT in the education system requires different levels of technical support. A practice in use in many of the IDB projects is to have at least one trained technical person per school district and to identify those teachers more technology-savvy in each school and to train them in basic trouble shooting and maintenance. Such efforts decrease the dependency upon a central unit or upon contractors for initial, quick response. Further technical support via help facilities, contracts with local technicians and companies should also be incorporated into such policies.

e.   Planning budget and resources

Recurrent costs are to be regarded as a key factor. An exercise frequently left out of project design is to include the recurrent costs once computers and systems are in place. Nevertheless, the aggregate expenses of replacing ribbons, toners, etc. are not negligible for small countries' budgets. It is important to carefully guide communities in what can be defined as "life after implementation", mainly in issues not covered by the original equipment maintenance warranty.

f.   Planning for continuous evaluation, research and assessment

Ongoing evaluation is crucial within the context of dynamic and changing ICT and its application to the education environment. All aspects of an ICT in education project must be evaluated and corrective action must be taken if necessary. The simple implementation of a computer laboratory or system is not the end of the process in itself; it is not a certainty that everything goes well. Constant evaluation ensures that improvements are made, reduces the possibility of future inaccuracies, and substantiates ongoing reviews of policies.

g.   Developing new ideas, collaborations and partnerships

Resources and human capital required for successfully implementing ICT in education systems entail substantial investments of money and skilled personnel.

Therefore partnerships between government and the private sector, development agencies, school communities and others become important. The identification of this approach is important to include in any policy document.

It is important to emphasize one significant highlight of the strategic view of the Bank with regards to ICT in education, and namely the recent creation of a sub-department in charge of Education, Science and Technology. This organizational unit will bring together, in a systematized way, activities in the fields of ICT, education and science and technology, providing a convergence of endeavors and skills among the three areas.

Resources from a new Knowledge Partnership Korea Fund for Technology and Innovation will sponsor activities aimed at technical support in the three areas, the new entity will be a focal point for the development of strategies, policies, operational guidelines and applied research agendas of the Bank, and will play a leading role in their dissemination and implementation both within the Bank and in the context of larger policy dialogues sustained with governments, the private sector, civil society and academia.

The new sub-department will also interact with IDB's partners, clients and stakeholders to promote coherence and effectiveness in international assistance in scientific, technological and educational development.

Some Projects from the IDB Portfolio

The following is a brief list of some recent IDB projects in education that reflects the specific application of the tenets that guide ICT in education at the Bank. In some instances, a particular characteristic, obstacle or innovative solution is mentioned. This list is by no means exhaustive.

a. *Bahamas – Education and Training for Competitiveness*

The government of the Bahamas is promoting a reform in the country's secondary education system, including the technical vocational part of it, in order to better prepare local youth to compete in the world scenario. The hospitality, construction and information technology sectors were identified as priority for such action.

The IDB is financing the programme and the SDS/ICT Division has been mainly working on some components in the programme: the development of an internal computerized information system for the Ministry of Education and the design and implementation of a plan for the application of ICT in teaching.

The first endeavour involves the recruitment and training of some seven new employees for the IT Section, the design and implementation of a new database, the reengineering of information flow among sections of the Ministry, new hardware and software and training of administrative personnel. An investment of US $1.2 million is estimated for this segment.

The second component, "ICT for teaching purposes", is geographically widely scattered in the country – eleven different islands have secondary schools that need assistance and technical support. In order to effectively implement the programme the IDB is proposing the contracting of a firm for the design and development of materials and to carry out the training seminars. The following levels of training have been identified: basic ICT skills, ICT supported general teaching techniques, ICT supported subject specific teaching techniques, and advanced ICT skills for those in charge of computer laboratories.

Each school will receive a computer laboratory for general use, and three subject specific laboratories and specifically: language, mathematics and sciences. In each school a teacher will be identified to take responsibility for the laboratories and assistance to users, besides some troubleshooting tasks. Budget for schooling and training, including training for all administrative staff, is estimated at approximately US $2 million, and equipment at US $1.8 million.

The development of an education portal to function as the depository of all materials and teaching resources, as well as for administrative purpose, is planned to be set up in the next months. Some 500 subject teachers are expected to be trained, and close to 1,600 teachers will receive ICT supported general teaching techniques training.

b.   Trinidad and Tobago – Secondary Education Modernization Programme

The starting point for the ICT contribution in this project is different: several donors have delivered computers to Trinidad and Tobago schools which were installed without having an operations plan in place. The Ministry of Education now tries to create a standard practice for the use, maintenance and enhancement of the installed equipment while expanding the network and creating clear policies for ICT in teaching.

The Bank has been assisting the country's authorities in the development of an ICT and Education master plan, which includes both administrative and teaching application of information and communications technologies. Internal to the Ministry an information system is being developed and the redesign of processes is being conducted. Decisions about the level of access to the central data bank by individual schools and by school districts are expected soon.

Additionally, wireless technologies will be used to serve the schools and districts for a better and more effective implementation. The country has a reliable system and distances between schools are not great in many cases. Suppliers have been asked to discuss general approaches to the topic with the Ministry ICT team.

Although the project is in its initial stages, it is estimated an investment of around US $320,000 in software to cover the entire country's school information system.

The calls for ICT in Teaching and for the ICT Infrastructure consulting services will be published in the very near future. In terms of ICT for Teaching the project is inclined to base its strategy on the "Red Enlaces" experience implemented in Chile.

c.   The International Virtual Education Network (IVEN)

Created for the enhancement of science and mathematics curricula, IVEN is a pilot collaborative cross-country project in the region. The project aims to harness the potential of ICT by combining conceptions of effective learning with appropriate computer, video and communications technologies.

Argentina, Brazil, Colombia and Venezuela have been active in the initial phase, which involved instructional design of teaching/learning activities, production of web-based multimedia curricular materials, staff training, a distribution communication network, learning achievement assessment and programme evaluation. The programme remains mainstreamed and active today in Brazil and Peru. In Peru IVEN has focused on the production of content in browser-based format for science and mathematics in upper secondary education.

Funding comes from participating countries, a grant and loans from the IDB, and a start up grant has been bestowed from UNESCO. The initial training was conducted at Brazil's ICT in Education Laboratory, a facility of the Brazilian Ministry of Education, with the objective of establishing a set of procedures commonly accepted and used by all participants, as well as to level the technical knowledge of all personnel involved in the project.

d.   Latin American Education Portals Network (RELPE)

RELPE was recently presented to the IDB by borrowing member countries and calls for financing the exchange of content and information among educational portals of 15 Ministries of Education throughout Latin America. The basic principle of the project is that of autonomy for each portal: members of the network remain independent to design its portal according to national policies.

RELPE, if approved, would not be a Latin American Education Portal but rather a platform to expedite the exchange of contents among portals. This would contribute to lower expenses in the development of materials and portals contents in general, and to the increase of materials and other resources available to the education community in each country.

A Technical Committee, chosen by member countries, will guide and supervise the tasks associated with the development of standards and the platform itself. Proposals from institutions able to provide/develop the portal would be analyzed and countries would count with technical assistance to implement their individual section of the project.

RELPE is funded through the Regional Public Goods fund (Bienes Públicos Regionales) and the total estimated investment is of US $5.8 million.

e.   Uruguay – Educational Connectivity Programme

The Educational Connectivity Programme (ECP) is a joint effort developed by several Uruguayan institutions: Presidency of the Republic, the National Board of Education (ANEP) and the National Telecommunications Administration (ANTEL). The SDS/ICT Division has played an active role in the design, implementation and assessment of the project. The resolution on Educational Connectivity approved by the 2001 America Summit served to the IDB as a basis for the conceptualization of ECP. Financed with funds for technical assistance of the Japanese Government and managed by the IDB, ECP fosters the teaching-learning process, providing Uruguay teachers with the qualifications and necessary resources to spread the use of ICT and Internet in schools. The ECP was designed to provide internet connectivity to public education institutes, train the teachers in the use of technology and e-contents and to provide an initial site of educational e-contents online, starting then the development of the incipient industry of educational e-contents.

The e-inclusion of future generations in the educational environment and the teachers' training, has created for the first ones a more promissory future and for the latter it meant a substantial improvement of the working conditions. The availability of educational e-contents, besides having become an innovative event in the country, will have a direct effect on the educational curricula, determining new directions in the educational system which has not had changes for decades. The programme allows the primary, secondary and technical Uruguayan educational systems to access ICT as instruments of the teaching-learning process.

By means of this programme, 5.000 teachers, who are 12.5% of the total amount, have been trained in the educational use of ICTs; 400.000 public schools students (50% of the total amount in the country) have access to the information society through their respective educational institutes; a new e-content industry has become a reality due to the teachers motivation to elaborate endogenous educational e-contents relative to the Uruguayan curricula and values in more than 200 applications. The production of local educational e-contents has started an industry, which has not been developed in the country as well as in the area. More than 4.000 educational e-contents items elaborated by public education teachers; more than 20 teachers received awards in their respective areas.

This programme has allowed 25% of the public educational institutes to access Internet. This is a significant number not only in Uruguay, but also in the region, where similar programmes could not achieve the same impact, influence and reach. Undoubtedly, the main success is that this has been achieved in a self sustainable manner. Approximately 70% of the "public education computers" have been incorporated to this programme and approximately 35% of them are connected to internet.

From the point of view of the know-how and its dissemination to other countries in the region, this programme has become main focus for different countries because of the effectiveness of its implementation due to an appropriate design and to the optimal use of the resources. In this sense, the SDS/ICT Division has worked from the very beginning to achieve the greatest efficiency with the appropriate and necessary resources available.

Likewise, the production of local educational e-contents has started an industry, which had not been previously developed in the country or in the Region. More than 4.000 educational e-contents have been elaborated by public education teachers, more than 20 teachers were rewarded in respective contexts, and more than 100 already available in digital support for its uses in educational curricula, are significant achievements and totally new in the region. When this activity is put into context in the short period of assistance of the programme and it is projected within the possibilities for regional expansion it shows its real dimension and justifies its recognition as an outstanding reference.

TEACHING THROUGH MOBILE TECHNOLOGY DEBUTS IN SCHOOLS IN THE PHILIPPINES

Sherry Lynn R. Peralta

When classes began this year, students in the fifth and sixth grades from selected public and private schools in the Philippines will not just be leafing through pages of their textbooks or listening to their teachers' lectures on science.

They will be also able to view educational videos – downloaded with the help of mobile phones and satellite communication systems – on subjects such as plant and animal life, matter and energy, the Earth and the solar system right in their classrooms.

Such high-technology instruction is part of the global "Bridge It" programme to deliver digital learning materials to schools with the use of mobile technology. The Philippines is the only Asian country in Bridge It, which will also have its initial run in three other countries – the United States, Britain and Finland this school year.

Locally called "text2teach" – which uses the abbreviations typically used in sending short messages through mobile phones – the programme is meant to facilitate access of teachers and students to distance-learning schemes in video and multimedia lessons.

The programme aims to merge high-technology methods with basic education needs in this south-east Asian country of 80 million people, one that has often been called the world's texting capital with more than two million messages sent each day from well over 13 million cellular phone users. "Text" is the way the short message service (SMS) function of mobile phones is referred to in the country.

Tri-sector Cooperation Bridges the Divide

Bridge It is a global programme that delivers digital education materials to schools using mobile technology. The program is implemented through a unique cooperation between Nokia, the International Youth Foundation, Pearson and United Nations Development Programme (UNDP).

What is Bridge It?

Quick and simple to use, Bridge It combines existing mobile products and satellite technologies to deliver digital, multimedia materials to teachers and students who otherwise would not have access to them. It makes distance-learning programmes immediately accessible to teachers and students.

In practice, teachers use mobile phones supplied by Nokia to access a library of more than 80 full-length science videos provided by Pearson, the world's leading learning company. Once selected, videos are downloaded via satellite to a Nokia digital video recorder connected to a television right in the classroom.

Through the programme, students can explore the same state-of-the-art educational programmes regardless of the location of their school or its academic resource budget.

Programme Pilot in the Philippines

Bridge It was initially launched in the Philippines in 2003 as a pilot project, with the support of local Philippines organizations. Bridge It was developed locally under the leadership of the Ayala Foundation and with the commitment and involvement of the Philippines Ministry of Education, SEAMEO Innotech, Globe Telecom, PMSI Dream Broadcasting, and Chikka Asia.

The Ayala Foundation is also working to extend the benefits of recent technological developments to a greater number of men, women and children. Through these new technologies, the Foundation continues to work for the cultivation of Filipino ingenuity and talent, as well as the preservation of the country's rich culture, history and traditions.

Positive Results

A research report completed by the University of the Philippines confirmed that the outcome of the Bridge It pilot was very positive. The students' performance was raised markedly and their attitudes toward science and technology became more positive as a result of their participation in the "text2teach" pilot. Teachers also welcomed the new teaching concept, as it improved their competence and attitude toward using technology. The positive impact went beyond the classroom, as the project motivated also school officials, parents and community leaders.

Pilot Results in a Nutshell

In brief, the pilot results were as follows:

- 40 schools in three cities in three project sites: Batangas/Laguna, Cotabato City and Quezon City/Manila ;

- More than 13,000 5th and 6th grade students benefited from the programme;

- Improved student performance in science;

- Improved teachers' competence in teaching science as a result of "text2teach" training;

- Development of a very easy-to-use mobile solution for science education; and

- Creation of a programme blueprint to guide expansion and replication.

Expanding Content and Reach

Three key principles – sustainability, scalability and replicability – are the backbone of the Bridge It programme. Sustainability refers to local relevance and ownership as well as affordability. Scalability means that when expanding to more subjects and to more schools reaching more students, there must be no technical or other obstacles and that the cost per student must become progressively lower. Replicability means that the Bridge It platform can easily be adopted in other countries and regions of the world.

Awarded Programme

Bridge It was honoured before the conclusion of its one-year pilot programme with two outstanding awards from an international group of business communication professionals. On March 30th, 2004 "text2teach", the Philippines-based pilot of the Bridge It programme, received two awards at the International Association of Business Communicators (IABC) – Philippines 2004 Gold Quill Awards.

The Gold Quill Awards Philippines is held each year to honour the achievements of professional communicators by recognizing excellence in communication. Bridge It received awards in two categories under Communication Management, which focuses on the communication aspects of programmes and campaigns.

The programme received an Award of Excellence for the entry "text2teach: a Bridge It Program – Community Relations". This award is for communication programmes targeted at community audiences, including non-profit and volunteer organizations.

The second award was an Award of Merit for the entry "text2teach: a Bridge It Program – International Launch – Marketing Communication". This award is given for communication programmes designed to help market products, services or places and targeted at an external audience.

Significance of Bridge It for Nokia

Veli Sundbäck, Executive Vice President, Nokia explains: "As a leading technology company, we expect to help bridge the digital divide. Bridge It places advanced digital communications at the service of education, showing that advanced digital communications technologies have a role to play in developing societies and that communications technologies and networks already in place can be leveraged for a lot of new purposes."

"The Bridge It programme brings together the public sector, civil society and the private sector in meaningful cooperation. We hope our example will stimulate others to search for mobile solutions that can deliver content and services to people who might not otherwise have access to them."

Section Four

CAPACITY-BUILDING FOR LEADERS, MANAGEMENT, TEACHERS AND ADMINISTRATORS

ICT AND SECONDARY EDUCATION: CHANGING LEARNING PATTERNS

Manuel Acevedo

Introduction

This article is a brief treatment on the influence of the Internet in the secondary cycle of education and related changes in the ways students learn.

Secondary school starts in most countries at between 12 and 14 years. We start from the assumption that in the secondary cycle it is possible to work on *explicit* pedagogical methods with the students. At this point in his education, the student possesses sufficient cognitive capacity about learning processes to enable teachers and students themselves to build on educational practices introduced in earlier years. In other words, this is the period for firming up learning/studying methods. Moreover, the student has attained sufficient social and intellectual capacity to consciously integrate the use of information and communication technologies (ICTs) – particularly Internet – as a set of tools for new ways of learning.

The article touches upon the three dimensions of educational processes, i.e. *"learning"*, *"teaching"* and *"(educational) environment"*, but focuses on the action of learning. It starts from the notion that all educational processes, particularly those said to be "student-centred", should converge towards good learning.

The problems of the digital divide and other development divides must be mentioned at the outset. Clearly, the greater challenge is in being able to educate all girls and boys in the world, which is moreover a well-accepted right of those children. The concepts hereby proposed imply prerequisites which are absent in too many cities and villages of the world, and therefore are more directly applicable where basic educational standards have already been met.

Yet quality education can and should be sought everywhere, and not only in more affluent contexts. ICT integration into educational processes should be part of the effort towards improving them and making the most of available resources, even when these are meagre as in most developing countries. As Moore (2002) points out, ICT also provides a glimmer of hope towards achieving the goal of quality universal education: "the developing country has to find new methods that will dramatically improve both its children's schooling and its continuing education system. As in every other walk of modern life, the answer to the challenge of education for economic development will lie, in part, with technology."

Learning how to Learn

If Internet changes educational environments along with the social context, it makes sense that students will need to adapt to these changes. This implies that the student should "*learn how to learn*" in the new educational context. To be sure, knowing how to learn is always one of the key objectives pursued in any proper pedagogical space. But at the level of a given educational environment (and perhaps more widely in the entire educational system), we could characterize the main pedagogical challenge as figuring out institutionally how to best empower students to learn.

It is assumed that pedagogical techniques in the secondary cycle are fully developed and formalized. While in the primary cycle the student has followed certain learning patterns, it is in high school when such practices can become explicit. The student is mature enough in cognitive terms to understand that besides the usual subjects (maths, literature, history) she can deliberately apply various learning methods. Most of us remember our best high school teachers more for the methods they made us discover than for the specific content they taught us.

Extending to the tertiary cycle (university), we could argue that while retaining only a small amount of the content we learned earlier, the university taught us to think (which is another way of saying "taught us to learn"). It is about reasoning and methodologies, about ways to formulate and analyse a given problem, about the tools we use; all of these remain valuable dividends of a good university education long after the "explicit" knowledge we gained has shrunk with time.

In this regard, Guitert/Coderch (2001) highlight some of the new informational skills, listed below, which offer particular value in present and future educational environments. Secondary school is an ideal period, and long enough, to gradually integrate these skills in the learning plans/processes. Those that we believe to be specifically new as a result of the Internet are marked with an "(n)".

- Navigating for notionally "infinite" sources of information; (n)

- Using information systems (n);

- Discriminating the quality of a source of information;

- Determining the credibility of a source of information;

- Managing informational overload, (n);

- Systematizing and communicating information effectively to others; and

- (applied to all the others), learning to utilize time, the only true scarce resource in the "network society", in the context of exercising informational skills.

Indeed, from the perspective of learning and the educational environment, the time factor appears as a resource to be explicitly integrated in plans and methodologies. For example, in the context of a given classroom, questions should arise like "how much can one learn, in a span of time 'x', about skills and knowledge related to the subject?" The Internet will help rationalize the time invested in any classroom. Technology tools can be included systematically in pedagogical models to make learning more *efficient* (less time for the same results), while maintaining or increasing its *effectiveness* (results in line with objectives).

Duart (1999) proposes a series of direct docent actions that while in the realm of *virtual learning environments* apply equally well to secondary education. He characterizes them as (a) tasks of orientation, motivation and monitoring, (b) tasks of resolution of doubts, (c) tasks of continuing evaluation, and (d) the definition of a docent plan. We could go further and ask whether a kind of virtual learning environment could not be integrated in secondary education environments, with a likely effect of enriching the ways of learning.

It is important not to lose track of the final objectives of any learning process. If learning may be considered an *end* in itself, for most people it is rather more a *means* to an end (indispensable, but a means nevertheless). After all, the point is to learn how to learn... *something*! Perhaps Resnick (2002) exaggerates when affirming that "As new technologies continue to quicken the pace of change in all parts of our lives, learning to become a better learner is far more important than learning to multiply fractions or memorizing the capitals of the world".

We cannot carry a notebook computer or personal digital assistant (PDA) to refer to any information object. Knowing how to solve differential equations is tacit knowledge that allows us to solve scientific problems, and even to formulate them correctly. Would we not associate someone who fails to recall Argentina's capital with a poor cultural level? Yet, we cannot underestimate what is at the core of Resnick's message: the importance of being a good learner.

Learner-centred Learning

Duart (2003) proposes that his models of learner-centred learning in universities could well be applied to secondary education. This includes greater freedom for the student/learner to use various types of supports, or the possibility to plan individual progress at the same time as regulating one's own working rhythm. It is a matter of adapting study plans and pedagogical methods in the secondary cycle, defining some minimum objectives to be achieved by all students. From that point onwards, there would be options according to the interests and possibilities of each student. For example, the case of the United States, not touted for the quality of its public secondary education, does allow a much higher degree of individual study plans than one of supposed higher academic quality like Spain's, where the option is basically between sciences or humanities.

But as pointed out by Werry and Duart, both the educational and the responsibility levels of the students should be significantly increased for the student/learner to manage her/his own learning with reliable results. While high school students may predictably respond better to improved learning methods, leaving the principal responsibility for learning in the hands of 15 year-old students seems a bit far-fetched at this time.

However, secondary schooling is precisely the best scenario to gradually transmit and transfer that learning responsibility, for two main reasons. One is that such practice will feed well into the next phase (university, technical college) where that student will be focusing on specific professional fields and should in any event exhibit greater personal responsibility. The other reason is that there exists a natural relation between assuming responsibilities, enjoying options/freedom and civic education. Teenagers are preparing to behave like adults.

The term "learner-centric learning" is sometimes used indiscriminately. One could claim that learning which is not centred on the learner is simply a consequence of poor educational methods and environments. Excluding considerably older educational systems (i.e. before the 1960's in most industrialized countries), few if any educational systems were at least intentionally "teacher-centred", or perhaps even "content-centred". In other words, if a school did not concentrate on the best possible learning for its students, it was a bad school, period. In pedagogical circles, at times the issue of "learner-centric learning" acquires connotations of a kind of branding for a new model. I prefer to take the side that new or renewed models in fact try to improve the "learner-centricity" of learning.

ICTs (especially the Internet) change the bases on which to focus learning more on the student/learner. This includes both *heteronomic* and *autonomous* learning practices, of which we can expect to have a mixture in secondary schools for some time.

Heteronomic learning is the traditional teacher-led learning process. ICTs can help teachers stimulate their students to learn more and to learn better. These technologies allow for high degrees of accumulation, breadth and compression of didactic presentation materials, which offer new opportunities for teachers and students. According to Peters (2002), teachers can take advantage at least four new types of possibilities based on ICTs:

- combination and integration of various methods of presentation;

- improvement of multisensorial instruction;

- quantitative/qualitative extension of interactivity; and

- improvement and expansion of support systems for the student.

Autonomous learning opens more options to the student, particularly to those that show a particular interest in a particular subject, as well as those who learn better without being forced to transit rigid pre-established channels. The student undertakes a great number of tasks related to planning, organization and evaluation. If to "autonomous" we add "individualized", then this style of learning gains even more value to allow students with special needs to enjoy good educational opportunities. ICTs provide additional opportunities for effective autonomy in secondary school learning, through:

- easy, fast and economical access to enormous volumes of content, which allow for possibilities of differentiated content for the individual;

- greater ease of communication, either in the same school or with other schools (students, teachers), experts, organizations, etc;

- didactic software that recognizes and tracks levels of knowledge and capacity in the student; this allows for the adaptation of contents, activities and the rhythm of learning for each individual;

- the possibility of learning in non-linear schemes based on logic and hypertextual connections[1]; and

- extending institutional resources that are valuable for learning, such as museums, media firms, government, NGOs, public utilities, companies, etc.

The co-existence of heterenomic and autonomous learning practices is beneficial and will contribute to improve learning more than the exclusion of either of the two models. A teacher has processed much information and generated significant knowledge over one or more subjects, and has experience on how students have responded to different ways to present and work on the subject. A certain degree of autonomous learning will complement the teaching function and overall improve learning. Moreover some situations will demand high levels of autonomous learning for a successful secondary education, like in remote rural locations or when there is a lack of qualified teachers.

Few of the changes highlighted above can occur without converting teachers into "accomplices of change". Certain conditions pointed out by Werry (2001) in university settings, like de-formalization of working conditions or teachers' loss of control over the academic process, are even more evident in secondary education (this includes developing countries as well). Add to this low salaries and the growing level of conflict in the classroom (as is occurring in Spain, for example). We can thus conclude that few changes will successfully be implemented without investing significantly in the over-worked and under-valued high school teachers. At the same time, a positive attitude from the teachers is also necessary; too often teachers who are well-versed in the theoretical discourse about pedagogy and educational innovation are in practice very traditional educators.

Learning by Doing, Learning by Making

In kindergarten, children learn by doing or by making things. This continues in primary school, where it is mixed with abstractions and descriptions of knowledge objects which

---

[1] Peters calls this last point a 'pedagogical paradigm change' and it may indeed be among the most important of the new learning possibilities afforded by ICT.

are meant to be processed by the student. Peters (2000) underlines that Aristotle went as far as postulating that even the most abstract knowledge is base in sensory perception.

But it is at the secondary school stage where students can truly become conscious of learning methods. Because of the benefits of constructivist methodologies to ease learning, they could be placed at the core of educational processes during that stage. Presently, ICTs and the Internet in particular have a lot to do with implementing constructivist approaches.

According to Rashke (2002), learner-centric learning does not aim so much at mastering pre-established educational contents, but rather on the capacity to generate new contents. In this regard, "the Internet is not just another resource for learning. It is fast becoming the incubator of knowledge." Denning (2003) speaks of "knowledge gardening" in relation to the ways in which the creation of knowledge should be fertilized, cultivated and cared for.

ICTs help to fertilize these "knowledge fields", in part thanks to their possibilities for creating and construction. Guitert/Coderch (2001) and Resnick (2002) underline that one of the main educational advantages of ICTs are that they facilitate and favour strategies of *construction* (to generate knowledge) in contrast to strategies of *instruction*.

That is not to ignore the critical importance of providing students with interpretative skills, abstract analysis and logic reasoning. Peters (2000) states that "…the use of a computer is often intuitive, which restricts the abstract-cognitive dimension, while the eventful-concrete dimension gains in importance."

ICTs are useful for learning because they let the student make things happen. Resnick (2002) describes computers as "construction machines", deriving their high educational value from this. In his opinion, ICTs are excellent channels to transmit and access information, but to limit them to that role means to minimize their possibilities for transforming learning processes. From a formative angle, he argues that computers are more like modelling clay than like television.

He maintains that " …the computer is the most extraordinary construction material ever invented, enabling people to create anything from music videos to scientific simulations to robotic creatures. Computers can be seen as a universal construction material, greatly expanding what people can create and what they can learn in the process". In the Computer Clubhouses supported by MIT's Media Lab (where Resnick works), youngsters come to learn, and learn by doing. If they are interested in video games, they do not play with them – they create them. Why not set up computer labs on a similar philosophy in secondary schools, as vehicles for constructionist learning strategies?

Network Learning, and Learning through the Internet

Learning in network fashion, and learning through the Internet bring together many of the ICT-supported learning aspects mentioned before. Secondary education is particularly well-suited to network learning since the students possess sufficient social skills and better communication capacities. In addition, many students form part of some social network.

Guitert/Coderch (2001) propose that the *fundamental characteristic of learning on the Internet is the possibility of working cooperatively*. Collaboration, a social feature which is not necessarily instinctive, allows for learning in different and arguably richer ways. One of the most important professional abilities today is to be able to work in teams. Network learning helps students develop this important psycho-social skill. It also strengthens their capacity to work independently. The student not only becomes used to fulfilling her responsibility within a team, but also to differentiate collective from individual responsibilities.

Learning with/through the Internet allows for hitherto unprecedented forms of collaboration both for students as well as teachers. Communication via the Internet allows common interests to drive the shared generation of knowledge, overcoming geographical limitations. Learning through the Internet expands learners' networks. Here we include both students and teachers, since teachers will be learning as well, experimenting with new learning structures.

Examples of collaboration among students in Guitert/Coderch (2001) illustrate the possibilities for learning in networks through Internet: (i) the participation in an electronic forum by two students; (ii) a videoconference with a high school in another country; (iii) creation of didactic materials accessible through the Web by a student; or (iv) inter-disciplinary and inter-school work by teachers and students. These are truly different ways to learn and to teach. Or even, to *educate*, in Duart's sense of education as the process of "forming one's own being".

Experiences about communication and joint projects among secondary schools from different countries and cultures demonstrate the possibilities of the Internet to construct global understanding and tolerance in the educational context. Better yet, they are not limited to the industrialized North. Initiatives like *World Links for Development* (http://www.world-links.org/english), promoting North-South and South-South inter-school communication, serve as a good reference. What better ways for a European teenager to learn about the geography and economy of Africa than together with other students of her same age who actually live there? Cooperative learning networks provide truly transformational opportunities for the educational process.

Conclusions

The Internet opens the educational process towards the world and converts it into a collaborative experience. By itself this does not make for student-centred learning, but it surely becomes essential in ending the classroom-centred learning approach which is still prevalent today. Museums, factories, radio stations; judges, pilots, nurses; other students and teachers (from the same city or in a different country) enter into a multi-nodal and changing classroom, in real as well as asynchronous time.

Modern pedagogical models like Piaget's were articulated many decades ago, but even in their initial steps have taken a long time to be put in motion. ICTs, and specially the

Internet, enable the acceleration of the changes required by such models, in all three dimensions of the educational process: teaching, learning and the educational environment. They improve the autonomy of students, the conduction and guidance of the teacher, and the dynamization of the environment.

This article has proposed that the secondary cycle of education is a proper scenario to make explicit to the students new forms of learning, such as collaborative learning supported by electronic networks. High school students are getting ready for both a professional and a civic education. In the primary cycle they will have learned instinctively, but from this point on they should become more deliberate in their learning approaches. A teenager is in the midst of the "learning how to learn" phase, and this kind of tacit knowledge will be among the most valuable things they takes in their backpack when finishing high school, legally an adult for most purposes (i.e. with civic rights and responsibilities). Knowing how to learn will be an essential skill for the rest of their lives.

Bibliography

Denning, Stephen (2002). "Technical Cooperation and Knowledge Networks". In: Sakiko Fukuda-Parr; Carlos Lopes; Khalid Malik (ed.). *Capacity for Development: New Solutions to Old Problems.* (pp. 229-246). United Nations Development Programme, New York

Duart, Josep M.; Sangrà, Albert. (1999). "Formación universitaria por medio de la web : un modelo integrador para el aprendizaje superior". En: Duart, J.M.; Sangrà,A. *Aprenentatge i Virtualitat* (pp. 23-49). Barcelona: Ediuoc-Proa

Duart, Josep M (2003). Educar en valores en entornos virtuales de aprendizaje: realidades y mitos. UOC, <http://www.uoc.edu/dt/20173/index.html

Guitert, Montse; Coderch, Jorge. (2001)."¿Como aprender y enseñar con Internet? " *Cuadernos de Pedagogía, 301* (pp. 56-63)

Moore, Michael C. (2002). "A personal view: Distance education, Development, and the problem of Culture in the Information Age". En: Venugopal Reddy, V; Manjulika, S. (ed.). *Towards virtualization: open distance learning.* (pp. 634-640). Kogan Page India, Pvt. Ltd

Peters, Otto (2000). "Digital Learning Environments: New Possibilities and Opportunities". *International Review of Research in Open and Distance Learning.* Vol. 1, no. 1

Raschke, Carl A. (2003) *The digital revolution and the Coming of the Postmodern University.* Routledge Farmer. London. Chapter 3, pp. 26–38

Resnick, Mitchel. (2002). "Rethinking Learning in the Digital Age". In *The Global Information Technology Report: Readiness for the Networked World*, edited by G. Kirkman. Oxford University Press. (pp. 32-37) < http://www.cid.harvard.edu/cr/pdf/gitrr2002_ch03.pdf>

Werry, Chris (2001) "The work of Education in the Age of E-college". *First Monday, Peer Review Journal of the Internet*, vol. 6, no. 5, May 2001, <http://www.firstmonday.org/issues/issue6_5/Werryy/index.html>

Web sites

World Links <http://www.world-links.org> Established by the World Bank in 1997, later becoming an independent foundation. It is a well-known project aimed at integrating ICT into education in developing countries, and promoting intra-school communication and collaboration around the world.

MIT Media Lab <http://www.mwdia.mit.edu> Founded by Nicholas Negroponte and others in MIT en 1980, houses one of the main research centres in the world dedicated to the interactions of technology and the human being.

BUILDING THE DEVELOPING NATIONS' UNIVERSITIES INTO THE ICT FOR DEVELOPMENT STRATEGY

Royal D. Colle

According to United Nations data, HIV/AIDS kills 6,000 people daily. Another 8,200 people are infected with the virus daily. Each year, 300-500 million people are infected with malaria, and approximately 3 million die as a result. The data continue on and on documenting the need for mobilizing forces, including information and communication technologies, to improve the welfare of the world's poorest people. We need bold action by the United Nations ICT Task Force and others to move nations along the path of information and communication technologies (ICTs) for development. Ideally, bold action would result in institutional changes that extend beyond the period of good intentions and the initial enthusiasm surrounding rhetorical declarations of goals. The Task Force's Eighth Meeting linking ICT and education is an appropriate place to consider the role that higher education – including both universities and institutes – might play in the ICT for development movement.

With the exception of technical connectivity issues, computer training, and distance learning courses for college level students, the record of higher education in information and communication technologies for development is dismal.[1] The record of university involvement with ICTs and the Millennium Development Goals is also virtually invisible. In regard to supporting and helping sustain community telecentres, universities are widely perceived as irrelevant – if they are even considered at all.

In India, the National Alliance for Information and Communication Technologies for Basic Human Needs came into being about a year ago. The National Alliance set a goal of bringing all of India's 600,000 villages into the modern "information society" by 2007, the 60th anniversary of the nation's independence. The National Alliance hopes to achieve its "Mission 2007" primarily through the creation of a network of "rural knowledge centers" (telecentres) across the country.[2] A proposal to an Alliance leader

---

[1] A substantial number of students have studied in distance learning courses throughout the world. The five largest programmes are based in developing countries. See The Task Force on Higher Education and Society, *Higher Education in Developing Countries, Peril and Promise*, The World Bank, Washington, 2000, p. 31.

[2] The programme was described by M.S. Swaminathan, Chairman of the National Commission of Farmers, at the 5th Annual Baramati Initiative on ICT and Development, March 3-6, 2005.

that the agricultural universities in India be explicitly included in the planning as partners for the knowledge centres received this terse response:

> "The universities have failed miserably in many respects. Most university faculty have no clue to life outside the campus nor have they any social concerns. Sorry for being very forthright or even blunt."

Yet a recent two-year study commissioned by the World Bank and UNESCO concluded that the contribution of higher education to social and economic development in developing countries has been "disappointing to date" including a failure to advance the public interest. One of the major obstacles is that "the social and economic importance of higher education systems is insufficiently appreciated" (p.93).[3]

In a recently-published paper Harvard University professor Calestus Juma suggests that "we need to reinvent the African university" so that universities can serve as engines of both community development and social renewal.

Universities and Telecentres

Telecentres are important in the discussion of ICTs and education because they are emerging all over the developing world: Taiwan, Vietnam, China, India and many other countries in Africa and Latin America. Typically a multi-purpose community telecentre is a public facility in the community that affords people the opportunity to use computers, networks, copiers, scanners, telephone, printed materials and audio and video resources for information searching, communication, training, and entertainment.

The services are free or available at an affordable cost. The primary mission of a telecentre is community service as compared to a cybercafé whose primary mission is profit. A telecentre has staff – often volunteers – who actively assist the public in solving information and communication problems. Ideally, the telecentre management also collaborates with other institutions such as those in agriculture, health, government, and education to mobilize information, training and distance learning resources.

Telecentres can be a local institution that parallels the local school system, providing a learning resource for reaching the rural and urban poor and millions of others, mostly in rural areas, who have been overlooked by the conventional education system.

There are important connections between universities and telecentres. First, a very large percentage of telecentres struggle for survival. The reasons vary, but prominent among them is the failure for telecentres to be demand-driven. This happens because telecentre people often lack an understanding of the communities' information, education and training needs, and the telecentre managers often lack the know-how and resources to build the content and services that could respond to those needs. There are four specific ways in which higher education can contribute to the sustainability of telecentres that – unlike cybercafés – have a community development mission.

---

[3] The Task Force on Higher Education and Society, *Higher Education in Developing Countries, Peril and Promise*, The World Bank, Washington, 2000

Research: Research helps telecentres become demand-driven. Research can identify communities' needs for information and related services. Research must be a long-term process, not a single start-up activity, because needs change over time especially if the community is developing. Telecentres generally have neither the skills, time, motivation, nor interest in systematic research about the communities around them. Telecentres also need research to evaluate continuously how well they are serving the needs of their communities. Many universities have research capabilities that could be applied to these telecentre needs. Students and university faculties in a range of disciplines (from computer science to rural sociology) can apply their knowledge and training to ICT-related research that will better link telecentres to their communities.

Local and relevant content: Too much content on the Web is not relevant to farmers and other rural people, nor to urban slum-dwellers. It is a common problem around the world, where externally-generated information often dominates locally-tailored material. This is where credible, useful and user-friendly information needs to be crafted. The UNDP has suggested that the most important reason for the failure of telecentres is their lack of suitable content. Universities such as agricultural universities have access to science-based information that could be tailored to regional, provincial and local agronomic, social, linguistic, and cultural characteristics, and could be matched with many of the education and training requirements related to the Millennium Development Goals.

Universities are also in a good position to design and administer distance learning and self-paced learning packages that people can use to negotiate successfully in contemporary society. For example, a woman who lives in a Delhi slum studied embroidery in a six week course at the telecentre, and ended up teaching embroidery in the community. In south India the Tamil Nadu University of Veterinary and Animal Sciences has produced video CDs on subjects ranging from remedial measures for infertility in cattle to "Cream, Butter and Cheese", all designed for rural populations.

Information management: People in telecentres need to be trained in how information can contribute to development. There are telecentre managers who know a lot about computers but do not know how to link telecentre potential to health clinics for community health education, or to schools, agricultural extension, or local government. Likewise, telecentres need to make their communities aware of the value of information, such as agricultural marketing, micro enterprise management, or the chances for more education through distance learning. Awareness of the value of information will help the communities realize the value of the telecentre. Universities have the capacity to teach and train, and these skills could be applied to these telecentre-related needs.

Human resources: Telecentres need volunteers who can help make telecentres good places to visit – volunteers who can help people search and understand the basic rewards of a digital experience and help those people navigate the various media in the telecentre. A major challenge for telecentres is to "gain, train, and retain" volunteers. Those in touch with today's young people are aware that they generally have the media and digital skills to be good volunteers – especially college students. Volunteers are important in welcoming persons in special groups such as women and the elderly who are frequently shut out of access to ICTs and telecentres by culture. Universities have human resources such as students who could serve as telecentre interns, and faculty members who could serve as content and development advisors.

Benefits to Universities

In addition to the benefits that they can bring to telecentres, the universities can benefit from an affiliation with telecentres, in at least three ways:

1. Telecentres provide universities with a means for reaching beyond their "ivory tower" to extend their knowledge and learning resources to the surrounding communities and to other populations in the region. This includes translating, adapting, localizing and re-packaging information from external sources to fit the agronomic and cultural characteristics of those local communities. This function is especially vital to the worldwide priorities identified in the Millennium Development Goals. Ultimately this makes universities more relevant and better candidates for support from the public and private sector.

2. Telecentres provide a laboratory for faculty and researchers to carry out ICT and extension-related research and development (R&D) projects, involving issues ranging from HIV/AIDS to small business enterprises and poverty alleviation, and to universities' involvement with these issues. Telecentres as extensions of the classroom can also strengthen student understanding of issues ranging from computer applications and community development to e-government and e-commerce.

3. Telecentres provide a learning environment for student volunteers to gain practical experience in helping people in the community. In some countries college graduates have a public service obligation for one or two years. While it is often associated with military service, attention can be drawn to adding community service in telecentres as a means for discharging this obligation.

An active, visible and successful university ICT for development programme can have two additional outcomes. One is the simultaneous building of the university's own internal ICT infrastructure – that is, its information and communication technology development – which will contribute to the quality and efficiency of its academic and administrative functions. And second is the reshaping of its relationship to the outside world as a more active agent of change. This addresses the observation of the Task Force on Higher and Society that "unlike primary and secondary education, there is little in the way of a shared vision about the nature and the magnitude of the potential of contribution of higher education to development."

Case Studies

In conclusion, here are three examples of relevant initiatives by universities, the first two from India, and the third from Africa.

The first is a 1969 initiative in which the Ford Foundation helped build the capacity of the G. B. Pant University of Agriculture and Technology (then in Uttar Pradesh) to produce radio programmes for Indian farm families. Radio was the major ICT at that time. In producing complete radio programmes and delivering them on tape to an All India Radio station (in Rampur), the university became the first non-governmental body in India to supply programmes for public consumption. Was it sustainable? Now, 35 years later, the university serves more than 20 radio stations in the region with information especially for the agricultural sector

The second case comes from Tamil Nadu where support from Canada's International Development Research Centre increased the capacity of the TN University of Veterinary and Animal Sciences (TANUVAS) to incubate and support three village information centres and six additional information centres especially serving self-help women's groups. All are community-driven and some are fully supported by their surrounding communities. The university continues to play a partnership role through some training and advisory initiatives and supply of content. This was one of the case studies featured in a United Nations ICT Task Force publication prepared for the Geneva meeting of the WSIS.[5]

In Africa, according to Professor Calestous Juma, the University of Zambia was the midwife of Zamnet, the country's largest Internet provider. It is a "shining example", says Juma, of business incubation by a university. There are also universities in Brazil that provide examples of how universities can be effective forces in ICT for development.

Conclusion

Telecentres (also known by other names such as "rural knowledge centers") are important local institutions that can provide education, training and information for people not served by conventional educational institutions. Universities can help these telecentres become more demand-driven, and thereby contribute to telecentres' sustainability.

In the process of supporting multi-purpose telecentres, universities can educate students about the potential of ICT for development and train them to apply ICTs to development issues in their communities, and ultimately to support local and national policies that build ICT resources into health, education, government, and economic programmes.

In a very practical way, initiatives that build the ICT capacities of universities will influence the future character of higher education and help them become, and be perceived as, more relevant to the people of their countries.

There are two main challenges for the United Nations ICT Task Force. The first is to sponsor a rapid appraisal to clarify why universities are on the sidelines regarding ICT for development, and gain a general picture of what it will take to bring about institutional

[5] Royal Colle & Raul Roman, "University-Based Telecenters" in Akhtar Badshah, Sarbuland Khan and Maria Garrido (eds), *Connected for Development: Information Kiosks and Sustainability*, UN ICT Task Force Series 4 available at http://www.unicttaskforce.org/perl/documents.pl?id=1361

change. What will it take to "reinvent" the African university and those on other continents?

The second is to support efforts that demonstrate models of universities becoming involved in ICT for development. At this time, initiatives regarding universities and ICT for development are being framed in China, Vietnam, India and various parts of Africa, but they require a strong push in terms of core funding. The core funding can leverage other resources such as computers from the World Computer Exchange as well as funding and services from other agencies and the private sector. For example, a project in India seems on the threshold of obtaining support from a private bank's social responsibility programme. A project in Vietnam has been designed and awaits funding from an Asian foundation and a private sector agency in Taiwan.

An endorsement of the university ICT for development telecentre concept by the United Nations ICT Task Force – reinforced with funds for planning and/or core activities – would give visibility to the idea and motivate others to examine the logic of this approach.

Along with the World Summit on the Information Society and various stock-taking meetings associated with the Millennium Development Goals, action now by the Task Force to move boldly ahead to encourage higher education to become a more active player in the ICT for development environment can have far-reaching and long lasting implications for positive change in the world.

CONNECTING THE GENERATIONS: INSIGHTS, CHALLENGES AND OPPORTUNITIES

Dianne Davis

The whirl of globalization, the 21st century information highway, and the expectation of all generations require re-examining traditional and institutional approaches to education. Thinking "outside the box" has stimulated a new generation of innovations, benefits and opportunities not foreseen. Over the past few years, efforts have been made to introduce information and communication technologies (ICTs) as a key element to enhance the quality of life for all generations. Such initiatives have resulted in the positive impact of ICTs toward reducing poverty and isolation, activating local markets, supporting decentralization, improving the quality of education and healthcare, and introducing new populations to the complex area of the virtual world.

To stimulate new insights the following four C's: Content, Creativity, Connection and Curiosity have been considered as important essentials for meaningful and innovative community education and contributions toward achieving the Millennium Development Goals. These factors stimulate a local/cultural approach by promoting helpful interactions that enhance social and economic improvement.

Every month over 1 million people turn 60 years old globally, and 73% of this growth is occurring in the developing countries. New educational solutions and products are essential to address the "global sleeping giant: the agequake" which is fast approaching. By 2050, for the first time in history, the number of those over 60 will exceed the number of those under 15. ICTs as an instrument of change and as the enabler of the information/knowledge/learning society of the future can enrich and ensure an inclusive "society of all ages".

Beyond the issue of connectivity, telecentres provide an opportunity for accessing and using appropriate digital technologies to solve problems and to promote human development. The point of departure is not installing equipment and connections, but rather organizing the community so that it can resolve its specific problems, which may vary from one setting to the next. The best way of instilling a social vision into a telecentre is to plan it and establish it in a way that integrates it with other spaces and communication activities that are already operating successfully within the community. These will typically be community radio stations, public libraries, cultural centres, community organizations or schools.

Some of the fields in which community telecentres are contributing to human development are: employment and microenterprises; health (facilitating access to information about diseases and treatments, preventive medicine, alternative treatments, hygiene and sexual education); education (supporting school activities and promoting informal education within communities, particularly among children and youth); strengthening self-esteem (helping to improve people's perceptions of themselves, of their own abilities and their prospects for the future, enhancing creativity, self-esteem and teamwork); community organization (fostering new forms of neighbourhood organization, and strengthening individual and collective capacities, encouraging new leaders, and helping to resolve concrete problems and needs in the community, helping marginal groups; and urban planning (helping to organize community input into the planning and execution of housing projects, disaster prevention and mitigation, and improving public services and community facilities)

The following are examples of projects that have contributed to development of new mindsets regarding education and human capacity building.

First Nations communities computer network (Canada)

- *Insight: the technology is directed by and for the community*

- *Challenge: to find a balance which ensures that everyone benefits*

- *Opportunity: to serve remote communities with quality services and prevent effects from isolation.*

Keewaytinook Okimakanak (Northern Chiefs) is a small, not-for-profit organization in northwestern Ontario referred to as the "tribal council" by Indian and Northern Affairs Canada (INAC). It is led by the chiefs of the member First Nations (six small, remote communities) who serve as the Board of Directors. Back in 1994, it began the development of a computer communication network that would connect and serve the schools in each of these communities. That original bulletin board system has grown to become a regional and national broadband network and service provider.

The network is formally known as the Kuh-ke-nah Network of Smart First Nations, or K-Net for short. The name is an Oji-Cree expression for "everybody" and this is the goal of the network. The communities represented in the Keewaytinook Okimakanak (Northern Chiefs) tribal council are 49 First Nations across an area roughly the size of France with a population of 25,000. The majority is aboriginal and live in remote communities with 300-900 inhabitants. For many communities, the only year-round access into or out of their area is by small airplane, though most have winter road access for five or six weeks during the winter season. In less than a decade, K-Net has gone from one phone for 400 people to accessing broadband service from individual homes. The most important insight has been the importance of paying close attention to the *process*. The vision has grown because it meets the community's unique needs and demands.

Multipurpose community telecentres (Jamaica)

- *Insight: utilizing the library system as network base*

- *Challenge: enhancing basic telecentres into multipurpose community centres*

- *Opportunity: to facilitate affordable information technology access to the widest cross-section of the general public*

Following a survey of telecentres in Jamaica, seven categories of telecentres were identified. The concept of multipurpose telecentres has been embraced, but in practice there was found to be a need for the development of services and activities to extend these centres from into multipurpose telecentres. It is planned that the extension of these sources should be in keeping with the actual needs of the local communities. The programme is a partnership between the Government of Jamaica, the Jamaica Sustainable Development Networking Programme, the United Nations Development Programme, and the Post and Telecommunications Department of Jamaica. The University of the West Indies, Mona, Information Systems Unit and Cable and Wireless, Jamaica provide technical support.

The Information For All Advisory Committee decided to work in collaboration with the Jamaica Library Service, which manages the national public library network. The Jamaica Library Service has fourteen parish libraries, and over one hundred branch libraries, which make up the national network. The basis for the collaboration was the capacity of the Jamaica Library Service to meet the criteria identified. This was particularly related to the existence of local community support and infrastructure, which will ensure medium- to long-term sustainability of the two multipurpose telecentres. It was also expected that the experience in the development of the multipurpose telecentres would have a multiplier effect on related activities in the Jamaica Library Service Network, and in the development of telecentres in Jamaica.

It was agreed to identify two rural branch libraries where there had been some commitment by the Jamaica Library Service and the local community to the development of telecentres. The two selected would then be further developed into multipurpose telecentres.

The multipurpose community centre was intended to approximate a rural village general store to provide services in some or all of the following areas: public telecommunications and Internet services, information services, distance education, telemedicine, and banking, with the different services introduced in stages. The following sequence was recommended: upgrading of public telecommunications and Internet services to enable users to log on to the system more easily and to increase the speed of accessing information on the Internet; identification of electronic information sources related to concerns of the local community; regular updating and expansion of the website to incorporate more local information; implementation of training programmes for users and staff; and development of a new section of the website to show how relevant information in the library can be accessed by users within and outside the library.

Postal system ICT centres (Jamaica)

- *Insight:* use post offices as e-service access points as well as the courier for products.

- *Challenge:* resistance of communities to utilize kiosks for Internet access in a post office location.

- *Opportunity:* postal network is especially well positioned to provide reliable ICT-based services to low-income communities in both urban and rural communities.

The postal system has been encouraged by the public telephone system, which has been opened up to competition and an official regulator established to regulate telecommunications. A separate authority has been established to regulate and monitor the issuing and use of radio licenses to include satellite linkage and cellular telephones. Access to ICT facilities is provided for all communities, including those in rural areas as well as in poor urban areas. ICT are used to enhance education, health and national security. These government initiatives are being funded by the sale of cellular licenses. Given the rapid rate of technological change, the government has realized that it cannot provide all the necessary funding and public/private partnerships are necessary to ensure the long-term sustainability of the country's ICT infrastructure. Above all it recognizes the crucial role of the public sector promoting ICTs and the knowledge economy.

In Jamaica the postal network is well positioned to provide a reliable mechanism as the main carrier of ICT based services to communities, and in particular to low-income communities in both urban and rural areas. Over 600 postal service points are available to be equipped with ICT facilities. A wireless partnership with the major provider Cable and Wireless has seen the implementation of a pilot project at 30 locations. The main challenge faced has been the resistance of communities to utilize kiosks for Internet access in a post office location. Plans to utilize a wireless digital network have been put on hold pending an increase in usage.

The use of IT-based over-the-counter financial services has been growing, however, with over 60 locations offering bill payment, money transfer, e-cards and other transactions. The Post Office also expects to finalize an arrangement to use post office counters as collection points for Government taxes, which will result in an expansion of the IT network.

An e-commerce facility with a focus on rural entrepreneurs, many of whom are women, is now on the drawing board. This project, which is executed by the Ministry of Commerce, Science and Technology, will utilize post offices as e-service access points as well as the courier for products.

The post office network aims to be a key player in bridging the digital divide .The post offices in Jamaica are almost all run by women who have been attending training courses to be able to use the new technologies. Learning how to use the technologies has encouraged the women to take on greater responsibility and become more entrepreneurial. Many are drawing up their own business plans and using the newly acquired skills to enhance their income-earning capacity.

Multimedia for Caribbean Communities (Caribbean)

- *Insight*: *linguistic, educational and technical barriers are overcome by radio browsing*

- *Challenge*: *development of local content*

- *Opportunity*: *widely-shared access to technology while also reaching thousands through the broadcasting component.*

This regional project was launched in September 2002. Its aim is to bring information, knowledge-packaging and networking to people particularly in marginalized urban, rural and remote areas, using modern communication and information tools and the hands-on training required to run all aspects of their centres. UNESCO is transforming four existing community radio stations into Community Multimedia Centres, complete with added facilities such as at least one computer, fax, telephone, e-mail and Internet services for public access.

Needs analyses, equipment procurement, assessment of competence levels and Web site development have been carried out. A specialised training of trainers programme is on-going. Initial participating stations include Roots FM in partnership with Zink Link Internet café (Jamaica), Radio Toco (Trinidad and Tobago), Radio GED (Barbados) and Radio Cocodrilo (Cuba). The four centres constitute a core regional network which will be expanded to include other regional community radio stations at a later phase.

As these Community Multimedia Centres develop, they are expected to serve as a springboard for further community development activities such as distance learning, micro-lending schemes and electronic commerce.

Luz das Letras literacy programme (Brazil)

- *Insight*: *enhances the independence and self-esteem of participants. Consumer driven programmes hasten literacy*

- *Challenge*: *enhancing corporate responsibility in bridging the digital divide*

- *Opportunity*: *connecting virtually 100% of the rural population the state of Paraná via the distribution grids*

Luz das Letras is a literacy programme developed by the Companhia Paranaense de Energia (Copel), the energy company of the Brazilian state of Paraná.

The programme was designed to educate illiterate teenagers and adults using the computer as its main tool. Its success is directly related to providing for an immediate feedback facility incorporated in the programme that encourages constructive, evaluative and interactive learning.

Developed with a multidisciplinary approach, the software is available free of charge to interested organizations, provided they have the necessary infrastructure and interested students. Using computer-based teaching there is no standardization of materials, allowing students to move forward as they feel ready. Computer-literate members are encouraged to return as teachers.

The programme promoted the establishment of local partnerships among NGOs, city administrators and offices, churches, universities and private companies. It encourages social work and bridges the gap among individuals. By 2003, over 1,413 students had received an education in the states of Paraná, Santa Catarina, São Paulo, Roraima and Goiás. Important to note: 294 older computers are being used instead of wasted. Also, 7.5 tons of paper have been spared according to calculations of how much paper is normally used in teaching.

Social benefits include enhanced individual and group confidence, ability and status. Most important, each student develops a sense of pride that they can read information by themselves. The dropout rate is virtually zero, because of the community spirit of all the stakeholders. Participation by the community is increased as a result of the flexibility of the learning process. Content relates to the needs of participants.

Street children and telecentres (Ecuador)

- *Insight: ICT can empower street children by providing economic and educational opportunities*

- *Challenge: Decrease tension between children and parents*

- *Opportunity: Opens doors and increases motivation for additional areas of information and training*

Sustainable telecentres in Esmeraldas, located on the coast of Ecuador, are a perfect example of "out of the box" thinking in resolving a universal problem. Today, after four years, over 200 street children who were given ICT training by the Fundación ChasquiNet are running telecentre. Self-motivated, they learned to read and write because they wanted to use the computers. This empowering programme indirectly enhanced their overall education. They were interested in using on-line courses mostly concerned with electronics, but the challenge is to find courses for them in non-electronic fields like midwifery, accounting, nursing, etc.

Moreover, besides opening several telecentres, they did not stop there; first they copied software and sold it on the street, then they opened a music recording studio to record and produce CDs with local marimba music that they sell. Often the children earn more money than their parents and social tension results. Thus, the programme should include coordination with education and jobs for their parents if at all possible.

Education Connectivity Programme (Uruguay)

- *Insight:* trilateral partnerships can be forged among government, sector users and private sector

- *Challenge:* how to maximize input of local content.

- *Opportunity:* creation of a new industry for production of local educational contents not previously available, thus encouraging educators to be involved in human services and ICT in the country and region.

The Educational Connectivity Programme (ECP) is a combined effort among Uruguayan institutions: the Presidency of the Republic, the National Board of Education (ANEP) and the National Telecommunications Administration. The Information Technology for Development Division (SDS/ICT) at the Inter-American Development Bank took an active part in its design, implementation and assessment.

The ECP was designed to provide Internet connectivity to public education institutes, train the teachers in the use of technology and contents and provide an initial site of educational contents on-line, starting the development of an incipient industry of educational content.

With a number of prospective beneficiaries totaling more than 750,000 public education students and more than 40,000 teachers, its main starting goals were largely overcome only after a few months from the beginning. The e-inclusion of future generations in the educational environment and the teachers' training has improved: for the first, a more promising future and for the latter, a substantial improvement in working conditions. The availability of educational contents, besides being an innovative event in the country, will have a direct effect on the educational curriculum, determining new directions and turns in the conservative educational trends that have not changed for decades.

The ECP is a clear example of how social and economic development can be made possible through ICTs. These technologies are the core of the operation. They have facilitated all the aspects of the follow-up and communication processes among actors geographically separated that would have been impossible by other means.

The programme also allows primary, secondary and technical Uruguayan educational systems to access the ICTs as instruments of the teaching-learning process.

Through the programme 5.000 teachers, 12.5% of the total number, have been trained in the educational use of ICTs; retired teachers were also reached and included; 335,000 public education students, 45% of the total number in the country, have access to the information society through their respective educational institutes; a new contents industry has been started by the teachers' concern to elaborate educational content relevant to the Uruguayan curriculum. Through competitions, more than 100 applications have been received.

Likewise, the production of local educational content has started an industry which was not previously developed in the country or the region. More than 4,000 pieces of educational content have been elaborated by public school teachers, more than 20 teachers have been rewarded in competitions and more than 100 pieces of content are already available in digital format for use in educational curricula. These are significant achievements that are totally new in the region.

Rural high-tech village, Yamada (Japan)

- *Insight: bring new life to a remote village*

- *Challenge: encouraging youth to return to village*

- *Opportunity: to create a cyber "town square".*

By connecting the generations, new life and economic recovery was brought to a remote Japanese village. The ICT enabling tool was Web site training developed by a few young technophiles with a government grant. For years, the village's young moved away leaving only the older people behind; now, young family members are returning seeing new opportunities. All are connected through the village's central server, a cyber version of a town square. For the first time in decades the population has stopped declining and outsiders are moving in. Farmers and pensioners claim to have the most wired community in Japan. Most importantly this new technology has fought off loneliness during the long winters. The most popular village event has been weekly sessions on Web site construction.

It is clearly not true that older people cannot learn to use a computer. Mr. Nobu Tanaka, 83, proudly states that he used to have trouble changing channels on his TV. But now he has his own Web page, chats with friends and neighbours, and finds the use of ICT for medical purposes most important in the convenience of sending information about his health to his doctor.

2005 ICT Student Design Competition

- *Insight: develop awareness of older persons' needs and contribution*

- *Challenge: stimulate inclusion of all ages in the Knowledge Society*

- *Opportunity: develop new solutions, hardware and software products.*

In response to addressing inclusion of the "graying society" in the information society, the International Council for Caring Communities has organized a 2005 ICT Student Design Competition as a means of fostering practical research among the next generation of professionals. University students from all regions of the world working in ICT research, design, application development and/or implementation are encouraged to apply their creative talents toward solutions that promote and enable the effective use of ICTs by older persons.

The competition is aimed at addressing unique and practical solutions adapted to reflect the situation in their or other specific regions. It emphasizes researching existing communities and endeavors to connect the generations resulting in new thinking and awareness. Awards will be presented at the World Summit for the Information Society in Tunisia, followed by an exhibition and discussion of winning students' insights at an international conference, "Caring Communities for the 21st Century: Imagining the Possible". This will be held on 10 February 2006 during the Commission for Social Development at United Nations Headquarters in New York.

NEW TECHNOLOGIES AND SOCIAL CHANGE: LEARNING IN THE GLOBAL CYBERAGE[1]

Bertram C. Bruce

Rapid technological change; social barriers breaking and re-forming; large scale immigration leading to a multicultural society; globalization of the economy; questions about the future of democracy; and major changes in literacy practices. Such a list comprises but a few of the touchstones for current discourse about the context of twenty-first century education. As we consider educational practices around the world we cannot avoid the conclusion that we are in a time of great change. Furthermore, we find ourselves questioning the traditional ways of teaching and learning, which seem outmoded in an age defined by the worldwide Web, biotechnology, and globalization.

In this context, there is a need for learning that builds upon the diverse experiences of learners, is open to change, and extends beyond the walls of the classroom and the standard curriculum. Learning based on inquiry in the face of new phenomena is more appropriate in these times than learning with limited and pre-established goals. Fortunately, the new technological context not only challenges the educational system, but offers new opportunities for this kind of learning. In order to understand better both the challenges and the opportunities, it is helpful to turn first, not to the latest *Scientific American* or *Wired* magazine, but to events of a century ago.

A New World in the Early Twentieth Century

The changes we see before us today have remarkable counterparts in the period of the turn from the nineteenth to the twentieth century. In fact, a case can be made that that period represents not only a forerunner, but a more marked example of each of the changes itemized above.

During the late nineteenth and early twentieth centuries, technological change transformed American life. The industrial revolution brought factories, and in turn the growth of urban areas. The family farm transformed with the introduction of mechanical harvesters, plows, and other equipment. Railroads, and later the automobile, reshaped the landscape, bringing distant points together and changing the social order.

---

[1] This article was originally published in L. Bresler & A. Ardichvili (Eds.), Research in international education: Experience, theory, and practice (pp. 171-190). New York: Peter Lang. The author would like to thank Ann Bishop for a number of helpful comments and suggestions on an earlier draft of this chapter.

Although we talk of today as the era of changes in the arena of information and communication technologies, a good case can be made that the earlier period experienced more dramatic changes. The telegraph and telephone for the first time made nearly instant communication possible across long distances. New techniques for recording and transmitting audio and video were embodied in the phonograph, the radio, and motion pictures.

Corresponding changes occurred in every domain. For example, this was one of the greatest periods in the history of children's literature. As Lewis (1998) details, the reduction of social barriers, the advent of compulsory education, and changes in the technologies of publishing essentially established new forms of literacy: Towards the end of the nineteenth century compulsory education for children, the invention of lithography, mechanical paper making and cloth binding coincided to enable the standardised mass production of books, which meant the possibility of greater quantities of any book and the consequent reduction of cost, the possibility of colour illustration and the wider attraction of books to a mass literate population.

The period of a century ago saw rapid social change as well along, with these technological changes. The emancipation of slaves did not result in equality for African Americans, but it did begin the long, unfinished process of their inclusion in mainstream American life. The women's movement of that time paralleled the struggle of African Americans. Meanwhile, massive immigration, especially in the early twentieth century, redefined the mix of languages and cultures in the country. The rate of immigration then was more than double that of recent years in the US.

These changes occurred at a time when the US was very much a player on the global stage, much more so than it is today. It is an important fact – though often misunderstood – that globalization is a return to normal for the American economy. Between 1890 or so and 1914, America was the world's biggest trading economy except for Britain. A very large proportion of the economy was either imports or exports. There were massive direct investments, which dwarf the level of foreign investment seen now (Smoler, 1998, pp. 65-66).

The combination of shifting demographics, new social relations, new technologies, and awareness of the international context led educators of that era to seek more appropriate means to support learning. Beyond the structural changes, which began the move toward compulsory education for all, educators recognized the need for learning that was more flexible and responsive to change. Mass literacy was seen as necessary for a technologically advanced economy that needed to interact with Europe, and increasingly, other parts of the world. The public library movement grew (Minow, 1997), enabled by Andrew Carnegie, as people saw the need for learning for all. Schools grew and began to serve a larger percentage of students for a longer period of their lives.[2]

---

[2] These movements were not solely in service of greater democracy. Libraries and advanced education also tended to shore up the class system by delineating the educated elites. Although new libraries and extended education for the masses created new learning opportunities, they also had a crucial function of fashioning 'civilized' production workers (see Bowles & Gintis, 1976, 1980).

Meanwhile, pragmatism provided the philosophical basis for the commonsense views that knowledge is ever-changing and that the future consequences of our beliefs need to be considered as much as their antecedents. It led to the progressive movement in education, built in large part upon the work of John Dewey, who articulated an educational philosophy which saw the need to build a more inclusive society with methods appropriate to the new contexts for learning.

A Twenty-First Century Reprise?

A consideration of the US society at the start of the last century does not lend much credence to the view that we are in an unprecedented time of globalization, technological change, and societal disruption. Quite the opposite: the changes of today all have precursors, and in most cases, the evidence is that the earlier period was more tumultuous. There was more immigration, more significant inventions, more social change, and greater consequences for education.

Does that mean then that the millennial headlines are all hyperbole? That the era of a globalized, technologized society is nothing new or noteworthy? Not exactly. There are reasons to think that what we see today could presage even greater changes than those experienced a century earlier.

For example, no one can discount the enormous impact of the new modes of communication introduced around the turn of the last century. Having achieved near light speed, one might see further developments as mere embellishments. And yet, the World Wide Web may surprise us even more than it has already.

Through what is called *convergence*, the Web/Internet is now becoming the fusion of all the communication technologies. Already we have print, graphics, databases, e-mail, fax, radio, and video available through a Web browser. The tools to access these technologies are becoming less expensive and more widely available throughout the world. Moreover, these technologies, once one-way, are becoming two-way, meaning that any individual or group can become a producer as well as a consumer. For example, one site alone[3] offers 29,119 radio stations from around the world through the Web (as of February 26, 2001). It already claims 75 million listeners.

Similarly, although the US is now more self sufficient economically, the trend of increased globalization appears irreversible. Already, multinational corporations act as supra-governments, controlling the movement of labor and environmental decisions. Work that was once tied to locale and culture can now be redirected overnight to sites around the world. This has led to the concept of umbrella cultures that transcend any local or nationally-based cultures. Asea Brown Boveri Ltd. (ABB) is a $36 billion-a-year multinational corporation divided into 1,300 companies in 140 countries; no one national group accounts for more than 20 percent of its employees. Percy Barnevik, the former CEO of the company, explained that his best managers were moved around periodically so that they and their families could develop "global personalities" by living and growing up in different countries. ABB management teams, moreover, were never composed of

---

[3] http://www.live365.com/

employees from any one country. Barnevik said that this encouraged a "cross-cultural glue." (Kaplan, 1997, p. 72).

What will be the consequences of a world of "global personalities"? Will it lead to greater peace? To more global understanding? Or do its threats to the cultural strengths and diversities of the world challenge democratic societies? Going further, Kaplan (1997) asks whether democracy was just a moment in history that will be replaced by other political formations through continuing globalization.

Meanwhile, demands for *knowledge workers* (Drucker, 1994) or *symbolic analysts* (Reich, 1991) have led to a renewed interest in lifelong learning. The new worker will supposedly need to understand more of the work process and to see work as inseparable from continual learning and re-learning. In *post-capitalism*, work will be more meaningful than in the *Fordist* economy based on assembly-line manufacturing. The extent to which this happens for the majority of workers remains to be seen (see critique in Gee, Hull, & Lankshear1(1996).

At the beginning of the last century we saw movements in education that served to open up possibilities for learners and to lay the basis for engaged citizenship. These very same movements also served to assimilate immigrant and rural workers into an increasingly mechanized and urbanized economy, by inculcating political and social values.

It is not surprising that at the beginning of this century we see similar conditions and a similar emphasis on education. The 2000 US Presidential election saw that as one of its major themes. As in the previous era, the energy derives in part from a sense that a normalizing education is needed to maintain the social order against the "disruptive" forces of immigration, new technologies, a changing economy, and new social relations. There are thus calls for restoring fundamental values in schooling and for increased accountability of students, teachers, and schools. A thorough account of how new technologies are re-shaping education on a global scale would need to explore the role they play in standardizing curricula and assessment for these purposes. Their major effect may be in reinforcing the normalizing function of schooling through on-line learning, computerized testing, and control of publication.

At the same time, the conditions of the present environment call for a renaissance in inquiry-based learning. The explosion in information now encompassing music, video, on-line databases, and other media demands new abilities to Integrate knowledge from multiple sources. It also requires citizens to think critically about information that can be found nearly instantaneously throughout the world. New forms of collaboration are both enabled by and required by new communication and information technologies. Many say that the need now is not so much to solve problems, in the sense of solving well-structured puzzles of the kind seen in textbooks, but rather, to engage with a complex situation and to turn the messiness of that situation into a problem that can be solved; thus, to find problems rather than just to solve them. And the age-old emphasis on learning how to learn becomes ever more relevant in a rapidly changing technological and cultural environment. These soft skills (Murnane & Levy, 1996) will be increasingly important in today's Internet world.

In order to make our way through the complex and dynamic set of issues associated with the new information and communication technologies and their impact on education in this century, we will use the inquiry cycle described above. Four examples, one each of Investigation, Creation, Discussion, and Reflection show how learners are making use of new resources in response to the new challenges of the twenty-first century.

Inquiry-Based Learning Through New Media

The fact that new information technologies have created bounteous opportunities to learn about the most obscure phenomena is now a commonplace. Most people in the US are now familiar to some degree, for example, with the variety of resources offered by the World Wide Web. But Internet content is considerably more diverse and much more extensive than most users realize. For one thing, the Web (HTTP protocol) is only a subset of Internet content. Other protocols include FTP (file transfer protocol), e-mail, news, Telnet and Gopher (BrightPlanet, 2001).

More Than You Know

Considering the Web alone, we can see a remarkable number of documents – text files, data sets, images, audio, and video. By some measures, the Web is approaching the size of the 20 million volumes of the US Library of Congress, although within that total are many duplicates and broken links. The Web currently contains an estimated 1 billion documents, a figure growing at the rate of 1.5 million documents per day (Inktomi, 2000). The search engines cannot keep up. The largest in terms of indexed files is Fast,[4] which claims to list 300 million documents.

But what has been called the *surface Web* is only a part of the story. The *deep Web* – information that is accessible through the Internet, but not through HTTP, is considerably larger. A study by BrightPlanet (2001) found that "public information on the deep Web is currently 400 to 550 times larger than the commonly defined World Wide Web... A full 95% of the deep Web is publicly accessible information – not subject to fees or subscriptions."

A few of the largest of the deep Web sites identified in the BrightPlanet study are shown below:

- National Climatic Data Center (NOAA)
  http://www.ncdc.noaa.gov/ol/satellite/satelliteresources.html – satellite images of the earth showing hurricanes, fires, volcanoes, snowstorms, and more

- Alexa http://www.alexa.com/ – a Web navigation tool that provides price comparisons, links to similar Web sites, address and phone number for sites, traffic ranking, news related to the site. and reference search on Merriam-Webster Dictionary and Thesaurus, Encyclopedia Britannica, Yellow Pages, White Page

---

[4] http://www.alltheweb.com

- Right-to-Know Network (RTK Net) http://www.rtk.net/ – "free access to numerous databases, text files, and conferences on the environment, housing, and sustainable development. ...you can identify specific factories and their environmental effects; analyze reinvestment by banks in their communities; and assess people and communities affected."

- MP3.com http://www.mp3.com/ – access to thousands of compressed digital audio files using the MPEG3 format; music of every country and genre

- Terraserver http://terraserver.microsoft.com/ – images of every location in the US and many in other parts of the world

- US Trademarks http://www.uspto.gov/tmdb/ – "more than 2.9 million pending, registered and dead federal trademarks."

- US Patents http://www.uspto.gov/patft/ – "Full text of all US patents issued since January 1, 1976, and full-page images of each page of every US patent issued since 1790."

- JSTOR Project http://www.jstor.org/ – on-line access to over 100 journals

What this massive collection of information means is that resource-based learning, long advocated by many educators, can become a practical reality for students throughout the world.

Learning about Sarawak

Consider just one example. Suppose we wanted to learn about Sarawak, that strip on the northwest coast of Borneo, which is a state of Malaysia. We could go to just one site, that of the Sarawak Tourism Office[5] and learn: [Sarawak's] rainforest... houses the world's richest and most diverse ecosystem. It is also home to the world's largest flower, the Rafflesia, the size of a coffee table, squirrels and snakes that fly, deer the size of cats, plants that eat insects (and small mammals) and species of flora and insects still waiting to be discovered... [It] is home to 27 ethnic groups; people each with their own distinct language, culture and lifestyle. ...[It also has] the world's most extensive cave system, 310 kilometers of passages.

The visitor to the site can take a virtual tour of cities and towns in Sarawak, or make an on-line visit to each of the many national parks. For example, we learn that "Lambir Hills [Park] is the world's most ecologically diverse area. Just a sample 52 hectares of the park's 7,000 hectares revealed 1,050 different species of tree, and each tree supports 1,000 species of insect life... Its forest is home to gibbons, tarsiers, bearded pigs, flying squirrels, deer and 157 types of bird."

---

[5] http://www.sarawaktourism.com/

At Niah National Park we learn that "Humans inhabited Niah Great Cave 40,000 years ago. Today, local Penan tribesmen venture into the cave to collect edible birds nests and the guano dropped by the myriad swiftlets and bats that live there."

From the site, one can link to various on-line newspapers as well, such as the *Sarawak Tribune*,[6] the *Borneo Post*,[7] or *The Star*.[8] Students could spend days studying the information on culture, history, and people of Sarawak, without even leaving this one site, and could discover additional opportunities to learn if they were to follow the links from there to other sources. For example, there are photos showing the making of *Pua Kumbu* – the famous double-ikat blanket. This is considered the most prized of Sarawakian handicrafts: "Traditionally woven by Iban women, acclaimed as the finest weavers in all of Borneo, Pua Kumbu is made from individually dyed threads on a back strap loom. It is a unique form of weaving, not only in technique, but also in design. The manufacturing of tie and dye materials is known as *kayau indu*, or 'women's war'."

Although one could explore this single site for a long time, the beauty of the Web is that one can quickly access additional sources. For example, you could go to the *Rengah Sarawak* site,[9] which has similar images of cultural production, supplemented with videos. You can see Sarawak images and listen to *Besati meh*, a Sarawak community song.[10]

Rengah Sarawak is a Penan language phrase meaning "Sarawak News", but although its site is an on-line paper, there is no link to it from the Sarawak Tourism site. That may be related to their mission statement. The second Web site contains stories and information about and related to the various struggles in Sarawak, one of the two East Malaysian States in the northern part of the island of Borneo. This site is the result of combined efforts by several Sarawak NGOs and communities to bring views and information on and about the people's struggles directly to the Internet community and beyond. The authors of the site state: "We aim to give you an accurate and alternative picture of what is happening here – mainly stories from and about communities, as well as those from NGOs."

One of the articles on the site (Joe, 2000) shows images of people, not unlike those on the Tourism Office site. But it also talks of the political struggles currently underway. Developmental projects such as roads, mining, logging, mono-crop plantations, dams, airports and golf courses have led to the loss of land and resources among many indigenous communities not only in Sarawak. At the same time, the traditional social, religious and political systems have undergone great stress as systematic proselytisation, centralised government decision-making, centralised education systems and the mass media have imposed themselves in obvious and subtle ways.

These two sites, Sarawak Tourism and *Rengah Sarawak*, are similar in many ways. They both help a Web visitor gain some understanding of the geology, biology, history, culture, economics, language, politics, art and music of Sarawak. The images and videos,

---

[6] http://www.jaring.my/tribune/
[7] http://www.borneopost.com/
[8] http://www.thestar.com.my/
[9] http://www.rengah.c2o.org/sarawak/
[10] http://www.rengah.c2o.org/ram/besati-meh.ram

though no substitute for the direct experience of a physical visit, do provide a feel for a fascinating region. Even a brief exploration raises all sorts of questions about rain forests, economic development, and cultural representation, any of which might be pursued through endless other sites and non-Web resources. Investigating through the Web in this way reminds us that the vision John Dewey and Lucy Sprague Mitchell had of geography as the organizing frame for the curriculum is potentially more powerful than ever before.

Telling Sarawak's Story

Our brief look at a couple of Web sites about Sarawak reminds us that it is important to assess the author's purpose when interpreting any information. The importance of this principle is amplified when we look at the Web as a whole. The diversity of stories it holds provides a strong reminder that different purposes lead to different constructions of meaning. It is also increasingly evident that the stories of people throughout the world are not always told by the people themselves (Bruce, 1999).

In the case of Sarawak, we see this pattern in the extreme. Consider the highland village of Bario, which has no phones or, for that matter, public electricity. When researchers polled 140 villagers a year ago, only one had even heard of the Internet, while fewer than 30 had heard of computers. The only way to get to the village is by a daily 20-seat flight, or by trekking through the jungle for a week (McFarland, 2000).

Bario is of course not alone. There is less than one telephone for every 1,000 people in most rural areas throughout the world. All the developing countries of the world put together own only 4% of the world's computers. Tokyo alone has more telephones than the entire African continent (Harris, 2001).

These realities show that the World Wide Web is far from worldwide, either in terms of access to the information it contains or in terms of the ability to create and influence the information that is there. But there are various projects underway to extend Internet access. Universiti Malaysia Sarawak (UNIMAS) has one in Sarawak in which they are pioneering waterborne Net surfing. They will provide a boat, an Internet boat, which will cruise the Rajang River, docking at villages every few hours to teach residents how to use computers and the Internet (Reuters, 2000).

In another project, UNIMAS is creating E-Bario (Eagar, 2000; Harris, 2000). This will be a centre in which the local community can gain access to the Internet, telephone, fax and other facilities. Equipment will have to be carried in by plane or on the backs of water buffaloes. The aim is to promote economic and social development through increased access to information on government, health, education, recreation, entertainment, and agricultural practices. In addition, the centre will provide opportunities to create content. This will enable the ability to engage in electronic business and to develop new industries. There is also a crucial cultural component. Developers and Bario citizens see the chance to promote Kelabit culture and to create an electronic record on all things Kelabit, from genealogies to recordings of traditional songs and dances, as well as, stories and *adat* (tribal law). E-Bario thus exemplifies the contrasts of local/traditional and global/new that Friedman (2000) describes in his survey of globalization trends.

Part of E-Bario will be to create a *Malaysian smart school*[11] there. The smart school project is a country-wide effort to create a technology-supported education system, which will in turn produce an IT-literate population. It is hoped that this will establish Malaysia as a developed nation by the year 2020 and give it a competitive edge in the global economy. Each smart school will have at least a computer lab with student work in four subject areas.

The E-Bario project and the Internet boat are examples of attempts to make the Internet accessible to the majority of people in the world, not just to those in economically-privileged nations. They still have a long way to go toward providing anything approaching equal access. But they do open the door, not only to finding resources, but to making it possible for ordinary people to create resources, and thereby allowing people to tell their own stories to the world.

Inquiry-based Learning in Contexts of Change

The expanding diversity of mainstream American society, brought about both by immigration, and by opening doors to minorities and women who had been excluded earlier, put pressure on schooling to become more democratic, both in means and ends. It also highlighted the age-old fact that learning begins with the learner. The learner's previous experiences and needs are not just constraints on what can be taught well; they are the very foundation for learning.

The Cycle of Inquiry

This reality for teaching and learning is further articulated in Dewey's (1956) description of the four primary interests of the learner: investigation – the child's natural desire to learn; communication – the propensity to enter into social relationships; construction – the pleasure in creating things; and expression, or reflection – the desire to extract meaning from experience. Dewey saw these as the natural resources, the uninvested capital, "upon the exercise of which depends the active growth of the child." Figure 1 places these primary interests of the learner in the framework of a cycle of inquiry. For any question or problem, one may then think of activities of Investigation, Creation, Discussion, and Reflection as means for its resolution.

Figure 1: The Cycle of Inquiry

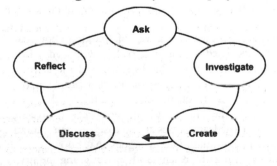

Although there are many nuances we might consider, for the purposes of this paper *inquiry-based learning* indicates a broad set of practices in which learners extract meaning from experience as they engage in efforts to address questions meaningful to them. These practices were central for progressive educators in their conception of the rapidly changing social fabric as both a challenge and an opportunity for democracy. They understood that democracy means active participation by all citizens in social, political and economic decisions that affect their lives. Inquiry was then not simply the process whereby an individual learns, but the means for a democratic society to continually renew itself. The education of engaged citizens, according to this perspective, involves two essential elements: (1) *Respect for diversity*, meaning that each individual should be recognized for his or her own abilities, interests, ideas, needs, and cultural identity, and (2) the development of *critical, socially engaged intelligence*, which enables individuals to understand and participate effectively in the affairs of their community in a collaborative effort to achieve a common good. These elements of progressive education have been termed "child-centred" and "social reconstructionist" approaches, and while in extreme forms they have sometimes been separated, in the thought of John Dewey and other major theorists they are seen as being necessarily related to each other (University of Vermont, 2001).

In the work of the progressive educators, these elements aimed toward fostering an attitude toward life that was experimental, questioning, and built more upon actual experiences than on tradition, authority, or established curricula. Lucy Sprague Mitchell, one of the founders of Bank Street College, expressed this well: "Our aim is to help students develop a scientific attitude towards their work and toward life. To us this means an attitude of eager, alert observations; a constant questioning of old procedure in light of new observations; a use of the world as well as of books as source material; an experimental open-mindedness; and an effort to keep as reliable records as the situation permits in order to base the future upon actual knowledge of the experiences of the past." (Lucy Sprague Mitchell, quoted in Bakken, 1999).

It is not difficult to see why the critical, socially-engaged intelligence that progressive education sought to foster could be threatening to the established order. As a result, the ideas that grew out of a reconstruction of traditional philosophy, and which called for a new moral and social order, were often reduced to no more than a set of methods which would allow the romanticized inner child to develop.

Inquiry Learning Today

The examples from Sarawak exemplify a way of thinking about curricula in relation to learning that Dewey articulated a century ago, but which may be even more relevant today. Rather than thinking of knowledge as static and the learner as an empty vessel whose job it is to absorb as much as possible of that pre-defined material, he saw the learner as an inquirer, learning through work on problems that were meaningful in the present circumstances. At the same time, the resources – objects, books, Web sites, curricular materials – that the learner uses are themselves representative of inquiry. As he did for so many other dichotomies, Dewey argues that books, curricula, disciplines, and technologies should be seen as representations of on-going inquiry, based on collective and historically-based understandings, but not fundamentally different from that of the individual learner. This is known as "psychologizing the curriculum". Aspects of curricula, even the driest textbook, can then be viewed not in opposition to the learner or to inquiry, but rather as another point on a continuum of inquiry.

The Web sites about Sarawak are then not material to be learned, but material in the process of being learned as they are created. As Dewey and Bentley (1949) might say they represent a "knowing" rather than "knowledge". Those who write these sites, where "write" means to produce text, images, sound, video, and interactive elements in hyperlinked documents, as well as those who read them, where "read" means to observe, study, and interact with them, are engaged in processes of investigating, creating, discussing, and reflecting, all the elements of the inquiry cycle shown in Figure 1. Learners today can be a part of these activities, and not merely passive participants destined to do no more than absorb the work of others. The Web is not a necessary technology for that shift in roles, but it invites it in a way traditional media do not.

The Inquiry Page

A site that makes the inquiry cycle more explicit is the Inquiry Page[12]. It is designed to help teachers weave a learner's interests with those of society by supporting them in sharing their successes and collective expertise (Bruce & Davidson, 1996; Bruce & Easley, 2000).

One aspect of the site is a tool for on-line creation of Inquiry Units by teachers (or by students). Each unit starts with a guiding question and provides a space for activities of Asking, Investigating, Creating, Discussing, and Reflecting. The user fills out a Web based form. When the unit is called up again by the same, or another user, it can be used as a guide for inquiry. A second teacher can *spin off* a copy of the unit, modifying it to fit new circumstances. Students can also do that, thus using the curriculum Inquiry Unit as a place for their own work. In this way, the site elides the lines between pre-established knowledge and knowledge-in-creation, between curriculum and student work, and between teacher and student, framing all of these as ongoing inquiries. The cycle presented in Figure 1 and employed in the Inquiry Page unit generator presents an idealized model for inquiry, not to constrain our account of inquiry, but rather to serve as a reminder of the range of activities that might be supported in a successful learning environment.

Conclusion

As Dewey recognized, schooling is not just about the individual. It is the coming together of the child's interests with those of the society, as manifested in the disciplines of the academy. These disciplines represent centuries of collective thought as well as the interests of the larger community in maintaining itself by communicating its knowledge and values to the next generation. Today, "society" or "the larger community" has come to mean the entire world. It is no longer viable to structure curriculum around a static and parochial view of the world.

---

[12] http://inquiry.uiuc.edu/

The globalization we see today in the economy, in cultural transformation, and in education has been accompanied by major technological changes. Whether these changes will someday be accounted as significant as those of the late nineteenth century, or as some say, comparable to that of mass printing, remains to be seen. Nevertheless, the changes are major, and have been both part and parcel of globalization.

These changes raise a number of important questions. What skills/knowledge/attitudes are needed in an environment seemingly changing along every dimension? What new forms of social arrangement will arise? What are the emerging alignments of power, communication, work? What are the new opportunities for learning? What kind of critique is needed? An article by Lester (2001) is telling here. Just as there is widespread agreement that personal privacy has eroded because of new technologies, such as video surveillance, monitoring of Web surfing, and data mining, there are signs that other new technologies are making it possible to maintain privacy at more secure levels than ever before. Zero-Knowledge,[13] for example, offers a tool suite to guarantee anonymous e-mail and Web surfing.

It is a daunting task to consider questions such as these, not only because of their complexity, but because conditions, particularly those associated with new technologies, change in unpredictable ways. Just as learners today need opportunities to develop their critical faculties through engagement with the dynamic complexities of new social relations and changing technologies, so do we in our efforts to assess and predict these changes and their implications for education. Rather than playing out well-established scripts, we need to frame those efforts as ongoing inquiries.

References

Antler, Joyce (1987). *Lucy Sprague Mitchell: The making of a modern woman.* New Haven, CT: Yale University Press.

Bakken, Marjorie (1999, March 23). *The new emphasis on standards and its effect on progressive educators.* Presentation Bank Street College of Education. [On-line http://www.bnkst.edu/html/news/speeches/Bakken.html]

Bijker, Wiebe E., Hughes, Thomas P., & Pinch, Trevor (Eds.) (1987). *The social construction of technological systems: new directions in the sociology and history of technology.* Cambridge, Ma.: MIT Press.

BrightPlanet (2001). *The deep web: Surfacing hidden value.* [On-line paper: http://www.completeplanet.com/]

Bruce, B. C. (1999, February). How worldwide is the web? *Journal of Adolescent and Adult Literacy, 42*(5), 382-385. http://www.readingonline.org/electronic/jaal/Feb_Column.html

[13] http://www.zeroknowledge.com/

Bruce, B. C., & Davidson, J. (1996). An inquiry model for literacy across the curriculum. *Journal of Curriculum Studies, 28*(3), 281-300.

Bruce, B. C., & Easley, J. A., Jr. (2000). Emerging communities of practice: Collaboration and communication in action research. *Educational Action Research, 8*(2), 243-259.

Dewey, J. (1956). *The child and the curriculum & The school and society.* Chicago: University of Chicago Press. (Original works published 1902 and 1915)

Dewey, J., & Bentley, A. F. (1949). *Knowing and the known.* Boston: Beacon.

Drucker, P. F. (1994, November). The age of social transformation. *Atlantic Monthly,* pp. 53-80.

Eagar, Toni (2000). *Potential applications and challenges of electronic business in Bario.* [On-line http://www.unimas.my/fit/roger/Toni/Home.htm]

Ellul, Jacques (1964). *The technological society.* New York: Vintage.

Friedman, T. L. (2000). *The Lexus and the olive tree.* New York: Random House.

Gee, J. P., Hull, G., & Lankshear, C. (1996). *The new work order: Behind the language of the new capitalism.* Boulder, CO: Westview.

Harris, Roger W. (2001). *Internet access by remote communitiesÂ in Sarawak: E-Bario.* [On-line at http://www.unimas.my/fit/roger/Bario/]

Inktomi Corp. (2000, January 18). Web surpasses one billion documents. [Press release: http://www.inktomi.com/new/press/billion.html and http://www.inktomi.com/webmap/]

Joe, K (2000, January). Land is our life: indigenous peoples of Sarawak. [On-line at http://www.rengah.c2o.org/sarawak/about.htm]

Kaplan, R. D. (1997, December). Was democracy just a moment? *The Atlantic Monthly, 280,* 55-80. [On-line version: http://www.theatlantic.com/issues/97dec/democ.htm]

Lester, Toby (2001, March). The reinvention of privacy. *The Atlantic Monthly, 287*(3), 27-39.

Lewis, Jacquelyn (1998, June). Children's publishing at the turn of the century - a lasting impression? *The Culture of Publishing.* [On-line journal: http://www.brookes.ac.uk/schools/apm/publishing/culture/lewis.html]

McFarland, Sofia (2000, December 27). Malaysia's digital dreams reach Bario's rice paddies. *The Wall Street Journal: Asia View.* [On-line http://www.wsj.com/asian/p/asiahome.html]

Minow, Mary (1997, December 1). Filters and the public library: A legal and policy analysis. *Firstmonday, 2*(12). [On-line journal: http://www.firstmonday.dk/issues/issue2_12/minow/]

Murnane, R. J., & Levy, F. (1996). *Teaching the new basic skills: Principles for educating children to thrive in a changing economy.* New York: Martin Kessler.

Reich, Robert (1991). *The wealth of nations: Preparing ourselves for 21st century capitalism.* New York: Alfred Knopf.

Reuters (2000, December 6). Malaysian Internet boat surfs into Borneo. [On-line http://www.cnn.com/2000/TECH/computing/12/06/malaysia.reut/]

Smoler, F. (1998, February/March). Paradise lost? An interview with Michael Elliott. *American Heritage, 49*(1), 58-60, 62-67.

University of Vermont (2001). John Dewey Project on Progressive Education [Web site: http://www.uvm.edu/~dewey/]

REACHING TEACHERS WORLDWIDE

Alvaro H. Galvis

Developed and developing countries alike struggle with improving the quality of teacher preparation and teacher professional development. One thing is certain in education worldwide: teacher impact on student learning makes a critical difference. However, many areas of the world face special challenges attracting and retaining good teachers and providing appropriate resources for students. For instance, in rural areas and in low-income communities, it is difficult to recruit certified teachers and to provide students with multiple resources for learning.

This twin set of problems is most severe in areas where there is armed conflict or a major health concern. The AIDS epidemic in rural Africa, for example, has virtually destroyed education; many untrained teachers head up classrooms. Worse still, these teachers face barriers that hinder their continuing professional development. The Internet provides opportunities for students in developing countries to interact with educational resources and with distant students and teachers.

But there is good news. Information and communication technologies (ICT) have opened new avenues for teaching and learning. The Internet provides opportunities for students in developing countries to interact both with a wide variety of educational resources and with distant students and teachers. The Concord Consortium has pioneered the educational uses of ICT. For a decade we have researched the essential elements to ensure success when technology is introduced in classrooms. Hardware and software alone are not enough. More important are good teaching and quality learning resources. Our efforts have, therefore, focused on developing research-based materials and high-quality teacher professional development.

CAPTIC project in Peru

The Concord Consortium is part of dot-EDU, an alliance for education funded by the U.S. Agency for International Development (USAID). The dot-EDU strategic alliance is a worldwide effort to enhance education in selected countries through the use of ICT. USAID Peru and the Peruvian Ministry of Education invited dot-EDU to create and pilot a model for professional development of rural elementary teachers that would enhance their students' learning. In response, the Concord Consortium partnered with EDC and Programa Huascarán, a national program in Peru that provides ICT infrastructure and advice for educational institutions to create CAPTIC (a Spanish acronym for ICT-based learning communities). Local and distributed collaborative, inquiry-based projects helped students to develop basic competencies. Teacher professional development provided by CAPTIC used both online and onsite discussions among teachers.

During the pilot, the project faced huge organizational and technological issues that are common in many developing countries. For instance, while the Peruvian Ministry of Education determines which competencies must be achieved at each grade level and outlines ways of achieving these competencies, it does not prescribe national curricula. Educational regions in Peru are thus autonomous from an administrative perspective. Each region has its own funds to provide free basic educational services at public schools and regional educational authorities appoint teachers at public schools. However, teacher preparation is not part of this regional administration; rather, teacher colleges are ruled and sponsored by the Ministry of Education.

The creation of a network of ICT-based learning communities was, therefore, not an easy task, requiring careful coordination with different groups and authorities. Technology readiness was also a major issue. While all of the institutions participating in the Programa Huascarán theoretically had working computers and Internet access, this was not the reality. At the beginning of the pilot, only four of the fifteen computer labs were fully operational; at the end, twelve were prepared. The original design of the project assumed that online interaction was possible between all institutions, but while computers were available everywhere, connection to the Internet was not. The project thus reimbursed participants for fees they spent for Internet connections at local cyber-cafés.

Networked Communities of Practice

The CAPTIC project tested an ICT-based network of communities of practice in Peru. The center of this network was at Programa Huascarán, which hosted the virtual space for interaction between project participants. A full-time national coordinator of the network was in charge of ensuring technological support from Huascarán and of leading the implementation of CAPTIC. Four regional bases, one at each of the participating rural teacher colleges, co-facilitated the in-service training of elementary teachers. Each local group was focused on creating and nurturing communities of learners composed of students and teachers who co-construct knowledge around inter-curricular and locally relevant educational problems. Twelve rural elementary schools in four regions, each with four or five participating teachers, took part in the project.

The teachers focused on two key educational ideas, both of them implemented in face-to-face and online learning environments: genuine dialogues between teachers and students, and CLIC-based projects. (CLIC is a Spanish acronym for Creative, Ludic (playful), Interactive, and Collaborative.)

Regional facilitators videotaped sessions of participating teachers' classes at the beginning, middle, and end of the school year. Teachers reviewed their own videos, selected episodes to study with colleagues, and participated in a local community of practice. The facilitator helped teachers build trust and develop expertise in reflecting and commenting on their classroom experiences. Videotapes revealed that at the beginning of the project, interactions between teachers and students were mostly didactic (focused on getting the expected answers from students); at the end, many teachers sustained genuine conversations with their students. When teachers took part in an online seminar about building online learning communities, they reported learning additional strategies for fostering pragmatic dialogue in their classrooms.

Teachers also participated in two workshops where they discovered CLIC pedagogy. Teachers were immersed in playful problem-based experiences. Problems were designed to require interdependency between groups as well as a variety of educational resources. After the first workshop, teachers created local collaborative projects that focused on school-based educational needs. Following the second CLIC workshop, teachers created global collaborative projects, focusing on a grade-specific educational need. The global projects were implemented across sites using information and computer technologies to manage the interaction between distant groups.

Through their involvement in ICT-supported reflective practice, teachers reported professional growth. The integration of educational media around problem-centered activities gave ICT another important role. Teachers and students participating in local and global collaborative projects found that this learning expands the borders of the classroom and allows them to go beyond the traditional role of transmitting or receiving knowledge.

Because teachers discussed local practices, face-to-face interaction was necessary. The Internet was essential for managing the interaction among teachers at different schools and among their students. Facilitation of the process was blended, with both face-to-face and online seminars and workshops. In the future, the hope is to move more quickly towards Internet interactions.

A Look into the Future

Is the Peruvian experience expandable and sustainable? Could it be used in different settings with similar problems and opportunities? We think so. The Ministry of Education in Peru is preparing for a second round, with only minimum intervention on our part. A similar initiative is being launched in Colombia, in partnership with the Colombian Ministry of Education and the dot-EDU program.

We hope to refine the process, methods, and tools in order to share this experience with many other countries that need to reach teachers and students in underprivileged areas. Online activities will increasingly become the dominant mode of interaction among teachers and students who participate in problem-based collaborative projects. But video case-based teacher professional development may still require some face-to-face interaction, at least initially, in order to create the local conditions in which educational innovations can prosper.

ON-LINE EDUCATION MUST CAPITALIZE ON STUDENTS' UNIQUE APPROACHES TO LEARNING[1]

Michael Arnone

To be successful in the long run, on-line education must allow students to learn according to their personal styles, says Nishikant Sonwalkar, principal educational architect at the Education Media Creation Center at the Massachusetts Institute of Technology (MIT).

Mr. Sonwalkar, founding director of the Hypermedia Teaching Facility at MIT and founder and chairman of Intelligent Distance Learning Systems, a company specializing in distance-education software, specializes in the pedagogical use of computers.

Q: What have you learned about online pedagogy? What is required for on-line pedagogy that isn't required for traditional pedagogy?

A: In my view, on-line learning provides tremendous opportunity for providing pedagogical choices to learners that cannot be provided by a single professor or teacher in a classroom situation. On-line education provides a unique opportunity to use multiple representations of knowledge in terms of media. At the same time, it also provides opportunity to sequence this knowledge in a way so that it makes more pedagogical sense, by providing different learning strategies.

Q: What are some of those learning strategies?

A: There are fundamental learning styles that appeal to the learner in order to process knowledge. One is acquisition of knowledge via different media – text, graphics, audio, video, animation, and simulation. The other part is how to process that information through fundamental learning models, like apprenticeship, incidental learning, inductive learning, deductive learning, and discovery-based learning.

With that framework we can provide various choices – if you took a six-by-five matrix, you could provide 30 different ways of learning. With that, we can accommodate individual learning styles of the students in a way we could not do in a classroom with an individual teacher.

---

[1] This chapter originally appeared as an article in *The Chronicle of Higher Education*, with whose kind permission it is reproduced.

For on-line education, there is an opportunity that has not been completely utilized right now by the page-turner courses, because they do not address the issue of individual learning styles and the media preferences.

Q: Are you saying that on-line education now hasn't taken advantage of the medium to promote better learning?

A: Yes. What I'm saying is that on-line learning has a lot more potential of accommodating the individual learning experience than the way it is currently used.

Q: What needs to be done for on-line education to meet that potential?

A: One, you have to provide a paradigm shift in terms of thinking about content in terms of learning strategies and putting the media in the context of learning strategies, rather than tacking on multimedia and static Web pages, which really don't help to engage students' learning models.

The second thing you have to do is to provide a framework so that the content they are using for static pages can be a dynamic page, and that dynamic page can change according to the learning style of the user.

The third element is to provide interactivity, so that based on the trajectory that the student takes through the content, a system should be able to provide meaningful feedback to the student about their success or failure in learning certain concepts.

PART THREE

ICTs IN EDUCATION: THE CHALLENGES AHEAD

EDUCATION EMPOWERED BY ICT – THE WORLD'S BEST INVESTMENT?

Hugh G. Jagger

Rates of return on investment in education in the developing world have been shown to be very high on average. They look set to become higher in the future, as education's socio-economic leverage increases in the developing world. In addition, after some ineffective early starts, ICT is now showing potential to enhance rates of return to education. Donors and developing country governments are aligned in wanting to increase investment in education but while some favour a strong ICT component, others are skeptical. Therefore effective investment appraisal tools and data are urgently required to support policy, strategy and investment decisions in education and ICT for education.

This is crucial to support decisions on scaling to achieve the MDGs. The full set of returns and dependencies need to be better understood and quantified. ICT impacts need to be researched and modeled in detail so that the next wave of donor investments in education incorporates an appropriate ICT component. The United Nations ICT Task Force through its education initiative GeSCI has recognized this issue, and in response a number of public and private sector organizations have started to collaborate on a project to develop strategic insights and practical tools to inform policy, strategy and investment decisions in education and ICT for education.

The extensive research available on education in developing countries over the past 50 years shows that rates of return on investment are generally very high. For example, incremental economic growth linked to focused education investments has been shown to yield average rates of return as high as 40-50% and routinely 15-30%. Looked at another way, a large proportion of economic growth in many of the better performing developing countries can be attributed to effective investments in education. By comparison stock market investors typically expect 5-15% rates of return and even venture capitalists hope for only 30%. Therefore 15-50% from education should re-invigorate the development community's commitment to invest in education and to focus on strategies capable of achieving the upper end of the range.

Furthermore, future rates of return on education could well be higher than those from past research, for several reasons. Firstly, most historical research almost certainly understates the returns. This is partly because it excludes elements of the economic returns, such as the spillover productivity effects of educated workers and other "externalities" which are difficult to analyse; this is an area of debate, but recent research increasingly demonstrates large externalities.

Secondly, nearly all of the research on economic rates of return on education (sometimes referred to as market returns) excludes non-market returns to education, such as those from health, social order and the environment. Some researchers are showing that externalities and non-market returns are of the same order of magnitude as market returns.

Thirdly many of the historical studies did not allow sufficient study horizons for the full returns (allowing for lag times) to be captured, nor did they allow for education quality, now recognized as a major driver of returns.

Finally, many developing countries' socio-economic leverage of education is on the increase, as they increasingly link into the global knowledge economy via the Internet, adopt new production technologies in agriculture and other industries, and start using ICT in public and private organizations; educated citizens enable each of these changes, with their consequent benefits, to be realized.

Thus, for a variety of reasons it is reasonable to expect investments in education made in the next five years to have very high rates of return, higher than those estimated in the past and higher than most of the alternative development opportunities. However the development community needs effective investment appraisal tools and data to give confidence that education investment strategies are focused on high returns and will indeed yield high rates of return. These are not currently readily available.

Use of ICT in education is much newer and therefore less well researched. However, there is growing body of evidence that ICT can make a substantial positive impact on rates of return in developed and developing countries, with the right ICT strategies. This is in contrast to many earlier uses of ICT in schools in both the developed and developing world which had more to do with political appearances ("we must have some computers in our schools") than with the transformation of core education processes such as teacher training, daily teaching and learning in the classroom and student assessment.

Of course, ICT is no "magic bullet" for education's ailments – or those of any other field for that matter. The history of ICT in private and public organizations in every sector has shown mixed results. High returns have occurred when ICT strategies have focused on business objectives, when application software and data have been used to transform business processes, and when ICT implementation projects have been well executed within change management programmes. Poor and negative returns have occurred in a minority of projects, most of which have not had these characteristics. Many of these failures were in the early days of computing when executives felt "we must have some computers in our business" without a clear strategy. Education is still finding its way with ICT and therefore it is not surprising to see some of the mistakes occurring that other sectors made in their early days with ICT.

Furthermore, while effective ICT for education strategies are now emerging and hold exciting potential for scaling to meet the MDG's, it is increasingly clear that they should be embedded in holistic education strategies, including strategies which:

1. Build the human capital actually needed by a country's economy and society, by focusing on the mix of grade levels, curriculum and pedagogy most likely to match the knowledge skills and attitudes required.

2. Raise the quality of education, since educational attainment in nearly all developing countries is extremely poor when benchmarked against developed countries.

3. Raise demand for education where it is weak, often because families bear over 60% of total cost of education (largely through foregone earnings) and perceive education's impact on subsequent earnings to be insufficient to justify their private cost.

4. Raise educational efficiency, especially teacher efficiency, because teachers represent around 70% of the public sector cost of education – and because the "youth bulge" is imposing an increasing strain just as teacher attrition rates are rising (due to HIV/AIDS, urbanization, etc.).

5. Build the capacity of education institutions to implement change and manage ongoing performance – because holistic and systemic reform programmes sustain high returns.

6. Invest in other socio-economic initiatives, which complement education investment, for example physical capital, technology transfer, openness to trade, institutional capacity, health and inclusion (especially inclusion of girls and women in the economy and health management).

ICT can contribute to each of the above. In particular high quality electronic curricula content for student and teacher learning shows great potential to raise education quality across the whole curriculum and to reduce the time taken to cover the curriculum. In addition, access to wider knowledge resources, via the global Internet can also raise education quality. Another example is school resource management software, which can increase teachers' administrative efficiency and facilitate the introduction of performance management across the education system.

Mention should also be made of including ICT as a curriculum subject, since it builds developing countries' capacity to use ICT in the economy, which in turn can improve business processes, international trade, institutional management, healthcare, and so on, thus multiplying socio-economic returns. In fact ICT seems to offer solutions for most of the drivers of high returns from education and therefore may become the developing world's trump card for success. However ICT costs may still be too high for immediate and widespread use in some least developed countries. This will change with time as ICT costs decline; therefore large-scale investments need to be timed for low enough ICT costs to ensure adequate rates of return and this will be different countries at different stages of development.

While the returns on investment in education in many areas are now quite well understood by academics, further research is needed to fill gaps and improve research methodology. Existing research needs to be integrated to include full socio-economic returns, including those from the economy, health, social order and the environment. In addition, the potential impacts of ICT on education urgently need to be better understood, so that ICT is appropriately included in future education strategies.

Donors and developing countries need to be able to easily model the total cost of ownership over time of traditional and ICT investments, and the associated returns, so that they can evaluate different strategies and compare rates of return. The required broader and deeper understanding of both education and ICT for education therefore needs to be embedded in tools to support policy, strategy and investment decisions and ongoing performance management. Finally a framework is needed for the next three to five years to fill research gaps, refine tools and disseminate useful information and tools widely.

The United Nations ICT Task Force recognized these needs at its meeting in Dublin in April 2005 and a number of public and private sector organizations have since collaborated to develop a project to address the needs, with the United Nations sponsored Global eSchools & Communities Initiative (GeSCI) acting in a coordinating role. To date, firm support has been received from the Government of Ireland, Cisco Systems and A.T. Kearney. Organizations with an interest are invited to contact GeSCI. This project will help the development community to understand the extent to which education is a good investment, perhaps one of the world's best investments, and the extent to which ICT can enhance returns.

IS THERE AN EVEN BIGGER DIGITAL DIVIDE JUST AROUND THE CORNER? THE CHALLENGES OF INTERNET2

Vic Sutton

The current technology gap between rich and poor countries may be set to grow even larger, once Internet2 arrives.

The ease of information and communication that is made possible by e-mail and Internet access is nowadays taken for granted around the world.

Yet the "digital divide" is real. It is the difference in access between rich and poor, within countries as well as internationally.

Internet users as a percentage of total population and as a percentage of world users, 2005		
Region	% of Population	% of World Users
Africa	1.5	1.5
Asia	8.4	34.0
Europe	35.5	29.2
Middle East	7.5	2.2
North America	67.4	24.9
Latin America and the Caribbean	10.3	6.3
Australia and Oceania	48.6	1.8
World	**13.9**	**100.0**

Source: Internet World Stats[1]

The digital divide can be measured in different ways. Most of us think of access to computers as the challenge. However, access to telephone lines is as important. And soon, it will be access to bandwidth[2] that determines what individual countries, and people within the countries, are able to do from their cell phone, computer or Internet kiosk.

---

[1] See www.internetworldstats.com for details and sources.
[2] bandwidth is the amount of data that can be transmitted in a fixed time, usually measured in bits per second (bps). For a useful on-line source of ICT definitions see www.webopedia.com

For many users in the developing countries, just to get hold of e-mail and information from a handful of Web sites, the "new technologies" still mean dial-up access using a 56 Kbps modem – able to send 56 kilobits[3] per second.

And even today, poor-quality analogue telephone lines, in many countries, mean slow connections and an endless wait for Web pages to download. Too often, "www" still stands for worldwide waiting.

Back in the days of teletype technology, the standard speed of news agency wire transmission, or telex transmission from offices, was 50 bauds – 50 bits per second. It takes eight bits to make a letter, so 50 bauds allowed the transmission of around six letters a second, some 3,000 words an hour.

A speed of 56 kilobits per second is over one thousand times faster. Even those of us who are using poor-quality telephone lines for dial-up access, are used to seeing our mail and file attachments vanish into the ether in next to no time.

It is only when we have to download the holiday photographs, running into megabytes,[4] that we start to complain.

However, speeds of 56 Kbps are going to be dwarfed by those planned for Internet2.

Internet2 is a research and development consortium led by some 200 US universities, and working with the US government and industry. They are planning for faster and more reliable networking links than are allowed by the existing Internet.[5]

The Internet, as we know it, was not planned. It grew out of research into packet switching communications carried out in the UK and the USA. in the late 1960s, and from the ARPANET, the first-ever network of different computers, which was set up at the end of 1969 to link computer nodes at the UCLA, Stanford Research Institute, UC Santa Barbara and the University of Utah.

Communications between the ARPANET nodes first ran at 50 Kbps.

The work to develop the Transmission Control Protocol/Internet Protocol, which make communication possible between large numbers of machines in an open-architecture network, was coordinated by Robert Kahn and Vint Cerf from 1973 onward.

The Ethernet technology which is now the most widely-used was developed by Bob Metcalfe at Xerox PARC in 1973.

The Internet grew steadily. At first this was thanks to use by the research community, but by the late 1980s it was well-established as a network for daily computer communications worldwide.

---

[3] a kilobit is 1,000 bits so 56 Kbps is 56,000 bits per second.
[4] a *byte* is 8 bits, a *kilobyte* is 1,024 bits and a *megabyte* is 1,048,576 bits.
[5] For more details see www.internet2.edu

The main early application was electronic mail, first developed from 1972 onward for communication between the researchers themselves. File transfer and remote login (Telnet) were other important applications in the early days. But with the development of the World Wide Web and browsers, and the growing power of personal computers, the Internet developed into what we know it as today, a global communications network with multiple uses, for both public-interest and commercial users.[7]

Quite a number of Internet start-up costs were subsidized, not only by the universities but also by federal agencies and the US National Science Foundation. And in the USA where many users pay a fixed monthly charge for telephone services, the ability to access the Internet over the telephone made it possible for service providers to offer communications links and content at modest additional cost.

This made possible the growth of a versatile and flexible global communication network using people's existing computers, software that is mostly free to users, and – usually – only modest charges for access to a user account on the host computer of an Internet Service Provider (ISP).

The main cost, for the very many who have to dial their ISP to be able to access the Internet, is the bill from their telephone company for what sometimes turn out to be many hours on-line. As mentioned earlier, in many parts of the world poor-quality telephone lines, switched through analogue telephone exchanges, make for unreliable communication links and slow access speeds.

In Europe and North America, and in some countries of the Arab world and Asia, faster options are available.

Where the telephone system allows it, these include higher-speed, digital telephone lines. The line known as a "T1" line will carry data at speeds up to 1.544 megabits per second (Mbps).

Speeds tested for Internet2 are many times faster.

The current speed record for Internet2 was set in November 2003 by a team from Caltech and CERN. They transferred more than a terabyte of data over more than 10,000 kilometres of network in less than an hour. That represented an average speed of more than 5.64 Gbps, more than 20,000 times faster than a typical home broadband connection.

A terabyte of data is 1,000 gigabytes or approximately one thousand billion bytes. It represents around five hours of high-quality DVD transmission. Internet2 compares the transmission speeds involved with the following graphic:

---

[7] For Internet history see *A Brief History of the Internet*, by Barry M. Leiner, Vinton G. Cerf, David D. Clark, Robert E. Kahn, Leonard Kleinrock, Daniel C. Lynch, Jon Postel, Larry G. Roberts and Stephen Wolff, published by the Internet Society at www.isoc.org/internet/history

Figure 1: Internet2 Land Speed Record[8]

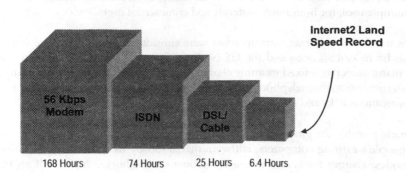

Who needs such high speeds of data transmission? Well, scientists and researchers use them to link computers, both to build powerful data-crunching networks and to make remote access possible.

For most of us, however, the most likely end-use of broadband links[9] is video transmission, for work and play. In particular, this can be used for video conferencing, which in theory allows face-to-face consultations in real time between remote users anywhere in the world.

In theory, because in practice time zone differences mean different working hours for different regions. However, these can be worked around.

Video transmission also allows for the whole range of uses of existing and new television channels, with their mix of entertainment, education and commerce. It also makes video on demand straightforward, a concept that the Internet has made familiar for music and other audio applications, but that bandwidth limitations have so far hampered when it comes to film and television.

There are of course copyright issues to be dealt with, but video distributors have taken these in their stride as products have moved from cellulose to cassette tape and to digital platforms, for both broadcast and non-broadcast distribution.

The challenges of introducing broadband services are more to do with infrastructure, the legislative environment and cost recovery.

---

[8] Reproduced with kind permission from the *2003 Internet2 Annual Report*, available on-line at www.internet2.edu.

[9] A *broadband* link can carry several channels at once over a single wire.

Ideally, broadband services should travel over fibre optic telecommunication links. But existing co-axial cable links can also serve.

This is where the digital divide could threaten to become an unbridgeable gulf. For example, there is no way that telecoms service providers in a region like Africa – where currently, whole communities lack telephone access – can envisage wiring up every household.

At the same time, the acceleration of mobile computing means that more and more users will use wireless links for many services (e.g. with access from cell phones or palm-held devices). And the experience of television shows that human ingenuity, and the resourcefulness of small-scale entrepreneurs, can overcome obstacles that may at first seem daunting.

On the face of it, television access in the developing countries may seem way below that in the developed world. To continue the African example, in 2000 there were 547 television sets per 1,000 people in Europe, while in Sub-Saharan Africa there were only 52 sets per 1,000 people.[10]

However, satellite transmission has brought the costs of providing a broadcast signal nationwide to all-time lows, and once a good-quality satellite signal is there, the costs of a television receiver, satellite antenna and decoder are within the reach of village entrepreneurs.

Internet kiosks have, similarly, brought e-mail and Internet access to millions of users who could never afford computers and on-line services from their home.

Nonetheless, while gaps between rich and poor remain it is likely that a digital divide will also persist, and perhaps grow.

There is little that policy-makers in the developing countries can do to bridge technology gaps, unless they have the capacity to invest in their own research and development. A more practical challenge may well be that of bridging gaps in the flow of content over the wires.

There have been some attempts to limit the spread of the new communication technologies. For example, as a result of US export restrictions, a number of US software providers warn users that their products cannot be downloaded – as of the time of writing – by citizens of Cuba, Iran, Iraq, Libya, North Korea, Sudan and Syria.

But there are many more examples from around the world of attempts to block access to content. These include government attempts to use both formal means – including legislation – and informal pressure, to prevent people from accessing services and content from abroad.

---

[10] Source: International Telecommunications Union, *World Telecommunications Indicators 2004*, cited by the World Resources Institute, http://earthtrends.wri.org

In this field the Internet has proved to be a very open medium. Web publishing is a relatively low-cost venture, accessible to all. But the key question remains: how many content providers will be able to afford to provide the volume of information and products that tomorrow's users will look for?

WHAT CAN YOU LEARN FROM A CELL PHONE? ALMOST ANYTHING![1]

Marc Prensky

How to use the 1.5 billion computers already in our students' and trainees' pockets to increase learning, at home and around the world

"When you lose your mobile, you lose part of your brain."– a Japanese student

One-and-one half billion people, all over the world, are walking around with powerful computers in their pockets and purses. The fact is they often do not realize it, because they call it something else. But today's high-end cell phones have the computing power of a mid-1990's PC (while consuming only one one-hundredth of the energy, by the way). Even the simplest, voice-only phones have more complex and powerful chips than the 1969 on-board computer that landed a spaceship on the moon!

In the US it is pretty much universally acknowledged that computers are essential for 21st century students, although there is still considerable debate about how and when to use them. But to most educators "computer" means PC, laptop or, in some instances, PDA. It is time we begin thinking of our cell phones as computers – even more powerful in some ways than their bigger cousins. Even the simplest, voice-only cell phones have microchips and perform logical functions just as bigger computers do. The main difference is that the phones began with, and still have, small size, radio transmission and communication as their core features, expanding out toward calculation and other functions. This has happened at precisely the same time as the calculation machines we call "computers" have expanded into communication and other areas.

Clearly the two are headed towards meeting in the middle, and we will wind up, when all the miniaturization problems have been solved, with tiny, fully featured devices that we carry around (or perhaps have implanted in our bodies.) But for now, most see these as very different animals, with the tiny cell phone being, among other things, a much more ubiquitous and personal device, especially among young people.

Students around the world increasingly carry these miniature "computing/communication devices" during the school day, using them almost

---

[1] This article was originally written for publication in *Innovate!* magazine

exclusively for personal purposes. Over 90 percent of Tokyo high schoolers have them, as do one in eight students in Botswana.

In America we do not fully appreciate the potential of these devices, since, from a cell phone perspective, we are a PC-centric laggard. The cell phone – generally called a mobile phone outside of the US – has proved so useful elsewhere that there are 1.5 billion around the world, with half a billion new ones sold every year. The country where the computer was invented, along with its northern neighbor, Canada, are the only places in the world where PC's outnumber cell phones. In the rest of the world it is the mobile that reigns, with countries often having 5 to 10 times the number of mobile phones than PC's. In some countries and groups – such as students in parts of Japan, Korea, Europe and the Philippines – cell phone penetration is over 100 percent, which means that individuals own and use two or more of these devices. And of course usage is growing like a weed around the world, where relatively inexpensive cell systems are bringing phones to places without land lines.

The Computers in Their Pockets

Today's young people – I call them our "Digital Native" generation – have, in an incredibly short time, adopted these tiny computers in their pockets, purses and backpacks as their primary means of communication. They are using their cell phones for communicating by voice, text, and, increasingly, digital photographs and videos. And, increasingly, they are using them for computing, such as the digital signal processing which allows them to play ringtones and mp3s.

Even in the PC-centric US, the penetration of student mobile phones is impressive. In high schools it is often over 75 percent, and in some schools it is almost 100 percent, as it is in most US colleges. In US elementary and junior high schools the number is over one-third, and fast approaching half the students. With dropping prices and increasing utility, it is almost a foregone conclusion that not too far into the future all students will have a cell phone, quite possibly built right into their clothing. Ski parkas with built in cell phones are already on the market.

Brain Extenders

"When you lose your mobile," says one student in Japan, "you lose part of your brain." The statement indicates an intuitive understanding of the link between Digital Natives and technology that has escaped educators. Most American teachers and administrators believe that cell phones have no place in the educational process. This is not totally surprising, since schools have never had an easy time integrating technology into teaching. Far too often, and certainly today with cell phones, educators' knee-jerk reaction is to view new technologies as a "huge distraction" from the education they are trying to provide. Some imagine dozens of these phones ringing constantly, despite the fact that the devices have off switches and penalties can be collectively established and enforced by good teachers. Others observe "cheating" during tests via mobile phones and think that banning the devices – rather than educating the students – is the appropriate answer.

I feel sorry for these short-sighted educators, but even sorrier for their students. For as US educators are busy banning cell phones in schools, millions of students in China and Japan, the Philippines, and Germany are using their mobile phones (respectively), to learn English; to study maths, health and spelling; and to access live and archived university lectures.

Here's my point: cell phones are not just communications devices sparking new modalities of interacting between people, they are also particularly useful computers that fit in your pocket, are always with you, and are always on. Like all communication and computing devices, cell phones can be used to learn. So rather than fight the trend for kids to come to school carrying their own powerful learning devices – which they have already paid for! – why not use the opportunity to our advantage?

How Do We Do That?

But how? Can cell phones really provide their owners with the knowledge, skills, behaviours and attitudes that will help them succeed in their schools, their jobs and their lives? I maintain the only correct answer to the "What can they learn?" question is "ANYTHING, if we design it right." There are many different kinds of learning and many processes that we use to learn, but among the most frequent, time-tested, and effective of these are listening, observing, imitating, questioning, reflecting, trying, estimating, predicting, "what-if"-ing and practicing. All of these learning processes can be done through our cell phones. In addition, the phones complement the short-burst, casual, multi-tasking style of today's "Digital Native" learners. Using cell phones as a learning device, whether in or out of school, requires a good deal of rethinking and flexibility on the part of educators. But given the opportunity, we can be certain that students, as they have been doing with all useful digital technology, will quickly embrace and use the tool and make it their own in various unexpected ways.

Feature Segmentation

So what and how can our students – including adult trainees – learn from their cell phones?

A useful way to answer this question is to consider the capabilities phones in use today possess, and to see what each capability brings us. With half a billion cell phones sold each year, the devices are hotbeds of feature innovation – the major ones being voice, SMS, graphics, user-controlled operating systems, downloadables, browser, camera (still and video), and geo-positioning – with new features, such as fingerprint readers and voice recognition, being added every day. In addition, there are optional hardware and software accessories, as both input mechanisms (thumb keyboards and styli) and optional output systems (such as plug-in screens and headphones).

Voice Only

But let's begin with the most basic of phones – those with voice capabilities only. These are still the most prevalent in the world, although they are fast being replaced and upgraded. They are basically radios, which pick up and send signals on certain predetermined frequencies.

Is there anything students can learn on a voice-only phone? You bet! Let me suggest just a few of them: Languages. Poetry. Literature. Public Speaking. Writing. Storytelling. History.

Of these, language is probably the most obvious. Given the huge demand and market around the world for English lessons and practice, it's the one kind of learning that's already readily available on cell phones. In the UK, a company called CTAD has created voice-only mobile phone learning for school dropouts with language needs. In Japan you can dial a number on your cell for short English lessons. In China, the BBC and others are providing cell phone English language training. One company is even subtitling pop songs with their lyrics, highlighting each word as it is sung. Language games, such as crosswords and Tetris-like word puzzles, are being added as well. Other types of voice-only learning applications also exist, and are growing in popularity.

In Concord, Massachusetts, you can use your cell phone for an historically accurate guided tour of Minuteman State Park, where "the shot heard round the world" was fired. A UK university has experimented successfully with using cell phones for exams, with the students' voice prints authenticating that they are the ones being tested.

And it doesn't have to stop there. Have you ever listened to "Car Talk?" Or "Fresh Air?" Or the BBC? Remember, cell phones are basically radios. You don't need anything more than a voice link and a person on the other end worth listening to in order to learn a whole lot. Why not offer cell-phone delivered lectures (really engaging ones) on basic subjects, with cell phones call-ins and multi-way discussions?

An immediate advantage of voice-only learning is that we know it works – for millennia it was the only type of learning humans had. While some "Digital Immigrant" adults may have a difficult time with, and even question the value of, non-face-to-face voice communication and relationships for learning, virtual relationships are now second nature to students, and often preferred.

Additional inspiration in the voice (and sound)-only area we comes from research done for the blind and sight-impaired. As Jenkins, Squire and others have pointed out, many extremely useful voice-only cell phone approaches developed for this group, such as voice-activated search engines and menus, can also be of great benefit to the sighted as well.

Short Text Messages (SMS)

Short Messaging Service (SMS), only recently introduced in the US, has been available on cell phones outside the US for several years. This feature has caught on like wildfire among young people in Europe and Asia, with literally billions of SMS messages being sent every day around the world. SMS messages, which can be written quickly, even in your pocket (especially with "predictive text"), offer enormous learning opportunities.

Currently, SMS messages provide timely "learning" reminders and encouragement for people trying to change their behaviour, such as quitting smoking. SMS is the technology used for voting on the TV show "America's Idol". It is used by marketers for informational quizzes about subjects of interest to young people, such as movie and TV stars. And innovative SMS games, many of which have strong educational potential, are attracting large playing audiences.

In schools, SMS can be used for pop quizzes, to poll students' opinions, to make learners aware of current events for class discussion (e.g. with messages from CNN Breaking News,) and even for tutoring and spelling and maths tests. Outside of school, test preparation companies such as Princeton Review are already offering cell-phone delivered SAT and other test preparation questions at specific user-preferred times. It would be a simple matter to use SMS technology to provide cell phone learners, individually and in competitive/collaborative groups, with data and clues in real time for analysis, diagnosis and response, whether in an historical, literary, political, scientific, medical or machine-maintenance context.

Graphic Displays

Just about every cell phone has some kind of graphic display, even if it shows only the signal and battery strength and the number or name of the person being called. But most new cell phones come with far more graphic power than that – they typically sport bright color screens that can crisply display words, pictures and animation. Many of these screens have resolutions of 320x240 pixels – half the screen size of the standard computer of not too long ago – and higher. They display thousands of colors and even 3D and holograms.

Such high-resolution screens allow for meaningful amounts of text to be displayed, either paragraph by paragraph, or flashed one quick word at a time, with the user setting (and generally greatly increasing) his or her own reading speed. In Asia, novels intended to be read on phone screens are already being written. Why not learning texts?

Better graphic displays also mean that such text can be accompanied with pictures and animation (and, of course, sound – it *is* a phone). Many schools are currently using computers and handheld devices for animations in subjects such as anatomy and forensics – cell phones can replace these devices. Japanese students have long learned everything from business to cooking through graphic novels or "manga", which are now becoming popular in the West as well. At a recent computer show, a Japanese company was handing out a manga pamphlet about its "middleware" software, that could easily be displayed one frame at a time on a cell phone. So in many cases our mobile phones will replace our textbooks, with the limited screen size of the phones being, in fact, a positive constraint that forces publishers to re-think their design and logic for maximum effectiveness, rather than just adding pages.

Downloadable Programmes

Now that cell phones have memories (or memory card slots) that accept downloaded programmes and content, entire new learning worlds have opened up. Cell phone users can download versions of the same kinds of tools and teaching programmes available on personal computers, and, given that the phones are communications devices, use the tools for collaboration in new and interesting ways. All manner of applications combining elements of voice, text, graphics, and even specially designed spreadsheets and word processors can be downloaded to the phones, with additional "content" added as needed.

Need review in any subject? Want to practice for your Nursing Boards, Graduate Record Exams, or Medical College Admission Tests? Just download a programme to your cell phone, call your friends, and start studying.

Internet Browser

Internet browsers are now being built in to a growing number of cell phones, especially those that use the faster "3G" (third generation) protocol. Web sites specifically designed for cell phones are becoming more and more numerous. A browser in the cell phone puts a dictionary, thesaurus, and encyclopedia instantly onto the hands of every student. It gives them instant access to Google and other text search engines, turning their cell phones into research tools. Students studying nature, architecture, art or design can search for images on the Web that match what they find in life in order to understand their properties, style and criticism.

Cameras

Almost a million camera phones were sold last year, and in many places such phones are already accepted as the norm. Educationally – once students learn that privacy concerns are as important here as anywhere else – they are a gold mine. In class, cell phones with cameras are tools for scientific data collection, documentation, and visual journalism, allowing students to gather evidence, collect and classify images, and follow progressions over time. Creative cell phone photos can inspire students' creative writing via caption or story contests. Phones can be placed in various (appropriate) places, and operated remotely, allowing observations that would be impossible in person. We can literally see what's going on around the world, including, potentially, in "sister classrooms" in other countries.

Global Positioning Systems

The initial crude ability of cell phones to "know where they are" quickly became the basis of some very innovative applications abroad, including a multiplayer search game in the UK. Now sophisticated GPS satellite receivers are being built in to many cell phones (and made available as add-ons for many others) that know the phone's precise position to within a few feet.

This feature allows cell phone learning to be location-specific. Students' cell phones can provide them with information about whatever location they happen to be at in a city, countryside or campus. (Some colleges already use this feature for orientation.) The ability of students to determine their precise position has clear applications in geography, orienteering, archeology, architecture, science and maths, to name only a few subjects.

Cell phones with GPS can be used by students to search for things and places (already known as "geocaching"), and to pinpoint environmental dangers, as in a recent learning game from MIT.

Video Clips

Finally, as I write, the first video cam phones are hitting the market, capable of taking and sending short, typically 10-30 second, video clips. This extends the phone's learning possibilities even farther, into television journalism (most TV news clips are less than 30 seconds), as well as creative movie-making. A terrific educational use of short video clips would be for modeling effective and ineffective behaviours relating to ethics, negotiation, and other subjects.

Connections and Caveats

My main purpose in writing this article is that, having searched quite a bit, I have found the number of people using or researching learning via cell phones to be exceedingly small, particularly outside of Asia. (In Japan, Masayasu Morita, working with ALC Press, has found that, using the same content formatted differently for computers and cell phones, 90 percent of cell phone users were still using the system after 15 days compared to only 50 percent of the computer users: http://csdl.computer.org/comp/ proceedings/ c5/2003/1975/00/ 19750128.pdf. Another Japanese company, Cerego, is also very bullish on cell phones for learning.)

While researchers such as Elliot Soloway and Eric Hopfer in the US, Jill Attenwell in Great Britain, and Georgio da Bormida in Italy are experimenting with "mobile devices" for learning, they typically are not using "cell phones" but rather PDAs, (which are often donated by manufacturers eager to find a new market for their devices.) But this is not the same, in my view, as using cell phones for learning. There are less than 50 million PDAs in the world but over 1.5 *billion* cell phones. Of course much PDA-based research will be useful, but it is not until we begin thinking of using the computing/communication device currently in the students' pocket for learning, that we will be on the right track.

As usual, the students are far ahead of us on this. As noted, the first use they have found (in large numbers) for putting their cell phones to use for learning is "retrieving information on demand during exams". Educators, of course, refer to this as "cheating". But they might better serve their students' education by redefining "open book" testing to "open phone", for example, and by encouraging, rather than quashing, student innovation in this and other areas. Just so that I am not misinterpreted, let me state that I am not "for" cheating. But I am for adjusting the rules of test-taking and other educational practices in a way that fosters student ingenuity and creativity in using their tools, and that supports learning rather than administration.

As these sorts of adjustments happen, new norms and ethics will have to emerge around technology in classrooms. But norms can change quickly when a new one is better. Perhaps you can remember how rapidly, in the 1970s, the norm went from "It's rude to have an answering machine" to "It's rude NOT to have an answering machine!"

Educators should bear in mind that cell phones can be used for context as well as content (as in the aforementioned tour of Lexington. Maryland.) Those concerned that students use their tools not only to retrieve information but to filter and understand it are the very people who should be figuring out how to use cell phones to do this. Just as we are designing and refining Web and PC-based tools for such tasks, so must we be designing similar tools for the cell phones – and in doing so the communication and social features of the phones are likely to be of great help.

Fully-featured as they are, it has also been pointed out that cell phones are not powerful enough to be students' only learning tool. "Well Duh!" most students would say. "We'll use whatever tools do the job – just make sure they all work together!" Our cell phones can be our students' interface to a variety of computing devices, just as they control their entertainment devices.

Although I have tried to provide a variety of suggestions and examples as to how cell phones might be used for learning, my goal here is not to present a fully-completed vision, but rather to open the eyes of those who are ignoring an important resource for learning that is real and untapped today. I am sure many will extend the vision and possibilities for cell phones in learning, and I welcome all suggestions. I am convinced that once cell phone-based learning is under way, the "world mind" of both educators and students will take it in a million useful and unexpected directions.

The Future

Cell phones are getting smaller and more powerful each day. The disposable cell phone, a mere 2" x 3" with the thickness of three credit cards and made entirely of paper (the circuit board is printed with metallic conductive ink) is already patented and being manufactured. Such phones, in volume, will likely cost less than a dollar a piece, with the air time for educational uses likely subsidized by carriers and others.

Imagine teachers handing out a phone in every class preloaded with all the software and contact numbers for a class task or project. Or imagine the United Nations dropping millions of disposable, single-button cell phones over places in the world sorely in need of learning. Pick one up, push the button, and suddenly you are no longer part of the "digital divide" but part of a world learning community, with your connection costs paid for by those with a stake in making your learning happen. (A project of just this type is happening today for Afghan rural women, but using bulky, proprietary machines at fifty times the cost.) Of course "adverphones" will no doubt appear as well, and we will need, just as we do with other media, to help our students understand the difference.

Finally, despite complaints we often hear from older "Digital Immigrant" adults (with fading vision and manual dexterity) about cell phones' limited screen and button size, it is precisely the combination of miniaturization, mobility, and power that grabs today's Digital Natives. They can visualize a small screen as a window to an infinite space, and have quickly trained themselves to keyboard with their thumbs.

And despite what some may consider cell phones' "limitations", students are already inventing ways to use their phones to learn what they want to know. If educators are smart, they will figure out how to deliver their product in a way that fits into their students' digital lives – and their cell phones. And instead of wasting our energy fighting their preferred delivery system, educators will be working to ensure that their students extract maximum understanding and benefit from the vast amounts of cell phone-based learning they will all, no doubt, soon be receiving.

PARTNERSHIPS IN ACTION

Stephen Nolan

Introduction

The Global forum was our opportunity to bring together leading thinkers, policy makers, practitioners and visionaries in the field of ICTs and education to draw their ideas on both the challenges and opportunities we face. We arrived at conclusions, mapped out future directions and laid foundations for many future impactful partnerships. The global forum was a undoubtedly a success. But like a forward to a book, a forum is mere prelude to the real body of work to come. In this case such work means the forging of multistakeholder partnership initiatives to ensure that the dividends of an unprecedented human experiment in digitalization and information communication technologies, can be extended to education systems and other areas of paramount human need around the world. We cannot, nor do not imagine that one forum, or series of forums however strong the number of experts in attendance, can deliver the sea change we need if we are going to raise an ailing standard of education and accelerate development globally. But it is a shot in the right direction. New forms of technology and communications are tremendous tools to place in the hands of the world's poor and disadvantaged. Realizing such potential requires comprehensive national and regional strategies. The global forum is a step closer on the road to such strategies.

The event itself was not only the first event for GeSCI to co-host but it also signified the next stage in GeSCI's work in two of our priority countries. Concurrent to the main plenaries and the breakout sessions that formed the Global Forum on ICTs in education, GeSCI organised two roundtables which each focused on two of our priority countries – Namibia and India. Though each had very different objectives, both roundtables produced highly successful results.

Namibian Roundtable

GeSCI was delighted to welcome the Honorable Nangolo Mbumba, the recently appointed Minister of Education for Namibia and his team of dedicated officials to Ireland for our Roundtable. His attendance at this event provided a key opportunity for the Minister to present his government's recently produced high-level policy for the application of ICTs for education in Namibia.

Roundtable participants enjoyed this opportunity to hear about the clear objectives and basic competencies that are now identified by the Namibian government for their country educational system. Interestingly, Namibia has placed greater emphasis on the pedagogical use of ICTs an integrated tool in the teaching-learning process at all stages of the educational system and Minister Mbumba described how this will be achieved through the clarification of national goals and the identification of clear ICTs tools complementary to their plan.

Throughout the course of this Roundtable, a number of issues and challenges for Namibia to be successful with their aims were identified – these include infrastructural support, curricula and content development, technical support and maintenance and more broadly, the impact of the HIV/AIDS crisis within their country. With the recognition of these challenges completed, GeSCI partners used this time with the Namibian government to frame the nature of potential solutions and explore possible areas for collaboration so to surmount the current issues.

With expressions of interest by a range of GeSCI partners voiced in this Roundtable, the GeSCI team will now be working in collaboration with our partners in Namibia and will continue to fine-tune with all stakeholders specific areas of co-operation. The Namibian government set for its next task the development of a specific implementation plan. Terms of reference for this were completed in the summer of 2005. Mr. Khalid Bomba, the GeSCI Country Programme Faciliator for Namibia is now assisting with both the implementation plan and the GeSCI partner interest in Namibia's work. With the leadership of Minister Mbumba and local stakeholders, Namibia's ICT in Education plan is turning into a reality.

Indian Roundtable

Chaired by Mr Ghanshyam Tiwari, the Rajasthani Minister for Education, the objective of this Roundtable was to assess the state of the ICT-for-Education sector in India, to identify critical gaps in this area and requirements for putting in place a complete end-to-end system. It also was set to explore ways in which GeSCI partners could support India's future work in the area of ICT for education.

The Indian government wanted to give an indication that ICT4E was a clear priority for their educational strategy and to signal to potential partners that they would welcome support. They achieved this through a series of presentations, from a range of senior officials from both the state and the federal level. Mr Madhavan Nambiar from the Ministry of Communications and Information Technology highlighted that while India has made significant advances in the area of ICTs, the deployment of these technologies in education has been a relevant recent trend. He saw that GeSCI and our global partners could develop models of positive international collaboration, which could leverage the competitive advantage of the various countries and partners involved.

Mr Keshav Desiraju, Joint Secretary of the Ministry of Human Resource Development also spoke and clearly identified to all present the formidable task at hand when tackling Indian standards of education. He noted that while India accounted for 17% of the global population, it also had 40% of the world's illiterates and though major initiatives launched since independence had halved this percentage from 80%, high levels of female illiteracy and school drop-outs were still persistent problems.

The debate was engaging and informative – and a number of our non-governmental partners made expressions of initial interest in the work that India hopes to achieve with ICTs in education. It is clear from the Indian delegation that the value for using ICTs as the tool for raising standards of education and now the process is to identify the best solutions to match for Indian educational needs. With the stewardship of our Country Programme Facilitator for India, Ms. Aruna Sundararajan, GeSCI India has now formally selected Rajastan in which to concentrate our work. Over time our work will be extended to other states.

The future is happening for us faster than we knew. The power of ICTs and the power of mulitstakeholder partnerships are combining to create a cross-geographical current of unstoppable momentum and drive – towards the millennium development goals, towards country-specific ICT for development implementation plans, and at long last towards the worldwide challenge to educate all.

DEPLOYING ICTS IN SCHOOLS: A FRAMEWORK FOR IDENTIFYING AND ASSESSING TECHNOLOGY OPTIONS, THEIR BENEFITS, FEASIBILITY AND TOTAL COST OF OWNERSHIP

Alex Twinomugisha, J. Paul Callan and Kate Bunworth

Abstract

We have developed a framework and approach that educational policy makers and school administrators can use to inform their choice of Information and Communication Technologies (ICT) for schools, in a way that ensures that they achieve their educational objectives. The framework advocates for a consideration of three elements: a focus on educational objectives as the overriding consideration, targeting an end-to-end approach, and considering the benefits, feasibility and total cost of ownership of any ICT choice. The approach involves 5 key steps that stem directly from the elements above.

Introduction

As educational policymakers and school administrators in developing countries increasingly consider information and communications technologies (ICTs) for education, they are faced with a number of problems. Chief among these is a lack of understanding of the different technologies that exist and what they can do for teachers and students. A decision to acquire ICTs is seldom driven by a careful analysis and consideration of needs, alternative technologies and the real costs involved. As a result, ICTs in many schools in developing countries have become synonymous with computer laboratories with high equipment breakdowns and low usage.

This state of affairs was evident to GeSCI staff who visited schools in developing countries during the conception stage of the organization. It led to many discussions about how this trend could be reversed, and how best to help schools effectively integrate ICTs in teaching and learning. A team composed of McKinsey and Company, Dalberg Development and GeSCI, supported by a financial contribution from Intel and pro-bono time and effort from McKinsey and Company, studied the problem early this year. The team developed an overall framework for thinking about benefits, costs and feasibility of ICT options for schools and created a sophisticated analytic electronic tool that models TCO for various ICT options. The framework and electronic tool have subsequently been revised extensively by GeSCI following feedback from various experts and are scheduled for public release by the end of this year.

This paper briefly presents the framework and some of the insights gained on the major problems facing the schools as they plan for, acquire and deploy ICTs. The paper draws heavily from a draft report[1] originally prepared by McKinsey and Company as part of the initial team effort and subsequently revised by GeSCI.

The Framework

The framework and corresponding approach is based on 3 key considerations that arise directly out of some of the major problems facing the deployment of ICTs in schools today.

- Focus on educational objectives

  ICTs are a tool and not an end in themselves. Schools should therefore focus on what they need to use the tool for, in the first place. Choosing and deploying ICTs for education must stem from, and be driven by the desired educational objective and outcome.

- Target an end-to-end approach

  Purchasing and installing ICTs in schools is not the end of the story. It is part of an integrated, comprehensive and on-going (end-to-end) system that requires that a plan be developed in advance, ICTs purchased and installed, users trained, adequate technical and user support provided, and continuous assessment and evaluation conducted to ensure that educational objectives are being met. The end-to-end system is illustrated in Figure 1, and consists of 5 major components: deployment of ICTs, content and applications that accompany the ICTs, user training and support to enable proper usage, maintenance and technical support to keep the ICTs working and monitoring and evaluation to ensure that the ICTs are being used for the educational objectives originally envisaged. It should be comprehensive, demand driven, capable and efficient and well coordinated.

Figure 1 – GeSCI end-to-end-system

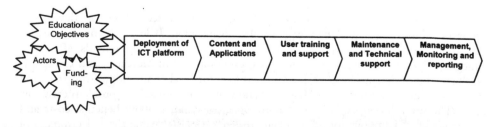

---

[1] The report entitled "Deploying ICTs in Schools- a framework for identifying and assessing technology options, their benefits, feasibility and total cost of ownership" is still under revision by GeSCI.

- Consider benefits, feasibility and long term costs

Benefits and feasibility of both the technology selected and the overall approach to deployment should be considered, along with the long term costs of introducing ICTs in schools. It is dangerous to focus on the immediate or initial costs such as those for buying and installing computers in a school without considering the long term recurring costs, which are critical to keep the computers working and usually much higher than the initial or immediate costs.

The feasibility of any given ICT determines whether that particular ICT is applicable in a given context irrespective of the inherent benefits. Feasibility is usually influenced by local conditions. There are 5 key constraints: existence of poor ICT infrastructure such as computer equipment and telecom infrastructure, availability of sufficient electricity for ICT usage, limiting physical school infrastructure (size and shape of classrooms; security; types of furniture; lighting conditions; ventilation), educator's technology skills and comfort in integrating technology into teaching, and access to developed local ICT industry that includes distance from services; capability of local ICT service industry and ease of procurement. For example, the lack of wired telecom infrastructure at a remote village may mean that the only connectivity options are satellite or none at all, or cultural considerations such as teachers' lack of readiness to use technology in the classroom may mean a deployment of technology in teacher offices only.

The Approach

Drawing from the considerations above, a strategy to select and deploy ICTs in schools was developed. It has 5 key steps as depicted in Figure 2:

Figure 2 – The approach

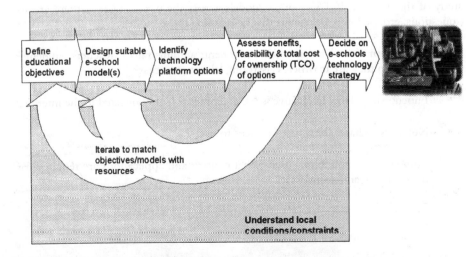

Step 1 – Define Educational Objectives

What are you trying to achieve with the technology?

The range of possible objectives divides into four broad categories: administration, teacher development, student learning resources, and ICT skills training as a subject in its own right. In all, there are eleven distinct objectives within these four categories, which are summarized in the table below.

Table 1 – summary of possible education objectives

Category	Objectives
Administration	Enhancing School productivity
	Enhancing data flow for policy making
Teacher Development	Developing teacher skills and knowledge
	Assisting effective lesson planning
Student learning resources	Accessing information (by students)
	Improving conceptual understanding
	Developing constructivist skills
	Facilitating collaboration
	Providing testing and feedback
ICT skills training	Developing basic ICT skills
	Developing advanced ICT skills

Step 2 – Design suitable "e-school model(s)"

Which e-school model best achieves the educational objectives above?

A study of the different ICT-in-schools models across the world suggests there are six key questions, grouped into 4 elements that help define those models:

- Usage approach: Who uses the equipment: administrators, teachers, students? Where do they use it: office, classroom, lab, open access?

- Functionality: How interactive is the equipment? Is it connected to the internet?

- Numbers: What is the ratio of devices to users?

- Content and Applications used: What content and applications are required for the educational objectives set?

Figure 3 – E-School model and Technology deployment model

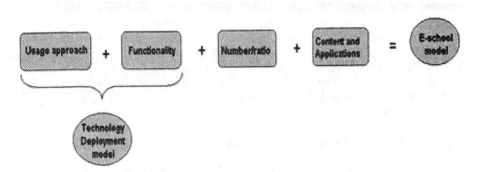

We have therefore defined an e-school model as a distinct combination of these four elements (Figure 3). The combination of only the usage approach and functionality is referred to as the "technology deployment model". Because there are six different usage approaches and three different levels of functionality, eighteen technology deployment models are theoretically possible. However, of these eighteen technology deployment models, four are not in fact meaningful, since they combine a functionality (non-interactive) with usage approaches that would not make sense together. Specifically, it does not make sense to consider use of non-interactive technology (e.g., TV, radio) only in office administration. The 14 possibilities are as illustrated in Figure 4:

Figure 4 – Possible Technology deployment models

		Functionality		
		Non-interactive	Interactive un-networked	Interactive w/ Internet
Usage approach	Teacher and admin office use	✗	✓	✓
	Mobile device assigned to teacher	✗	✓	✓
	In classroom single device mainly used by teacher	✓	✓	✓
	In classroom multiple devices used by teacher and students	✗	✓	✓
	Computer lab multiple devices used by teacher and students	✗	✓	✓
	Open access	✓	✓	✓

Note that a school may implement more than one e-school model to achieve its objectives.

A careful analysis of the 14 deployment models, and therefore the e-school models, shows that some models are more suited to achieving certain education objectives than others. "Suitability" in this particular case is based on a combination of the benefits rendered and the feasibility of the given model. The chart below in Figure 5 summarizes the suitability of any model to the range of educational objectives. It uses "circles" – a blank circle represents zero suitability and a completely filled-in circle represents maximum suitability. Mounting degrees of suitability are represented by quarter-, half-, and three-quarter-filled circles.

Figure 5 – Comparison of e-school models and educational objectives

e-school models			Administration		Teacher development		Learning development					ICT skills	
			Enhancing school productivity	Enhancing data flow for policy making	Improving teaching practice	Assisting effective lesson planning	Accessing information (by students)	Improving conceptual understanding	Developing constructivist skills	Facilitating collaboration	Providing testing and feedback	Developing basic ICT skills	Developing advanced ICT skills
Teacher and admin office use	Interactive un-networked	①	◕	◔	◕	◕	○	○	○	○	○	○	○
	Interactive w/internet	②	●	●	●	●	○	○	○	○	○	○	○
Mobile device assigned to teacher	Interactive un-networked	③	◑	◔	◕	◕	○	●	◕	◕	◕	◕	○
	Interactive w/internet	④	◕	◕	●	●	○	●	◕	◕	◕	◕	○
In-classroom single device mainly used by teacher	Non-interactive	⑤	○	○	◔	○	○	◕	○	○	○	○	○
	Interactive un-networked	⑥	◔	○	◔	◔	○	●	◔	◔	◔	◔	○
	Interactive w/internet	⑦	◑	◑	◑	◑	○	◔	◔	◔	◔	◔	○
In-classroom multiple devices used by teacher and students	Interactive un-networked	⑧	◔	○	◔	◔	◔	●	◑	◑	◑	◑	●
	Interactive w/internet	⑨	◑	◑	◑	◑	◑	●	●	●	●	●	●
Computer lab with multiple devices used by teacher and students	Interactive un-networked	⑩	◔	○	◔	◔	◔	●	◑	◑	◑	◑	●
	Interactive w/internet	⑪	◑	◑	◑	◑	◑	●	●	●	●	●	●
Open access	Non-interactive	⑫	○	○	◔	○	◑	◔	○	○	○	○	○
	Interactive un-networked	⑬	◔	○	◔	◔	◑	◔	◑	◑	◔	◑	○
	Interactive w/internet	⑭	◑	◑	◑	◑	●	◔	●	●	◑	●	○

Step 3 – Pick the specific technology platform to buy

There are so many various ICTs that a school can choose from. To simplify the process of choosing among them, the decision is broken down into five main choices: the access device; the software; the display device; to-school connectivity; and in-school connectivity (*See*

Figure 6). All these are supported by new or modified physical infrastructure and power backup systems.

Figure 6 – Components of ICT platform

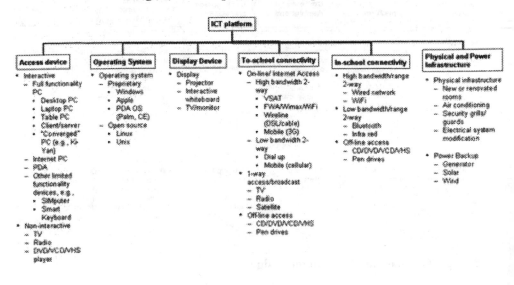

A combination of these 5 choices is termed the "ICT platform". There are also various ways of deploying any particular platform (termed the "ICT deployment model").

Step 4 – Calculate the Total Cost of Ownership (TCO)

Work out how much this technology will cost, not merely to buy in the first place, but throughout the life of the project using the Total Cost of Ownership (TCO) concept.

The TCO captures all the costs of a particular purchase from "cradle to grave" i.e. from making the decision to purchase, through the useful life of the purchase to retirement or end of life. TCO differs from a regular budget because the budget usually focuses on the immediate (or initial) costs, encompassing one time purchases and the more obvious operating costs. TCO is therefore vital to understanding the full implications of any purchase one makes. The TCO of any technology platform selected must take account of all the five main categories of spending, aligned with the GeSCI end-to-end system.

Each of these categories involves initial capital expenditure and then ongoing operating expenditure as depicted in Figure 7.

Figure 7 – Initial and Ongoing costs

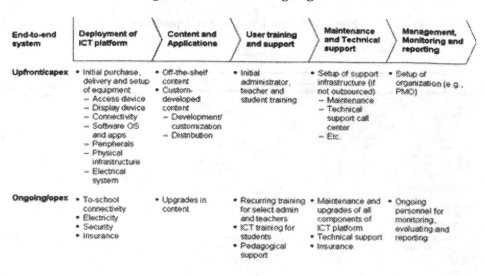

Step 5 – Compare this TCO to the budget

If it is within the budget, you can move forward to design a strategy around the chosen technology platform. If it is too expensive, you must go back and review the earlier choices, starting off with your selected technology platform and then the e-school model. Finally, if the cost is still too high, you must go all the way back to your educational objectives, and make compromises in an iterative manner until the TCO falls to an acceptable level.

Remember that every stage of this process will be shaped by local conditions and constraints, which could influence or limit the choices at any point of the approach.

Conclusion

The framework and approach we have developed will help educational planners and school administrators make the right ICT choices that will fulfill their particular education objectives. We understand that the approach to choosing an e-school technology strategy is a complicated one does and not necessarily have a "right" answer. It requires different users to come up with different solutions appropriate for different circumstances. This framework and approach will help the decision maker faced with these difficulties to choose the right technology for their given circumstances. The reader may well have come across numerous other frameworks that strive to achieve the same goal; we believe that our framework provides a lot of flexibility. Therefore the approach described above in Figure 2 is not meant to be a definitive one, but merely one that we have found to be useful in guiding our thinking. Most importantly, this framework will make it much more likely that the ICTs acquired have a direct impact on your school administration, management, teaching and learning.

ANNEXES

INFORMAL SUMMARY OF THE GLOBAL FORUM ON A MULTISTAKEHOLDER APPROACH TO HARNESSING THE POTENTIAL OF INFORMATION AND COMMUNICATION TECHNOLOGIES FOR EDUCATION (DUBLIN, 13-14 APRIL 2005)

INTRODUCTION

The Global Forum on "A Multistakeholder Approach to Harnessing the Potential of Information and Communication Technologies for Education" was attended by almost 300 representatives of interested stakeholders, both members and non-members of the United Nations ICT Task Force, including a number of Ministers and other high-level government officials, prominent educators, representatives of civil society, the private sector, academia and youth representatives. Building on the tradition of the previous three Global Forums, the meeting was characterized by its open and inclusive procedures, and by a comprehensive, realistically critical and solutions-oriented interactive discussion among well-informed and committed actors. The tone and thrust of the discussion were set by the message of the United Nations Secretary-General, in which he welcomed the theme of the Forum and stated that "we must ensure that ICT is used to help unlock the door to education" so that people everywhere "can fully seize economic opportunities, and live lives of dignity, free from want".

The Global Forum comprised four plenary sessions, four concurrent break-out meetings and a keynote address. The first two plenary sessions presented both challenges and achievements in the area of ICT for education. Break-out sessions on the morning of 14 April afforded an opportunity for an interactive discussion in smaller groups on a range of related issues. The concluding plenary sessions in the afternoon defined areas for action and collaboration and explored ways to engage stakeholders and create innovative partnerships.

The keynote address, delivered on the second day of the Forum by Prof. Jeffrey Sachs, provided a stark review of progress on the achievement of the Millennium Development Goals (MDGs) and highlighted the need for donor governments to meet the aid obligations to which they have committed themselves. The role of ICT in increasing the likelihood for success in attaining the goals by 2015 was highlighted.

The intensive two-day discussion once again demonstrated that all of the different stakeholders have a distinctive role to play in harnessing the potential of ICT in the fight against poverty and allowing education to unlock the door to a better future for the poor. The Forum highlighted that education is not only a goal in its own right, but also essential for the achievement of the other seven MDGs. Forum participants underlined that education empowers people to fully realize human capabilities, creates choices and opportunities and gives every individual a stronger voice in society. Education prepares workers to participate in the global economy and provides citizens with the tools for full engagement in public life. Education is vital to controlling the spread of disease, to ensuring adequate food supplies, and to safeguarding natural resources and the environment.

Throughout the Forum meetings, there was a genuine dialogue focusing on opportunities to achieve reduction of poverty and enhance development by promoting the cognitive, creative, expressive and technological skills necessary to master digital technologies in productive ways. There was broad consensus that the real revolution is not "information" but the digital revolution: education is not about swallowing information but about new ways to learn and produce. It was fully recognized that teachers shape the future through their work and that they should have all available tools at their disposal, including the full range of information and communication technologies. It was emphasized that new models of capacity development for teachers, administrators, facilitators in neighborhood tele-centers are key to the success and sustainability of education strategies and to a systematic approach in the use of ICT for education. Participants reiterated in this context that multistakeholder partnerships could maximize complementary strengths.

The following is an informal summary of the proceedings of the Forum.

OPENING SESSION

Mr. Brendan **Tuohy,** Department of Communications, Marine and Natural Resources, Ireland and Vice-Chairman of the Task Force, chaired the meeting. In his opening statement, he introduced twelve-year-old Patrick Dempsey, an active member of the Intel clubhouse in the Liberties district of Dublin. Patrick described how, in working with computers, he has developed skills, confidence and knowledge that he will use throughout his life.

Mr. Noel **Dempsey**, Minister for Communications, Marine and Natural Resources, Ireland, delivered a welcoming address on behalf of the host, the Government of Ireland. He reflected upon the importance of education in building a modern and thriving society and as a means of tackling issues such as the AIDS crisis, gender inequality and poverty. He highlighted some of the ways in which ICT can improve the quality and quantity of education and make the world more inclusive. He illustrated that falling costs of ICT make their use more economical. He also described some ways in which the Government of Ireland was supporting ICT and education initiatives, including the Global e-Schools and Communities Initiative (GeSCI), the co-organizers of the Global Forum.

Mr. José Antonio **Ocampo**, Under-Secretary-General of the United Nations for Economic and Social Affairs, delivered a message to the Forum from the Secretary-General. In it, the Secretary-General highlighted the necessity of harnessing the potential of ICT in order to achieve the Millennium Development Goals by 2015 and of fully integrating the global ICT agenda into the broader United Nations development agenda. He also noted the need to improve the use of ICT within the United Nations itself "so that the Organization's collective mindset and methods of work are brought fully into the digital age".

The Secretary-General congratulated the ICT Task Force on bringing together governments, civil society and the private sector to work toward common goals. He urged participants "to be creative and ambitious" and "to think and act urgently and boldly to ensure that ICT is used to advance education and development".

Mr. Ocampo underscored the significance of 2005 as a potential tipping point in international development efforts. He urged the participants of the forum to advocate applying ICT as a tool for development at all levels. On education, he quoted statistics on children who do not have access to primary schooling. He emphasized the centrality of partnership and collaboration among all stakeholders in the various sectors, countries and regions to overcome obstacles that deprive children of their right to education and to move toward innovative and sustainable solutions for development.

The Chairman then introduced the rules of procedure and time management of the Forum.

PLENARY SESSION I: ICT IN EDUCATION – A REALITY CHECK

The session was chaired by Mr. **Ocampo** and moderated by Amb. David **Gross**, Department of State, United States.

Amb. **Gross** opened the session by sharing his personal experience with ICT being introduced into communities through his role as a board member of a local school. This experience had taught him that people learn in different ways and that ICT could help broaden the methods of learning. He introduced the three lead discussants, who then made brief introductory statements. All three picked up the challenge of "reality check" contained in the title of the Session and shared their candid assessments of the current role of ICT in education.

Ms. Titilayo **Akinsanmi**, Programme Manager, Global Teenager Project, shared her personal experience and highlighted how important it was for her to have access to the Internet in order to be able to conduct her work. Ms. Akinsanmi challenged the donor community, highlighting that many excellent ICT-for-education projects cannot be implemented on a large scale or in a sustainable manner for lack of support. She commended GeSCI on its coordinating role of existing initiatives. Ms. Akinsanmi emphasized the need to look at learning as a life-long process determined by individuals and not by technology. She stressed the importance of knowing what is happening on the ground relating to ICT and education in order to be able to translate policies into action. In this context, she challenged participants to consider the knowledge they have of their community educational systems, the government's policies on ICT and education that apply to their community, and the subsequent impact these policies have.

Ms. Esther **Wachira**, Capacity Building Manager, Computer for Schools Kenya, described the work done by her organization in providing secondary schools with computers in Kenya. Ms. Wachira stated that providing computers is only the first step toward integrating ICT into educational systems and stressed that most important is building capacities within the schools. She emphasized that it is critical to train teachers and principals and sensitize them on the benefits of using computers in schools. Ms

Wachira described the teachers as authority figures and agents of socio-economic change who must be empowered. She urged the private sector not only to be innovative in addressing hardware, software and connectivity issues, but also to invest in schools and to support teacher-training programmes. Ms. Wachira also emphasized the importance of localizing content development in order to make it relevant to the local reality and population. She stressed the importance of applying ICT to the broad range of subjects (such as art, history and language) and not only to science in order not to exclude girls from the use of ICT since in many cultures science interests only boys.

Mr. Alfred **Ilukena,** Director, National Institute for Educational Development, Ministry of Education, Namibia, reiterated the need to provide teacher training if ICT is to make an impact since teachers are not the end but the start of ICT in education. He stressed the importance of targeting pre-service training which is cheaper and allows teachers to become champions and multipliers once they complete their training programmes. Mr. Ilukena noted the importance of building the appropriate infrastructure and establishing legal frameworks conducive to innovation and to the integration of ICT into the educational systems. He also emphasized the importance of creating an enabling environment that would facilitate access by everyone to the ICT facilities of the community centers. He concluded by stating that although the challenges are many, they should not keep developing countries from moving forward.

An interactive discussion between Forum participants and panelists followed the statements. Many participants supported the approach that teachers shape the future through their work, are multipliers and agents of socio-economic change who must be empowered. They should have all available tools at their disposal, including the full range of information and communication technologies – not just the Internet, but also standalone computers, radio, TV and telephones. However, in order to provide them with the skills they need to transfer knowledge to their students, to improve their own effectiveness and to insure that the computers that are finding their ways into schools in the developing world are put to good use, teachers urgently require training in ICT. It was recognized that educators who had been trained in ICT often abandon their teaching careers for jobs that pay better salaries.

It was stressed that there are many adults who miss educational opportunities, and that community centers play a crucial role in providing access to them. Universities in the South were also encouraged to act as incubators and supporters of community centers to bring educational opportunities to adult learners. Participants recognized that capacity-building initiatives enabling teachers to use ICT are also a source of employment leading to social value and recognition for young people, thus providing a creative way to combine use of technologies and social recognition for meaningful and sustainable outcomes. The discussion reiterated that hardware and software tools as well as educational material must be adapted to meet the specific needs of local communities. Human resources were highlighted as a key component necessary for the sustainability of ICT in education initiatives.

PLENARY SESSION II: THE CONTRIBUTION OF ICT TO EDUCATION INITIATIVES

The session was chaired by Mr. Khalil **Saeed**, Secretary, Ministry of IT and Telecom, Pakistan. Three panelists made brief introductory statements.

Mr. Abdul **Waheed Khan**, Assistant Director-General, UNESCO, briefed the audience on the Education for All (EFA) initiative and on the role of ICT in contributing to the achievement of EFA's mission, which is to provide access to education worldwide. This is expected to be achieved through meeting six goals: early childhood education, free primary education, equitable access to learning, improvement of adult literacy, gender equality and improvement of the quality of education. Mr. Khan highlighted the link between education and development as well as the two education-related MDGs (goal 2: achieving universal primary education and goal 3: promoting gender equality) and illustrated trends and progress at the regional and local levels toward their attainment.

He defined the main challenges relating to education (access, equity, quality and relevance) and stressed how ICT can contribute to responding effectively to these challenges. ICT can provide increased learning opportunities for underprivileged categories of population, enhance diverse and collective learning processes, it represents an enabler for developing non-formal learning environments and can shift learning processes from a one-time event to a life-long learning process.

Mr. Khan presented the three educational initiatives that UNESCO will be implementing in 2006: 1) Literacy Initiative for Empowerment (LIFE); 2) Teacher training in Sub-Saharan countries; and 3) HIV/AIDS and Education. He also brought to the attention of the audience one of UNESCO's twelve strategies that is directly related to ICT and education. It specifies the need to harness the new ICT to help achieve EFA goals. In the framework of the EFA initiative, UNESCO's work on ICT and education focuses on four main areas: ICT support to decision makers, improvement of the quality of teaching and learning, capacity building, and content development and knowledge sharing. Mr. Khan concluded his presentation by highlighting the importance of the numerous existing multistakeholder partnerships for the achievement of the EFA goals.

Ms. Victoria **Garchitorena**, President, Ayala Foundation, Philippines, emphasized the importance of ICT in delivering education in those countries, such as the Philippines, that need to leapfrog geographical as well as infrastructural limitations.

Ms. Garchitorena presented the "text2teach" programme, a partnership among the Ayala Foundation, NOKIA, Pearson, the International Youth Foundation and UNDP, that delivers digital learning materials to schools using mobile technology. Each school targeted by this program is equipped with a satellite dish, 29-inch television set with rack, a 40-gigabyte digital video server/recorder to record and store video clips and two to three mobile phones. The programme was first initiated in the school year 2003-2004 in 40 public elementary schools of different socio-economic levels. It was subsequently replicated in another 41 schools and finally, in 2005, was implemented in 120 schools. Ms. Garchitorena expressed the hope that the programme could be further extended both in terms of outreach and content, and serve as an example for other countries while still being deep-rooted in the local reality.

Mr. Henry **Chasia,** Executive Deputy Chairperson of the NEPAD e-Africa Commission, presented the NEPAD e-school initiative that provides a framework and a systematic approach for ICT and education in the African continent. He highlighted the three main goals of the initiative: a) providing ICT skills to participate in the knowledge society; b) enhancing teachers' capacities through ICT; and c) improving school administration. The initiative is being implemented in four phases: phase one, which targets 20 countries, aims at creating a business plan by the end of 2005; phase two will have as main objective the development of a demo; phase three will create a satellite infrastructure; and phase four will result in the development of a national executive agency. The initiative is led in partnership with a number of global and local private sector companies.

The interactive discussion that followed the presentations emphasized that achieving universal primary education is not only one of the Millennium Development Goals, but it is also critical to the attainment of all the other goals. Several speakers highlighted the great value in sharing experiences and practices and in scaling-up successful educational programmes utilizing ICT. The discussion also stressed that ICT need to be integrated into all national education systems in order to realize higher quantity and quality of education. But in order to succeed in this effort, it is imperative to have a strong institutional commitment and political will. The integration of ICT into education systems is of particular value to developing countries because it gives them an opportunity to leapfrog inherent limitations and to acquire new resources and formulate innovative strategies. It was emphasized that new models of capacity development of teachers and administrators are key to the success and sustainability of education strategies and to a systematic approach in the use of ICT for education.

BREAK-OUT SESSIONS

Please see the Annex for the summaries of the break-out sessions.

KEYNOTE ADDRESS

A keynote addressed was delivered by Prof. Jeffrey **Sachs,** Special Adviser to the Secretary-General on the Millennium Development Goals.

Prof. Sachs insisted that the MDGs can be met everywhere but a decisive change of course would be required for that to happen. He summed up the essence of that challenge with the two words: "investing" and "practical". Prof. Sachs assessed that there are different rates of progress in the implementation of MDGs, ranging from very good in Asia to Africa still lagging behind. He went on to demonstrate that public investment, as a pre-requisite for a vigorous private sector, is critical to meeting the MDGs. Prof. Sachs insisted that currently, public investment does not come close to the level needed to break out of the poverty trap and urged governments to meet the ODA-target of 0.7% of GNP.

Prof. Sachs stressed that ICT were critical on the path to the end of poverty. He called for practical intervention requiring modest financing at the grassroots level. He stressed that connectivity enables aid in new ways, allowing more effective monitoring and delivery of aid where it is most needed. He noted the progress already made in developing countries through the spread of cellular telephony. Prof. Sachs made a plea for engaging the private sector to bring connectivity down to the local level in order to help people meet their basic needs. He finally called on all stakeholders to come to the Millennium+5 Summit in September 2005 with practical, bold, country-scale models of connecting the poor with the rest of the world, stressing that models showing education as "the way" were not yet in place.

PLENARY SESSION III: REPORTS OF THE BREAK-OUT SESSIONS

This session was chaired by Mr. Nii **Quaynor**, CEO of Network Computer Systems, Ghana.

The Rapporteurs of the break-out sessions presented their summary reports.

Many interventions were heard following the summaries of the Rapporteurs. One speaker emphasized that in order to raise sufficient money to fund ICT for education initiatives, there must be a greater focus on monitoring and measuring impact, benefit and return on investment in order to offer a compelling business case. Another statement asked participants to keep in mind the differential in gender and to address gaps in access and find opportunities to specifically engage girls in the use of ICT.

Several speakers linked Prof. Sachs' keynote address to issues they had discussed in the break-out sessions. The power of connectivity at the community level to transform the way aid is distributed, monitored, used and evaluated was underscored. Another speaker asserted that public investment is not sufficient to achieve modern universal access for education. Innovative, multistakeholder financial schemes are needed, with the cooperation of international financial institutions, commercial banks and suppliers. A private sector representative observed that ICT is not yet mainstreamed in the development finance institutions nor in the broader development agenda, but that ICT can be financed on the private market with the right business model. Public-private partnerships are, therefore, the key to mobilizing private funds and stretching public money: governments, in essence, provide a partial subsidy and the private sector develops business models and brings in private financing. A representative of an African government, however, argued that investment from the private sector has not materialized, and that market failure does exist. More support to the public sector in financing the expansion of infrastructure, therefore, is needed.

Proposals advanced in the course of the discussion:

- The ICT Task Force should assemble and make available through its website a selection of best practices regarding the formation and implementation of multistakeholder partnerships.

- A model similar to GeSCI should be applied to the pursuit of other MDGs, bringing different sectors together and to incorporate ICT throughout (Oxfam Ireland)

PLENARY SESSION IV: NEXT STEPS

The final session was chaired by Mr. Art **Reilly,** Senior Director, Cisco Systems and Vice-Chairman of the Task Force, and moderated by Mr. Sarbuland **Khan**, Executive Coordinator, Secretariat of the United Nations ICT Task Force.

Mr. Khan praised the fact that the discussions in the break-out sessions promoted creation of a common culture and understanding among the various stakeholders. He noted that the suggestions made out of the break-out sessions were good ideas. He then challenged the audience to find non-traditional measures to use public sector ODA to promote growth, particularly calling on civil society to bring the public and private sectors together.

Ms. Julia **Fauth,** Chair, Working Group on Global ICT Policy and Youth, highlighted the fact that the youth intervention was a welcome innovation of the Global Forum. She stressed that youth, through the Youth Caucus, has proven to be an important stakeholder of the WSIS process, and that youth should be seen as knowledge consultants helping shape policies. She agreed that global approaches are useful but insisted that the kind of education necessary could only be identified in national context. Ms. Fauth stressed that technology had no bias for a particular way of learning; rather, it played a role in enabling innovative thinking. Ms. Fauth re-iterated the need for youth inclusion in policy making and underlined the importance of inter-generational dialogue, remarking that by 2015, the target year for the achievement of the MDGs, a new generation of decision makers would re-think the policies made today. She stressed the need for continuity, as embodied by the proposed Global Alliance. She suggested that the meaningful involvement of young people in future work is a logical next step, calling on participants to turn policy making into an inter-generational dialogue.

Other interventions from representatives of the WSIS Youth Caucus supplemented Ms. Fauth's statement. Mr. Diogo de **Assumpçao** presented a national platform to reach young people in Brazil through training programmes. Mr. Mike **Griffin** said that it was time to teach the next generation how to learn, not what to learn. Ms. Maja **Andjelkovic** said that young people could serve as a powerful catalyst for building dialogue, as demonstrated by the more than 30 national youth campaigns (in the WSIS process) around education.

In the discussion that followed, it was reiterated that youth should be involved in policy-making, stressing that long-term intensive use of technology is changing the way young people think, learn and behave. One speaker called on the audience to nurture the potential of the youth and the development of a research framework to transform what is learned into practice. Noting that the keynote address by Mr. Sachs left great concern for the future of Africa and the world, one participant emphasized that it was dangerous to rely only on digital technology. Even though technology was important for capacity building and empowerment, it was crucial to foster and prepare youth as early as possible to face their future and generate income and creativity. One speaker stressed the need to devise appropriate business models for ICT and education. Another participant called for the development of the capacity of developing countries' universities to participate actively in the ICTD field. The need for continued and focused discussions on ICT and education was reiterated.

In his closing remarks, Mr. Khan called on ICT Task Force members and partners to generate the follow-up to the many proposals and ideas that emerged throughout the Forum. He invited volunteers with ideas to participate in online discussions on the ICT Task Force website and take up opportunities for partnership building. Ideas gathered will be published on the ICT Task Force website.

Proposals:

Foster the appraisal of readiness of universities in developing countries to participate in ICT4D activities (Dr. Colle)

Develop a research framework to learn from and work with young people to nurture their potential as users of technology and contributors to society (Ms. Malyn-Smith)

Create consortiums of universities for greater research cooperation on topics to be specified for their relevance and usefulness to the fields of ICT for development and ICT for education. (Ms. Haglund-Petitbo)

Involve universities in the North and South in identifying models for sustainability for ICT for development projects (Ms. Diop Diagne)

Create a database of key resources and involve business and donors as experts and to provide case studies and impact assessments (Ms. Mallalieu)

Provide guidance on how to build public-private partnerships and viable business models in ICT4D and ICT4E (Mr. El din Ismail)

Create a GeSCI Forum under the leadership of the Irish Government, to bring together the various existing initiatives (Ms. Shope-Mafole)

The Task Force should engage more closely with Ministries of Education at national and state level (Mr. Gupta)

FORMAL CLOSING OF THE GLOBAL FORUM

A short video, capturing comments by participants to the Global Forum on ICT and their use in education, was shown. The chair, Mr. Brendan Tuohy, recalled some of the key issues addressed throughout the Global Forum. He described the first session as a forceful reality check, which indicated that teachers play an important role and special attention should be paid to their training. He noted the calls for sustainability and private sector involvement. The second session gave participants good insight about what is possible and showed that strong political will was needed for success. Mr. Tuohy then praised the increased participation by developing countries speakers and the youth involvement as stakeholders. Acknowledging Prof. Sachs' challenges at the global level, Mr. Tuohy called on participants to take initiatives back at the local level.

The meeting was closed.

ANNEX

Four concurrent break-out sessions were held to discuss with greater depth and interactivity issues related to ICT and education.

Break-out session I on Maximizing Complementary Strengths

Chair:

- *Ms. Martina **Roth**, Education Director, Europe, Middle East and Africa, INTEL*

Discussants:

- *Ms. Clotilde **Fonseca**, Executive Director, Omar Dengo Foundation, Costa Rica*

- *Mr. Madhavan **Namibiar**, Additional Secretary, Ministry of Communications and IT, India*

- *Ms. Elena **Pistorio**, Director of Operations, STMicroelectronics Foundation*

- *Rapporteur: Amb. Klaus Grewlich, German Foreign Office*

Peace and prosperity in the 21st century depend on increasing the capacity of people to think and work on a global, intercultural basis. As technology opens borders, education opens minds.

In her introductory statement the Chair, Ms. Martina **Roth** explained that in recent years, multistakeholder partnerships (MSPs) were explored as a way to address complex development challenges. MSPs are alliances between the public and private sectors and civil society and promise an efficient, holistic and inclusive approach to development – one where organizations working together in complementary ways may achieve more in concert than each could alone. The Chair proposed to examine the role and structure of MSPs pertaining specifically to the education and technology sectors and suggested the following subtopics: 1) digital technologies and education for poverty reduction; 2) structure of MSPs; building and sustaining effective partnerships; and 3) applying MSPs to ICT for education.

Referring to the opportunities provided by digital technologies for education and poverty reduction, one discussant argued that not so long ago, experts and international agencies considered the introduction of new technologies to developing countries as something too costly and inappropriate ("pentium vs. penicillin"). Today, however, many conceive technology as a new "deus ex machina". Nuancing this position, it was stressed by the discussant that the poor will not become less poor because today they have more access to information. Reduction of poverty and increased development cannot be seriously considered unless a conscious effort is made to develop the cognitive, creative, expressive and technological skills necessary to appropriate and master digital technologies in productive ways. The real revolution is not information but the digital revolution, i.e. new ways to learn, produce and live. This requires redefining the use of technology for education and work. Education is not about swallowing information but about new ways to learn and produce.

In this context, another discussant underlined that the potential involvement of university education with ICT and the Millenium Development Goals is underestimated. Multi-purpose community telecenters affording people in the developing world the opportunity to use computers, networks, copiers, scanners, telephone, printed materials and audio and video resources for information searching, communication, training and entertainment are ideal places for university involvement. Students may act as volunteers who actively assist the public in benefiting from the digital revolution; research may help telecenters to become demand-driven. Telecenters would need research to continuously evaluate how well they are serving the needs of their communities. Locally-tailored material should more and more complement and replace externally-generated information. Business and NGOs may become excellent partners in this endeavour.

The training of teachers was put into the forefront as one of the most important components for success in harnessing the potential of ICT for education.

At the same time it was underlined that the teachers themselves must have a voice in this training process.

It was argued that education in principle is a fundamental responsibility of the state but that for a number of reasons some governments were not able or willing to live up to this responsibility. Thus there is scope for contracting out and compensating for governmental weaknesses. Private business in partnership with NGOs and regional or local governmental entities may play an important role in this respect.

It was underlined that such partnerships for enhancing promising forms of education at different levels are complex because of the multifaceted character of the various actors. Private businesses, like governmental entities, play several roles at the same time. Private business search for profit, are tax payers, are corporate citizens with social responsibility – sometime they define, without knowing, via software development ("embedded code") regional, national and even global education policies. Governments, on the other hand, are policy makers, guarantors of order and security, arbitrators, investment promoters, contractors and evaluators.

Given such complexities, the chair suggested to establish, as possible, basic characteristics of MSPs and to reach an improved understanding of the conditions that would help sustaining effective MSPs. The chair suggested the following principles as criteria for success: trust between partners; long-term commitment and strategic approach; dialogue and communication; leadership and evaluation of performance. These criteria were generally accepted and constructively discussed in more depth.

Several discussants underlined the importance of being clear and honest in the formation phase of MSPs. Responsibilities must be clearly established and genuine core responsibilities should never be transferred to other partners. Roles, expectations and interests such as profit and power must be openly put on the table and clearly understood by all partners. In doing this, realism is required: forming partnerships, notably building trust and co-operative attitudes is time consuming. Several participants recognized that in some cases of MSP formation it was a grave mistake to unduly shorten the consultation phase and to enter too quickly into agreements.

Furthermore it was stressed that there must be a "catalyst", a driver stimulating the formation of an MSP. The bigger the program the more important is the role of the catalyst. In certain cases the catalyst may become later on the leader of the MSP. In other cases it may hand over operational leadership to partners and concentrate for instance on the evaluation of progress.

The crucial importance of understanding local and regional cultures, e.g. in the formation of telecenters, was underlined by several speakers. Local NGOs could be particularly helpful in reaching this objective. The point was made that equally important is the understanding of corporate culture in the case of strategic business participation. Here again the universities could play a role as agencies to provide intercultural insight as well as instruments for fostering human growth and development.

At this point of the discussion an attempt was made to propose several models for successful MSPs. One speaker expressed reluctance towards the idea of having ONE model that would drive the very different partnerships. This speaker stressed that there were many variables because of different local cultures, societal and political instabilities at the local and regional levels. Therefore each case should be dealt with on its own merits. Partners would build the respective MSPs on very specific circumstances. It was stressed however that in any case there must be three things: 1) trust, 2) common goals, and 3) some form of an "evaluation, assessment or monitoring agency" depending on the specifics of the respective MSPs. This "agency" would feed back its knowledge into the specific MSP. The assessment agency itself could be local or regional (a government entity or a private foundation) or global (e.g. a subcommittee of the proposed Global Alliance for ICT and Development).

Long-term commitment in terms of sustainable finance was mentioned as a particularly important key factor for success. Pulling out funds (or lack of proper financing) at an early stage could be a terminating factor for the project. But also delays in calling off existing funds was mentioned in the discussion; also delays because of interdepartmental communication issues were referred to. It was said that the private side should show, as necessary, an appropriate patience and understanding towards the public sector and its specific international working mechanisms. It was stressed that in private business longer-term commitment must happen at board level. Alternatively the establishment of foundations would be a promising way to guarantee sustained financial stability for MSPs.

The chair made the point that "being project-centered" is a particularly valuable guarantee for the stability of the MSP. Projects must be as specific as possible and really engage the responsibility and creativity of all partners. In many cases the specific nature of the project commands the particular composition of stakeholders. It was mentioned in this context that, in a number of projects involving "ICT for education" on the local level, the private sector and NGOs were not particularly interested in dealing with local governmental entities.

The importance of making the media co-owners and partners of "ICT for education" projects was underlined by several speakers. Media support was considered essential for reaching established goals.

In concluding the chair summed up on the basis of a rich discussion the critical factors for success of MSPs, stressing the following: goals & strategy; building of capacities to be taken forward; vision & leadership; effective evaluation and feedback into the MSP.

Break-out session II on Access to ICT in Education – Opportunities and Challenges

Chair:

- *Amb. Astrid Dufborg, Ministry for Foreign Affairs (Sweden)*

Discussants:

- *Mr. Rahul Tongia, Assistant Research Professor, School of Computer Science (ISRI)/ Department. of Engineering and Public Policy, Carnegie Mellon University (USA)*

- *Ms. Leigh Shamblin, Director, Education Office, USAID/Macedonia*

- *Mr. Martin Curley, Director, Intel Innovation Centre*

- *Rapporteur: Mr. Peter Hellmonds, Director, Public and International Affairs, Siemens AG, Communications Group*

The Chair, Ms. Astrid **Dufborg,** suggested addressing three topics within the realm of access: infrastructure, efficient deployment models and innovation, and research. She hoped that the session would reach a common understanding of, for example, an e-school concept, low-cost solutions, and school participation in innovation and research, as well as come up with recommendations for further action.

The first discussant attempted to provide a framework for access. The digital divide was a manifestation of other underlying divides and access could be a building block for empowerment to reduce the others. The discussant presented four levels of the digital divide, easily remembered as the four "A's": <u>awareness</u> (knowing what can be done with ICT), <u>availability</u> (proximity to hardware and software), <u>access</u> (literacy, e-literacy and language) and <u>affordability</u> (ideally, the costs should be less than 10% of one's income).

It was highlighted that the total cost of ownership (TCO) was very differently priced around the world today with highs in Africa of more than 800% of people's income for a 20 hour/month dial-up connection. It was explained that reducing the digital divide required improvements across all dimensions of ICT, summarized in four "Cs": computing (PCs are today prohibitively expensive for most people; PCs are difficult to use and even experts spend too much time on maintenance and upgrading); connectivity (innovation has been seen in this area with mobile telephony and wireless connectivity); content (meaningful content is lacking in many languages; today's system tends to make people passive consumers of information instead of active producers of locally relevant information); and human capacity (users need to be aware, literate and innovative to harness the power of ICT).

The second discussant provided the session with an account of USAID's efforts to connect schools to the Internet in Macedonia. USAID had decided to not only do a pilot but actually to connect all secondary schools in the country – approximately one hundred computer labs plus security, maintenance and insurance. In implementing the project a number of hurdles were overcome. No local company had the capacity to do the installation and maintenance, so most computers arrived but could not immediately be installed, which led to frustration. The licenses for the software arrived late which led to the installation of open source alternatives until the licenses were received. Once the computers were installed, it was realized that there was not that much Internet to use due to the existing telecom monopoly. There was also a problem finding content in Albanian. Lessons learned had been to involve the schools in the security and fund-raising for maintenance as well as to provide teacher training. USAID has now trained 4000 teachers in ICT in Macedonia.

The third discussant emphasized the need for revolutionary thinking and taking an innovative approach in ICT and education. Technology innovation brings "disruptive" approaches to communication. The need for integrated information society strategies to address regulatory and policy challenges are great. He emphasized innovative approaches using the latest disruptive technologies. One example was, instead of building separate labs in schools, one should move towards mobility in computing, providing a more natural integration of ICT into learning making use of technologies like Wi-Fi and Wi-Max that are cheaper and good quality. He also highlighted peer-to-peer computing, which could lead to a more effective use of CPU power. The hardest part of ICT in education is not installing hardware but developing viable business models for their sustainability.

The ensuing discussion was interesting and spanned several areas regarding access in education.

A number of participants talked about the importance of making ICT training valuable for teachers and engaging them in welcoming and integrating these new methods and technologies into their learning environment. One would also have to accept that all teachers working today will not be interested in ICT skills. Sometimes students could learn by teaching teachers about ICT since young people were often more knowledgeable in this area. One participant suggested adopting four "M's": monitoring (how ICT in schools is being used), measurement (measure the usage), mentoring (mentor students' talents adding positive feedback) and management (develop the students' talents into a viable business model for her/his future). Participants also brought up that education was not limited to a school setting but was a life-long process that could be conducted in many environments.

Another issue that was highlighted was the movement towards next generation networks (NGN) where all devices were able to do all things. In the near future there would not be any difference between a phone and a computer. You will be able to phone and compute with either of them. Participants discussed that wireless would become more important and hoped for the further spread of technologies such as Wi-Max. If wireless would become more widespread the PC might no longer be the appropriate tool for accessing the Internet. It was suggested that something more robust using peer-to-peer computing might be more suitable for developing countries and poor communities. In this context it was also discussed whether it was realistic to expect a 100% penetration of ICT or whether that even should be an ambition. By instead focusing on a slightly smaller number, great achievement could be made and the poorest of the poor would benefit from a trickle-down effect. There was no consensus on this issue.

The main reasons for the high TCO in developing countries was also of interest to the group. One discussant suggested factors like lack of competition but mainly blamed it on bad regulatory design that was not able to handle technological progress. A lot of regulatory environments deal more with technology than with the results. New technologies therefore become disruptive. There was a new slowly emerging model for passive infrastructure but it could not be implemented. These are complex issues that need to be discussed with regulators as well as being brought to the public's attention.

Many participants questioned Macedonia's choice of reverting from open source applications in favor of proprietary software from Microsoft. A government representative from Macedonia said it was because the Macedonian Government had struck a deal with Microsoft but he also said that the computers allowed users to choose whether they wanted to use the open source or the Microsoft software. One participant explained that the open source software was not only operating system but also office applications, and since there is no concerted marketing effort the spread is slow. There is also plenty of free educational content on the Internet that needs to be promoted (UNESCO, MIT, etc), as well as content that is being developed among online communities of professors and teachers. The need for ICT4D enthusiasts to publicize these was raised.

Providing a perspective from an international organization, a participant from UNFPA drew participants' attention to the fact that ICT4D proponents often are not aware of how donor money was disbursed. He explained that the Poverty Reduction Strategies (PRS) of countries determine the allocation of donor resources and that today ICT is part of the PRS in on very few countries. This is why it is tremendously difficult to convince donors to spend money in this area. ICT is also missing in the United Nations and World Bank guidelines on how to draw up a PRS.

The Chair concluded the discussions by thanking the participants and expressing that there had been many interesting interventions from the whole spectrum of stakeholders. She made five observations of the discussions:

- Development. Can all people be reached by ICT? Should we be realists or keep the 100% ambition? Who can decide who to "leave behind"?

- Technology. We must start from a needs perspective. When integrating new technology, ownership must be developed. Exposure is important to help people realize what their needs are and how ICT can help.

- Risk-taking. We have to take risks in order to reach progress. We cannot wait for the perfect solution but must test different options.

- Policy regulation. The regulatory environment can control your maneuverability. The education system is not isolated and is affected by many policy areas.

- Education goes beyond schools. It is a life-long process.

Break-out session III on Learning Strategies

Chair:

- *Mr. Amaldo Nhavoto, Mozambique*

Discussants:

- *Ms. Michelle Selinger, Educational Strategist, Cisco Systems*

- *Mr. Jim Wynn, School Strategies Manager, Microsoft*

- *Ms. Shafika Issacs, Executive Director, Schoolnet Africa*

- *Rapporteur: Ms. Bonnie Bracey, The Thornburg Centre, USA*

The Chair suggested organizing the discussion around three related themes: 1) national development goals and e-learning strategies; 2) teacher capacity-building; and 3) content development.

On **national development goals and e-learning strategies**, the Jordan Education Initiative was used as a case study. The initiative provided an example of a government making a concerted, systematic effort to drive education reform to generate a knowledge economy to bring about a real change in the national educational system. Discussants explained that this initiative was about much more than content (i.e. production of new textbooks), but rather a part of a country-wide, economy-wide integrated model to build capacity. It is an exercise in change management. It provides opportunities for private sector involvement in the reform process through content production and technology development/provision in partnership with the Education Ministry, which is leading the transformation. Working in this systematic, strategic way, Jordan hopes to achieve a high level of return on its investment. Other governments, one example of which is the United Kingdom, have taken smaller steps to integrate ICT by mandating its incorporation into the national curriculum, which has the effect of slowly driving a change in teaching practice. A speaker from Ghana observed a need to change the way teaching is conducted throughout the African continent – to shift from didactic learning to emphasizing learning-to-learn, problem-solving and independent thinking.

It was noted that for change to be of value, it must be sustainable and replicable. Participants discussed whether the best practices that were identified in the Jordan Education Initiative would be adaptable to other cultures, regions and political systems. One speaker observed that, although ICT had successfully been introduced into classrooms in many countries, alignment of student assessment had lagged.

On teacher **capacity-building**, it was emphasized that training is different than support, and that both are needed if teachers are to successfully integrate ICT into their pedagogical methods. A participant warned that introducing ICT without training was very costly because the expensive technology would not be effectively applied; teachers tend to continue old practices with new resources. The session also discussed the need to teach teachers about better classroom management, without which it is difficult to create an enabling environment for learning. Participants and discussants generally advocated a blended learning approach, using a combination of electronic content, online collaboration tools and classroom teaching to enhance the learning process by improving effectiveness and/or efficiency.

Teacher trainers need sufficient skills (e.g. coaching, leadership and technical) themselves or they cannot be effective. The session agreed that teachers needed support, training, access to resources, mentoring and initiatives for professional development. An Indian participant shared his experience in training teachers: 1) training works best in pairs using the technology together, 2) effectiveness drops when teacher training class size is above 25, 3) teachers must be revisited within 10 days of their training to review that they are using what they learned, 4) have teachers trained using technology teach other teachers, and 5) teach using practical, not empirical, examples.

Teachers go through stages of change following training and need continued support, but often funding is lacking even when the need is acknowledged. The session was reminded that computers are important tools in teaching, but they can only help learning; they do not replace teachers. Teachers must be taught when not to use computers as well as when to use them.

One participant reflected on the lack of indicators by which to measure success of ICT-enhanced education, noting that it is much easier to count the number of computers than it is to measure how effectively they are used to improve education.

A discussant cited a statistic of a shortfall of five million teachers in Africa. Distance learning for educating teachers is being employed on the continent in an effort to retain or replace large numbers of teachers who leave the classroom (or country) to pursue higher education or other work, or who succumb to HIV/AIDS or other disease. Distance learning utilizes Internet, radio, television, videos and CDs. In Jordan, distance learning has also been applied to build teacher skills and provide subject-specific knowledge in the form of just-in-time, just-enough training.

A speaker noted that in order to keep teachers from leaving for more lucrative work, salaries need to be improved. Another participant suggested that policy changes are needed to provide moral, not material, incentives to encourage teachers to stay in their positions and execute their responsibilities competently. A speaker relayed the Indian experience, in which teachers became more excited about their jobs when computers were introduced into their schools and student attendance increased markedly. In India's society, he explained, computer knowledge enhanced individual's social value.

A study on ICT-enabled teacher training programs in Africa is available at schoolnetafrica.net. It reveals that such initiatives in Africa are largely project-based, extracurricular, short-term and small-scale. There are not many national strategies that provide systemic intervention at a pre-service level. A French participant asserted that problems of a digital divide are not confined to Africa, but is found in developed countries as well.

Some participants felt that teachers, who tend to work independently, do not easily and naturally share experiences and collaborate with one another, and that poses a challenge requiring even a bigger change in mindset than incorporating ICT in pedagogy. Nonetheless, participants suggested there was merit to a global platform through which teachers could share their experiences. Some speakers cited successful examples of teacher collaboration, including an online community through New York University's distance-learning course. The Africa Teachers Network, a nascent network looking at pre-service training from a regional perspective, has emerged. The UNESCO web portal also provides relevant information and contact with an online community of teachers. One participant stressed the value of learning from mistakes and suggested that "bad practices" also need to be shared, and that platforms through which teachers could reach out for help and advice might be useful.

Content remains a challenge, principally in determining whether to use or buy existing content or develop it through local learners and instructors. Local content can interest children more because it is seen to be directly relevant to them. Participants discussed whether it is possible/desirable to adopt or adapt other content for local conditions or promote the production of original local content. A combination, drawing on global resources for adaptation while still encouraging local content creation, was suggested. This is potentially limited by local capacity to develop content and by access to technology to facilitate content production and dissemination. Bridging content creation and teacher training was suggested to increase the levels of local content development. Open content which can be shared and repurposed should also be encouraged. Teachers, therefore, should receive instruction on intellectual property rights and also Internet safety.

When selecting existing content, teachers need to be taught to evaluate online learning objects in terms of interface, learning, feedback and fit as part of the pedagogical process. Poor quality content can cause confusion; it was suggested that quality standards might be needed. One participant suggested assembling editorial guidelines to define quality content, which would help a teacher assess quality on his/her own in light of what is appropriate for their particular culture.

ICT were commended for their potential to be utilized in the classroom to support individualized learning, especially to meet the needs of different types of learners or to suit particular subject matter. For example, games can be good for visualization and modeling.

Recognizing that connectivity is often an issue, one participant noted that if information doesn't need to be online, it shouldn't be. Students and teachers can interact with modules that have been downloaded to desktops or use CD ROMs in order to avoid problems surrounding Internet connections.

Break-out session IV on Capacity-building for leaders, management, teachers and administrators

Chair:

- *Mr. Alfred Ilukena, Director, National Institute for Educational Development, Ministry of Education, Namibia*

Discussants:

- *Ms. Celia Moore, Manager, Corporate Community Relations, Europe, Middle East and Africa, IBM UK*

- *Mr. Dudley Dolan, Senior Lecturer, Trinity College, Dublin*

- *Rapporteur: Ms. Susan Teltscher, Economic Affairs Officer, e-Commerce Branch, UNCTAD*

Mr. Dolan stressed the importance of ICT capacity building in order for everyone to be able to participate in and benefit from today's knowledge society. He emphasized that today's interconnected world poses new challenges for education systems such as producing citizens and workers who are adaptive to new technologies and receptive to life-long learning. Mr. Dolan identified a number of key elements for the successful implementation of capacity-building programmes: a) realistic plans developed by those who understand the local needs and have a good knowledge of the available resources; b) managers and educators who appreciate the potential of ICT and can actually implement the strategies; c) educational facilities where senior civil servants, managers and educators can have access to best practices and the latest applications of the technologies.

Mr. Dolan then set the stage for the subsequent discussion by addressing to the audience a number of questions such as: What are the goals for the capacity-building for leaders, management and administrators? What environment will be created to encourage these goals? What infrastructure is required? How can we educate government Ministers and senior civil servants regarding best practices in the use of ICT?

Ms. **Moore** provided an overview of two global capacity-building programmes implemented by IBM (Reinventing Education and KidSmart Early Education Programme). She reiterated the need to raise educational standards at all levels and to focus on building knowledge society skills amongst both teachers and students. Ms. Moore emphasized the importance of working in partnerships to create sustainability.

The following discussion focused on three main issues: a) what is the scope of the target group; b) what kind of capacity-building programmes should be implemented; and c) how to implement capacity-building programmes.

On scope of the target groups, there was broad consensus on the three groups that were outlined for the session. However, participants felt that it was necessary to specify the different types of leaders, such as political leaders, community leaders, civil society leaders etc.; similarly, administrators (in the public sector) needed to be addressed at different levels of operation, including school administrators. Several interventions stressed the importance of the role of teachers. The group also agreed that ICT in education should target people at all age groups, young students as well as adults who were considered to be also drivers of change.

The discussion on **what kind of capacity-building programmes should be implemented** benefited from many good examples of programmes that are being successfully carried out (examples were provided from Intel, Microsoft, IBM, UNESCO, UNECA and others). Several speakers made the distinction between training and education. The group felt that, while ICT training was important, capacity building for leaders should focus more on raising awareness on the potential of ICT to harness education. It was emphasized that ICT educational programmes should not be too tool- or technology-oriented since technology changes rapidly, but should rather deal with the broader concept of the information society.

On **how to implement capacity-building programmes**, the group felt that leadership and a strong commitment at the highest level (such as at the level of Head of State and Minister) is necessary to have a successful implementation of any ICT-related strategy and programme. The United Kingdom and Bolivia were mentioned as examples of countries where leaders are strongly committed to integrating ICT into educational programmes. Some speakers also stressed that implementation strategies need to take into consideration both long-term and short-term results since politicians need tangible results, whereas learning is a life-long process.

The group emphasized that there is a need for realistic and sustainable plans that take into consideration available resources and are developed by local people. The importance of proper institutions and facilities was also stressed. In this context Ireland and Mozambique were referred to as examples of countries that have successfully established institutes for public education for civil servants.

Several speakers stressed the role of the private sector in delivering capacity-building programmes and, in particular, in providing resources; however, representatives from the private sector highlighted the importance of a partnership approach between governments and business, to get into a long-term engagement, to share mutual aims, resources, expectations and responsibilities. They stressed the need to move to a different model, from industry-as-a-donor to industry-as-partner.

Building networked communities of practice was considered a successful implementation strategy. The communities could be initially established at the local and regional levels and then spread to the national level.

The discussants stressed that capacity-building programmes need to be tailor-made to different audiences; training programmes for politicians and civil servants should be different from those for school administrators or educational authorities.

The group agreed that capacity-building models need to be shared as much as possible and recognized that there is a range of templates and good practices already available that could be adapted to specific environments and to the local context. Some speakers called for the creation of a "body" that would collect and make available the information about existing educational programmes and models. GeSCI and NEPAD were referred to as possible drivers of this process.

SOME EXAMPLES OF GENERAL ON-LINE RESOURCES FOR TEACHERS

African Virtual University

http://www.avu.org

The African Virtual University (AVU) is a first-of-its-kind, interactive, instructional telecommunications network established to serve the countries of Africa. The objective of the AVU is to build capacity and support economic development by leveraging the power of modern telecommunications technology to provide world-class quality education and training programmes to students and professionals in Africa.

Agora Project

http://www.agoramed.gr/1.intro_en.htm

In the Mediterranean the Agora Project is teaching new ways of using media for all of the countries around the Mediterranean.

Citta della Scienza, Napoli

http://www.cittadellascienza.it/

In Italy the Citta della Scienza in Naples is an interactive museum dedicated to scientific phenomena where the guest is involved in interactive itineraries, experiments, exhibitions and practical demonstrations.

European SchoolNet

http://www.eun.org/portal/index.htm

European SchoolNet's online community building tools are bringing together communities of teachers and learners from all over the continent.

George Lucas Educational Foundation (GLEF)

http://www.edutopia.org/foundation/courseware.php

In the United States, GLEF provides educators with free teaching modules developed by education faculty and professional developers. They can be used as extension units in existing courses, or can be used independently in workshops and meetings. Each module includes articles, video footage, PowerPoint ® presentations, and class activities. They draw from the wealth of GLEF's archives of best practices.

SchoolNet India

http://www.schoolnetindia.com

SchoolNet India provides programmes for diverse learning segments, for children with learning disabilities, corporate training and formal training courses. SchoolNet India will also provide teachers with Internet access to pass on information to students. While a part of the content will be directly sourced from Morgan Media and adapted for domestic conditions, a new joint venture will also develop content specific to India, in subjects like history, geography etc.

SchoolNet South Africa

http://www.schoolnet.org.za

SchoolNet SA is at the forefront of ICT implementation strategies in South African schools. It has developed a successful implementation strategy as a result of its experience and analysis of a wide range of past ICT implementation projects. As part of this process it has developed a teacher development framework that has seen its continued leading involvement in the education network, a distance-based ICT integration educator development programme.

USING ON-LINE RESOURCES IN THE CLASSROOM: THE EXAMPLE OF GEOGRAPHY

There are powerful on-line resources available for use in education, provided the educators know where to find them.

Here are two small examples of the power of online content:

Big Blue Marble

http://antwrp.gsfc.nasa.gov/apod/ap030426.html:

or this one: http://antwrp.gsfc.nasa.gov/apod/ap050302.html

Information literacy is the key, and we will explore how it can be used in teaching geography, with brief notes about resources for other science subjects.

Geography Matters

"There is a basic ingredient for significantly improving decision-making that involves the location, distribution, or impact of people, places, and events in the world. Proximity of customers to a store location, the routing of emergency vehicles to an incident, and the change over time in a habitat – all share the common component of geography.

"Just about anyone or anything can be associated with a known location in the world – a street address, a service region, a climatic zone, a voting district, a latitude/longitude coordinate. Geographic information systems (GIS) software is the ideal tool for extracting the patterns and trends inherent in location-based information.

"Mapmaking and geographic analysis are not new, but a GIS performs these tasks better and faster than do the old manual methods. And, before GIS technology, only a few people had the skills necessary to use geographic information to help with decision-making and problem solving.

"Geography is information about the earth's surface and the objects found on it, as well as a framework for organizing knowledge. GIS is a technology that manages, analyzes, and disseminates geographic knowledge.

"GIS engages students and promotes critical thinking, integrated learning and analysis, and multiple intelligences and sciences at any grade level.

"With the use of ICTs to explore the world, learning becomes more powerful. GIS technology is one of the hottest new tools in education and research and is one of the fastest growing high-tech careers for students today. GIS training helps students develop computer literacy, analytical approaches to problem solving, and communication and presentation skills." [1]

The Case for Geography

"Geography is not just an academic subject, it is a serious discipline with multibillion dollar implications for businesses and governments. Choosing sites, targeting market segments, planning distribution networks, responding to emergencies, or redrawing country boundaries – all of these problems involve questions of geography. Learn more about why geography matters."[2]

Geographic Information Systems

"GIS is a technology that is used to view and analyze data from a geographic perspective. The technology is a piece of an organization's overall information system framework.

"GIS links location to information (such as people to addresses, buildings to parcels, or streets within a network) and layers that information to give you a better understanding of how it all interrelates. You choose what layers to combine based on your purpose."[3]

Teaching With GIS

Geographic information systems (GIS) can help learners of all ages understand the world around them. GIS helps students and teachers engage in studies that promote critical thinking, integrated learning, and multiple intelligences, at any grade level.

In classrooms across the country and around the world, educators are using GIS in the study of topics as varied as Environmental Studies, History, and Economics. The resources below show how GIS is being used in schools and by educational organizations, and to help you start using GIS in your own classroom.

Educational Projects Involved with GIS

Many of these projects or groups are making use of GIS in powerful ways for helping education. Some are producing data that is tailor-made for use with GIS. All of them work to help teachers engage their classes in activities that involve critical thinking about spatial information. Geography is global, of course. You remember the tsunami event and how it affected the whole world.

* NCGE - National Council for Geographic Education
* NGS - National Geographic Society
* JASON Project

---

[1] from: http://www.gis.com/whatisgis/geographymatters.pdf
[2] cited from: http://www.gis.com/whatisgis/index.html
[3] Source: http://www.gis.com/whatisgis/overview.html

* The GLOBE Program
* Journey North
* GEODESY - Berkeley Geo-Research Group
* TERC
* Various Sectors of the United Nations in specialized content
* Union Géographique Internationale
* International Network for Learning and Teaching (INLT)
* International Symposium for Learning and Teaching Geography

Some Resources

World Wind

http://worldwind.arc.nasa.gov

World Wind lets PC users zoom from satellite altitude into any place on Earth. Leveraging Landsat satellite imagery and Shuttle Radar Topography Mission data, World Wind lets you experience Earth terrain in visually rich 3D, just as if you were really there.

Virtually visit any place in the world. Look across the Andes, into the Grand Canyon, over the Alps, or along the African Sahara.

Map Machine

http://plasma.nationalgeographic.com/mapmachine

National Geographic's redesigned online atlas gives you the world – your way. Find nearly any place on Earth, and view it by population, climate, and much more. Plus, browse antique maps, find country facts, or plan your next outdoor adventure with trail maps.

Google Earth

http://earth.google.com

Want to know more about a specific location? Google Earth combines satellite imagery, maps and the power of Google Search to put the world's geographic information at your fingertips.

Exploring Earth

http://www.classzone.com/books/earth_science/terc/content/visualizations/es0101/es0101page01.cfm?chapter_no=visualization

Exploring Earth provides animated resources and animation from NASA/Goddard Space Flight Center – Scientific Visualization Studio, Smithsonian Institution, National Science Foundation (NSF), Defense Advanced Research Projects Agency (DARPA),

Global Change Research Project (GCRP), National Oceanic and Atmospheric Administration (NOAA), Dimensional Media Associates (DMA), New York Film and Animation Company, Silicon Graphics, Inc. (SGI), Hughes STX Corporation.

IKONOS

http://www.spaceimaging.com/gallery/default.htm

Space Imaging's IKONOS earth imaging satellite has provided a reliable stream of image data that has become the standard for commercial high-resolution satellite data products. IKONOS produces 1-meter black-and-white (panchromatic) and 4-metre multispectral (red, blue, green, near infrared) imagery that can be combined in a variety of ways to accommodate a wide range of high-resolution imagery applications.

NASA Observatorium

http://observe.arc.nasa.gov/nasa/education/reference/main.html

NASA's Observatorium provides a number of on-line resources for science teachers, with a focus on remote sensing.

The WorldWatcher Project

www.worldwatcher.northwestern.edu

The WorldWatcher Project encourages students to use visualization tools for inquiry, for example, to compare temperature patterns in different places at different times. They also engage in communication, by sharing their visualizations and writing in a scientific notebook. The WorldWatcher Project also enables students to use scientific visualizations as expressions of their beliefs and hypotheses in three ways.

One is through the customization of the display of visualizations using the features for changing resolution, colour schemes, and magnification described under interpretive visualization. The second is through the mathematical creation of new data using techniques for analytical visualization. The third is through a direct manipulation interface using a paint metaphor.

Modeling and Visualization

http://faculty.ed.uiuc.edu/j-levin/taxonomy.html

"From a 19th century scatter plot used to isolate the source of a cholera epidemic to supercomputer-based weather models, visualization tools have revolutionized problem solving, research, and communication in science, mathematics, engineering, and technology. Today, researchers can explore and combine images of complex weather events like hurricanes, molecular structures such as pockets on the surface of proteins, or the environmental impact of factors such as deforestation. Advances in technology have led to personal computers capable of generating powerful visualizations and simulations in real time, while the rise of the Internet has increased access to the high end tools and datasets of scientific and engineering practice."[3]

Interactive Web-based Tools

AgentSheets

http://agentsheets.com

AgentSheets is a unique authoring tool to build interactive simulations in Java. It can be used to create interactive virtual worlds, modifiable simulations, training demos, and put them online fast with music, speech, video, and Java.

Maya

http://www.alias.com/eng/index.shtml

Maya is a high-end 3D computer graphics software package used in the film and TV industry, as well as for computer and video games, by Alias. Maya, used in most films today, is named for the Sanskrit word meaning "Illusion" and is the industry standard integrated 3D suite, evolved from Alias PowerAnimator. Maya comes in two main versions, Maya Complete (the less powerful package) and Maya Unlimited. Maya Personal Learning Edition (PLE) is available for non-commercial use, and is completely free.

Berkeley Madonna

http://www.berkeleymadonna.com/features.html

Berkeley Madonna is a fast, general purpose differential equation solver. It runs on both Windows and Mac OS. Developed on the Berkeley campus under the sponsorship of the U.S. National Science Foundation and National Institute of Health, it is currently used by academic and commercial institutions for constructing mathematical models for research and teaching.

Biology Student Workbench

http://bsw-uiuc.net

The Biology Student Workbench provides curricular materials centred around molecular biological investigations, links to educational, scientific, computational, and informational resources, and communication tools to bind together a contributing community of educators.

---

[3] From Bruce, Bertram C. **Modeling and visualization across learning contexts**. In M. Linn, L. Bievenue (NCSA), S. Derry, M. E. Verona, and U. Thakkar (Eds.), Workshop to integrate computer-based modeling and scientific visualization into teacher education programs. Champaign, IL: NCSA/EOT-PACI.

BugScope

http://bugscope.beckman.uiuc.edu

Bugscope is an educational outreach project of the Beckman Institute, University of Illinois for K-12 classrooms. The project provides a resource to classrooms so that they may remotely operate a scanning electron microscope to image "bugs" at high magnification. The microscope is remotely controlled in real time from a classroom computer over the Internet using a Web browser.

ChickScope

http://chickscope.beckman.uiuc.edu

ChickScope, developed by the Beckman Institute at the University of Illinois, allows students to raise chicken embryos in the classroom and obtain magnetic resonance images through the Internet.

ChemViz

http://chemviz.ncsa.uiuc.edu

ChemViz (Chemistry Visualization) is an interactive programme which incorporates computational chemistry simulations and visualizations for use in the chemistry classroom. The ChemViz tools, developed by the U.S. National Center for Supercomputing Applications, include an image generator (Waltz), a structural database (CSD) and a molecular editor (Nanocad).

Interactive Tools for Physics and Maths

http://www.mathsnet.net/asa2/2004/tech.html

Contains information about a number of interactive tools for teaching physics and maths, with links.

The Shodor Foundation

http://www.shodor.org

The Shodor Foundation is a non-profit research and education organization dedicated to the advancement of science and maths education, specifically through the use of modeling and simulation technologies. The Foundation provides interactive activities and instructional materials for students, educators, and parents.

National Science Digital Library

http://www.nsdl.org

The NSDL is a digital library of resource collections and services, organized in support of science education at all levels. It was created by the U.S. National Science Foundation to provide organized access to high quality resources and tools that support innovations in teaching and learning at all levels of science, technology, engineering, and mathematics education.

Computational Science Education Reference Desk

http://cserd.nsdl.org

Computational science – using computers to do science – involves the appropriate use of a computational architecture (possibly a computer, calculator, abacus, dice, poker chips, etc.) to apply some algorithm, or method, to solve a scientific application, or problem. When students learn to build models of the world around them in an attempt to answer specific questions, they learn to inquire in an authentic manner, and build their own understanding. Computational science provides a content-rich method of putting inquiry-based learning into classrooms. The Computational Science Education Reference Desk provides more information and a digital library.

Alexandria Digital Library Geospatial Network

http://webclient.alexandria.ucsb.edu/mw/index.jsp

The Alexandria Digital Library (ADL) is a resource of the University of California, Santa Barbara. It contains more than 15,000 holdings, such as maps, images, and datasets, that are available online for public download over the Internet.

ABOUT THE CONTRIBUTORS

Manuel Acevedo has been involved in information and communications technology (ICT) for human development since 1994, when he joined UNDP in Cuba and helped set up the INFOMED national public health network. Later in UNDP NY (96-97) he was focal point for ICT at the Regional Bureau for Latin America and the Caribbean, and was part of the UNDP Info XXI group which promoted the integration of ICT into UNDP's culture and operations. In 2000 he set up a novel 'e-Volunteering' unit at the UN Volunteers agency, where initiatives like UNITeS (the United Nations Information Technology Service) or the pioneer UN Online Volunteering Service were launched. Mr. Acevedo served as co-chair of the Capacity Building Committee of the UN ICT Task Force (2002-2003), and represented the UN Volunteers programme during the 1st phase of WSIS, advancing the awareness about ICT Volunteering. Mr. Acevedo is now an independent consultant on ICT4D, while doing research for a Ph.D. on ICT mainstreaming in large development cooperation agencies as well as on the crossover between the Human Development and Network Society paradigms. Mr. Acevedo is also introducing ICT4D into the curricula of some university programmes about Development and Cooperation in his native Spain, as well as promoting ICT mainstreaming into Spain´s international cooperation. He lives in Madrid.

Titilayo Akinsanmi currently works with SchoolNet Africa as Program Manager of the Global Teenager Project. She has experience spanning the private and public sector working in the broadcasting industry (radio and TV) and in mobile telecommunications. She has a passion for connecting people, ideas and resources. Ms. Akinsanmi works towards being a valuable part as concerns not just bridging the digital divide but in contributing to the development of each life on earth – one at a time. She is an avid volunteer around issues of Youth, Young Women, Local Content and how ICTs serve as an enabling tool; and believes in the principle of "Ripples" – all it needs is an initial ring, and it keeps growing beyond expected boundaries. She currently volunteers on the AFARA (in Nigeria) and IKAMVA youth project (in South Africa) as well as facilitating the WSIS Youth Caucus and the project. Ms. Akinsanmi holds a B.A degree in English, majoring in Language from Obafemi Awolowo University.

Edna Aphek is a linguist and educational researcher at David Yellin School of Education (Jerusalem), specializing in the introduction of computer literacy, with a particular interest in educational and social systems. She has designed and implemented virtual learning environments and partnerships for children and senior citizens and has published stories and poetry for children and adults.

Michael Arnone is a reporter at the The Chronicle of Higher Education.

Bonnie Bracey is a teacher-agent of change, working on technology integration projects with classroom teachers and national organizations. She also works internationally with Global Information Infrastructure initiatives as a consultant and in outreach for The

George Lucas Educational Foundation. A former Fulbright Exchange Teacher in India and an elementary school teacher in Virginia, Ms. Bracey was selected as a Christa McAuliffe Educator by the National Education Association in 1993. She has been involved with all of NASA's youth projects and is on the NASA review board for youth projects. She serves on the faculty of the Challenger Center and is a NEWEST Graduate, Langley, and NEW graduate of Goddard Space Center. She was a traveling teacher instructor for the White House Initiative CyberED, which was a project that spanned the United States working in empowerment and enterprise zones to teach the effective use of technology. The third Outstanding Service to Digital Equity Award was presented in 2004 to Ms. Bracey from SITE by Sir Johon Daniel, of UNESCO for her work as a change agent and reformer within the US and abroad. A holder of honors in a variety of fields including technology, aerospace, physics, geography and multicultural education, Ms. Bracey attended Virginia State University, received a graduate degree from the Marymount University SED program, and completed education technology training at George Mason University.

Bertram C. Bruce has been a member of the faculty at the University of Illinois at Urbana-Champaign since 1990 where he teaches in masters and doctoral programs in Library and Information Science, in Writing Studies, and in the undergraduate minor in Information Technology Studies. Before moving to Illinois, Mr. Bruce taught Computer Science at Rutgers (1971-74) and was a Principal Scientist at Bolt Beranek and Newman (1974-90). He has led workshops and presented on inquiry learning and new technologies with teachers, librarians, museum educators, community groups, university faculty, researchers, corporate and government groups in Australia, China, Russia, Haiti, and throughout Europe and North America. Mr. Bruce has received the Council of Graduate Students for Education Faculty Award for Excellence in Graduate Teaching, Advising, and Research and has regularly been selected for the University's "Incomplete List of Teachers Ranked as Excellent." He received the College of Education Senior Scholar Award, the Faculty Fellows Award, and is a Fellow of the National Conference on Research in Language and Literacy. He received a B.A. in Biology from Rice University in 1968 and a Ph.D. in Computer Sciences from The University of Texas at Austin in 1971.

Natasha Bulashova is, with Gregory Cole, co-developer and Co-Principal Investigator of the US GLORIAD program funded by the US National Science Foundation. She has served for six years on the NSF and Russian Ministry of Science funded NaukaNet program, helping to coordinate activities between US and Russian team members and building an effective Russian consortium of science and networking organizations. With Mr. Cole, Natasha has designed and implemented a traffic monitoring and utilization database and software system (http://www.gloriad.org/madasd/) that provides information on uses of the network. She has served as Principal Investigator or Co-Principal Investigator on many other joint US-Russian programs – including Principal Investigator on nearly $700,000 of Ford Foundation funding establishing the US-Russian Civic Networking Program (now operating in six Russian cities). Ms. Bulashova has also co-directed other US-Russian activities funded by such sponsors as NATO, US State Department, Eurasia Foundation, International Science Foundation, Sun Microsystems and others.

Kate Bunworth, Programmes Analyst with the Global e-Schools and Communities Initiative, joined the team in the summer of 2005, fresh from completing her BA in Economics from University of Dublin, Trinity College. During her undergraduate years she specialised in detailed economic research and analysis, specifically relating to labour economics as well as infrastructural costing and benefit techniques. Her research into the long-term effects of trade restrictions on less developed countries was published in the 2005 Trinity Student Economic Review. Since commencing employment, Ms. Bunworth has worked closely with Alex Twinomugisha to develop a holistic cost and benefit framework to simplify the decision-making process for GeSCI's partner countries. She also works closely with the consultant in Ghana and with Khalid Bomba, the Country Programme Facilitator in Namibia.

J. Paul Callan is Director of Programmes with the Global e-Schools and Communities Initiative, leading the team of Programme Facilitators and Specialists who implement GeSCI's work of mobilising, facilitating and supporting national and regional e-schools initiatives. His work with GeSCI goes back to the beginning; Paul was project team leader for the development of the concept and "business plan" for GeSCI. From 2000 to 2004, Paul worked at McKinsey & Company, the international consulting firm, serving a range of government agencies, non-profit organisations and private sector companies. Paul is now a Partner at Dalberg Global Development Advisors, a consulting firm that advises leading international development institutions on issues of strategy, organisational design, operations and performance management. In addition to GeSCI, Paul has served the World Bank, the Inter-American Development Bank and the United Nations while at Dalberg. He is now on secondment from Dalberg to GeSCI. Paul holds a BA in Theoretical Physics from Trinity College, Dublin and a Masters degree and PhD in Physics from Harvard University. Paul has been actively involved in educational administration in several contexts, serving at various times on the Board and the Academic Council of Trinity College, Dublin, and on the Harvard Faculty of Arts and Sciences and the Harvard University Library Committee.

Gregory Cole serves as co-Principal Investigator, with Natasha Bulashova, of the NSF-funded program establishing GLORIAD, as well as the program's predecessor, NaukaNet. NaukaNet established the primary high performance Internet network between the US and Russian S&E communities and has led to an effective consortium of US and Russian academic and networking organizations. In December 2001, the project realized its goal of routing S&E traffic from across the whole of both US and Russia. The number of users (hosts) of the network exceeds 2 million today and traffic to Russia exceeds 3 terabytes monthly. With Co- Principal Investigator Ms. Bulashova, Greg has designed and implemented a traffic monitoring and utilization database and software system (http://www.gloriad.org/madasd/) that provides information on uses of the network. The NaukaNet network program has provided the network infrastructure, the organizational support, the experience with advanced applications, and the relationships on which the new GLORIAD program has been built. Greg has also co-directed (with Ms. Bulashova) the US-Russian Civic Networking Program (funded by the Ford Foundation and the Eurasia Foundation) and directed several other US-Russia network infrastructure and community development programs funded by such organizations as NATO, US Department of State, Eurasia Foundation, Sun Microsystems and others.

The US-Russia project that he and Ms. Bulashova started more than 10 years ago is known as Friends & Partners.

Royal D. Colle is a Professor Emeritus at Cornell University where he has been a member of the Cornell University faculty for almost 40 years, 10 of which were as Chair of the Communication Department. He has lived and worked abroad in countries ranging from India and Indonesia to Western Samoa and Guatemala. Mr. Colle has served as a consultant for a variety of international organizations including the World Bank, FAO, the UN, UNFPA, UNESCO, USAID, and the Ford Foundation. His work has focused on the design of communication strategies and innovative uses of information technology for development. He continues to teach, write and work on projects such as telecenters and building the ICT4D capacities of universities in developing nations. He is co-author of A Handbook for Telecenter Staffs.

Martin Curley is Senior Principal Engineer and Global Director of IT Innovation at Intel Corporation, managing a network of Intel IT Innovation centres developing advanced IT solutions. Previously, Mr. Curley held a number of IT Management positions for Intel including Director of IT Strategy and Technology based in Sacramento, California and Fab14 Automation Manager based in Dublin, Ireland. He has also held IT management positions at General Electric in Ireland and Philips in the Netherlands. Mr. Curley has a degree in Electronic Engineering and a Masters in Business Studies from University College Dublin, Ireland. Martin is author of Managing Information Technology for Business Value published by Intel Press January 2004 and now in its third re-print.

Terry Culver has more than ten years experience in partnership and community development, education, and communications. From 1998 to 2005, he was Director of Development at New York University from, and a faculty member at the University's Gallatin School, where he taught courses in technology and community development, and the arts. Previously, he was project development officer at the Harvard Institute for International Development where he was involved in a number of education, health, and economic projects in West Africa, Southern Africa, and Eastern Europe. He has sat on the Board of a number of community organizations, including Groundswell Community Murals and Art Resources Transfer, and has served as special advisor to the Gowanus Canal Community Development Corporation. He has a B.A. and MFA from New York University.

Dianne Davis is the Founding President of International Council for Caring Communities (ICCC), a non-profit organization in Special Consultative Status with the Economic and Social Council of the United Nations. An international public speaker and consultant, she specializes in integrated products and services for the hospitality, healthcare and educational industries. Currently her work focuses on the impact of the "longevity factor" on society: mainstreaming ageing issues especially within the areas of the built environment, e-health and information and communication technology by the approach of connecting the generations. She has designed international ICT and architectural student competitions and developed unique "Cross-Sectorial" Dialogues for local authorities and international decision-makers. Ms. Davis received her graduate degrees from Columbia University and since 1966 has been cited in "Who's Who of

American Women." She serves on United Nations NGO Committees and various international boards. Known as an industry catalyst, change agent, and futurist, her goal is to develop "cross over" ventures and stimulate traditional "sleeping" organizations or programs to move into the forefront of performance and impact.

Diogo André de Assumpção has been interested in technology since an early age and has developed expertise in many fields including programming and networking. He is passionate about technology and science and interested in innovation and knowledge. Mr. de Assumpcão is an activist. The spark came when he joined the scout movement at the age of 13, which gave him his initial opportunities to work on social issues and be proactive to cultivate positive change. In 2001, he joined a recently founded youth organization, Grupo Interagir, with a different proposal: to use information and knowledge to help young people strengthen their proactive participation in the society. In 2002, Mr. de Assumpcão, already a computer sciences student, became interested in ICT for development and began researching and studying the subject. Later that year he got involved in the World Summit of Information Society, which was consolidated in 2003 when participated in two preparatory meetings as a member of the youth caucus, and at the summit as a member of the official Brazilian delegation. Mr. de Assumpcão is today a international relations student, is still working with Grupo Interagir and also working for a worldwide digital communications company.

Geraldine de Bastion studied political sciences at the Freie Universität Berlin and worked in a number of political institutions, including the German parliament and the German Federal Ministry for Economic Co-operation and Development (BMZ) before joining the Junior Experts Programme of the German Gesellschaft für Technische Zusammenarbeit (GTZ) in September 2004. She has been active in a number of cultural and political initiatives, focusing on issues such as sustainable consumerism and youth participation and worked as the editor of a youth magazine and Internet portal during her time at University. As a member of GTZ's ICT4D Team, Ms. de Bastion is currently working on topics such as e-Government and Open Source in development programmes, Open Government, and scientific electronic publication systems.

Irene Hardy de Gómez is the Director of the AME Program of the Cisneros Foundation. She is an adviser with an extensive experience in training, research, education and agro-industry issues in organizations of sustainable development. She was the Executive Secretary of the Electoral Commission of the Universidad Central of Venezuela. Ms. Hardy de Gomez studied at the Universidad Central de Venezuela and the holds a master degree in biology from the Instituto Venezolano de Investigaciones Cientificas.

Astrid Dufborg is Ambassador and ICT Adviser at the Swedish Mission to the United Nations in Geneva, leading the Swedish government's work in relation to the WSIS. Ms. Dufborg is also a member of the United Nations ICT Task Force where she, among other things, serves on its Bureau and convenes the Working Group on the Enabling Environment. She is also currently the Vice-Chair for the Global e-Schools and Communities Initiative (GeSCI). Ms. Dufborg has vast experience working with development issues, having been employed by the Swedish International Development cooperation Agency (Sida) for more than 30 years of which 10 years have been spent in various African countries. Her last position was as Assistant Director General. Ms. Dufborg has a political science educational background.

Julia Christina Fauth is chair of the working group on Global ICT Policy in the German Scholarship Foundation Villigst and a scholarship holder of this institution. Prior to these assignments, Ms. Fauth carried out research work on HIV/AIDS and worked for them as journalist focusing on humanitarian assistance, gender inequalities and international youth networking. Ms. Fauth earned a Bachelors degree in Communications from the University of Muenster, Germany in February 2004 and is a member of the Global Politics Discussion Board of the London School of Economics and Political Science. She has been engaged as organizer and pre-educator in international student programs in Aushwitz and Berlin and, within this scope, is a liaison person to the International Auschwitz Committee.

Clotilde Fonseca is Executive Director of the Omar Dengo Foundation, a Costa Rican non-profit organization created to promote socio-economic and human development through the appropriation of new technologies. She was Executive President of the Costa Rican Institute for Social Assistance (IMAS), which is in charge of the country's anti-poverty programmes, and has done consultancy work for UNDP, USAID and CABEI. At present she is a member of the Hemispheric Advisory Board to the Institute of Connectivity of the Americas. She is also a member of the Executive Committee of the Global Knowledge Partnership (GKP). Ms Fonseca has published extensively on issues of education, technology and socio-economic development. She has a Master in Public Administration with emphasis on Education and Technology Policy from Harvard University. She also completed graduate studies on mass media at the University of Navarre,Spain.

Alvaro H. Galvis is a Senior Researcher at The Concord Consortium, creating and leading research and development projects that involve applications of information and communication technologies to pressing educational problems. He is also interested in international cooperation as a way of helping developing countries overcome some of their educational problems with support of computers and information technologies. Mr. Alvaro is research director for the Seeing Math Telecommunications Project and pedagogic director and principal investigator of CAPTIC (Comunidades que Aprenden usando Tecnología de Información y Comunicación). His areas of interest include online / virtual learning environments, highly interactive playful learning environments, teacher professional development, and strategic uses of informatics in developing countries. Through Metacursos, the Spanish division of Metacourse Inc., Mr. Galvis offers eLearning Seminars to Spanish speaking educators.

Mona Grieser is a senior development professional with over 20 years of overseas living and working experience in such countries as Mali, Mauritania, Chad, and Jordan and working in an additional 30 countries. Her fields of specialization include the technical fields of education, health and the environment, while her process specializations include communication, social marketing and strategic planning for development using systems thinking. She has published extensively, has owned her own development firm and is currently Program Director at the Academy for Educational Development (AED) managing a USAID-funded worldwide Hygiene Improvement Project. Ms. Grieser was the project Director in Jordan responsible for the design and implementation of the National Water Conservation Program funded by USAID (WEPIA) which included the development of a national curriculum emphasizing water conservation in schools. Ms. Grieser was born in Iran, raised in Kenya and completed her studies in the United States at Mills College (BA), The University of California at Los Angeles (MPH), the University of Minnesota (MA) and the University of Southern California.

Mike Griffin has an honours degree in Social Science from University College Cork. He is the Director of Synchronicity and Research with the Morgan Institute of Advanced Learning, specialising in the evolution of consciousness and its spiritual applications in providing innovative programmes in learning and training designed to access and develop the true natural resources of the whole person.

Sophia Huyer is the founding Executive Director of Women and Global Science and Technology (WIGSAT), an international NGO based in Canada which promotes women's use of ICTs for gender equality in the global context. She has published and spoken widely on international gender, science and technology issues policy, including ICTs and social development. She is also Senior Research Advisor for the Gender Advisory Board of the UN Commission on Science and Technology for Development, and has done work for international agencies such as the Canadian International Development Agency, the International Development Research Centre (IDRC), UNESCO, the Organisation of American States, the UN Institute for Training and Research on Women (INSTRAW), and others. Recent publications include "ICTs, Globalisation and Poverty Reduction: Gender Dimensions of the Knowledge Society" for the Gender Advisory Board–UNCSTD, and "Overcoming the Digital Divide: Understanding ICTs and their Potential for the Empowerment of Women", synthesis paper of the INSTRAW Virtual Seminar Series on Gender and ICTs. She is a member of the International Advisory Committee of the Global Women's Leadership Centre at Santa Clara University. She received her Ph.D. from York University, Toronto.

Shafika Isaacs is currently the Executive Director of SchoolNet Africa (SNA), one of Africa's first African-led, pan-African NGOs which promotes learning and teaching through the use of ICTs in African schools, in partnership with schoolnet practitioners and policymakers in 35 African countries. Previously, she worked as a Senior Program Officer with the International Development Research Centre (IDRC)'s Acacia Program which promotes development in Africa through the use of information and communication technologies. Ms. Isaacs was formerly the Director of the Trade Union Research Project (TURP) at the University of Natal in South Africa for 10 years, where she specialised in research, training and writing publications on globalisation, gender issues and the impact of changing technologies on the labour market. Ms. Isaacs serves on a number of advisory committees and boards. She is known for her role in the first phase of the WSIS Gender Caucus where she served on its Steering Committee and as Interim Coordinator in 2003. She also served as chairperson of the United Nations Division for Advancement of Women-led (UNDAW) Expert Group Meeting on ICTs as an Instrument for the Advancement of Women. Ms. Isaacs won the Mandela Scholarship Award in 1996 to complete an M.Sc in Science and Technology Policy at the Science Policy Research Unit (SPRU) at the University of Sussex.

Mayyada Abu Jaber is currently the Head of an NGO focused on public education started by Her Majesty Queen Rania. She was the Director of the WEPIA education Project at the Royal Society for the Conservation of Nature (RSCN) in Jordan, which was designated as the lead agency to implement the national water conservation curricula. She is a recognized expert in education having taught in the Baccalureate School in Jordan (the premier English language K-12 school), and receiving considerable training in curriculum development through that institution. Her work in developing a digital curriculum has been applauded by His Majesty and become a model for other electronic education programs in Jordan and in neighboring countries where it has won awards. She obtained her graduate education in the United States from Duke University in Environmental studies.

Hugh G. Jagger is a Consultant of CISCO Systems working on the Jordanian Education Initiative. He is a senior partner in "big five" management consultancies, operating internationally with the world's premier telecoms, media technology companies, with senior management experience in industry.

Dabesaki Mac-Ikemenjima is Executive Director of Development Partnership International, Co-Founder and Task Force Member of the Global Youth Coalition on HIV/AIDS and currently Nigeria's representative to the Commonwealth Youth Caucus. Mr. Mac-Ikemenjima has been involved in various ICT4D initiatives in Nigeria including UNESCO's National Virtual Library Feasibility.

Joyce Malyn-Smith plays key roles in several national IT projects. She is the Principal Investigator on three National Science Foundation projects, the ITEST (Information Technology Experiences for Students and Teachers) Learning Resource Center and IT Across Careers (I and II). Previously, Dr. Malyn-Smith served as Project Director for the Information Technology Career Cluster Initiative funded by DOE's Office of Vocational and Adult Education to develop and pilot a framework for education programs leading to "IT producer" careers. In partnership with ITAA (Information Technology Association of America), Dr. Malyn-Smith lead EDC's activities for the Techforce Initiative funded to highlight and expand IT employer involvement in school-to-work nationally. Dr. Malyn-Smith developed and produced several seminal products including the IT Pathway/Pipeline Model: Rethinking Technology Learning in Schools and has co-authored skill standard implementation guides, including Making Skill Standards Work (National Skill Standards Board/DOL). Dr. Malyn-Smith received her BA from Universidad Interamericana in Hato Rey, Puerto Rico, her M.Ed. from Boston State Teachers College and her Ed.D. from Boston University.

Claudia Morrell is the Executive Director of the Center for Women and Information Technology (CWIT) at the University of Maryland, Baltimore County (UMBC) in the U.S. The Center houses several major initiatives intended to increase the participation and leadership of girls and women in IT, from middle school through college and university to the workforce and technology entrepreneurship at the regional, national, and international levels. Her recent efforts have resulted in a CWIT Scholars program which retains 93% of its students; increased funding of $7 million in scholarships, research, and program support; an international award-winning women and technology video entitled, You Can Be Anything; and the establishment of the first statewide

Governor's Taskforce on the Status of Women and IT in the US. The Center's website, www.umbc.edu/cwit, is recognized internationally as "the best resource for women and IT on the web." Ms. Morrell has spoken at state, national and international events, including the United Nations and World Bank. Ms. Morrell serves on multiple statewide, national, and international advisory boards.

M. Madhavan Nambiar is Additional Secretary in the Department of Information Technology in the Ministry of Communications and Information Technology in India. Previously, he served as Executive Director of the National Institute of Disaster Management, Ministry of Home Affairs; Chairman and Managing Director of Tamil Nadu Industrial Development Corporation Limited; Chairman and Managing Director of Electronics Corporation of Tamilnadu Limited; and held several other positions within the Indian government. He has taught at Columbia University and Oxford University. Mr. Nambiar has a B.A. in Economics and Statistics and an MBA from the Delhi School of Economics, Delhi University.

Juan Carlos Navarro is Chief of the Education Unit of the Sustainable Development Department at the Inter-American Development Bank. He led the preparation of the new consolidated education and training strategy for the Bank. He has extensive field experience gained through participation in the design and supervision of education and science and technology projects across Latin America and the Caribbean, and has led several applied research and technical cooperation initiatives of the Bank, accumulating a number of publications in areas such as teacher's careers and incentives, higher education, integration of technology in the school systems, education financing, private-public partnerships and political economy of education reforms. Before joining the Bank in 1997, Mr. Navarro was a professor of social and education policy at the Institute for Advanced Studies in Administration (IESA), and at the Andrés Bello Catholic University, in Caracas, his native city. At the time, he consulted on education and social policy for several international organizations and Latin American governments. He was also, in 1995, a visiting scholar at the Harvard Graduate School of Education. Mr. Navarro is a policy analyst (Master in Public Policy, Georgetown University) and political scientist (doctoral studies at the Central University, Venezuela).

Stephen Nolan is the Executive Director of the Global eSchools and Communities Initiative. For three years previous to this, Stephen was the Special ICT Advisor to Secretary General of the Irish Department of Communications, Marine and Natural Resources, advising on a range of issues pertaining to the Department's portfolio for Communications and also any matters arising from Secretary General Tuohy's position as Vice Chairman of UN ICT Task Force. Mr. Nolan has been instrumental in the development of Ireland's domestic and international ICT for Development program – initiatives he has led include the creation of an international ICT for Development unit within the Irish Government and the Centre of ICT4D which deals with international telecommunication regulation and policy dissemination. He also led the project development team that established the European Biometric Forum founded to provide thought leadership in the new issue of biometrics. Mr. Nolan is a contributor to a number of international forums that deal with the global issues regarding ICT such as Development Cooperation Ireland's ICT Task Force and the International Advisory Group to the European Biometrics Forum. In addition to this, he has co-chaired the

Working Group on Human Capacity Building and Development of the UN ICT Task Force and acts as an ICT Advisor to the UN ICT Task Force Secretariat. He holds a B.A. in Business and Economics from Trinity College Dublin and a post-graduate Diploma in Information Technology from Dublin City University.

Sherry Lynn R. Peralta is the Executive Director of the Ayala Foundation USA based in Redwood City, California. Ayala Foundation USA (AF-USA) is a private, 501(c)3 non-profit organization established in 2000 to promote meaningful involvement in addressing areas of greatest need in the Philippines. From 2002-2005, she served as Executive Director of the Filipino American Human Services, Inc. (FAHSI) providing organizational leadership and management in the areas of fund development, program development, fiscal management, staff development and supervision, community relations, and advocacy. She has worked for over 10 years in the field of community and social services, particularly in the area of youth programming. She received her B.A. in English and Psychology in 1996 from the University of California at Berkeley. For two years, she worked as Program Director for Project C.A.R.E. (Children At-Risk Excelling), an after-school enrichment program for at-risk youth in the San Francisco Bay Area. She received her Masters in Social Work (M.S.W.) degree from the Columbia University School of Social Work, with concentration in Social Administration for Children and Families.

Danilo Piaggesi has been the Chief of the Information Technology for Development Division (SDS/ICT) at the Inter-American Development Bank since 1999. From 1992 to 1998, he served as a technical staff of TELESPAZIO, Societá per Azioni per le Comunicazioni Spaziali, TELECOM-Italia Group in Rome and was in charge of the Strategic Alliances and International Activities Division. From 1981 to 1991 he worked for the United Nations Food and Agriculture Organization (FAO) at different duty stations in Africa and Latin America. He also served as a consultant to the European Union in Brussels in which he evaluated project proposals for funding in the field of telecommunications and environment. Mr. Piaggesi received professional training in remote sensing, digital image processing and analysis, technical cooperation project formulation and appraisal, and telecommunications and technology transfer. He holds a Masters degree cum laude in Physics with a diploma in geophysics from the University of Rome (1980). He also obtained an Executive International Business Certificate from Georgetown University/John Cabot University in Washington D.C-Rome in 1996.

Elena Pistorio, born in Milan in 1970, graduated from Brown University in 1992 with a BA in Economics and a BA in Media Culture with Honors. Upon graduating, she worked first as a Business Analyst in Ansaldo, based in Genoa, Italy. In 1995 she moved to Paris to join the Media department of Euro-RSCG. Attracted to the film industry, she spent one summer studying film at New York University and one year working as Production Assistant for Merchant Ivory Productions in Paris. In 1998, she completed her Masters Degree in Film and Television Production at Goldsmith College in London. Her graduation film, a short film which she wrote, directed and produced, was screened at the BBC Short Film Festival. In 1999, she married and moved to Geneva, Switzerland, devoting a few years to being a full-time mother. Driven by a strong passion and concern for issues concerning the Environment and Development, she was the first

employee to join the newly founded STMicroelectronics Foundation and became Director of Operations in January 2004.

Marc Prensky is an internationally acclaimed speaker, writer, consultant, and designer in the critical areas of education and learning. He is the author of Digital Game-Based Learning (McGraw-Hill, 2001), the founder and CEO of Games2train (whose clients include IBM, Nokia, Pfizer, and the US Department of Defense) and creator of the sites http://www.dodgamecommunity.com and http://www.socialimpactgames.com. Mr. Prensky has created over 50 software games for learning, including the world's first fast-action videogame-based training tools and world-wide, multi-player, multi-team on-line competitions. He has also taught at all levels. He has been featured in articles in The New York Times and The Wall Street Journal, has appeared on CNN, MSNBC, PBS, and the BBC, and was named as one of training's top 10 "visionaries" by Training magazine. He holds graduate degrees from Yale (Teaching) and Harvard (MBA).

Jeffrey D. Sachs is the Director of The Earth Institute, Quetelet Professor of Sustainable Development, and Professor of Health Policy and Management at Columbia University. He is also Director of the United Nations Millennium Project and Special Advisor to United Nations Secretary-General Kofi Annan on the Millennium Development Goals, the internationally agreed goals to reduce extreme poverty, disease, and hunger by the year 2015. Mr. Sachs is internationally renowned for advising governments in Latin America, Eastern Europe, the former Soviet Union, Asia and Africa on economic reforms and for his work with international agencies to promote poverty reduction, disease control, and debt reduction of poor countries. He was recently named among the 100 most influential leaders in the world by Time Magazine. He is author of hundreds of scholarly articles and many books. Mr. Sachs was recently elected into the Institute of Medicine and is a Research Associate of the National Bureau of Economic Research. Prior to joining Columbia, he spent over twenty years at Harvard University, most recently as Director of the Center for International Development. A native of Detroit, Michigan, Mr. Sachs received his B.A., M.A., and Ph.D. degrees at Harvard University.

Leigh Shamblin is the Education Office Director for the U.S. Agency for International Development in Macedonia. Prior to joining USAID, Leigh spent 11 years guiding economic growth and education projects in Central Asia, Central and Eastern Europe, Russia, the Balkans, Thailand, and the US, including such responsible positions as the Dean of the MBA Program at the University of International Business in Almaty, Kazakhstan. She holds a Master's degree in Business from Kenan-Flagler Business School and is a doctoral candidate in adult education at North Carolina State University. In addition to managing the education office, her work with USAID/Macedonia focuses on education policy and reform, ITC deployment and integration, and effective donor and host country coordination.

Vic Sutton has long experience of ways to use information and communication technologies to promote economic and social development goals. He worked for more than 20 years for the international news agency Inter Press Service (IPS) in Rome, Italy, first as journalist and editor, then as project manager, helping to build the IPS reporting and news distribution network in Africa, Asia, Europe, North America and the

Caribbean. He also managed IPS fundraising and relations with the donor community. More recently he spent five years making television programmes for broadcast in southern Africa, based in Johannesburg, South Africa. He is currently conducting research on the impact of new developments in technology on the digital divide.

Rahul Tongia is a research faculty member at Carnegie Mellon University (CMU), in the School of Computer Science and the Department of Engineering and Public Policy, where he focuses on interdisciplinary issues of technology policy. He is also Senior Fellow in the Centre for Study of Science, Technology and Policy (CSTEP), a non-profit think tank under incorporation in India. His core interests are in infrastructure development, with an emphasis on technology, policy, economics, and security. Mr. Tongia is active in the telecom sectors (including digital divide and access technology issues) and in the power sector (including reform, regulation, and IT/smart metering). He is presently Vice-Chair of the UN ICT Task Force Working Group on Enabling Environment (formerly, Low-cost Connectivity Access), and has organized global conferences on ICT and Sustainable Development for the United Nations, World Bank, and National Science Foundation. His undergraduate education was in Electrical Engineering from Brown University, and he holds a doctorate from CMU.

Alex Twinomugisha is currently the ICT Specialist at GeSCI based in Dublin where he is responsible for generating, maintaining, acquiring and sharing knowledge and expertise in ICTs for Education and Community Development. Prior to this, he was a technical consultant to the World Bank in Washington DC for the African Virtual University (AVU) project responsible for setting up and managing the online and satellite technical infrastructure for course delivery and management to over 34 learning centers in over 15 African countries. He later established and managed the ICT department for the independent AVU organization based in Nairobi, Kenya. He has undertaken other special assignments as a lead technical consultant including work for the Ugandan Ministry of Education, in designing an ICT network for course delivery and management for a planned open university, a VSAT network for universities in Somalia under a joint World Bank-UNDP capacity building mission for Somalia and obtaining cheaper VSAT bandwidth for universities supported by the Partnership for Higher Education in Africa. He has over 7 years experience in ICTs for Education and Development in the areas of planning, design, implementation and management.

Mwiyeria Wachira is the Training and Communication Manager of Computers for Schools Kenya (CFSK). She has been educating Kenyans on the use of ICT for the last 15 years. She has been active in training professionals in the public and private sectors in the country. In 2003, Mwiyeria was among those who founded CFSK and started a procedure of donating pre-owned PCs to Kenya public secondary schools in the rural areas and disadvantaged communities. This started with a nascent team of four persons but now is a team of 20 full-time employees and 25 volunteers actively bringing ICT to Kenyans young generation. Ms. Wachira received her formal education in Kenya and graduated in 1990 with a BSc. in Education majoring in Mathematics and computer studies. She plans to pursue a post graduate degree in technology applications in teaching and learning (Telematics) in the Netherlands.